PAKISTAN
Founders' Aspirations and
Today's Realities

PAKISTAN
Founders' Aspirations and Today's Realities

Edited by
Hafeez Malik

OXFORD
UNIVERSITY PRESS

Great Clarendon Street, Oxford OX2 6DP
Oxford University Press is a department of the University of Oxford.
It furthers the University's objective of excellence in research, scholarship,
and education by publishing worldwide in

Oxford New York

Auckland Bangkok Buenos Aires Cape Town Chennai
Dar es Salaam Delhi Hong Kong Istanbul Karachi Kolkata
Kuala Lumpur Madrid Melbourne Mexico City Mumbai Nairobi
São Paulo Shanghai Taipei Tokyo Toronto

Oxford is a registered trade mark of Oxford University Press
in the UK and in certain other countries

© Oxford University Press 2001

The moral rights of the author have been asserted

First published 2001

All rights reserved. No part of this publication may be reproduced,
translated, stored in a retrieval system, or transmitted, in any form or by any
means, without the prior permission in writing of Oxford University Press.
Enquiries concerning reproduction should be sent to
Oxford University Press at the address below.

This book is sold subject to the condition that it shall not, by way
of trade or otherwise, be lent, re-sold, hired out or otherwise circulated
without the publisher's prior consent in any form of binding or cover
other than that in which it is published and without a similar condition
including this condition being imposed on the subsequent purchaser.

ISBN 0 19 579333 1

Second Impression 2003

Typeset in Times
Printed in Pakistan at
Print Vision, Karachi.
Published by
Ameena Saiyid, Oxford University Press
Plot No. 38, Sector 15, Korangi Industrial Area,
Karachi-74900, Pakistan.

Contents

	page
Preface	vii
1. Founders' Aspirations and Today's Realities: An Introduction *Hafeez Malik*	1
2. Constitutional Development *S.M. Zafar*	30
3. The Judiciary and Constitutional Crises in Pakistan *Javid Iqbal*	61
4. The Role of the Military in Politics: Pakistan 1947-97 *Khalid Mahmud Arif*	82
5. Political Development in Pakistan *Craig Baxter*	126
6. Development and Significance of Pakistan's Nuclear Capability *Munir Ahmad Khan*	149
7. The Nuclear Subcontinent: Political and Economic Realities *Walid Iqbal*	172
8. Pakistan's Economy: Achievements, Progress, Constraints, and Prospects *Robert E. Looney*	195

CONTENTS

9. The Sunni-Shia Conflict in Pakistan   244
   Anwar H. Syed

10. The Sipah-e-Sahaba Pakistan   263
    Afak Haydar

11. A Ride on the Roller Coaster: US-Pakistan 287
    Relations 1947-1997
    Dennis Kux

12. Pakistan's Relations with the
    Soviet Union and Russia   313
    Hafeez Malik

13. Foreign Policy: Relations with the West,
    China and the Middle East   352
    Abdul Sattar

14. India-Pakistan Relations and the Problem of Kashmir   413
    Robert G. Wirsing

    Contributors   453

    Index   457

Preface

At Pakistan's fiftieth birthday, it was appropriate to have an assessment of its performance as a state, especially in the light of its founder(s)' aspirations. Quaid-i-Azam Muhammad Ali Jinnah was indeed the founder of Pakistan, the leader of Pakistan's national movement, the President of the first National Assembly, and the first Governor-General. Conceptually, however, Dr Muhammad Iqbal, the poet-philosopher, had articulated the architectural design of a Muslim state in the northwest, and another one in northeast of India in 1930, when he delivered the presidential address at the annual session of the Muslim League in Allahabad. In 1940, the All-India Muslim League adopted the 'Pakistan Resolution', and just before the dawn of freedom in 1947 East Bengal was hitched onto Pakistan, with disastrous consequences to Pakistan's national security.

In the 1940s, when the Pakistan national movement was at its peak, the citizens expected the new state to live up to the founders' aspirations: (1) Pakistan would be a liberal and democratic Muslim state, which would treat Muslim and non-Muslim citizens as equals; (2) it would be economically prosperous, as the leaders would devote their energies to economic development; (3) it would be a shining star of science and technology, and modern education for all citizens; and (4) it would be the light to Islamic world in its adaptation of Islam to the modern age.

Ever since 1947, Pakistan has been plagued by the issues of provincial autonomy, sectarian violence, military *coup d'etats*, and endless polemics over power sharing between Punjab, the most populated, and relatively more developed province of the federation and the smaller provinces. The never-ending phenomenon of Islam, which should have been definitively resolved with the establishment of the state, keeps surfacing as the process of Islamization, which spawns further fragmentation. Instead of nation-building, economic development, scientific and technological progress, the national energy has been squandered on superficial and obscurantist theological issues, which continue to be divisive and corrosive of national solidarity.

From 40 million in 1947, the population has exploded into 130 million in 1998, while economic resources have not developed proportionately. Yet no effective family planning programme has been adopted, which would control the population explosion. Pakistan's leaders are accused of bribery, taking kickbacks from foreign companies, misappropriating state resources, and transferring funds in western banks in order to purchase or lease villas or luxury apartments in European countries. The so-called leaders have brought Pakistan's prestige to its lowest ebb. No wonder that some foreign scholars of Pakistani politics despite their empathy with Pakistan, have drawn its future in sad and grey colours.

In 1971, after losing the East Bengal territory, primarily due to the military regime's ineptness, Zulfikar Ali Bhutto initiated the nuclear programme, which has now guaranteed the territorial integrity of Pakistan against any foreign aggression. Yet internal contradictions continue to multiply. Pakistan has fallen into the Indian trap the way the Soviet Union was ensnared by the United States in an economically ruinous race for bigger and better weapon systems, leading to the Soviet collapse and economic meltdown of Russia, the successor state. With limited resources and smaller economy, Pakistan cannot afford to spend gargantuan sums on military preparedness year after year. US Arms Control and Disarmament Agency stated that in 1995 Pakistan's military expenditure was $3.24 billion. In contrast, eight times larger and economically better developed India spent $7.83 billion. Pakistan's per capita military spending was $30, while India's was only $8. With the development of nuclear weapons and missiles, Pakistan needs to restructure its security doctrine in regard to India in order to scale down military expenditures. It is appropriate at this stage to redirect national resources to national integration and development.

PREFACE

Since its inception, Pakistan's foreign policy of forging closer relations, verging on an alliance with the United States, was correct until 1991. This was the period of the cold war, and Pakistan accordingly derived strategic advantages. At the global level, the geostrategic environment has undergone a sea change. No great power, especially the United States, is going to pull chestnuts out of the fire for Pakistan, especially in its conflicts with India. The natural habitat of Pakistan's foreign policy, if it is imaginatively crafted, is the Middle East, Persian Gulf region, Central Asia, and China. Yet Pakistan would remain quagmired in its confrontational interaction with India over Kashmir and would be unable to play a meaningful regional role in its "natural political habitat."

The inescapable disparity of economic strength, size, population, military power, and other resources mandate Pakistan to maintain friendly, but 'distant', relations with India. Pakistan's national interest will be best served if it turns its back on India, and let it be the 'greatest power' in the world, which would hopefully satisfy Indians' historically scarred psyche. Exogenous powers for their own reasons would contain Indian ambitions. In order to find a secure niche in the world, Pakistan must shed its Indian liability.

Also, Pakistan would be well advised to improve its relations with Russia. Russia is no longer a superpower, but remains a great Eurasian power and will continue to have strong influence in Central Asia, as well as in South Asia. Nor should one ignore the fact that Russia has officially assumed the role of a successor state to the Soviet Union, while it controls 60 per cent of the former Soviet territory and has a population of 150 million. Moreover, 20 million Russians live in the former republics of the Soviet Union, including the Central Asian states.

Russia has inherited from the Soviet Union a large number of assets: 90 per cent of the oil; nearly 80 per cent of the natural gas; 62 per cent of the electricity; 70 per cent of the gold; and 70 per cent of the trained technical workers. Russia has also inherited nearly 80 per cent of the industries, including metallurgy, aeronautics, space, aircraft and nuclear industries, and a vast military-industrial complex, which were established by the Soviet Union. Despite Russia's fall from the pinnacle of superpower status, it still can be an alternative source of technology and defensive military hardware, and a partner in diplomacy for Pakistan, especially in Central Asia and South Asia.

In order to assess as objectively as humanly possible Pakistan's performance as a state over a period of fifty years, I organized an international seminar at Villanova University on 24-25 October 1997 under the auspices of the Pakistan-American Foundation, and in cooperation with the Center for Arab and Islamic Studies. Scholars and public figures from the United States and Pakistan presented their well crafted papers on specific topics: these constitute the chapters in this volume. Without their collective endeavours and cooperation, neither the seminar nor this comprehensive and multidimensional analytical study would have been possible.

Villanova University has not only been an intellectual haven for me, but it has also generously supported over the last twenty-three years the *Journal of South Asian and Middle Eastern Studies*, the Pakistan-American Foundation, and the American Institute of Pakistan Studies, which have also received generous support from the Ministry of Education of the Government of Pakistan. I am equally indebted to Fr. Edmund J. Dobbin (President), Dr John R. Johannes (Vice President of Academic Affairs), and Fr. Kail C. Ellis (Dean of Arts and Sciences, and Director of the Center for Contemporary Arab and Islamic Studies) of Villanova University. Dr Javid Iqbal, former Justice of the Supreme Court of Pakistan, and currently a member of Pakistan's Senate and a ranking member of its Committee on Foreign Relations, presided over one of the sessions and managed to keep the level of discourse very high between hotly contested political views, Curt Weldon Professor Congressman, Pdelivered a keynote address, highlighting US relations with Pakistan.

Among my friends, I single out Nadia Barsoum, who helped me in many ways to make this seminar a successful enterprise.

Some of my friends, both in the United States and abroad, have always been a source of encouragement and support: Yuri V. Gankovsky, Afaq Haydar, Jack Schrems, Naim Rathore, Lori Kephart, Syed Abid Ali, Zaheer Chaudhry, Igor V. Khalevinski, Vyacheslav Ya. Belokrinitsky, Ralph Braibanti, and (Akhuna) Khalil Ilyas. I value their friendship and cherish their affection. Professor Masood Ghaznavi Presided over another Session, and kept the discussions at a sophisticated level. My programme coordinator, Susan K. Hausman, handled the details of the seminar with her usual efficiency and her imaginative skills. Last, but not least, a colleague at Villanova University, my wife, Lynda P. Malik, a sociologist specializing on Islamic societies, not only participated in the seminar, but also acted as a cheerful host.

Hafeez Malik
Villanova University

1

Founders' Aspirations and Today's Realities: An Introduction

Hafeez Malik

Pakistan's political, social and religious life today is in glaring contrast to what the founding fathers—Quaid-i-Azam Muhammad Ali Jinnah (1876-1948) and Dr Muhammad Iqbal (1877-1938)—had aspired it to be. Contemporary reality would be disappointing to both.

Today's Pakistan is filled with the stench of sectarian violence, rabid religious fanaticism, the law of blasphemy, which has spawned an oppressive milieu against minorities, and the rush to pass the fifteenth amendment. The latter is done ostensibly to enforce Islamic provisions in the provinces, but would in all probability, whittle down provincial autonomy, and cause incalculable harm to national solidarity. All this is done in the name of Islam!

Jinnah and Iqbal espoused Muslim nationalism, and envisaged for Islam a progressive role: an Islam at once tolerant, and respectful of non-Muslim citizens and their faiths, enabling them to live in Pakistan as equal citizens, suffering from no legal or political discrimination. They expected Pakistan to be a democratic state under the rule of law, not to be periodically ruled by Martial law, imposed by the so-called 'historical scavengers.' Pakistan was expected to be a prosperous state, where science and technology (instead of theology) were to flourish. Pakistan was to be a beacon of enlightenment and progress in the Muslim world.

Sadly, economic development has almost come to a grinding halt, educational opportunities are starved of funding, and existing universities and colleges have become intellectual wastelands. Medical care for a mushrooming population (from 40 million in 1947 to 130 million in 1998) is woefully inadequate and substandard. Drawn mainly from the feudal and multi-millionaire industrialist classes, the political leadership has enriched itself by plundering ('borrowing') the nationalized banks, and receiving kickbacks from foreign sellers of industrial and military hardware. This may sound like excessive generalization, but is not without truthful content.

***

An eminent poet and a thinker, Iqbal articulated the two nation theory: Muslim India within India or without India. In 1930 in his presidential address at Allahabad, and thereafter in his letters to Jinnah, Iqbal proposed one or more autonomous Muslim states. Specifically, in the north he proposed a state which later came to be known as Pakistan.

Clearly, Iqbal's projected Muslim state in South Asia was a realistic choice. However, this State of Iqbal's vision was not to live in antagonism with India. He declared: 'Nor should the Hindus fear that the creation of autonomous Muslim states will mean the introduction of a kind of religious rule in such states.' Moreover, Iqbal assured India that the Muslim state would not collaborate with a Muslim invading force from abroad. In his vision, the Muslim state was supposed to be a political space to protect the Muslims' cultural personality, wherein as a numerical majority they would have the opportunity to mobilize the progressive spirit of Islam.

Islam in the Muslim state was to be dynamic, and relevant to modern times. Iqbal supported Ata Turk's abolition of the Ottoman Caliphate in 1922 as a relic of the past and applauded his religious reforms, especially the licensing of the *ulema* (religious scholars) and abolition of polygamy. Also, Iqbal applauded the elected Turkish national assembly, which was in consonance with the principle of *shura* (consultation) in Islam. Ideologically, he was opposed to nationalism, yet pragmatically he endorsed Turkish and Iranian nationalism. Obviously, secular nationalism was objectionable to him, especially where Muslims are in a minority, because its political milieu would lead Muslims to lose their distinct identity in a secular national life.

Iqbal was equally concerned about the distribution of wealth in society. Although he rejected its atheism, he was sympathetic to the Socialist movement. The question of whether or not he was actually a Socialist is still debated. Some of his followers, including the late Dr Khalifa Abdul Hakim, have described him as a 'Muslim Socialist',[1] who thought of Islam and Socialism as supplementing each other. Others claim that Iqbal agreed with all the economic aspects of Socialism and even approved of the destruction of all outmoded social institutions, because they hindered the spiritual growth of the individual.[2] Yet some scholars have suggested that Iqbal believed in a 'spiritual democracy', whatever it may mean.

Iqbal's conception of Socialism may appear to be utopian; however, the free market economy of capitalism is no panacea of all social and economic problems, as the world has begun to realize. However, deeply rooted in spiritual values, the paradigm of Iqbal's Socialism (or egalitarianism) is a midway paradigm between the Soviet totalitarianism and economic *laissez-faire* of the West. In light of this paradigm, Iqbal predicted that Asia in general, and Muslims in particular, would one day create a new world order, which would combine spirituality with material development of societies. Addressing an audience of the All-India Muslim National Conference, Iqbal developed this thesis:

> The peoples of Asia are bound to rise against the acquisitive economy which the West has developed and imposed on nations of the East. The faith you represent recognizes the worth of the individual, and disciplines him to give away his all to the service of God and man. Its possibilities are not yet exhausted. It can still create a new world order where the Social rank of man is not determined by his caste or colour or the amount of dividend he earns, but by the kind of life he lives; where the poor tax the

rich...where an untouchable may marry the daughter of a king, where private ownership is a trust and where capital cannot be allowed to accumulate so as to dominate the real producer of wealth. This superb idealism of your faith, however, needs emancipation from the medieval fancies of theologians and legists.[3]

Yet Iqbal's great contribution to the Pakistan idea lies in his relentless persuasion of Jinnah to opt for the Pakistan state. In a letter of 21 June 1937 Iqbal advised Jinnah: '...it is obvious that the only way to a peaceful India is a redistribution of the country on the lines of social, religious and linguistic affinities.' In the same letter, Iqbal asked Jinnah a rhetorical question: 'Why should not the Muslims of Northwest India and Bengal be considered as nations entitled to self-determination just as other nations in India and outside India?'[4]

Between 1936-7 Iqbal wrote eight letters to Jinnah, which were published by Jinnah with a Foreword after Iqbal had died in 1938 in which he acknowledged that Iqbal's views finally led him 'to the same conclusions as a result of careful examination and study of the constitutional problems facing India, and found expression in due course in the united will of Muslim India as enumerated in the Lahore Resolution of the All-India Muslim League, popularly known as the "Pakistan Resolution", passed on 23 March 1940'.[5]

***

Jinnah was indeed the builder of Pakistan. His Hindu and British opponents called him 'fanatic', 'most frigid, haughty and disdainful' and full of 'negative attitudes'. Yet they all grudgingly admired his incorruptible personality, intellectual brilliance, upright character and his unchallenged leadership of Muslims. His liberal and humane political philosophy became brightly visible after Pakistan had come into existence in August 1947.

The majesty of his liberal political vision steeped in the democratic values filtered through his monumental address, which he delivered to the Constituent Assembly of Pakistan on 11 August 1947. He admitted that at this point in time, he could not make a 'well-considered pronouncement' on the nature of the Constitution, but he emphasized some fundamental principles of governance:

(1) The first duty of a government is to maintain law and order, so that the life, property and religious beliefs of its subjects are fully protected by the State.
(2) Society was suffering from the biggest curses of bribery and corruption. That really is a poison. We must put that down with an iron hand.
(3) The evil of nepotism and jobbery...must be crushed relentlessly.
(4) The partition of the Punjab and Bengal—is now final and binding on all.
(5) 'If we want to make this great state of Pakistan happy and prosperous we should wholly and solely concentrate on the well-being of the people, and especially of the masses and poor.

If you will work in cooperation, forgetting the past, burying the hatchet, you are bound to succeed. If you change your past and work together in a spirit that every one of you, no matter to what community he belongs, no matter what relations he had with you in the past, no matter what is his colour, caste or creed, is first, second, and last a citizen of this State with equal rights, privileges and obligations, there will be no end to the progress you will make.

I cannot emphasize it too much. We should begin to work in that spirit and in course of time all these angularities of the majority and minority communities, the Hindu community and the Muslim community—because even as regards Muslims you have Pathans, Punjabis, Shias, Sunnis, and so on, and among the Hindus you have Brahmins, Vashnavas, Khatris, also Bengalees, Madrasis, and so on—will vanish.

Also, he articulated the notion of Pakistani nationalism which combined religious freedom, political equality, and the state's detachment from religious and sectarian squabbles. With emphasis he added:

> You are free; you are free to go to your temples, you are free to go to your mosques, or to any other place of worship in this State of Pakistan...You may belong to any religion or caste or creed–that has nothing to do with the business of the State...We are starting in the days when there is no discrimination, no distinction between one community and another, no discrimination between one caste or creed and another. We are starting with this fundamental principle that we are all citizens and equal citizens of one State. The people of England in course of time had to face the realities of the situation and had to discharge the responsibilities and burdens placed upon them by the government...Today, you might say with justice that Roman Catholics and Protestants do not exist; what exists now is that every man is a citizen, an equal citizen of Great Britain...all members of the Nation.[6]

Finally, he carried the logic of his reasoning to an ultimate and inescapable conclusion, which is the majesty of modern and liberal Islam:

> I think we should keep in front of us as our ideal and you will find that in course of time Hindus would cease to be Hindus and Muslims would cease to be Muslims, not in the religious sense, because that is the personal faith of each individual, but in the political sense as citizens of the State...I shall always be guided by the principles of justice and fairplay without any, as is put in the political language, prejudice or ill-will; in other words, partiality or favouritism. My guiding principle will be justice and complete impartiality, and I am sure that with your support and cooperation, I can look forward to Pakistan becoming one of the greatest Nations of the world.[7]

By August 1947 Jinnah's health was precarious. A year before his physician had predicted that the hectic pace of life would lead him to death in 'no more than eighteen months'.[8] 'He had consumption, soon to be compounded by cancer of the lungs', and when he died on 11 September 1948 'all that remained of him weighed only seventy pounds'.[9] If Jinnah had survived for another period of three years, he certainly would have led the Constituent Assembly to complete a democratic Constitution for Pakistan, although it is difficult to predict if he would have preferred the presidential or parliamentary system. Knowing his political and psychological proclivities one could wager that he would have recommended the presidential form of government for the republic.

***

From 1946-8, frail and consumptive Jinnah conducted the most arduous and delicate negotiations with the British government and the All-India National Congress, which was ideologically committed to a united and secular India. Led by Mahatma Gandhi, Jawaharlal Nehru, Sardar Vallabhbhai Patel, Abul Kalam Azad, Acharya Kripalani, and assisted by some lesser luminaries in the central working committee the Congress was politically well equipped to share the physical wear and tear of complicated negotiations with the British as well as the Muslim League. While the Congress maintained collective leadership, in fact the division of labour was also established. For instance, Patel was primarily responsible for the integration of 584 princely states into the Indian union. Mahatma Gandhi provided political and charismatic leadership, but by no means made decisions for the Congress.

Jinnah's associates, especially Liaquat Ali Khan and Sardar Abdur Rab Nishter, who often accompanied Jinnah in negotiations looked up to him to articulate negotiating strategy as well as tactics. The All-India Muslim League's Working Committee and the Council invariably ratified Jinnah's decisions, once he had firmly taken a position. Unlike the Congress, there was no division of labour among the Muslim League leaders. There is no evidence to indicate that any planning had been undertaken in regard to the issue of the princely states' accession to Pakistan, or the division of British India's assets, or the nature of East Bengal's relations with Pakistan should India be partitioned. Jinnah was indeed a one man 'collective leader'.

In addition to the burden of negotiations, the League leadership had to cope with the Muslim religious organizations' opposition to the creation of Pakistan. Most notable among them were: (1) Jamiat Ulama-i Hind; (2) the Deoband Dar al-Ulum; (3) Jamaat-i Islami of Maulana Abul Ala Maudoodi; (4) Majlis-i-Ahrar; and (5) the Khaksar Movement.[10] The followers of the latter twice attempted to assassinate Jinnah.

During this very tense and emotionally charged period (1946-48) and under very heavy pressures, the Muslim League leadership made two strategic errors of judgement: (1) the first error was the handling of the issues of accession by the rulers of Kashmir, Junagadh, and to a lesser extent that of Hyderabad. The embittered relations with India spawned by the 'vivisection of Mother India' (in Mahatma Gandhi's idiom) were further poisoned by the mismanagement of these states' accession to India or Pakistan. Subsequently, three wars were fought (especially two over Kashmir) and the end of conflict with India is not in sight even after fifty years of independence; and (2) the second error was the yoking of East Bengal with Pakistan.

Emergence of Pakistan: Accession of Kashmir, Junagadh, and Hyderabad

Instead of cooperating with the British during World War II, the Congress, under Mahatma Gandhi's leadership, started in 1942 the 'Quit India' campaign, forcing the British to declare Indian independence. Jinnah described it as 'blackmailing the British' in order to establish the Hindu Raj. In the wake of British defeat in Malaya, Singapore and Burma, many Congress leaders were doubtful of British victory and many were indifferent to the war effort. To solicit Indian cooperation, the British government sent Lord Privy Seal Sir Stafford Cripps to India in March 1942, who assured India in a declaration that (1) after the war 'an elected body would be set up with the task of framing a new constitution.' The second point in the declaration was most reassuring to Jinnah. It stated (2) 'the right of any province that was not prepared to accept the new Constitution to retain its existing position, provision being made for its subsequent accession.' The British government 'would be prepared to agree with a non-acceding province for a new constitution, arrived at by a similar representative process, and giving it the same status as the Indian Union itself'.[11] The Congress rejected the Cripps plan, Jinnah did not commit himself because the plan contained 'the implicit acceptance of Pakistan'.[12]

From now on Jinnah's negotiating strategy became crystal clear: he would let the British or Congress make an offer, which he would turn down, and ask for more. This enabled him to exploit their errors of judgement and to demand Pakistan. In this spirit Jinnah accepted the Cabinet Mission Plan of 1946, and when Nehru fumbled in establishing Congress' sovereignty over the plan's implementation, Jinnah wriggled out of it. The net advantage to Jinnah was that the basis of Pakistan was inherent 'in the grouping of the Muslim areas in Section B and C of the plan.[13]

Conceptually, the two independent states had come into existence in 1946, yet there is no evidence available to suggest that the League leadership had developed any cohesive strategy to deal with the issue of the princely states' accession, and especially that of Kashmir to Pakistan. In July 1947 the Indian Independence Act created two *de jure* states, which was an occasion to rethink the negotiating strategy. The transfer of power to India was to be accomplished no later than June 1948. This was announced on 20 February 1947. Jinnah was no longer negotiating with a political party, but the sovereign and independent State of India. While the issue of states' accession was rooted in the governance of British India, that the accession of states to India would be achieved through machiavellian techniques remained beyond the Muslim League leadership's intellectual horizon.

Like the accomplished lawyer that he was, Jinnah attempted to tackle the accession issue in a legal framework. Yet the strategy in the transformed political milieu called for the technique of *realpolitik*. This implied that the Muslim League leadership should have bargained with the Indian leadership: giving to India, what at that time India wanted most—smooth and non-disruptive transfer of the states of Junagadh and

Hyderabad to India, where Pakistan exercised decisive influence, and in a quid pro quo to receive Kashmir, if not all, then those parts of this heterogeneous state which were predominantly Muslim. Jinnah had already accepted the principle of partition within partition, that is, the division of the Punjab and Bengal, along the line of the Hindu-Muslim divide. This led him to call the new Muslim state 'a moth-eaten Pakistan'. Mortally afraid of India's 'balkanization', the Congress leadership would have been in all probability receptive to this bargain. This is not merely a conjecture, a great deal of circumstantial evidence lends credence to this thesis.

Granted, that the State of Jammu and Kashmir had a population of 4,021,160 (in 1949) of which 78-85 per cent was Muslim. But this Muslim population was concentrated in certain parts: (1) Gilgit; (2) Hunza; (3) Baltistan; (4) Poonch, and (5) the Kashmir valley. Jammu was predominantly Hindu, with the exception of two or three Muslim *tehsils* (sub-districts). Ladakh was (and still is) Buddhist, where the population is ethnically related to the Tibetans. Following the principle of self-determination, the Ladakhis should belong neither to India nor Pakistan. The Kashmir valley is no more than 10 per cent of the total area of the historical Kashmir state. Currently, Pakistan retains control over Gilgit, Hunza and Baltistan, the redesignated northern areas, and Azad Kashmir which includes parts of Poonch. Pakistan's real loss has been the Kashmir valley, which was incorporated into the Indian Union with force. This loss could have been avoided in quid pro quo negotiations with India before August 1947.

Instead of territorial bargaining, Jinnah accepted in a statement on 19 June 1947:

> ...the Indian [princely] states will be independent sovereign states on the termination of [British] paramountcy...it is open to them to join the Hindustan Constituent Assembly or the Pakistan Constituent Assembly, or to decide to remain independent...we do not wish to interefere with the internal affairs of any state, for that is a matter primarily to be resolved between the rulers and the peoples of the states'.[14]

In legal terms it meant that a ruler could sign the instrument of accession, to join either India or Pakistan. On 15 August 1947 Junagadh state announced its decision to accede to Pakistan, while the Hindu ruler of Kashmir joined India on 26 October 1947.

In Junagadh the population was overwhelmingly Hindu, the ruler was indeed Muslim, and the reverse was true in Kashmir. However, Junagadh was sacred to Hindu sentiment because it was believed to be the death-place of Lord Krishna, and is the site of the famous Temple of Somnath, which was sacked by Sultan Mahmud Ghazanvi in 1024. (Incidentally, when India took over Junagadh 'the temple was restored at great expense.')[15] India, as well as Pakistan, rejected the accessions of Junagadh and Kashmir.

In a court of law, Jinnah would have successfully argued his case by striking a plea bargain: Pakistan withdraws its claim to Junagadh, and India should do the same in regard to Kashmir. Jinnah's tactical and legal shrewdness would have paid off. But this case was not in a British court of law. Here two sovereigns were playing a zero-sum game for high geo-strategic advantages. On the other hand, a political strategy of demanding plebiscite in disputed areas, especially in Kashmir, Junagadh (and in Hyderabad) might have secured the Kashmir valley for Pakistan in light of the principle of partition within partition. This approach could not be considered outlandish since the Indian leadership had successfully insisted on a plebiscite before 15 August 1947 in the Northwestern Frontier Province of Pakistan.

For this strategy to have a chance of success, Jinnah needed to have the goodwill of Lord Mountbatten, the last British Viceroy of India. Their relations were problematic: two titanic egos had a head-on collision, both determined to protect their place in the sun. One represented the waning imperial power, operating in collusion with Indian leadership, and presiding over an established state, which had inherited the material and intellectual resources of the British Raj; the other, who considered himself the equal of Mountbatten, if not his superior, was confident of his political skills and unchallenged leadership over the Muslims, who were completely mesmerized by his charisma. Mountbatten had offended Jinnah by using the principle of partition within partition in the case of Punjab and Bengal. Jinnah wounded Mountbatten's ego by denying him the opportunity to be even the part-time Governor-General of Pakistan. How bitter was their relationship can be gathered from a dialogue, which was recorded by Mountbatten on 2 July 1947:

> Mountbatten: 'I pointed out to him if he became the constitutional Governor-General of Pakistan his powers would be constitutionally restricted, and that he would act only on advice, but that as Prime Minister he could run Pakistan.'
> Jinnah: 'In my position it is I who will give the advice, and others will act on it'.
> Mountbatten: 'Do you realize what this will cost you?'
> Jinnah: 'It may cost me several crores of rupees in assets.'
> Mountbatten: 'I replied somewhat acidly: It may well cost you the whole of your assets, and the future of Pakistan.' He added, 'I then gave up and left the room.'[16]

What was the major cost to Pakistan? Kashmir! India, with Mountbatten's collaboration, managed to obtain Kashmir's accession to India and cheated Pakistan out of a legitimate inheritance. Kashmir's disposition in this unjust manner sowed the seeds of enmity and distrust between the two states, and Mountbatten must be held responsible in large measure for this unfortunate consequence. On a personal level, Mountbatten turned the table on Jinnah and hoisted him on his own petard in a face to face conversation of three and a half hours over Kashmir on 1 November 1947 at Lahore:

> Jinnah: 'Expressed surprise at the remarkable speed at which we [Government of India] had been able to organize sending troops into the Srinagar plain'...
> Continuing: 'The accession was not a bona fide one since it rested on "fraud and violence" and would never be accepted by Pakistan'.

Mountbatten: 'I asked him to explain why he used the term 'fraud', since the Maharajah was fully entitled in accordance with Pakistan's own official statement about Junagadh—to make such accession. It was, therefore, perfectly legal and valid'.

Jinnah: 'This accession was the end of a long intrigue and that it had been brought about by violence'.

Mountbatten: 'I entirely agree that the accession had been brought about by violence; I knew the Maharajah was most anxious to remain independent, and nothing but the terror of violence could have made him accede to either dominion...the violence had come from tribes for whom Pakistan was responsible'.[17]

To inflict further damage on Pakistan, Mountbatten also interfered with the work of the Boundary Commission. As he himself admitted, Kashmir's accession to India would be 'a practical proposition' only if the three eastern *tehsils* (sub-districts) of Gurdaspur district were allotted to India, which would make Kashmir a contiguous territory with that of India. The first schedule of the Indian Independence Act of 18 July 1947 had given the entire district to Pakistan. In the final Boundary Commission award of 12 August which was not published until 15 August 1947, through Mountbatten's intervention, the three *tehsils* of Gurdaspur were awarded to India.[18] This cartographic dishonesty created a safe and all year round route from India to Kashmir!

Mountbatten lived up to his words: 'Mr. Jinnah, it may well cost you the whole of your assets, and the future of Pakistan.' It did!

***

Joining of East Bengal with (West) Pakistan

This was against the best judgement of Iqbal, and the Muslim League leadership. In his presidential address at Allahabad in 1930 and in his letters to Jinnah, Iqbal had visualized two states, one in the north-west (Pakistan), and the other in the East. The same formulation was reiterated on 23 March 1940 at the session of the Muslim League in Lahore. Specifically, it was stated 'that the areas in which the Muslims are numerically in a majority as in the North-western and Eastern zones of India, should be grouped to constitute independent states in which the constituent units shall be autonomous and sovereign'.[19]

However, meeting in Delhi on 9 April 1946 the Muslim League legislators bypassed the Lahore Resolution of 1940 to include Bengal in the State of Pakistan. This may have been a shrewd tactic to pacify the Congress that British India would not be balkanized and only two states would emerge as the consequence of partition; yet Jinnah remained unconvinced that a two winged Pakistan, separated by 1000 miles of hostile Indian territory, would be a feasible state. In recognition of this impossibility, Jinnah demanded that a corridor across India should be allowed to connect the two separated parts of Pakistan. Needless to say that the Congress leadership rejected the proposal out of hand.[20]

Not all Bengali leaders were interested in joining the two-winged state. An alternative proposal was advanced by Hussain Shaheed Suhrawardy for Mountbatten and Jinnah's consideration: Would it be acceptable to Jinnah if Bengal remained united 'at the price of its remaining out of Pakistan.' Mountbatten recorded his interview with Jinnah on 26 April 1947. 'Without any hesitation,' Jinnah said, 'I should be delighted. What is the use of Bengal without Calcutta, they had much better remain united and independent; I am sure they would be on friendly terms with us.'[21]

Like Jinnah, Liaquat Ali Khan (who later became the first prime minister of Pakistan), had the same view on a united and independent Bengal. He informed Sir Eric Mieville 'that he was in no way worried about Bengal as he was convinced in his own mind that the province would never divide. He thought it would remain a separate state, joining neither Hindustan [India] nor Pakistan'.[22]

However, when the Punjab and Bengal were divided, Jinnah accepted divided (East) Bengal in the new state of Pakistan. In addition to the separated geography of Bengal, its union with

Pakistan created a demographic anamoly: much smaller in size the fifth province of Bengal contained more than 50 per cent of the country's population compared to the four provinces of (West) Pakistan, and the acquired territories of Kashmir. Not knowing the depth of Bengali (sub-) national sentiment, Jinnah made another error of judgement. Ill and tired, Jinnah flew to Dhaka and delivered on 21 March 1948 a stunning speech in English before an estimated crowd of 300,000 non-Urdu speaking Bengalis and said: 'The state language of Pakistan is going to be Urdu and no other language'.[23] The negative reaction of the crowd was loud and clear.

Geographically, linguistically, and culturally, Bengal was a 'foreign' territory. With the exception of Islam, it had nothing in common with the people of Pakistan. It should have been allowed to go its own way, either in union with West Bengal or India, as Jinnah had originally preferred in April 1947, or as an independent state, which it became in 1971 as Bangladesh. Pakistan would not have suffered the trauma of defeat at the hands of India, and Pakistan would have developed realistic policies in consonance with its size and resources.

***

India-Pakistan wars, spawned by Kashmir and Bangladesh have generated so much bitterness and alienation between the peoples of India and Pakistan that not a shred of confidence is left between them. This is the greatest tragedy!

Political dynamics in recent history have demonstrated that when multi-national states break up violence invariably ensues. The splintering of Yugoslavia in the 1990s is a painful reminder and so is the case of the former Soviet Union. Unresolved issues generate mistrust and deepen a sense of grievance against the dominant nationalities. The American Civil War took a little more than 100 years to significantly diminish rancour so that a southerner, like Jimmy Carter, could be elected President. One does not expect a smooth friendly relationship to develop in the near future between India and Pakistan. All one can hope for is the start of a peaceful co-existence, which might extend its therapeutic impact.

In this positive spirit the seminar at Villanova University examined fifty years of Pakistan's existence, neither to indict it for its failures nor to gloss over them. A candid appraisal was expected of American and Pakistani scholars and the notable Pakistani public figures; the latter have had profound experience in the working of Pakistani governments at the highest levels. Their collective endeavours in this volume provide a variety of interpretations regarding Pakistan's performance as a state.

Constitutional and Political Development of Pakistan and the Role of the Military in Pakistani Politics

Pakistan's three well-known public figures—S.M. Zafar, Javid Iqbal, Khalid Mahmud Arif—and a well-known American scholar, specializing on Pakistan, Craig Baxter, have exhaustively explored the constitutional development of Pakistan. All four perceive the process of development through different prisms.

A former Minister of Law under President Ayub Khan, and currently Pakistan's premier attorney, Zafar has offered a detailed constitutional analysis of Pakistan. He has described Jinnah as the *Rehbar* (leader), (incidentally, a term which has been used in the Iranian Constitution for the Supreme head of the Islamic Republic of Iran). As Governor-General, Jinnah 'participated in the cabinet responsibilities', functioned as president of the Constituent Assembly, and its constitutional adviser. All three functions rolled into the *Rehbar* concentrated an enormous amount of power in Jinnah. He died one year after the advent of Pakistan. There is no clue in Zafar's analysis as to what kind of political system—presidential or parliamentary—would have emerged under his stewardship; however, in March 1949 the Constituent Assembly adopted the Objectives Resolution, which 'combined federalism, democracy and popular sovereignty with Islamic principles'.

Liaquat Ali Khan, the first Prime Minister, submitted a draft constitution, which he withdrew after two months, that provided enormous powers to the head of state, including the power to suspend the Constitution in whole or in part, and to dismiss the provincial governments. Here, Zafar speculates that Liaquat probably preferred the presidential to parliamentary form of government for Pakistan. By the time Liaquat was assassinated in October 1951 no constitution had been adopted.

This situation encouraged the upper crust of bureaucracy to assume the leading roles. Consequently, the politicians surrendered their right to govern the state. A bureaucrat turned Governor-General, Ghulam Muhammad, struck the first fatal blow to the draft constitution of 1954. Muhammad Ali, another bureaucrat turned Prime Minister, had the Constituent Assembly adopt another Constitution, which was enforced on 25 March 1956. Two years later this Constitution was abrogated by President Iskandar Mirza, who was then overthrown by General Ayub Khan, who became the President and established the presidential form of government.

Ayub Khan's regime lasted until March 1969, when he was forced to resign. He transferred power to his Commander-in-Chief, General Yahya Khan, who clamped Martial Law on Pakistan, and by his short-sighted policies, led the country to a civil war with East Pakistan, and a military defeat at the hands of India. Zulfikar Ali Bhutto, who succeeded General Yahya Khan, was subsequently overthrown by the Chief of the Army Staff, General Ziaul Haq, in July 1977.

However, a new Pakistan was ushered in by Bhutto with a new Constitution in 1973 which established a parliamentary form of government in Pakistan. For the last twenty-five years, Pakistan's political culture has evolved under this Constitution, which was one of Bhutto's significant contributions to Pakistan. Zafar's chapter meanders through Pakistan's constitutional development, and finally speculates on the 1973 Constitution's relative popularity, and its future prospects.

A former Justice of the Supreme Court and currently a Senator of Pakistan, Javid Iqbal has presented the role of the judiciary in the constitutional crises of Pakistan. Iqbal has highlighted the role of the federal judiciary in every struggle for power between the Governor-General/President and the federal legislature. The first constitutional phase under the Government of India Act 1935 (modified by the Act of Independence in 1947) lasted from 1947-56. During this period, two crises erupted: One in October 1954, when Governor-General Ghulam Muhammad dissolved the Constituent Assembly because it planned to reduce his powers. The Federal Court upheld his action, but restrained him from legislating on constitutional matters. The 1956 Constitution was abrogated by President Mirza, who proclaimed Martial Law on 7 October 1958. Mirza, in a short period of time, was sent into exile by General Ayub Khan. When Martial Law was challenged in the Supreme Court, the Chief Justice Muhammad Munir in his judgment of 27 October 1958, proclaimed: 'a victorious revolution or a successful *coup d'état* an internationally recognized method of changing a legal order.'

After the secession of Bangladesh in December 1971 Yahya Khan abdicated, and Bhutto took control of the country. Iqbal believes that from March 1969 to December 1971 Pakistani courts 'receded into the background', because 'the jurisdiction of the superior courts was curtailed' retroactively from 25 March 1969. However, between December 1971-April 1972 the Supreme Court delivered some important judgments: (1) Yahya Khan was 'declared a usurper, who had no authority to abrogate the 1962 Constitution and to impose Martial Law'; (2) the Supreme Court sentenced a 'general to a simple imprisonment until the rising of the court' for committing contempt of the court'.

Under Bhutto, Iqbal maintains, five constitutional amendments were made to control or curb the independence of the judiciary. However, Bhutto's government lasted for less than six years and he was deposed in July 1977. Once again, Martial Law was imposed. The Supreme Court, once again, justified the imposition of Martial Law by General Ziaul Haq, who proceeded to curtail the independence of the judiciary by 'numerous devices'. In the last section of his analysis, Iqbal has drawn some conclusions about the role of the judiciary. He says: (1) Whenever Pakistan was ruled by a constitution, the judiciary was 'prompt to uphold the supremacy of the Constitution and the rule of law'; (2) Recently (1998), the Chief Justice of Pakistan engaged in a head-on collision with the Prime Minister 'without any judicial restraint'. The result, indeed, was not a compliment either to the Chief Justice or the Prime Minister; both behaved equally gracelessly. Finally, the Chief Justice was removed, but the Supreme Court continued to function effectively.

A former Commander of the Pakistan Army from 1984-1987, General Khalid Mahmud Arif has very thoughtfully examined in detail the Pakistan Army's take-over of the civilian governments three times over a period of fifty years, and speculated upon the lessons that might be learned for the future. The history of Pakistan is riddled with political instability. Arif pointed out that of Pakistan's 'eleven heads of state, six were either soldiers or bureaucrats.' Their cumulative tenure lasted for thirty-six years. Their 'achievements' included 'the dismissal of eight out of the fifteen prime ministers, dissolution of seven out of the ten national assemblies, and banning five out of the seven political parties that were outlawed.' In between these episodes Pakistan experimented with four different types of political systems—parliamentary, presidential, military, and 'a half-breed between the parliamentary and presidential system.'

What are the factors which caused this instability? Arif has enumerated several factors: (1) Pakistan inherited a country without the infrastructure of a state; (2) the immediate influx of millions of refugees from India; (3) the early death of the founding father, Jinnah; (4) Pakistan's nascent political system 'suffered a double jeopardy', internal difficulties, which were 'compounded by the aggressive policies of India'; and last, but not least (5) the inexperienced and inefficient politicians of Pakistan, who 'made a mockery of democracy.' These factors, Arif has argued 'created a vacuum that started a chain reaction', leading the armed forces to intervene intermittently in the political process of the governance of Pakistan.

While Arif has highlighted the military's positive contributions, he has not overlooked some of the damage that was done to the army's professional role. They are (1) starting in 1947, there was 'a bonanza of promotions,' which raised inexperienced junior officers to positions of higher command; (2) 'swift promotions from junior to senior ranks', bred indiscipline, which led to the first left oriented aborted coup of 1951, which came to be known as the Rawalpindi Conspiracy case; (3) during the middle 1950s, General Ayub Khan was included in the Federal Cabinet, which 'set in motion a process that eventually sucked the military into the political quagmire'; (4) grant of extensions of service to staff officers from a term of four to more years created 'non-professional ideas in the minds of the affected commanders'; (5) senior army officers were cultivated by political leaders, which encouraged the officers to career opportunism; (6) during martial law periods, the military governments co-existed with the higher judiciary, but the implication was that the judiciary played second fiddle to the military; and finally, (7) Arif forthrightly admits that 'martial law retarded the growth of democracy, weakened the political system, caused constitutional crises and hindered the development of institutions.'

A well-known American scholar, who for some years served in Pakistan as an American Foreign Service Officer, Craig Baxter has examined Pakistan as a 'failed state'. He has judged Pakistan in the light of 'five factors', that 'are the goals of every state', including: (1) state building, (2) nation building, (3) economy building, (4) participation; and (5) distribution. Baxter sees the development of institutions, governmental, and non-governmental, as parts of state building. In these matters, he believes Pakistan has failed, while 'it inherited a functioning form of government from British India.' He adds: 'There were in place the elements of government that are described as executive or administrative. There existed a civil service that administered governments at the Centre and in the provinces, a police force, a military establishment, and other essentials necessary to administer this new entity, the state of Pakistan.'

In other words, according to Baxter's thesis, all the state institutions were in place, when Pakistan came into existence in 1947; except that the Pakistani leaders failed to function appropriately. The first part of his thesis does not stand up in the light of historical facts, as General Arif has so convincingly demonstrated in his chapter. One might add (as an eye witness) that the provincial institutions indeed existed in 1947, but that the infrastructure of the federal government was non-existent. Moreover, the federal leaders, including Jinnah, and his 'close' associates, migrated from India in August 1947, and were in a sense 'strangers' to the cultural milieu of (West) Pakistan. These factors very substantially contributed to the many failures of Pakistan, which Baxter has highlighted.

Nuclear Capability of Pakistan and Explosions in India and Pakistan in April-May 1998

A former Chairman of the Pakistan Atomic Energy Commission, Munir Ahmad Khan has presented a very comprehensive history of nuclear development in India and Pakistan. He maintains that 'some leaders in India and Pakistan still regard nuclear weapons as the hard currency of power and as means of domination [India] or deterrence [Pakistan].' Against this moral and political assessment Munir Khan has laid out the milestones of Pakistan's efforts to become a nuclear power: (1) Prime Minister Z.A. Bhutto's initiative in 1972 (in response to India's progress in nuclear development) to establish the Ministry of Science and Technology under his own leadership, and authorizing the Atomic Energy Commission to build the infrastructure, and develop the necessary manpower; (2) reaction to India's nuclear explosion in 1974; (3) the development of various nuclear facilities, including nuclear fuel and enrichment plant; (4) the United States aid cut-off to Pakistan in April 1979 and (5) Pakistan's efforts for non-proliferation, especially involving India. These efforts included proposals for India and Pakistan to sign the NPT, accept full-scope safeguards, calling for reciprocal inspections, signing a bilateral treaty banning nuclear tests, establishing a nuclear free zone in South Asia, and issuing a joint declaration of non-acquisition or manufacture of nuclear weapons. None of these proposals were accepted by India.

Munir Khan pointed out that the 1980-90 decade was a troubled period for US-Pakistan relations over the nuclear issue. The US imposed sanctions on Pakistan, which were multiplied in the wake of Pakistan's nuclear explosion in May 1998.

Walid Iqbal, an attorney-at-law with the prestigious New York law firm of Cromwell and Sullivan, has discussed exhaustively the US reactions to the India-Pakistan explosions. The US Senator, Jesse Helms, commented acidly: 'The Indian government has not shot itself in the foot—it has most likely shot itself in the head.' Walid Iqbal contends, on the other hand, that the Indian strategists had carefully and 'meticulously planned' their move. The Indians had calculated that the Indian economy, with its output in goods and services totaling $350 billion in fiscal 1996, could sustain the harshest of sanctions.

Iqbal has argued that Pakistan's economy and other resources, which are indeed smaller than India's, cannot easily absorb the negative input of the sanctions. While the Indian government 'brushed off the idea of sanctions', the Pakistan government initially 'issued cautious statements like *the nature and duration of sanctions*, and 'panicked in the face of the aftermath'. Also, Iqbal has argued that 'economic sanctions are a preferred apparatus of Congress', while the administration considers them counterproductive.

Finally, Iqbal has attempted to look into the future. The United States is now into a bilateral dialogue with India and Pakistan 'to settle' the nuclear issue. What does the US want? The answer was recently provided by the Secretary of State, Madeleine Albright, on 30 September 1998:

(1) signing and ratifying the CTBT (Comprehensive Test Ban Treaty); (2) finding a formula for a moratorium on producing fissile material; (3) structuring a restrained regime on nuclear weapons, and their means of delivery; (4) to demonstrate their [India and

Pakistan] intent to avoid a nuclear arms race; and (5) actually strengthening their export control regime.

Bilateral negotiations of the United States with India and Pakistan would stretch into the future. For how long? That is anybody's guess.

In the wake of nuclear explosions, US-imposed sanctions have indeed placed tremendous strains on Pakistan's economy. Yet a reputable American economist, Robert E. Looney, who is Professor of Economics at the Naval Postgraduate School in Monterey in California, has presented a rather optimistic picture of Pakistan's economic development. 'Since independence, Pakistan can look back on fifty years of steady, sometimes spectacular economic advance. Pakistan's growth has been the fastest in South Asia.' Looney maintains that 'Pakistan started behind India at the time of independence, but its income per capita is now 75 per cent higher. In spite of high population growth, per capita income has more than tripled in the past two decades.'

Despite these accomplishments, Looney has pointed out some shortcomings, which include: (1) 'large budgetary and balance of payment deficits; (2) increasing inflationary pressures; (3) population explosion and rising unemployment; (4) physical infrastructure constraints, and (5) inadequate human resources development.' Finally, Looney has raised some basic social and political questions about Pakistan's economy: Is progress sustainable, and why are its people so poor when the economy has made such rapid progress? And the mother of all questions—to what extent can democracy be sustained in light of the massive economic and social difficulties the country currently faces? His analysis of these issues is critical, but is by no means pessimistic.

Sectarian Conflict in Pakistan

Two well-known Pakistani-American scholars, Anwar H. Syed and Afaq Haydar, have dealt with the perennial Shia-Sunni conflict, which has periodically erupted into violence. The bifurcation of the Muslims into two denominations can be traced back to Prophet Muhammad's (PBUH) death in June 632 AD. Soon after the Prophet's death was announced, the people of Medina (the Ansars) congregated at Saqifa Banu Sa'ida (an old Assembly hall of Banu Sa'ida) to choose their leader. The *Muhajireen* (the immigrants) led by Abu Bakr and Umar Ibn al-Khatab, persuaded the Ansar (the Prophet's helpers) to accept Abu Bakr as the first Caliph of the Muslim community. At this meeting, some people advanced Ali, the cousin and son-in-law of the Prophet (PBUH), as the most desirable successor. Consequently, the Saqifa 'should be taken as a generic name for the first split among the Muslims'.[24] This initial split later in July 657 AD exploded into a civil war between Ali and Mu'awiya, when the latter accused Ali of instigating a rebellion against Osman, the third Caliph, and Osman's assassination on 17 June 656 AD.[25]

Destined to endure with the life of Islam, the Shia-Sunni split periodically gets out of control and causes immense harm to Pakistan's national solidarity. It is not out of place to point out that the Founder of Pakistan, Jinnah, hailed from a Khoja family of Ismailis, a branch within the Shia denomination.[26] Syed has very thoroughly analyzed the religio-social factors of discord between the Shia and the Sunni in Pakistan. He has skillfully highlighted the issues where the two agree with each other and where they disagree.

In dealing with the prospects of conflict control, Syed has highlighted several possibilities, but in the final analysis has ended up hoping not very strongly that 'while conflict cannot be abolished, it can be managed and controlled.' Can it be done now in Pakistan? Syed has responded negatively. This is the saddest chapter of Pakistan's history.

Anwar Syed and Afak Haydar have agreed on the nature of catalytic forces, which have ignited Shia-Sunni conflict in the current phase. They are:

(1) General Ziaul Haq's unfortunate rule of eleven years, and his thirty-three policies of Islamization, signalling the

establishment of Sunni (Hanafi) interpretation and application of Islamic laws.

(2) Iran's Shi'a revolution, which triumphed in 1979, and the Saudi policies for religious affairs in Pakistan.

(3) 'The socio-political environment' of Jhang city, and the district, and its impact on the religious sensitivities of the people of Punjab.

(4) The emergence of extremist groups among the Shia and Sunni organizations.

(5) The Shia and Sunni ulema's ambitions to play political role in Pakistan, and to harvest economic benefits, which accompany political power.

Pakistan's Relations with the United States, Russia, China, and the Middle East

Two former ambassadors and an academic, including Dennis Kux, Hafeez Malik, and Abdul Sattar, examined Pakistan's relations with the United States, the former Soviet Union, and its successor state, Russia, China, and the Middle East.

A former foreign service officer, Ambassador Dennis Kux maintained that

> 'a graph of the first fifty years of US-Pakistan relations shows a series of highs and lows, of sharp and uneven fluctuations.' He added that 'there have been three periods of close, even intimate, ties—the alliances of the 1950s, the Nixon-Ford years in the early 1970s, and the Afghan war partnership during the 1980s. There were also three periods of friction—during the Kennedy-Johnson years of the 1960s, at the time of the Carter administration in the late 1970s, and again after George Bush infused nuclear sanctions under the Pressler amendment in 1990'.

Finally, Ambassador Kux pinpointed

> two middling periods of superficially friendly, but substantially thin relations—during the Truman presidency and the latter 1990s.

One might add that at present there is indeed a great need to restructure 'the friendly and normal' relations between the two states, especially in the wake of the nuclear explosions.

Hafeez Malik, who has worked for two decades in specializing on Soviet/Russia-Pakistan relations, maintained that 'Pakistan's graph of fifty years of its relations (1947-91) first with the Soviet Union, and then with Russia, shows no highs, but a series of lows, reflecting a calculated disregard for the geostrategic imperatives of Eurasia. Malik then highlighted some of the significant 'lows', including: (1) the early options for some strategic decisions; (2) the crisis of Bangladesh; (3) attempts at bilateralism, and (4) the Soviet debacle over Afghanistan. Finally, an analytical word or two were added about Pakistan-Russian relations to cover the period of 1991–98.

Malik posited the thesis that after December 1991, when the USSR collapsed, Pakistan had the best opportunity to cement new relations with Russia in order to unlock India's claim on an exclusive friendship with Moscow. Russia could have become an alternative source of military hardware for Pakistan, as it has been for India, especially at a time when President Bush imposed nuclear sanctions in 1990. Thoughtlessly, those opportunities were squandered by Pakistan. In order to develop constructive relations with the newly independent Central Asian states, Pakistan needed Russia's confidence, if not its support.

Ambassador Abdul Sattar pointed out that Pakistan wanted to promote close relations with the countries of Asia and the Middle East, but also looked to the West for cooperation for its economic development of the western states. He is highly critical of Britain, especially the last British Viceroy, Lord Mountbatten, who 'pursued London's preference [for India] with simple-minded enthusiasm, believing that if independent India joined the British Commonwealth, its value to the United Kingdom both in terms of world prestige and strategy, would be enormous.'

In the East, Pakistan had great luck with China, who ignored Pakistan's anti-Communist rhetoric, and cultivated relations with Pakistan. In 1965, when Chinese Premier Zhou Enlai visited

Pakistan, the two powers stated that 'there is no real conflict of interests between the two countries.' This commonality of national interest became the solid foundation on which China and Pakistan have built an edifice of collaborative relations ever since 1965, which includes economic and technical aid, and nuclear cooperation.

Pakistan's relations with the Arab states have not been trouble free for several reasons: (1) Pakistan's alliance policy, especially with the United States during 1947-1978; (2) Pakistan's stance during the Suez crisis of 1956 was perceived by the Arabs to be almost hostile; and (3) Pakistan's partnership with Iran and Turkey first in the Baghdad Pact, and then in CENTO. In the last part of his chapter, Sattar has thoroughly explored Pakistan's role in confronting the Soviet Union in Afghanistan. In contemplating Pakistan's foreign policy over a period of fifty years, and especially the selection of alliances, Sattar concluded that 'the policy of alliance Pakistani leaders instinctively followed after independence was not flawed conceptually though it suffered at times from errors of judgment.'

India-Pakistan Relations and the Kashmir Problem

Unlike other states, India-Pakistan relations fall in a unique category: neither 'peace' nor 'war', and neither cooperation nor even the semblance of normal relations. These 'relations' are based upon protracted conflict over Kashmir, and its origins are embedded in the division of India in 1947. India was then and now bigger and stronger and could grab the territory of Kashmir by sheer power, and Pakistan could do really very little to remove Indian occupation of Kashmir. Robert Wirsing, who has done a great deal of research on this conflict, has presented an up to date survey of both countries' public opinion. This is by no means a 'scientific survey' as a methodologist would understand, but is the product of a kind of random survey conducted among the elites of India and Pakistan, who are generally well informed.

In Pakistan, Wirsing detected 'surprising willingness to rethink Pakistan's long-standing official position on Jammu and Kashmir...[and] recraft those aspects of it that had proven unproductive.' In India, on the other hand, there is universal view that 'India was in a powerful position to ward off any challenge to its control of Kashmir from Pakistan or elsewhere'. Moreover, Indians generally perceive Pakistan as 'a nation in social, economic and politial tatters', who has 'lost the strategic advantages granted it by the cold war'.

Within the framework of these perceptions, what are the possibilities for a settlement? From the Indian perspective, the solution seems to be Pakistan's acceptance of the present Line of Control, leaving the Kashmir Valley on the Indian side. The recent nuclear explosions by both states have made any radical solution a wellnigh impossibility. So the stalemate would continue!

NOTES

1. Dr Khalifah Abdul Hakim, *Fikr-i-Iqbal* (Lahore: Bazm-i Iqbal, n.d.), p. 255.
2. Ibid., p. 258.
3. For full text see, 'Shamloo', *Speeches and Statements of Iqbal* (Lahore: Al-Manai Academy, 1948), p. 54.
4. Muhammad Ali Jinnah, *Letters of Iqbal to Jinnah* (Lahore: Shaikh Muhammad Ashraf, 1956), p. 14. See also, Hafeez Malik, *Iqbal: Poet-Philosopher of Pakistan* (New York: Columbia University Press, 1971), pp. 383–8.
5. Ibid., pp. 384–5.
6. *Speeches of Quaid-i-Azam Muhammad Ali Jinnah as Governor-General of Pakistan* (Karachi: Sindh Observer Press, 1948), pp. 4–5.
7. Ibid., pp. 9-10.
8. Muhammad Munir (Retired Chief Justice of Pakistan), *Quaid-i-Azam Muhammad Ali Jinnah* (Lahore: Punjab University Press, 1976), p. 13.
9. Stanley Wolpert, *Jinnah of Pakistan* (New York: Oxford University Press, 1984), p. 370.
10. For the ideological position of these Muslim religious organizations see, Hafeez Malik, *Muslim Nationalism in India and Pakistan* (Washington, DC: Public Affairs Press, 1963), Chapter IX.

11. H.V. Hodson, *The Great Divide: Britain-India-Pakistan* (Oxford University Press, 1969), p. 96.
12. Ibid., p. 98.
13. Ibid., p. 153.
14. The Indian Annual Register (Delhi: 1947), p. 112.
15. Hodson, op.cit., p. 428.
16. *Report on the Last Viceroyalty* and *Viceroy's Personal Report*, No. 11, 4 July 1947; also Hodson, op.cit., p. 331.
17. *Mountbatten's Personal Report*, pp. 347–52 in Wolpert, op.cit., p. 352.
18. For details see, Lamb, op.cit., pp. 111–14.
19. For the text of the Lahore resolution see, Sharif Al-Mujahid, *Quaid-i-Azam Jinnah: Studies in Interpretation* (Karachi: Quaid-i-Azam Academy, 1981), pp. 497–8.
20. For details see, G. Allana, *Quaid-i-Azam Jinnah: The Story of a Nation* (Lahore: Ferozsons Ltd., 1967), pp. 445–6.
21. Record of Interview with Jinnah, 26 April 1947, pp. 452–3 in Wolpert, op.cit., p. 322.
22. Ibid., p. 323.
23. *Quaid-i-Azam Speaks: Speeches of Quaid-i-Azam Muhammad Ali Jinnah* (Karachi: Ministry of Information and Broadcasting, 1950), pp. 133–6.
24. For a detailed expositon of Shiaism, see an excellent study by S. H. M. Jafri, *The Origins and Early Development of Shia Islam* (London: Longman, 1979), p. 27.
25. For details on these issues, see an excellent study by Wilferd Madelung, *The Succession to Muhammad* (Cambridge: Cambridge University Press, 1997), Chapter 3.
26. Allana, op.cit., pp. 7–13.

2

Constitutional Development
S.M. Zafar

The constitutional history of Pakistan began even before Pakistan was legally constituted as a state. The Constituent Assembly of Pakistan had met on 10 August 1947,[1] and had the dual responsibilities of framing the Constitution and acting as a federal legislature or Parliament until a Constitution for the new state came into effect. Quaid-i-Azam Muhammad Ali Jinnah was elected its first President and he addressed the Constituent Assembly of Pakistan on 11 August 1947. The state of Pakistan later came into existence on 15 August 1947.[2] Lord Mountbatten, the last British Viceroy, wanted to be the Governor-General of both states, as the Indian Independence Act had provided that, unless a provision to the contrary is made by a legislative enactment of either of the two dominions, the same person may be Governor-General of both.[3] Jinnah rejected this option, and became the first Governor-General of Pakistan.

By virtue of the Indian Independence Act, the Governor-General was to be appointed by His Majesty (the Sovereign of Britain) to represent him in administering the government of the Dominions. The oath of the office of the Governor-General then in use was 'to bear true faith and allegiance to His Majesty'. Jinnah changed it to 'bear true allegiance to the Constitution…' and under the new oath assumed the office of Governor-General. He made it clear that the loyalty of the Governor-General of the new state was to the Constitution and not to any other person— legal, extra-legal or conventional.[4] Accordingly, he would give assent to any law as the Governor-General owing allegiance to the Constitution and not bearing 'true allegiance to His Majesty.' In case of a Constitutional Bill, he would affix his 'signatures as the President of the Constituent Assembly, and not as Governor-General.[5] Consistent with this imperative Section 6 (3) of the Indian Independence Act which provided for assent to every law in His Majesty's name was subsequently amended by omitting His Majesty's title and making it an assent by the Governor-General.[6] Thus began the history of constitution-making in Pakistan.

Quaid-i-Azam acted more in the capacity of a *Rehbar* (leader) than as a mere constitutional head. He kept under his control the portfolios of the Ministry of Rehabilitation & Refugees and that of States and Frontier Regions. He was a Governor-General who participated in Cabinet responsibilities. In addition to being the President of the Constituent Assembly, he also accepted the office and responsibility of constitutional adviser to the same Assembly. Obviously, he had to lead the nation to statehood. Jinnah died on 11 September 1948 and the sovereign Constituent Assembly was called upon to fill the vacuum of leadership and also to complete the drafting of the Constitution.

The Indian Independence Act, while a world class piece of legislative drafting, did not provide for a timeframe for completing the Constitution. Not being so constrained, the Constituent Assembly proceeded at its own leisurely pace, which progressively slowed down due to insurmountable problems faced by the new state, including the controversial issues between the two wings of East and West Pakistan, and the lack of cohesive leadership. The self-interest of its members in not framing the Constitution was evident as the delay prolonged their own life as members of parliament—it being tied to the enforcement of the Constitution. However, in March 1949 a constitutional document was approved by the Constituent Assembly, in the form of a resolution called the 'Objectives Resolution.' This is an 'enactment' which retained its importance in Pakistan's constitutional life long after the Constituent Assembly itself was dissolved. While the later constitutional documents were intermittently drafted and then discarded, the

Objectives Resolution was always there as the centre-piece to serve either as the preamble of a new Constitution or as a constitutional *Grundnorm*, and in 1985, it was incorporated as an operative part of the Constitution.

While delineating the state structure, the Objectives Resolution combines federalism, democracy and popular sovereignty with Islamic principles. The generality of its terminology was in reality an attempt to accommodate Islamic modernists and traditionalists alike. The Objectives Resolution received wide approval except from the minorities, while generally the members of the Constituent Assembly shared the enthusiasm of Liaquat Ali Khan, the first Prime Minister of Pakistan, who said, 'I consider this to be a most important occasion in the life of this country next in importance only to the achievement of independence...'.[7] However, the vagueness of the Resolution which may have been the reason for its general acceptance and for its durability, in due course became a source of conflicting interpretations. One section of opinion believes that the Objectives Resolution, if implemented honestly, can override and repeal certain substantive parts of the Constitution that come in conflict with the *Shariah*, as interpreted by them. The Judiciary in Pakistan was also frequently called upon to determine the status of the Resolution.

Ironically, Liaquat Ali Khan, who had successfully piloted the Objectives Resolution through the Constituent Assembly in 1949, submitted a draft constitution as an 'Interim Report' which provided for a head of a state with extensive emergency powers, including the power to suspend the Constitution in whole or in part; also, the head of the state had the power to dismiss the provincial ministries.[8] One critical member of the Constituent Assembly aptly remarked: 'If Mr Churchill had been the leader of the house, he would have drawn such a constitution'.[9] The reaction to the draft constitution was so negative that it was quietly and unceremoniously withdrawn after two months of its appearance on the agenda of the Constituent Assembly; ironically, the Objectives Resolution was its preamble. It remains an enigma why Liaquat Ali Khan, while holding the office of the Prime Minister, produced a constitutional draft which gave such extensive powers to the Governor-General. Or, did he believe that between the two historically constitutional paths of presidential rule as against parliamentarianism, Pakistan would benefit more by the former? Pakistan's constitutional history highlights a divide among the political leaders along these lines.

When the first Prime Minister of Pakistan, Liaquat Ali Khan, was assassinated on 15 October 1951, very little progress had been made towards framing the constitution.

Pakistan's political leaders failed to address promptly the most crucial issue of constitution-making. The higher echelons of bureaucracy became restless and distrustful of the politicians. They gradually became political leaders. A cavalcade of civil servants made their way to the highest political slots.[10] On the death of Liaquat Ali Khan, the Minister of Finance, Ghulam Muhammad, who had started his career in the audit branch of the Indian Civil Service, became the Governor-General on 18 October 1951. Iskandar Mirza, an Indian Army officer, who had graduated from the Sandhurst Military Academy of Britain and later opted for the Political Service of British India, became the closest associate of Ghulam Muhammad. Another member of the audit branch of the British-Indian government, Chaudhry Muhammad Ali, became a Secretary General to the Government of Pakistan and subsequently rose to the office of Prime Minister. Hailing from East Pakistan, Muhammad Ali Bogra, serving as Pakistan's ambassador in Washington, was catapulted to the high office of Prime Minister. Clearly, the politicians were surrendering their right to govern the state.

Against this backdrop of bureaucratic ascendancy, Governor-General Ghulam Muhammad dismissed the entire cabinet through a proclamation: 'that the cabinet of Khawaja Nazimuddin has proven entirely inadequate to grapple with the difficulties facing the country'.[11] The constitutional convention of the British Commonwealth which states that the Prime Minister who retained the confidence of the legislature could not be removed by the head of the state was brushed aside by a self-serving assertion: 'those conventions could not be read into the Constitution of the new state'. Ghulam Muhammad arrogantly presumed himself the inheritor of the prestige and authority of the Quaid-i-Azam Muhammad Ali Jinnah,—a misconception which also afflicted some of his successors. The arbitrary dismissal of the Cabinet, which enjoyed the confidence of the Assembly, was a serious setback to the prestige and authority of the legislature. The members of the Constituent Assembly merely accepted the Governor-General's highhandedness, more so when Muhammad Ali Bogra, a diplomat, was summoned to become the Prime Minister.

While the Assembly was progressing towards the final version of the constitution, it somehow decided to react (though belatedly) to the dismissal of Nazimuddin's Cabinet. On 21 September 1954, the Constituent Assembly amended the Government of India Act precluding the Governor-General from acting except on the advice of his ministers. On the same day, the Constituent Assembly voted its approval of the draft constitution, later fixing 25 December 1954 as the day for its enforcement. No satisfactory answer is available to explain why Muhammad Ali Bogra or the members of the Constituent Assembly introduced an amendment to the Government of India Act 1935, curtailing the powers of the Governor-General, and did not promulgate the Constitution immediately, since the provision relating to the advice of the Prime Minister, (binding on the Governor-General), was part of the draft constitution of 1954. Whatever may have been the strategy, the timelag was fatal and the Governor-General struck. On 24 October, Ghulam Muhammad issued a proclamation stating therein that the 'constitutional machinery has broken down...the constitutional assembly at present constituted has lost the confidence of the members and can no longer function.' This proclamation along with the state of emergency was treated as equivalent to the dissolution of the Constituent Assembly and so the draft constitution of 1954, a stillborn child, was thrown aside along with the dissolution of the assembly.

A few words about the draft constitution may be appropriate. The Objectives Resolution was its preamble. The Constitution made a few concessions to (1) the Islamic faction; (2) contained comprehensive and enforceable fundamental rights, along with the power of judicial review; (3) the country was to be a republic with a federal structure within the parliamentary system; (4) a bicameral legislature with equal representation from the units in the upper house would constitute the parliament; (5) the president could not dissolve the assembly and was bound mostly by the advice of the cabinet, and finally; (6) the Constitution itself and not the parliament was declared to be the supreme law. This was a fairly good constitution and its passage demonstrated the ability of the secular and religious political leaders to reach a compromise on a modern constitution.[12]

With the dissolution of the Constituent Assembly, the venue of constitutional matters shifted from the political field to the judicial forum. The President of the Constituent Assembly, Maulvi Tamizuddin, challenged the action of the Governor-General (it would not be possible to enter into the details of the litigation). Two aspects of this struggle are noteworthy: What the Federal Court of Pakistan did decide and what it did not decide. The Federal Court decided that the assent of the Governor-General was essential to all types of legislation, be it constitutional or otherwise. Thus, the power of issuing writs conferred on the High Court through a constitutional amendment of the Government of India Act, 1935 (not having received the assent of the Governor-General) could not be availed of by the courts in enforcing the rights of Maulvi Tamizuddin, the President of the Constituent Assembly.[13] The case was thrown out on this ground. What the court did not decide is more important and that related to the draft constitution. Ghulam Muhammad had objected in its proclamation to the 'unrepresentative capacity' of the Constituent Assembly, but made no criticism of the constitution itself. During the legal battle, the draft constitution was not referred to at all.

The Governor-General triumphed, but he was left with no legislature and Pakistan was left with neither a Constitution nor a Constituent Assembly. The Federal Court, the second player in the field of developing the constitutional basis of the country, forced the Governor-General to hold an election to a new Constituent Assembly. Justice Muhammad Munir observed that 'on no democratic principle can the power to dissolve vest in the executive unless the exercise of that power is followed by an appeal to the people'.[14] The country was brought back to its democratic roots. Its judgement also demonstrated the judiciary's ability to prevent autocracy. The newly elected Constituent Assembly met in the cool and breezy hill-station of Murree on 7 July 1955 and later elected Chaudhry Muhammad Ali as the new Prime Minister. In the leap year of 1956, the Assembly sat until nearly midnight of 29 February and just before the stroke of twelve, the final clause of the Constitution was approved. The Speaker's announcement was greeted with shouts of Allah-o-Akbar[15] (God is great). On 25 March 1956, the Constitution was enforced and Pakistan became an Islamic Republic under a new Constitution.

The Fate of the 1956 Constitution

The Constitution provided a federal parliamentary system based on a unicameral legislature in which parity was artificially established between East Pakistan and a newly created West Pakistan, as one unit out of the erstwhile four provinces. Supremacy of the Constitution was sought by empowering the courts to give full effect to the Constitution. It was said that 'the government thus established by the Constitution may well be described as a government by the judges.' However, the political forces in the country did not see it that way. Chaudhry Muhammad Ali, (who earned the credit of creating the national consensus for the Constitution) did not survive long. Ineptly dealing with the political dynamics of the House, he had to resign on 8 September 1956. In the next one and a half years three more prime ministers followed in his footsteps. Clearly, the bureaucrat-turned-politicians had also failed. The Constitution by itself could not hold the country. The time was ripe for the 'Man on Horseback' to enter the scene.

On 8 October, Iskandar Mirza, who had taken oath as the President to preserve the Constitution of 1956, made an announcement 'that the Constitution has been abrogated, Martial Law was proclaimed and General Ayub Khan appointed Chief Martial Law Administrator'. 'Next morning it was business as usual in the government offices, courts, bazaars and public institutions. The people welcomed the change openly. They had become fed up with the ministries and the ever growing corruption and inefficiency'.[16] This public response (or apathy) was later treated as the rationale for staging the *coup d'état* of 27 October, which was in a manner of speech, a silent revolution.

The new regime headed by General Muhammad Ayub Khan, promulgated The Laws (Continuance in Force) Order of 1958 which confirmed the abrogation of the 1956 Constitution, but provided for administering the country as nearly as possible by the defunct constitution, allowing the judiciary to function albeit with restricted jurisdiction. In other words, the regime rejected the political basis of the 1956 Constitution, but considered its administrative rules adequate and workable. The Supreme Court of Pakistan accepted these Orders as the newly law-creating organ as 'a revolution itself becomes a law-creating fact because thereafter its own legality is judged not by reference to the annulled constitution but by reference to its own success.' The coup of October was accepted as a successful revolution judged by the efficacy of its operation and general acceptance by the people.[17]

The October (Coup) Revolution established parallel military and civil structures to operate at the pleasure of the regime. It may not be inappropriate to compare the new system with the first civilian government which was headed by the founder of the nation, who was able to maintain a tight hold over the government by virtue of his accomplishment and status, and particularly as the guiding force, to the one established under the new dispensation, a military-cum-civilian regime headed and controlled by the 'defender of the nation' (Commander-in-Chief of the armed forces), primarily because of the failure of the political parties and the politicians under the hope that the intervener will lead the nation to a workable Constitution and solution.

If the Supreme Court had not given recognition to the Laws Continuance in Force Order, the Martial Law regime would have been a pure military system, and the judicial system might have been substituted by new courts. The Supreme Court provided the nation, political elements and to itself some space to collect their wits and react to the new realities.

General Ayub Khan had a definite plan to change the political culture of the country by introducing a Presidential system instead of Parliamentary rule and by replacing adult franchise with the provision of a limited electorate of basic democrats to elect the National and Provincial Assemblies.[18] With this presidential system in view, he promulgated a new Constitution after consulting a Constitution Commission headed by Justice Shahabuddin, of the Supreme Court, although he did not adopt the Commission's recommendations *in toto*. The 1962 Constitution adopted a federal structure as created by the 1956 Constitution consisting of two provinces with parity *inter se* in a unicameral legislature. The Judiciary retained the power of judicial review *sans* fundamental rights. Basic democrats were to be elected on adult franchise without the political parties. Basic democracy functioned in the absence of political parties as Ayub Khan wanted to keep it free from what he said was 'the curse of party intrigue, political pressures and fist thumbing politicians that characterized the Assemblies.'

In 1964, the Supreme Court rendered a judgment in the case of Jamaat-i-Islami which was banned under the Criminal Law Amendment Act, 1908. Relying on the provisions of the regulatory law, viz. Political Parties Act of 1962, (which was passed by the Assembly elected under the 1962 Constitution), the Supreme Court emphasized the national role of political parties and one of the judges on the Bench made an observation that 'one should remember that the opposition of today may be the government of tomorrow'.[19] The Court's verdict was an effort to re-politicize the State. Finally, a comprehensive list of fundamental rights and the role of political parties was integrated into the 1962 Constitution by an amendment in 1965. (At this point, I joined the ten-member Cabinet of Ayub Khan on 3 March 1965 as Minister for Law & Parliamentary Affairs.)

President Ayub Khan's interest in political parties remained minimal. He considered them relevant in controlling and disciplining the members of the Assembly. Since Ayub Khan, as the President of the country, was not obliged to please or cater to the needs of parliamentarians, he had an opportunity to undertake social reforms and enforce bureaucratic efficiency for economic development. Pakistan saw appreciable improvement in the economic, industrial, and agricultural sector. On the social side, the Family Laws Ordinance, Auqaf Acts and Land Reform Regulations were a quantum leap.

President Ayub Khan's system invites speculation: is the presidential system appropriate to the genius of the people of Pakistan? The debate is still alive, since people fondly recall the Ayub era when the country made significant progress in the industrial field, and a vibrant private sector came into operation. However, Ayub's system of basic democrats, though successful at the local level, failed to inspire confidence to the level of the presidential electorate college. Eighty thousand members from each wing proved to be comfortably manageable. A belated attempt to increase the number was made when the basic democrats from each wing were increased from eighty thousand to one hundred and twenty thousand. This too was not without resistance from some politicans, who asserted that 'any increase in the electoral college shall give an opportunity to the enemies of the country to influence the politics of the country'.[20] Obviously, they were referring to everyone in the opposition as an 'enemy' of the country.

The presidential system under the 1962 Constitution was of its own kind and cannot be compared to the presidential system of the United States, which is structured delicately on the doctrine of checks and balances. The 1962 Constitution was specifically structured to strengthen the centre even against the provinces. The Constitution further limited the powers of the

National Assembly, which did not have control over a major portion of the budget. Some reforms were initiated to give additional powers to the National Assembly, but they did not mature. By and large, political parties existed around known personalities and did not penetrate in the social fabric of the society; they hardly held elections for their leaders within their own ranks.

A war broke out between India and Pakistan and peace efforts at Tashkent culminated in the Tashkent Declaration on 11 January 1966. People in West Pakistan felt betrayed as they believed that the gains of the war were lost on the negotiation table, and a movement started against the regime. Ayub realized that his party, the Pakistan Muslim League, had left him to his own devices to deal with the crisis. To cope with the situation, he utilized such powers as were available to him under the Constitution.

Ayub's government declared an emergency,[21] suspended fundamental rights, detained political opponents and imposed censorship. A strong lobby pressured Ayub to curtail powers of the Judicial Review, which I resisted and the constitutional amendment drafted for this purpose was dropped.[22]

Consequently, the Judiciary intervened to protect the procedural rights of the citizens. In a number of notable cases judges of the Supreme Court made pertinent, though essentially political observations, for example: (1) In a democratic system it is the right of any party not in power to criticize measures adopted by the government in order to discredit it in the public eye, so as to oust it by constitutional means;[23] (2) Even in detention cases, it is illegal (for the government) to presume the citizens guilty through procedural innovation;[24] (3) Emergency provisions did not create new conditions for interpreting laws.[25]

In protecting the procedural rights of the citizens regarding fair play, objective satisfaction, and reasonableness the courts firmly inducted the doctrine of due process in the national norm. Perhaps this happened due to an article of the 1962 Constitution which reads: 'To enjoy the protection of law and to be treated in accordance with laws is the inalienable right of every citizen, wherever he may be, and of every other person for the time being within Pakistan.' In particular: a) No action detrimental to the life, liberty, body, reputation, or property of any person shall be taken except in accordance with law; b) No person shall be prevented from or hindered in doing that which is not prohibited by law; c) No person shall be compelled to do that which the law does not require him to do.

This article like the Objectives Resolution has outlived the constitution in which it was initially contained and is now a part of the 1973 Constitution, and is a favourite of the lawyers and judicially active judges.

Ayub Khan surrendered to the opposition[26] and finally agreed in a Round Table Conference (which consisted of political parties of combined opposition and some others) to revert to a parliamentary form of government and adult franchise thereby going back to the point from where he took the nation on a new course; a fortorari declining to undo one unit or parity. Notwithstanding this reversal and concession, the agitation did not cease. Opposition leaders had lost control of the public unrest that they had generated and, as observed by the Supreme Court in one of the cases 'sometimes politicians play with fire that becomes conflagration'.[27] Consequently, on 24 March 1969, an unnerved President wrote to General Yahya Khan, his Commander-in-Chief, 'to undertake his legal and constitutional responsibility to defend the country not only against external aggression, but also to save it from internal disorder and chaos.'

General Yahya Khan perceived that the only way he could perform his constitutional duty was to ignore the 1962 Constitution and to elect a new Constituent Assembly. He imposed Martial Law on 25 March 1969, and then promulgated the Legal Framework Order (LFO) of 1970,[28] for electing a house with the dual purpose of framing the Constitution within 120 days and acting as the federal legislature. Through the LFO he did away with parity and one unit of West Pakistan. This was the Indian Independence Act, 1947 revisiting the scene, except that a time-frame of 120 days was envisaged to complete the new Constitution.

In a fair and free election based on the principle of one-man-one-vote and direct adult franchise, a Constituent Assembly was duly elected.

The political backdrop influenced the outcome. The Awami League dominated the position in East Pakistan and thereby secured a majority in the Constituent Assembly. The Pakistan People's Party (PPP) won overwhelmingly in the Western Provinces. Political dialogue on the basic structure of a new Constitution, particularly under its control, dragged on and led to a hardening of positions. A civil war broke out on 17 January 1971 leading East Pakistan to secede with the help of the Indian Army. Consequently, Bangladesh appeared on the map of the world.

General Yahya Khan and his Martial Law regime were replaced in Islamabad by Zulfikar Ali Bhutto and his 'Civilian' Martial Law. The Legal Framework Order and the rump of the Constitutional Assembly, consisting of members from the Provinces of West Pakistan (and two from East Pakistan) remained to provide the constitutional base and political mechanisms to start all over again. Bhutto was elected the President of the Constituent Assembly as well. Referring to his multiple roles with pride, he stated that 'I am wearing four hats being the President of Pakistan, President of the Constituent Assembly, Chairman of the PPP, and Chief Martial Law Administrator, whereas, on the day of independence Quaid-i-Azam wore only three hats'.[29] Mr Bhutto did not realize that his additional fourth so-called distinction of Chief Martial Law Administrator was in contradiction to the other three positions held by him, whereas Quaid-i-Azam was free of such contradictions.

During the span of time stretching from 1971 to 1973, the saddened nation looked to the judiciary for help. The Supreme Court assuaged national anguish and anger by declaring Yahya Khan an usurper and refused to accord his regime a revolutionary legitimacy. In another judgement, it declared that notwithstanding the illegitimate and non-condonable nature of usurpation, the Legal Framework Order could provide legitimacy at least to the elections which were held under it and a Constitution framed by such an assembly would be legitimate. On a reference by the President, the Supreme Court rendered the advice that the National Assembly may debate and decide the issue of extending recognition to Bangladesh.

Clearly, with these astute views the Supreme Court helped the battered nation to come to terms with new political realities. The Supreme Court was aware that status quo ante could not be restored. Thus, the Judiciary became a venue for political dialogues on national issues, and indeed offered catharsis to a bewildered and confused nation.

The Emergence of the New Pakistan

The Constituent Assembly started the task of framing a new constitution suitable for the four provinces only since East Pakistan, though not yet recognized by Islamabad, was not represented in the Assembly.

The joint Opposition Parliamentary Party nominated a Constitutional Committee headed by Ghous Buksh Bizenjo, who later became the Governor of Balochistan. (I was invited to be its Constitutional Adviser and was present at most of the important meetings.) The political leaders involved in the constitutional dialogues were convinced that a parliamentary system would be more suitable to Pakistan. In a presidential system, they apprehended that Punjab, with its demographic majority, would generally elect a Punjabi president, and in case of a president from a minority province, the Punjabi majority in parliament may not allow him to function.

Finally, the Constitution was completed containing a parliamentary form of government, and a federal structure with adequate provincial autonomy and satisfactory safeguards for provincial rights. To harmonize the interests of the Centre and the provinces, the Constitution established a Council of Common Interests. Not only were Islamic provisions incorporated, but Islam was also declared the religion of the State. Fundamental rights were comprehensive, but there was a visible socialist bias, as ceiling on private property could be legally imposed. The dilemma of a powerful President as against the Prime Minister was resolved in favour of the Prime Minister. Consequently, the President under the 1973 Constitution became the ceremonious head of State. The Prime Minister became the Chief Executive, whose advice was binding on the President in every matter.

The power of the Prime Minister over parliament was further strengthened through an innovation which made the removal of the Prime Minister by a simple majority most difficult, if not impossible. Some critics called it a Prime Ministerial form of government rather than a parliamentary form of government. Abrogation, repeal, or subversion of the Constitution, was declared treason and punishable—a reaction to the two previous Martial Law regimes. The due process clause from the 1962 Constitution was incorporated and the Objectives Resolution became the preamble.

On 12 March 1973, the Constituent Assembly passed the draft of the new Constitution and then promulgated it. The nation heaved a sigh of relief. Chaudhry Fazal Elahi became the President and Zulfikar Ali Bhutto assumed the office of the Prime Minister.

Bhutto: The Populist Leader

The role of Bhutto was that of a populist leader; his major policies included nationalization of industry from the private sector, nationalization of education, and eliminating constitutional protection for the higher bureaucracy. However, when his government held elections in 1977, the opposition accused him of massively rigging the elections. The combined opposition of nine political parties established a political alliance called Pakistan National Alliance (PNA). Also, the religious forces joined this movement as they found the liberalism of the PPP unacceptable. So two equally balanced forces were engaged in a zero-sum game. There was no institutional force, including the President, with equal clout left in the field to mediate the conflict. The dialogue between the PPP and the PNA was prolonged to a near dead end. Despite the newly added article declaring abrogation as high treason, the third Martial Law was imposed on 5 July 1977. The Constitution of 1973 was suspended and the leaders of the PPP and the PNA were taken into 'protective custody'. General Ziaul Haq, the master of the *coup d'état*, announced that elections would be held within nintey days. The promise was never honoured.

The Judiciary was once again called upon to determine the legitimacy of the Martial Law regime. This time, departing from the previous two precedents, the Court neither treated Zia's take-over as a revolution, nor declared him a usurper. This time around, it examined, through the assistance of detailed arguments, the material and historical factors that led to the take-over. Finally, justifying it, the Supreme Court based its decision on the law of necessity, and extended its application, beyond validating the extra-constitutional action of taking over to further continue the exercise of judicial review with respect to the deeds of the Martial Law Administrator, and to judge if they were 'for the furtherance of the public good.'[31] The Supreme Court thus attempted to legitimize a regime in which the military was to function within the parameters of the law of necessity.

Recognizing that a new relationship between the Executive and the Judiciary had come into existence, the Judiciary entertained certain cases which enabled it to review the actions of the Martial Law Administrator. Zia showed patience for some time, but when the Chief Justice of the Lahore High Court, while hearing a constitutional petition, asked the Attorney General to inquire from his 'client' when would he fulfil the obligation of holding the election, Zia called it a day. Bhutto had already been executed on 4 April 1979 and the members of the PNA who had joined the Zia Cabinet, had been sent home. Consequently, Zia felt free to act against the judiciary. He promulgated the Provisional Constitutional Order of 1981

(PCO), which effectively controlled the judicial review. A large number of confirmed judges of the Supreme Court and High Courts were eliminated. The ghost of Dosso's judgement controlled the atmosphere. So, rather quietly, the Supreme Court started to refuse to entertain petitions against the Martial Law Administrator, by simply returning the petitions with a stamp indicating 'Hit by PCO'.

Zia attempted to create a political base for himself through his nominated *Shura* (Parliament), but finally settled for an elected Assembly on a non-party basis. He found a ready ally in Pir Ali Mardan Shah of Pagara, the President of the Pakistan Muslim League. I was then the Secretary General of the party. Realizing the dangers of an election without political parties, I vehemently opposed this action. My arguments were that 'such an election will give rise to provincial, sectarian and ethnic prejudices, encourage *baradari* system, and help local and monied mafia to capture the National and Provincial Assemblies, and it will then be difficult to dislodge them.' The President of the party, the Pir of Pagara, saw it differently. He was convinced that those who would get elected on a non-party basis would eventually join the Muslim League. Elections without the political parties were held for the National and Provincial Assemblies in 1985. Unfortunately, both of us turned out to be right. All the demons that I had identified came to life and spread their strong influence in the society as well as in the legislative assemblies. However, the majority of the elected members, as Pir Pagara had predicted, joined the Muslim League under the Prime Ministership of Muhammad Khan Junejo. I had no alternative but to withdraw from the party.[32]

The National Assembly met under the umbrella of Martial Law; after it passed the Eighth Amendment, the Constitution of 1973 was revived and subsequently Martial Law was lifted. The eighth amendment gave unprecedented immunity to the perpetrators of Martial Law and their actions, and extensively amended the Constitution. The powers of the president were enhanced and he could, within certain parameters, dissolve the National Assembly at his discretion. The power to dissolve the legislature was, however, subjected to holding new elections through an appeal to the people; (these principles were relied upon by Justice Muhammad Munir to compel Governor-General Ghulam Muhammad to elect a new Constituent Assembly). The Objectives Resolution was made a substantive part of the Constitution by adding a schedule at the end of the Constitution which now begins with the Objectives Resolution as its preamble and also ends with the words of the 'Objectives Resolution' repeated in the schedule.

From 1985 to 1987, Pakistan's political system moved from a party-less to a party-based system. In exercising power under the eighth amendment, Zia dissolved the National Assembly of Pakistan in 1988, and terminated Muhammad Khan Junejo's government. He announced 17 November 1988 as the date for elections, but he died in a plane crash on 18 August 1988. It is doubtful if he would have held the elections with political parties if he had lived. At this time, however, the Supreme Court upheld the right of a political party to get an election symbol of its own choice, setting the stage for party-based elections.[33]

The PPP, under the leadership of Benazir, the daughter of Zulfikar Ali Bhutto, won the majority and formed the government. The PML was the party in opposition. From 1990 to 1996, the PPP and the PML(N) followed each other in quick succession, since both were dismissed by presidential decrees and the legislature was dissolved. The Supreme Court dealt with each dissolution, but there was a public outcry against the non-elected executive exercising the power to dissolve an elected legislature. Four elections within a period of eleven years were held, which did help in creating some political awareness in the public; each election indicated improved maturity of the electorate. A two-party system has unmistakably emerged. Strong feelings have developed against legislators who defected their party after the election, and easily 'auctioned' their affiliation. More important, the electorate is demanding accountability of legislators' performance.

The powers of the executive to dissolve the Assembly have been withdrawn through the thirteenth amendment, and a number of functions have been transferred from the President to the Prime Minister. Parliament had tried, unsuccessfully, to establish its supremacy over the President in 1954; it has now been accomplished a little more than forty years later in 1997.

I have earlier briefly referred to the Supreme Court deciding the issue of four dissolutions by the President under Article 58(2)(b) of the Constitution on a case to case basis;[34] however, one trend needs to be noted: the Supreme Court, which ignored corruption as a non-constitutional issue in the first case, has finally termed it as the bane of the nation, and the last dissolution was upheld, *inter alia*, on the grounds of massive corruption of various forms which resulted in eroding the constitutional machinery. The judiciary could not remain indifferent to the executive's devious interventions into the realms of independence, one related to the separation of the judiciary from the executive[35], and another elevated the opinion of the Chief Justice of the Supreme Court to primacy, and in certain matters finality, especially in cases of the appointment of judges to the higher judiciary.[36] Public-spirited litigation and judicial activism is now in vogue.

Finally, it may be appropriate to make an assessment of Pakistan's achievements and failures in matters of constitutional development, and attempt to see what our future path should be: First, why has the 1973 Constitution survived, whereas the other two, of 1956 and 1962, did not?

The Survival of the 1973 Constitution and its Reasons

The 1956 Constitution did not survive and was displaced by a 'silent revolution' because it was passed by a legislature which was elected through indirect elections by an imperative judgement of the Federal Court.[37] The legislature did not reflect the peoples' choice. The 1962 Constitution was not even specifically abrogated; it became irrelevant a day after General Yahya Khan took over. It too was a constitution given by one person and approved by the basic democrats elected through indirect franchise. Neither the giver of the constitution nor those who approved it were directly chosen by the people. However, the 1973 Constitution was adopted by the chosen representatives of the people elected in a fair and free election. Consequently, this Constitution could not be abrogated (only suspended) by the third Martial Law which operated in the country for eight years. The same Chief Martial Law Administrator, who had caused its suspension, had to revive it, albeit with some amendments. This demonstrated that Pakistani society has an innate respect for democratic principles and any attempt which does not have the support of the people cannot survive long.

Another important reason for the survival of the 1973 Constitution is that it had satisfactorily settled the issue of provincial autonomy with the consent of leaders from the smaller provinces. The leaders of the opposition, and that of the Constitutional Committee of the combined opposition, were from the smaller provinces of NWFP and Balochistan. There was no artificial device of parity against the principle of one-man-one-vote. Thus, a consensus arrived at between the national leaders and leaders of the minority provinces can survive and receive homage from successive generations.

Another reason for the survival of the 1973 Constitution is that it satisfied Islamic ethos by declaring Islam as the State religion. I recall a meeting of the major political parties in Karachi during the Martial Law, when a declaration for the Movement for Restoration of Democracy was being prepared, including a demand for the revival of the Constitution of 1973. A well-known religious leader, Maulana Fazalur Rehman demanded: 'Why not just ask for establishing an Islamic Constitution?' When I informed him that the 1973 Constitution contains a clause making Islam the State religion, he, and many of his colleagues, were satisfied. No constitutional formula in Pakistan could be considered suitable to the genius of the people unless it contained the ideological base providing for Islamic aspirations.

Lastly, General Ziaul Haq, unlike General Ayub Khan, was drawn to the game of politics by events while he did not have any specific plan or alternative constitutional programme of his own. He could not afford to open a Pandora's Box by abrogating the Constitution. The stratagem of suspending the Constitution was resorted to, leaving room for its revival when so desired. The eighth amendment effectively altered fifty-three articles in the Constitution, and the amendment was undertaken by an assembly elected without parties under the umbrella of Martial Law. A Prime Ministerial Constitution was changed into a parliamentary system with a powerful President; the imbalance has been corrected through an amendment. Clearly, playing with the Constitution is not a healthy exercise; efforts should now be made to create a constitutional culture. Amendments undertaken in a hurry, howsoever laudable the objective may be, adversely effect the growth of constitutional culture.

The Judiciary: Its Future Role

The Judiciary has played a significant role in Pakistan's constitutional history. Like the US Supreme Court, there is hardly any important political issue which does not come before the Supreme Court of Pakistan. I have already referred to some significant and important decisions. I have handled scores of cases before the High Courts and the Supreme Court, where they have rendered verdicts on political or ideological issues.

The judiciary in Pakistan had to function under a greater burden than the charter and the design of the institution envisaged. At times, when confronted with an extraordinary situation, it acted with pragmatism bordering on judicial pacifism. But when there was some normalization or notable political recovery, the courts came forward to protect the procedural rights of the individual, gave importance to the Constitution and provided guidance on the issue of ideology. The courts have not been able to escape criticism; some of which is justified. Reliance on the law of necessity, or accepting the absence of public protest against a coup as the basis of a 'revolution', or working under a Martial Law regime which could and did retire judges at will, are such matters for which no defence can be offered. However, it goes to the credit of Pakistan's judiciary that it managed to act as a bulwark against autocracy, helped political institutions to return to constitutionalism, advanced political party culture and respect for the due process of law; also, at times it delienated the contours of ideology. The judiciary is a delicate apparatus; it can operate efficiently if other institutions and the vital limbs of the state are healthy and work properly. To depend entirely on the judiciary in order to correct all the ills of the society is asking for the impossible.

The members of the higher judiciary owe it to their institution to undo the adverse impression about the pacifist image of the courts. Public spirited litigation (within the four corners of the Constitution) is highly appreciated. The members of the judiciary would do well to enter the areas of human rights, environment, equality before law and, wherever possible, accountability of public office holders, with confidence.

Political Parties versus Movements

Political parties have a bearing on constitution making and the constitutional history of Pakistan. Pakistan was achieved through a constitutional struggle supported by a massive political movement organized by the All-India Muslim League under the dynamic and visionary leadership of Quaid-i-Azam Muhammad Ali Jinnah. Established in 1906, the Muslim League initially had a limited objective: 'to remove misunderstanding between Indian Muslims and British India and to represent the interest of the Muslim community.'[38] However, it passed a resolution in 1940 not to accept any constitutional arrangement which did not create a separate homeland for the Muslims. In the final stages of negotiations, it achieved success and Pakistan emerged on the map of the world within seven years (1940-47). The

Muslim League's success was largely due to its effective strategy, which could be implemented because the Quaid-i-Azam maintained very tight control over the party apparatus. Some critics have mistakenly referred to this strategy as authoritarianism.

A question may be asked: Was it a political party (the Muslim League) or the political movement (Tehrik-i-Pakistan) which mobilized the masses to win both freedom and a state? The reality lies somewhere in between. The Muslim League as a party launched the Pakistan movement, but the latter engulfed the party in the 1940s. When the fervour of the movement fell victim to its own success the inner contradictions of the party re-emerged in the 1950s. The Muslim League Party failed to focus on the needs of the people, and became an instrument of political dominance for the upper class. While an independent Muslim state was established, a free and independent society, which was the ultimate goal, did not flourish. Unfortunately, the Muslim League leaders came to believe that establishing a new country was the end of their struggle. The subsequent history of Pakistan's political parties is a repeat performance of the League; namely, various movements succeeded each other, but the parties spawning them failed to consolidate the results.

The Pakistan Democratic Movement (PDM) which was mobilized against Ayub Khan was an alliance of various political parties. Initially, the PDM succeeded in winning concessions from Ayub Khan in order to revert to the parliamentary form of government and adult franchise; finally, its units dispersed and its component parties failed to consolidate their gains, leading the country tragically into the second Martial Law. The massive movement against the PPP government on the issue of election rigging was well planned by a consortium of nine political parties; namely, the Pakistan National Alliance (PNA). Gradually, the movement acquired the popular name of Tehrik-i-Nizam-i Mustafa (Movement for the Restoration of the Prophet's Political System). It electrified a vast section of society across the country. Although the PNA movement brought the PPP to the negotiating table, lack of inner cohesion and discipline led to the struggle ending in the third Martial Law. Surprisingly, the members of the PNA later joined the Martial Law Cabinet (I was the only member of the Pakistan Muslim League, a component of PNA, who though specifically invited by General Ziaul Haq, declined to do so).[39]

The movement against General Zia was a daring effort. This too was initiated and carried on by a conglomeration of various parties, who called it the Movement for the Restoration of Democracy (MRD). The movement forced Zia to talk of elections and this led to an inconclusive debate amongst the members of the alliance: whether or not to participate in the non-party based elections. Consequently, the MRD Movement achieved at best non-party based elections in a *quid pro quo* for a blanket validation of the Martial Law, and the Eighth Amendment, which altered the parliamentary structure of the 1973 Constitution.

From 1987 to 1996, when the cabinets of political parties were installed, their successive removals were obtained by mini-movements, which were aided and abetted by presidential interference or intrigues. Each change has, unfortunately, eroded the financial and moral base of the country and the outraged people are asking for *Ehtesab* (accountability) or *Inqilab* (revolution).

In other words, when a movement is initiated by an ill-prepared political party, the initial gains erode party solidarity, and soon highlight its inner contradictions which overwhelm its achievements and revert the players of the game to square one. Movements are no substitute for political struggles, which may take longer to materialize and bear fruit, but eventually benefit both the party and the cause.

The Army and the Constitution

The causes for the imposition of Martial Law by Muhammad Ayub Khan and Yahya Khan were not examined by the Supreme Court. In Ayub Khan's case, the takeover was accepted as a 'revolution', whereas Yahya Khan was adjudged to be a usurper on the grounds that, when invited to perform his constitutional duty, Yahya Khan transgressed the same by imposing Martial Law. But the causes of the third Martial Law were fully discussed by the Supreme Court, which by that time had evolved into a forum for national debate. An examination of various arguments before the court indicated that the rationale for military intervention had been the continuous downward spiral in society, which was unchecked by political governments or caused by them, along with a threat to the security of Pakistan emanating from hostile India. The three bloodless coups indicated some degree of acceptance by the people, who might have hoped that military intervention may prove beneficial. However, the inept handling of constitutional and political issues by all the three Martial Law regimes convinced the public, (and I am confident, even the forces), that the solution of the political problems is not in the hands of a military Messiah. (Appearing in a television interview, I had the occasion to sum up this feeling by saying that with Ayub, Yahya, and Zia, the A, Y, and Z of the Martial Law is over. The military only intervenes in political crises due to a political vacuum, or an ineffective functioning of the state institutions, which encourage the armed forces to act.)[40]

Military intervention disturbs the constitutional and political culture. Pakistan must find a solution to its problems within the Constitutional framework. However, if the political integrity of the leaders is not restored and corruption continues, then individuals who talk of revolution with or without the army will be heard with credence.

Corruption and Constitution

Corrupt politicians have influenced the course of Pakistan's constitutional development. I have stated in the beginning that, at the dawn of Pakistan in 1947, the members of the Constituent Assembly took advantage of the absence of a time limit to delay the framing of the Constitution, and thus extended their own term as legislators. If they had been required to seek re-elections at the end of three years they would have completed the Constitution in 1950, and Pakistan's constitutional history might have been different.

Similarly, if after the dissolution of the Cabinet of Khawaja Nazimuddin, a number of ministers of his Cabinet had declined to join Muhammad Ali Bogra's Cabinet (his successor), the Governor-General may not have had the courage to dissolve the Constituent Assembly. If the duly elected members of the National Assembly in 1956 had not played the musical chair game in the corridors of power, the first Martial Law might not have been so welcomed as to earn the adjective of a 'silent revolution.' If the political leaders had not been seduced by the prospects of personal gain and had accepted the amendments in the 1962 Constitution, changing it into a parliamentary form of government, as was agreed upon in the round table conference, Ayub Khan might not have panicked and asked Yahya Khan to perform his constitutional duty. If the leaders of East Pakistan and West Pakistan, who had been elected in a fair and free election, had put their heads together to arrive at a consensus and had avoided confrontation, which led to secession, we might have continued as a united Pakistan. Had the subsequent politicians not corrupted and rigged the elections to perpetrate their power, the history of Pakistan after 1977 may have been different, and lastly, if from 1985 onward horse trading had not been the hallmark of Pakistan's politics, four dissolutions may not have been possible. The Supreme Court could not resist commenting on corruption and has considered it a factor which can erode the constitutional functioning of a government.[41]

Constitutional Culture

In order to develop a constitutional and political culture in the nation, senior leaders of all walks of life have to take the Constitution seriously. An incompetent lawyer having lost a case, blames the judge rather than the facts of his case or his own presentation. Immature leaders pass on their blame and their failure to the Constitution. For some time, arguments have been raging in political circles which only generate heat, but no light. The parliamentary form of government is not suited to Pakistan and, therefore, it has failed; the presidential system cannot work due to its delicate checks and balances, and so our experiment with it was a political disaster; we need a parliamentary system with a strong president, but there can be no two rulers in the same state, so we have had four dissolutions of the assembly. We should have a parliamentary form of government in which the president is merely decorative, but this has led to Martial Law. Arguments like this reflect intellectual frustration and lack of political focus. We do have a good Constitution; the time has come to take every word of it seriously, and to run a government in the letter and spirit of this Constitution.

Ideology and Constitutional Development

We are aware of the famous and oft-quoted speech of Quaid-i-Azam Muhammad Ali Jinnah, which he delivered on 11 August 1947 with the following famous words:

> Now, I think we should keep [this fundamental principle] in front of us as our ideal and you will find that in course of time Hindus would cease to be Hindus and Muslims would cease to be Muslims, not in the religious sense, because that is the personal faith of each individual, but in the political sense as citizens of the state.[42]

In order to create one nation (*umma wahida*), a Constitution was necessary. When the Constituent Assembly enacted the Objectives Resolution it was a clear indication that the future Constitution would spell out the ideological base, as well as the instrument to govern it. All the Constitutions contained the same pattern and indicated the ideological basis, and, inter alia, provided rules of governance, including the ideological thrust about the state religion being Islam (since 1973), and the President a Muslim, and that no law shall be passed against the Quran and Sunnah. Moreover, there will be an Islamic Advisory Council, and the Shariat Court (since 1985) would declare any law repugnant to the Quran and Sunnah as void.

The rules of governance are similar to those that can be found in any modern democratic country. Each Constitution provided a synthesis (or compromise) between the traditionalists and modernists. This was easily achieved at the time of framing the 1954 Constitution, although ideological debate did consume a lot of time. The 1956 and 1962 Constitutions represented the same spirit of compromise. The 1973 Constitution conceded to the traditionalists a clause that Islam is the state religion, and also provided a definition of 'Muslim', the latter through an amendment in the Constitution.

Ever since the Objectives Resolution was made a substantive part of Pakistan's Constitution and the Shariat Courts were established, the emphasis on ideology *vis-à-vis* the principle of Constitution has increased. While introducing these amendments in the Constitution, General Zia had remarked that the *qibla* (the ideological direction) of the nation was set right. The traditionalists have since then started to claim that the part of the Constitution dealing with the governance of the country be reread (or rewritten) in the light of the principles which are enunciated in the Constitution. The declaration that sovereignty belongs to Allah is supposed to provide enough basis for cancelling some of the substantive provisions of the Constitution as repugnant to the Quran and Sunnah (as understood by the traditionalists). The Supreme Court has so far kept the distinction between the ideological part of the Constitution and the provision relatable to the governance of the country.[43]

Whether the ideology will overshadow the provision of governance depends on how the parliamentarians work the system.

The Hope

The capacity of Pakistani society to sustain the stress of making and unmaking three constitutions, living through various Martial Laws, suffering the tragic shock of losing East Pakistan as part of the country, and witnessing massive corruption in politics, and yet being able to preserve national identity and seek to establish a system based on ballots and accountability is an exceptional phenomenon in itself and a source of great hope. Very few nations have the track record of being able to rid themselves of three successive Martial Laws. A two-party system has emerged out of our previous experience, resulting in alternative governments between the Pakistan People's Party and the Pakistan Muslim League, on each dissolution of the Assembly. It is now for the leaders to strengthen the system. Horse trading, called derisively *'lota-cracy'* has aroused national condemnation against it. The parliament has also passed the fourteenth amendment as desired by the electorate.[44] Judicial activism is being used to correct not only the constitutional violations, but to provide social justice and to strengthen ethical norms. If the Bar of the country provides proper assistance to the courts, a great deal can be achieved. The armed forces of Pakistan have recognized that the imposition of Martial Law cannot help the country, and it is appropriate to help the civilian administration to correct itself. Parties based on religion have lost their appeal in the electoral process.

The issue of ideology is being dealt with in a pragmatic manner, and parameters have been established by the parliament and by the judiciary which could provide scope for *ijtihad* (reasoning). *Ehtesab*, or accountability, is a public demand and it must be significantly satisfied. In a word, Pakistani society appears to be learning from its failures and shortcomings and that is a good beginning. I do see a ray of light in the future.

NOTES

1. Dr Safdar Mahmood, *The Constitutional Foundations of Pakistan*, p. 9.
2. Fifteenth day of August was fixed for both the dominions of India and Pakistan by Article 1 of the Indian Independence Act.
3. Proviso to Article 5 of the Indian Independence Act, 1947.
4. *Dawn*, 15 July 1947.
5. Rules of the Constituent Assembly, 1948.
6. Constitution (Amendment) Act, 1950.
7. Mahmood, op.cit., p. 47.
8. Constituent Assembly, Debates Vol. VII (1956), pp. 13-50.
9. Ibid., p. 181.
10. S.M. Zafar, *Through the Crises*, p. 46.
11. Order of Governor-General dated 17/04/53—see, Syed Nur Ahmad, *From Martial Law to Martial Law*, p. 321.
12. Report of The Basic Principles Committee adopted on 06/10/54.
13. 'Federation of Pakistan vs. Maulvi Tamizuddin Khan', PLD 1955 FC 240.
14. Article 58(2)(b) contains this principle and makes dissolution of National Assembly conditional with 'an appeal to the electorate.' Also see, 'Yusuf Patel vs. Crown', PLD 1955 FC 387.
15. Noor Ahmad, op.cit., p. 354.
16. Dosso's case; PLD 1956 SC and *Martial Law to Martial Law*, p. 402.
17. PLD 1958 SC 533 'Dosso vs. Federation of Pakistan'.
18. Muhammad Ayub Khan, *Friends not Masters*.
19. 'Syed Abul Ala Moududi vs. Government of Pakistan and others', PLD 1964 SC 673.
20. Zafar, op.cit., pp. 11 and 14.
21. Declared under Article 30 of 1962 Constitution on 06/09/95.
22. Zafar, op.cit., pp. 78-9.
23. 'Government of East Pakistan vs. Roshan Bijaya Shaukat Ali Khan', PLD 1966 SC 286.
24. 'Government of West Pakistan vs. Begum Agha Abdul Karim Shorish Kashmiri', PLD 1969 SC 14.
25. Ibid.
26. For reasons see, *Through the Crises* by S.M. Zafar.
27. 'Malik Ghulam Jillani vs. The Government of West Pakistan', PLD 1967 SC 373.
28. President Order No. II/70.
29. Rafi Raza, *Bhutto and Pakistan*, see *Dawn* 16/06/97.
30. President Reference under Indian Courts of Pakistan – PLD 1973 SC 563.
31. 'Begum Nusrat Bhutto vs. Chief of Army Staff' – PLD 1977 SC 657.
32. S.M. Zafar's statements, in *Jang* 06/01/85; *Dawn* 06/01/85; 02/03/86.

33. 'Benazir Bhutto vs. Federation of Pakistan' – PLD 1989 SC 66 (see also 'Benazir Bhutto vs. Federation of Pakistan' – PLD 1988 SC 416 in which political rights of the political parties were held to be substantive and enforceable).
34. For Dissolution of 1988, see 'Federation of Pakistan vs. Haji Saifullah' – PLD 1988 SC 338. For Dissolution of 1990, see 'Khawaja Tariq Rahim vs. Federation of Pakistan' – PLD 1992 SC 464. For Dissolution of 1993, see 'Mian Muhammad Nawaz Sharif vs. President of Pakistan' – PLD 1993 SC 473. For Dissolution of 1996, see 'Benazir Bhutto Vs. President of Pakistan' – 1997 SCMR 353.
35. 'Government of Sindh Vs. Sharif Faridi' – PLD 1994 SC 105.
36. 'Aljihad Trust vs. Federation of Pakistan' – PLD 1996 SC 324.
37. After the advisory judgement of Federal Court, Governor-General issued Constitutent Assembly Order providing for an election on 21/06/54 by an electorate consisting of Members of Provincial Assemblies.
38. The Aligarh Institute Gazette, dated 4 August 1907.
39. National newspapers of April 1978.
40. Ibid.
41. 'Mohtarma Benazir Bhutto vs. President of Pakistan' – 1977 SC Monthly Review 353.
42. Syed Nur Ahmed, op.cit., p. 283.
43. PLD 1992 SC 595 'Hakim Khan vs. Government of Pakistan'.
44. 14th Amendment does control defection but the amendment has overreached its purpose and appears to stifle democratic working of the political parties.

3

The Judiciary and Constitutional Crises in Pakistan
Javid Iqbal

In the fifty year history of Pakistan, the country has passed through numerous constitutional crises, and the superior courts have been called upon to resolve them. In the first decade, one of the reasons for these crises was the peculiar nature of the Provisional Constitution of Pakistan based on the Government of India Act 1935, with some modifications wrought by the Act of Independence in 1947 which remained in force for a period of nine years (1947-56). This Provisional Constitution retained the office of the Governor-General who represented the Crown and enumerated his broad discretionary powers. On the other hand, it laid down the structure of a democratic government. The Constituent Assembly enacted laws for the day to day affairs of the state and was also expected to frame the future Constitution. This is the background in which a struggle for supremacy started between the Legislature on the one hand and the Executive Authority on the other. The struggle assumed the form of a conflict between democracy and autocracy, and the judiciary, whose autonomy and independence were guaranteed under the Provisional Constitution, had to define and distribute power between the contesting parties.

The History of Judicial Review

The Constituent Assembly, while drafting the future Constitution, contemplated reduction in the powers of the Governor-General. But on 24 October 1954 Governor-General Malik Ghulam Muhammad, in a pre-emptive move, dissolved the Constituent Assembly on the ground that it had lost the confidence of the people and could no longer function.

The President of the Constituent Assembly, Maulvi Tamizuddin Khan moved the Sindh Chief Court against the Federation of Pakistan.[1] A Full Bench of that court unanimously held that the Legislature's supremacy in the Constitution-making field could not be questioned. The main thrust of the judgement was that the people were given the freedom to frame any Constitution they liked, and to do what they liked with their own Constituent Assembly. Thus, the action of the Governor-General was disapproved. The unanimous decision of the Sindh Chief Court, with its strong bias in favour of legislative supremacy, was actually an attempt to pave the way for the firm establishment of a democratic order in Pakistan.

The Federation of Pakistan appealed against the decision before the Federal Court of Pakistan.[2] The matter was heard by a Full Bench of that court, and the leading judgement was delivered by Chief Justice Muhammad Munir, who held that the Constituent Assembly acted merely as legislature of a dominion and that the assent of the Governor-General was necessary for each and every legislation made by it. According to the reasoning of Chief Justice Muhammad Munir, the Pakistan Governor-General represented the British Crown and his power to dissolve the Constituent Assembly was founded in the royal prerogative. The judges of the Full Bench, with the exception of Justice A. R. Cornelius, agreed with him. Justice Cornelius, in his dissenting opinion, maintained that the assent of the Governor-General was unnecessary because the Constituent Assembly being a supra-legal body could make its own rules for legislation. He expressed the view that the Governor-General owed nothing to the British Sovereign except his warrant of appointment issued upon the recommendation of the Government of Pakistan, and that he owed allegiance to the Constitution as amended from time to time.

Thereafter, when the Governor-General proceeded, through an ordinance, to validate all the laws previously made by the Constituent Assembly without his assent, he was restrained from doing so by the Federal Court on the ground that he was not competent to legislate on constitutional matters which could be done only by a representative assembly.[3] As a result, the Governor-General moved a Reference before the Federal Court invoking its advisory jurisdiction as to how the problem regarding the establishment of a new Constituent Assembly was to be resolved.[4] The answer was that the Governor-General was competent to set up a new representative body which would act as a Constituent Assembly. It was eventually this new Constituent Assembly which framed the first Constitution of Pakistan i.e., the Constitution of the Islamic Republic of Pakistan, 1956.

Although the Federal Court had upheld the action of the Governor-General in dissolving the Constituent Assembly, it did not permit him to proceed to legislate on constitutional matters and advised him to set up a representative body for that purpose. The Federal Court therefore, according to some jurists, 'restored the rule of law in a situation where the executive fiat appeared all pervasive'.[5]

The 1956 Constitution remained in force for about two years only. It was abrogated by President Iskandar Mirza on 7 October 1958. The Assemblies were dissolved, Martial Law was imposed and General Ayub Khan was appointed Chief Martial Law Administrator. The reason given by President Iskandar Mirza for his action was that in the background of the ruthless struggle for power, corruption, exploitation of the masses, and the prostitution of Islam for political ends, a chaotic internal situation had been created which could not be improved by elections.

In certain matters before the Supreme Court of Pakistan, a question arose as to what was the effect of the abrogation of the late Constitution and its replacement by the Laws (Continuance in Force) Order, 1958 on writs issued under some existing pieces of legislation. The Supreme Court, headed by Chief Justice Muhammad Munir delivered a judgement on 27 October 1958 in four appeals generally known as Dosso's case[6] to the effect that a victorious revolution or a successful coup *d'état* was an internationally recognized method of changing a legal order, and citing Kalsen's General Theory of Law and State, gave legal sanctity to the *coup d'état* in Pakistan. Here again, Justice Cornelius dissented, as he did not think that the *coup* could be legally justified. The following day, President Iskandar Mirza was made to resign and was replaced by General Ayub Khan as the President of Pakistan.

Justice Dr Nasim Hassan Shah, retired Chief Justice of Pakistan, maintains that although the doctrine that a new legal order created by a revolution is itself a law-creating fact, is of doubtful validity, it ensures governance according to law rather than on the whims of a military Commander. He is further of the view that, in the light of this ruling, the Martial Law regime was made to realize that under the President's Order 1 of 1958, also called the Laws (Continuance in Force) Order 1958, Pakistan was to be governed as nearly as may be in accordance with the late Constitution (of 1956) except to the extent where its provisions were modified through an express order by the President or the Chief Martial Law Administrator.[7]

The other view is of another retired Chief Justice of Pakistan, Justice Yaqoob Ali who had observed that the judgements delivered in the cases of Maulvi Tamizuddin Khan, Governor-General's Reference No. 1 of 1955 and State vs. Dosso had a profound effect on the constitutional development of Pakistan; that a country which came into being with a written Constitution providing for a parliamentary form of government with distribution of state power was soon converted into an autocracy, and eventually degenerated into a military dictatorship.[8]

From 1958 to 1962 the position of the Judiciary had been well illustrated in the case titled the Province of East Pakistan vs. Muhammad Mehdi Ali Khan Panni.[9] In that case the principle enunciated in Dosso's case was challenged. But Chief Justice Muhammad Munir, while defending the concept of revolutionary legality, held that the military regime of Ayub Khan had unfettered legislative power and could even annul or alter rulings of the court.

Martial Law was lifted when Ayub Khan promulgated his own presidential form of constitution in 1962. Fundamental Rights were added to this Constitution in 1964. Thereafter the courts became assertive again and proceeded to consider the matters involving constitutionality of Martial Law regulations as well as the ouster of the jurisdiction of the Courts.

The first opportunity came when the presidential ordinance making power was challenged. Ayub Khan wanted to amend the Constitution so that members of his council of ministers could address the house even if they were not members of the National Assembly. The matter was considered by the Dhaka High court which held that a presidential order cannot amend the Constitution.[10] The Supreme Court rejected the appeal.[11] Chief Justice Cornelius held that the written Constitution gave the courts powers which they could exercise with vigilance. In this judgement it was laid down that only the courts had the power to judge the proper use of the presidential authority under the 1962 Constitution, the presidential authority was not unlimited, and that in the instant case the President had not exercised his authority constitutionally.

The second important case decided during the Ayub era was Maulana Maudoodi's case.[12] The Government dissolved the political party of Maulana Maudoodi, namely Jamaat-i-Islami, by closing its operations under the 1908 Criminal Law Amendment Act. The Supreme Court upheld the rights of political parties to function and disapproved the governmental action of depriving a political party from functioning on the basis of its 'opinion' that it was interfering with the maintenance of law and order. The 'opinion' of the executive authority was held to be subject to judicial review. The Court laid down that absolute rights and controlled democracy could not co-exist and that constitutional rights once given cannot be withdrawn.

Another case of conflict between public order and individual rights was the matter of Malik Ghulam Jilani.[13] In that case the question involved was the interpretation of the expression 'satisfaction' in terms of Rule 32 of the Defence of Pakistan Rules. Malik Ghulam Jilani was detained on the ground that the detaining authority was 'satisfied' that his detention was in the public interest. The Supreme Court ruled that if the grounds were not 'reasonable' detention could not be justified.

In 1969, when Ayub Khan's Government was in trouble due to large scale public demonstrations against him, he transferred power to General Yahya Khan, Commander-in-Chief of the Pakistan Army, rather than to the Speaker of the National Assembly as required by his own Constitution of 1962. Yahya Khan abrogated the 1962 Constitution and placed the country under Martial Law.

He held general elections under the Legal Framework Order 1971. The results indicated that in East Pakistan, the Awami League of Mujibur Rehman secured all the seats of the Constituent Assembly whereas in West Pakistan, the People's Party of Zulfikar Ali Bhutto won with an overwhelming majority. This indicated that politically, the country was divided.

After the secession of East Pakistan and the establishment of Bangladesh in December 1971, Yahya Khan was compelled to abdicate and Zulfikar Ali Bhutto, the leader of the PPP (Pakistan People's Party), the majority party in West Pakistan, became the first civilian Martial Law Administrator. He held this office till the implementation of the Interim Constitution on 20 April 1972.

The reassertion of the Judiciary for upholding the rule of law which had commenced from the enforcement of the 1962 Constitution lasted only uptill March 1969 when the 1962 Constitution was abrogated. Thereafter, from March 1969 to December 1971 the courts receded into the background particularly after the implementation of Jurisdiction of Courts (Removal of Doubts) Order, 1969 whereunder the jurisdiction of the superior courts was curtailed with retrospective effect (i.e. from 25 March 1969). This Order held the field until the removal of Yahya Khan.

However, between December 1971 and April 1972 the Supreme Court did deliver some important judgements. The first was Asma Jilani vs. Government of Punjab etc.[14] In this case, the detention of some eminent persons under Martial law Regulation 78 was challenged and the Supreme Court was called upon to examine the validity of Yahya Khan's imposition of Martial Law. The leading judgement was written by Chief Justice Hamood-ur-Rehman in which the principle enunciated in State vs. Dosso was overruled as laying down incorrect law and placing the country on wrong lines; Yahya Khan was declared a usurper who had no authority to abrogate the 1962 Constitution and to impose Martial Law. Martial Law Regulation 78 issued by Yahya Khan was accordingly declared as void and of no legal effect. The judgement also attempted to warn future military adventureres that if they took advantage of the concept of revolutionary legality and considered themselves as the new lawgivers, then they would be treated as usurpers.

The second case was Hashmat Ali vs. Lt-Col Muhammad Shafi Durrani etc.[15] In that case, two sitting judges of the Lahore High Court had called upon respondent Lt-Col Durrani to explain under what authority he had taken a particular action against a civilian. The notice of the High Court so annoyed the Commanding Officer, General Mitha, that he ordered the said judges to show cause why they should not be proceeded for having committed contempt of Martial Law. But the crisis was averted on the intervention of the Zonal Martial Law Administrator who assured that Mitha would be dealt with departmentally. Since no action was taken against him during the prevalence of Yahya Khan's Martial Law, the High court took up the matter soon after Yahya Khan's ouster and held that Mitha had committed gross contempt of the High Court by issuing the aforesaid notice to the High Court Judges. The General tendered an unconditional apology before the Court. As he had ceased to be a Martial Law officer, he was sentenced to simple imprisonment till the rising of the court.

In the third case, State vs. Zia-ur-Rehman,[16] the question of the validity of the 1972 Interim Constitution was considered.

Under the Interim Constitution, the National Assembly, consisting of elected members of only West Pakistan was summoned and Zulfikar Ali Bhutto was inducted as President. The Supreme Court held that the National Assembly, as constituted, was a competent body to frame the Constitution and that the Constitution it framed would be a valid document. In short, the effect of judgements in the cases of Asma Jilani and Zia-ur-Rehman was to re-emphasize the power of judicial review and to widen its scope so as to include reversing the principle of *stare decisis*.

The 1973 Constitution, authenticated by Zulfikar Ali Bhutto, was based on consensus of the elected representatives and the leaders of all political parties. But Zulfikar Ali Bhutto, as Prime Minister with a rubber-stamp majority in the National Assembly, made numerous amendments in it, including those pertaining to the curtailment of the powers of the superior courts.

The independence of the Judiciary was first curtailed by the Executive when Ayub Khan started the practice of interviewing the judges before appointment to the High Courts. During the time of Yahya Khan the powers of the judges of the superior courts were taken away almost completely under the Jurisdiction of Courts (Removal of Doubts) Order, 1969.

The constitutional amendments made for controlling the Judiciary during the Bhutto era were: First Amendment (notified on 8 May 1974) which made provision for the transfer of a judge from one High Court to another without his consent; Fourth Amendment (notified on 25 November 1975) which curtailed the jurisdiction of High Courts in the matter of granting bail in detention cases; Fifth Amendment (notified on 15 September 1976) which limited the tenure of Chief Justices of the Supreme Court and High Courts to five and four years respectively. They were given, thereafter, the option either to retire from office or to assume the office as senior most judge of that court. A judge of the High Court who did not accept an appointment as judge of the Supreme Court would be deemed to have retired from his office. In this Amendment, further curbs were placed on the powers of the High courts to grant bail.

Sixth Amendment (notified on 4 January 1977) laid down that the Chief Justice of the Supreme Court may continue to be in office although he had attained the age of sixty-five years and that he would retire only after he completed the term of five years in office; and Seventh Amendment (notified on 16 May 1977) deprived the High Court of their constitutional jurisdiction under Article 199 in relation to any area in which the Armed Forces of Pakistan were acting in aid of civil power.

Fifth Amendment was made in order to remove Chief Justice Sardar Muhammad Iqbal of the Lahore High Court who declined to accept an appointment as judge of the Supreme Court and was deemed to have retired. Chief Justice Yaqoob Ali of the Supreme Court was enabled to retain his position even after attaining the age of sixty-five years under the Sixth Amendment. But he was removed on 22 September 1977 by General Ziaul Haq under CMLA Order No. 6 of 1977.

Zulfikar Ali Bhutto's civilian government lasted for less than six years, when because of the rigging of elections the opposition parties launched a country-wide agitation against him. The Bhutto Government tried to suppress the demonstrators by deploying armed forces and the imposition of mini-Martial Law in Lahore, Hyderabad, and Karachi. This action was challenged before the Lahore High Court and a Full Bench held that Martial Law cannot be imposed under the 1973 Constitution.[17] But the Sindh High Court held the contrary view.

However, before the appeal of the Federation as to whether or not localized Martial Law can be imposed under the 1973 Constitution, could be heard by the Supreme Court, the army struck and Martial Law was again imposed in the country on 5 July 1977. The operation of the 1973 Constitution was held in abeyance although it was not abrogated. General Ziaul Haq, as Chief Martial Law Administrator, in his address to the nation on 5 July 1977 spoke in the same tone as had been previously used by Ghulam Muhammad, Iskandar Mirza, Ayub Khan, etc., about the failure of the politicians to steer the country out of the crisis and that therefore the armed forces were left with no other alternative except to intervene.

Zulfikar Ali Bhutto was arrested on the charge of murdering the father of Ahmad Raza Kasuri MNA. Begum Nusrat Bhutto challenged his detention and the imposition of Martial Law before the Supreme Court.[18] A Full Bench of the Court reconsidered the two previous judgements in Dosso's case and Asma Jilani's case. The court held that the conditions prevailing in the country justified the imposition of Martial law under the principle of 'state necessity'. The leading judgement was delivered by Chief Justice Anwar-ul-Haq who maintained that since the 1973 Constitution had not been abrogated there was constitutional continuity, and that as it was held in abeyance for a limited period, it did not amount to a revolution of the nature described in Dosso's case but only a constitutional deviation necessitated by the circumstances prevalent in the country.

During Ziaul Haq's Martial Law, the Judiciary's independence was again curtailed by numerous devices. The Supreme Court had conferred upon Ziaul Haq the power to amend the Constitution. Taking advantage of this position, he made major amendments to the 1973 Constitution, particularly to oust the jurisdiction of the superior courts to review the orders passed by the Martial Law authorities, to prolong the duration of Martial Law, to transfer the judges to the Federal Shariat Court by way of punishment, and to remove judges from the High Courts and Supreme Court appointed by the Bhutto Government as well as those who were not acceptable to the establishment.

The controversial trial of Zulfikar Ali Bhutto along with others on the murder charge was held on the original side of Lahore High Court before a Full Bench which convicted and sentenced him to death *vide* Judgement dated 18 March 1978. The appeal before the Supreme Court was dismissed by the majority judgement on 6 February 1979. Subsequently, a review petition filed by Zulfikar Ali Bhutto was dismissed on 24 March 1979. He was executed on 4 April 1979.

After obtaining a five-year term to continue as President through a Referendum in 1984, Ziaul Haq held general elections on non-party basis. The parliament thus elected in 1985 adopted the heavily amended 1973 Constitution by means of the Revival of the Constitution 1973 Order (President's Order 14 of 1985). The amendments passed by the party-less parliament included the Eighth Amendment containing Articles 270-A and 58(2)(b). Thereafter Martial Law was lifted.

The superior courts managed to assert themselves once again when Martial Law was lifted. They straightened out some of the problems created by the drastic amendments of the existing provisions of law.

The first important case in this connection was Federation of Pakistan vs. Malik Ghulam Mustafa Khar,[19] in which the Supreme Court ruled that immunity granted under Article 270-A to orders passed by the military courts would not be available when there had been a malafide exercise of power, or orders had been passed without jurisdiction, or in violation of specific constitutional provisions.

The second case was Ms Benazir Bhutto vs. Federation of Pakistan,[20] in which amendments made in the Political Parties Act 1962 were challenged as violative of the Fundamental Rights guaranteed under the Constitution. The petition was accepted and the objectionable amendments of the Political Parties Act 1962 were struck down by the Supreme Court.

The third case was also brought by Ms Benazir Bhutto against the Federation of Pakistan.[21] In that case amendments made in the Representation of the People Act, 1976 were challenged whereby restrictions were imposed on the allocation of a common election symbol to candidates of a political party. This petition was also accepted by the Supreme Court holding the amendments as violative of the Fundamental Right of Political Association.

On 29 May 1988, the Government of Prime Minister Muhammad Khan Junejo was dismissed by Ziaul Haq while exercising his presidential power under Article 58(2)(b) of the Constitution. About two and a half months later on 17 August 1988 Ziaul Haq was killed in a plane crash near Bahawalpur.

The dismissal of the Government of Muhammad Khan Junejo and dissolution of the National Assembly by Ziaul Haq were challenged by Haji Saifullah Khan before the Lahore High

Court. The High Court set aside that order holding that the grounds on which the impugned order was passed by the President were vague, general, and non-existent. However, it did not grant relief of the restoration of the Assembly. The matter came up in appeal before the Supreme Court which upheld the judgement of the Lahore High Court. It ruled that the impugned order did not fulfil the requirements of Article 58(2) (b), therefore it was illegal and unconstitutional. But, like the High Court, relief was declined because general elections had already been announced and were being held on 16 November 1988.[22]

As a result of the general elections Ms Benazir Bhutto, leader of the PPP was sworn in as Prime Minister. But her Government lasted for about one year and eight months only. She was dismissed on 6 August 1990 on charges of corruption, nepotism, inefficiency, and violation of the Constitution; and the National Assembly was dissolved by President Ghulam Ishaq Khan in exercise of the discretionary power under Article 58(2) (b) of the Constitution.

A number of writ petitions were filed in the Sindh High Court against the presidential order. But in the Judgement delivered in Khalid Malik vs. Federation of Pakistan,[23] a Full Bench upheld the dissolution order as constitutional and valid. However, a Full Bench of the Peshawar High Court, by a majority judgement declared the dismissal of the Provincial Government of Aftab Ahmad Khan Sherpao and dissolution of the Provincial Assembly NWFP, as illegal and without lawful authority.[24] An appeal was filed against the judgement of the Peshawar High Court and the judgement was suspended by a single judge of the Supreme Court. The judgement of the Sindh High Court was likewise assailed in the Supreme Court but it was upheld. The judgement of the Peshawar High Court was set aside by a short order without incorporating detailed reasons.[25]

In the elections that ensued, the Muslim League obtained a majority in the National Assembly and Mian Muhammad Nawaz Sharif was sworn in as Prime Minister of Pakistan. But on 18 April 1993, President Ghulam Ishaq Khan, in exercise of the powers conferred on him under Article 58(2) (b) of the Constitution, again dismissed the government and dissolved the National Assembly on the ground that the Government of the Federation could not be carried out in accordance with the provisions of the Constitution.

Muhammad Nawaz Sharif assailed this order before the Supreme Court. The petition was heard by the Full Court. By a majority judgement, the Court accepted his petition, holding that the discretion conferred on the President under Article 58(2) (b) was not absolute. It was qualified and circumscribed by the object of the law that conferred it. The Supreme Court arrived at the conclusion that in the instant case the action taken did not fall within the ambit of this provision and was also violative of Article 17 of the Constitution. The order of the President was set aside, and the National Assembly was restored. Mian Muhammad Nawaz Sharif obtained a vote of confidence and again became Prime Minister.[26]

This judgement was a departure from the previous tradition. It has been considered a leap towards supremacy of the Constitution and independence of the Judiciary. However, it disturbed the establishment, including the army. Prime Minister Nawaz Sharif inexplicably resigned and the National Assembly was dissolved. New elections were held and Ms Benazir Bhutto became Prime Minister for the second time.

Benazir Bhutto's government was apprehensive of the new-found assertiveness of the Judiciary. Therefore, like her predecessors Ayub Khan, Yahya Khan, Zulfikar Ali Bhutto, and Ziaul Haq, she embarked on a course to make the Judiciary subservient to the Executive. Numerous devices were adopted in order to tame and emasculate the Judiciary. The Constitutional amendments made by Ziaul Haq, in respect of the appointment, tenure, and terms of service of the judges, were used by Ms Benazir Bhutto to her own advantage. The superior courts were packed through temporary, additional, *ad hoc* appointments. The length of the tenure of these judges depended on the pleasure of the Executive. In disregard of the principle of seniority, hand-picked Acting Chief Justices were appointed in the Punjab and

Sindh High Courts who blindly followed the directions of the Executive and appointed judges who were favourites of the Executive. Many of them did not even meet the Constitutional requirements for elevation to the High Court.

These manipulations were designed to erode the independence asserted by the Judiciary, particularly after the judgement of the Supreme Court presided over by Chief Justice Dr Nasim Hasan Shah which led to the restoration of the National Assembly and Muhammad Nawaz Sharif's Premiership.

Habib Wahab Al-Khairi filed a writ petition before the Lahore High Court challenging the appointment of the new judges in which, among others, twenty Additional Judges of the Lahore High Court, appointed by Benazir Bhutto's Government, were arrayed as respondents. The petition was dismissed by the High Court. But on appeal, a Full Bench of the Supreme Court, presided over by Chief Justice Sajjad Ali Shah passed a historic judgement in March 1996 setting aside all these appointments.[27]

The Supreme Court laid down that a judge of a superior court is to be appointed by the President after meaningful consultation with the Chief Justice of Pakistan as well as the Chief Justice of the High Court concerned, and that the candidate recommended by the Chief Justice has to be appointed unless sound reasons are recorded against the appointment by the President; that an Acting Chief Justice cannot be a consultee under the relevant provision of the Constitution; that an *ad hoc* judge cannot be appointed in the Supreme Court in the presence of permanent vacancies; that since the senior most judge of a High Court has a legitimate expectancy to be appointed as the Chief Justice of that court, he is entitled to be so appointed unless valid reasons against his appointment are recorded by the President; that a sitting Chief Justice or judge of a High Court cannot be appointed against his consent to the Federal Shariat Court; that the transfer of a judge from one High Court to another can only be made in the public interest; that the constitutional requirement of ten years practice as an advocate before being appointed as a judge means actual practice at the Bar and not merely the period of enrolment.

Mahmood Khan Achakzai's case[28] can also be included in the series of important judgements after Nawaz Sharif's case and the Judges' case. In this judgement, it has been laid down by the Supreme Court, *inter alia*, that no enactment can be made in respect of the provisions of the Constitution relating to the Judiciary by which its independence and separation from the Executive is undermined or compromised, since this would militate against the basic features of the Constitution.

Benazir Bhutto's Government was dismissed and the National Assembly dissolved under Proclamation dated 5 November 1996 by President Farooq Ahmed Khan Leghari exercising his powers under Article 58(2) (b) of the Constitution. The charges against her government included non-implementation of the judgement of the Supreme Court in the Judges' case as well as not implementing the direction of the Supreme Court regarding separation of the Judiciary from the Executive. Ms Benazir Bhutto's petition against her dismissal was dismissed by the Supreme Court. In the subsequent elections held in February 1997, the Pakistan Muslim League won with an overwhelming majority and Mian Muhammad Nawaz Sharif became Prime Minister. An Amendment deleting Article 58(2) (b) from the Constitution was expeditiously and unanimously passed by both the Houses of Parliament, bringing to an abrupt end this chapter of Presidential authoritarianism.

This brief survey of the fifty years' history of the Judiciary in Pakistan reveals that the judges of the superior courts performed their functions to the best of their abilities in order to uphold the rule of law despite the successive constitutional crises through which the country passed. Three judgements i.e., Maulvi Tamizuddin Khan's case, Dosso's case and Begum Nusrat Bhutto's case authored by two eminent Chief Justices of Pakistan, namely Muhammad Munir and Anwar-ul Haq, have been particularly subjected to criticism. But this criticism does not appear to be justified if the circumstances and the milieu in which they were passed are dispassionately kept in view.

Judicial Activism: Interpretations

The constitutional crises which led to the delivery of these judgements, were not the creation of the Judiciary. The superior courts were called upon to resolve conflicts which were political in nature and at the same time they had to maintain a tradition of judicial independence. Furthermore, these judgements were either passed unanimously or a large majority of the other eminent judges of the Benches had agreed with the author judges. They also had to exercise judicial self-interest i.e., to preserve the Judiciary as an institution in each of these constitutional crises. They were aware that an opinion which ran contrary to the interests of the establishment would not be acceptable. If they delivered a judgement which was not likely to be implemented, its defiance would be detrimental to the prestige of the Judiciary, particularly when there was no pressure of public opinion and the Press for upholding the independence of the Judiciary. In this background, the method employed by Chief Justices Muhammad Munir and Anwar-ul Haq can be described as one of judicial prudence or judicial realism as opposed to judicial purism or judicial idealism.

As for the controversy regarding the trial of Zulfikar Ali Bhutto, there are divergent opinions. Some commentators, like Roedad Khan (*Pakistan—A Dream Gone Sour*), Ramsay Clarke (*Trial of Ali Bhutto And The Future of Pakistan*), and Victoria Schofield (*Bhutto: Trial & Execution*) contend that his murder trial was biased. The others maintain that the trial gained prominence because an eminent political figure was involved. Otherwise, apart from its political dimension, the trial was like any other criminal trial in which the accused was convicted and sentenced unanimously by a Full Bench of the Lahore High Court on the original side, and on appeal his conviction and sentence were maintained by the Supreme Court by a majority of four as opposed to three dissenting judges on the Bench. Thereafter, his review petition was unanimously dismissed by the Full Bench. Had the trial been biased, there would not have been a split decision in the Supreme Court.

The Judiciary in Pakistan is the creature of the constitution. It was marginalized when Pakistan had no constitution, but whenever Pakistan has been ruled by a Constitution, the Judiciary as an institution has been prompt to uphold the supremacy of the Constitution and the rule of law.

The recent new-found independence of the Judiciary which has taken the form of judicial activism in Pakistan, actually commenced in 1988, when the Supreme Court passed a series of judgements upholding the rights of political parties to participate in the elections, removal of restrictions imposed on the allocation of a common election symbol to candidates of a political party, and reiterating the separation of the Judiciary from the Executive. These judgements paved the way for the successful working of a parliamentary form of democracy in the country. These were followed by the judgements in Nawaz Sharif's case and the Judges' case, which are water-sheds in the judicial history of Pakistan. With these judgements, the constitutional role of the Judiciary has been institutionalized. If this assertiveness is consistently maintained, the Judiciary will be fulfilling the role assigned to it by the Constitution.

In this new trend of Judicial activism, the Courts are interpreting Articles 184 and 199 of the Constitution for the benefit of disadvantaged and oppressed persons, instead of merely deciding disputes between private parties. In 'public-interest litigation' or 'class actions' the superior courts have, *inter alia*, banned activities leading to environmental pollution; upheld the rights of bonded labour in the brick kiln industry, women and children in hazardous occupations, and nurses or air hostesses who were not allowed to get married. Public hangings have been stayed as being violative of human dignity. *Suo moto* notice has been taken against police excesses, and the executive has been called upon to explain as to what steps are being taken to curb sectarian violence in the Punjab, and terrorist activities in Karachi.

After the deletion of Article 58(2) (b) from the Constitution, any selected Prime Minister of Pakistan with a heavy mandate would have unfettered powers. The only effective check against manipulation of the Superior Judiciary by the Executive, is the preservation of Judicial independence, supported by a strong public opinion and vigilant Press, provided this judicial independence does not degenerate into judicial autocracy.

It is unfortunate that during the year of the Golden Jubilee Celebrations (1947-97) Pakistan witnessed another constitutional crisis in the form of a confrontation between Sajjad Ali Shah, Chief Justice of the Supreme Court of Pakistan, and Muhammad Nawaz Sharif, Prime Minister. The confrontation brought home the fact that judicial activism without judicial restraint can be self-destructive. The detailed narration of the story of the conflict cannot be undertaken in this paper.

Briefly, while laying down the principles of appointment of judges to the Superior Courts in the famous Judges' Case, Sajjad Ali Shah, Chief Justice did not apply the 'legitimate expectancy' principle in his own case as he had superceded three of his colleagues on his appointment as Chief Justice by the ex-Prime Minister Benazir Bhutto. As a result, his fellow judges remained alienated from him and he could never really succeed in carrying them along with him.

The dispute between Sajjad Ali Shah and Muhammad Nawaz Sharif initially started when the viewpoint of the Chief Justice on the functioning of the newly created Speedy Trial Courts was rejected by the Prime Minister. Thereafter, the Chief Justice asked for the elevation instead of conceding the demand, the Prime Minister flirted with the idea of reducing the number of judges of the Supreme court by making an appropriate amendment in the Constitution. However, this did not happen and the requisition of the Chief Justice was accepted after some delay. But in the meantime, contempt proceedings had been initiated against the Prime Minister before the Chief Justice, and the threat was held out that after the conviction of the Prime Minister, he would be unseated and disqualified to hold his office. Petitions were simultaneously moved by the interested parties before the Chief Justice to suspend the operation of the Thirteenth and Fourteenth Amendments of the Constitution unanimously adopted by both the Houses of Parliament. The

Chief Justice particularly attempted to suspend the operation of the Amendment whereby Article 58(2) (b) had been struck down. The objective behind this move was to restore the Presidential power to dismiss the Prime Minister and to dissolve the National Assembly. Thus, under the garb of judicial activism, Sajjad Ali Shah politicized the Supreme Court. Muhammad Nawaz Sharif and an over-whelming majority of members of Parliament genuinely apprehended that the Chief Justice and the President of Pakistan (Farooq Ahmad Khan Leghari) were together conspiring against the Prime Minister and his Government. In this background, at a hurriedly called Parliamentary meeting of the ruling party it was resolved that the President should be impeached. As a consequence thereof the President tendered his resignation. On the other hand, the Supreme Court building was attacked by the workers of the ruling party and the hearing of the cases could not be carried out. In this state of utter confusion, petitions were moved before the Quetta and Peshawar Benches of the Supreme Court against the Chief Justice. The Chief Justice was put under restraint through the orders of his own colleagues. However, he retaliated by holding such orders in abeyance. A fight ensued among the judges of the Supreme court. Eventually, the appointment of the Chief Justice was held as illegal by a large Bench of the Supreme Court and soon after, he retired as an ordinary judge of the Supreme Court.

The moral of the story is that in this quarrel between the Executive and the Judiciary, the Executive survived unhurt but the Supreme Court was bruised and mauled. It will have to lick its wounds for a considerably long time until its health is fully restored. An illegally appointed Chief Justice by the Executive is not in a position to teach a lesson to it, if he so desires, in isolation from his colleagues.

The Superior Judiciary, as an institution, must always keep itself equipped with a consensus of the judges particularly on the issue of maintaining independence. A division or a split among them in this matter can provide an opportunity to a mischievous Executive to imperceptably manipulate a cooperative Chief Justice from the rest of his colleagues and to use him as an instrument for political purposes under the garb of administering justice.

If the supremacy of the Constitution is upheld in a way that the three organs of the state perform their responsibilities independently within their own spheres, democracy can flourish and the people can savour the fruits of independence. In the words of John Agresto, 'Real democracy can function, only with inter-active understanding of the people, their representatives and their judges together'.[29]

NOTES

1. PLD 1955 Sindh 96.
2. PLD 1955 FC 240.
3. PLD 1955 FC 387: Usif Patel vs. The Crown.
4. PLD 1955 FC 435: Special Reference No. 1 of 1995.
5. Justice (Retd.) Dr Nasim Hasan Shah's Address titled Role of the Judiciary in Maintaining Rule of Law in Pakistan.
6. PLD 1958 SC 533: State vs. Dosso.
7. Address by Justice Retd. Dr Nasim Hasan Shah: Role of the Judiciary in Maintaining Rule of Law in Pakistan.
8. Observations in Asma Jilani's Case: PLD 1972 SC 139.
9. PLD 1959 SC (Pak) 387.
10. PLD 1963 Dacca 669.
11. PLD 1963 SC 486.
12. PLD 1964 SC 673.
13. PLD 1967 SC 473.
14. PLD 1972 SC 139.
15. Cr. Original No. 5/1972 decided on 7.3.1972.
16. PLD 1973 SC 49.
17. PLD 1977 Lah 846: Darvesh M. Arbey vs. Federation of Pakistan.
18. PLD 1977 SC 639: Begum Nusrat Bhutto vs. the Chief of Army Staff.
19. PLD 1989 SC 26.
20. PLD 1988 SC 416.
21. PLD 1989 SC 66.
22. PLD 1989 SC 166: Federation of Pakistan vs. Haji Saifullah Khan etc.
23. PIJ 1991 Karachi 1.
24. PIJ 1991 Peshawar 1: Aftab Ahmad Khan Sherpao vs. Governor of NWFP.

25. PLD 1992 SC 646: Khawaja Ahmad Tariq Rahim vs. Federation of Pakistan.
26. PLD 1993 SC 473: Main Muhammad Nawaz Sharif vs. Federation of Pakistan.
27. PLD 1996 SC 324: Al-Jehad Trust vs. Federation of Pakistan.
28. PLD 1997 SC 324: Mahmood Khan Achakzai vs. Federation of Pakistan.
29. The Supreme Court and Constitutional Democracy, p. 10.

4

The Role of the Military in Politics: Pakistan 1947-97

Khalid Mahmud Arif

Introduction

Pakistan emerged through a political and constitutional process. The legal and peaceful struggle for its achievement demonstrated the passion of its founding fathers, led by Quaid-i-Azam Mohammad Ali Jinnah, for the rule of law and the aspirations of her people for a free society. With the replacement of the Union Jack by the green and white flag of the new country on 14 August 1947 the new nation did adieu to the colonial era and welcomed freedom. Pakistan was created to be a democratic polity and a progressive country.

The price tag was heavy. Massive communal riots engulfed Northern India in which one million people,[1] lost their lives in a savage orgy of violence. Other writers feel that, 'One million dead would be a conservative figure'.[2] Another fourteen million refugees migrated[3] across the Indo-Pakistan border in search of safety and honour. In the annals of human history this was the single largest trans-border migration of a population in peacetime. Much of this human distress might have been averted if the Viceroy, Lord Louis Mountbatten, had not virtually abdicated his constitutional responsibility to ensure a smooth and orderly transfer of power in India. His inexplicable callousness is condemnable. So also is the indecent haste in which he dismantled the Indian Empire, 'built over three hundred years, in just over seventy days'.[4]

During the crucial phase of the transition, Mountbatten played an active role in persuading the rulers of undivided India's Princely States to accede to India. The geographical proximity and other factors had offered opportunities to some of these states to join either India or Pakistan. Mountbatten's compelling advice to them was to join the dominion of India. In critical cases political expediency dominated his decisions. The accession of Bikaner to India is one example.[5]

So visible was Mountbatten's pro-India tilt that his tampering with justice showed rather prominently. One such act planted the seeds of the Kashmir dispute, perhaps deliberately. An Indian scholar argues that it was to promote 'British strategic interests in the post transfer of power era'.[6]

The Golden Jubilee year of Pakistan is an appropriate occasion for an analysis of her power politics in general and the stumbling performance of her democratic order in particular. Pakistan's three military takeovers and the role of the army in her national affairs may provide lessons for the future. The military factor has dominated Pakistan's political performance in the last fifty years. But it is not without a silver lining. Overwhelming evidence shows that setbacks to democracy have strengthened the people's commitment for an undiluted democratic order.

The Problem Defined

What went wrong, where and why is the burden of this narration. How robust was the democratic system inherited in 1947? How was it derailed? Were the political institutions inherited at the time of independence strong? Why did they fail? Did bureaucracy become a silent or active participant on the national political chessboard? What factors influenced military intervention in the political field, and has the army become a permanent pillar of power? Is this role reversible? How have the military takeovers affected its own professional performance and responsibilities? What does the future hold in this field? The list is long.

This study presents one view. The functioning and the malfunctioning of the political system reveals that flawed democracy and self-serving dictatorship alternated between themselves. Democracy has emerged out of this contest like a phoenix out of the ashes of authoritarian rule. This provides hope for the future.

The military dictators were not the sole spoilers of the democratic order. The performance of some elected leaders was no less ruthless and undemocratic. This chapter is divided into four parts:
1. The Political and Military Background
2. Extra-Constitutional Measures
3. Non-Military Influencing Factors
4. The Analysis of Military Role

The Political and Military Background

The Form of Government

Pakistan has had four martial laws, three imposed by the military dictators (Generals Mohammad Ayub Khan, Mohammad Yahya Khan and M. Ziaul Haq) and the fourth by a civilian elected dictator (Z.A. Bhutto). Collectively, the country remained under Martial law for about sixteen years. In addition, parts of the country remained under martial law in March 1953 and in April 1977. Ironically, both the mini martial laws were imposed by the elected civilian governments in order to extricate themselves from their self-created political quagmire. It was also a civilian government that first introduced Martial Law in the country in city of Lahore.

Of Pakistan's eleven Heads of the State, six were either soldiers or bureaucrats. Their cumulative tenure lasted three dozen years. Their 'achievements' in the power saddle include the 'dismissal of eight out of fifteen prime ministers; dissolution of seven out of ten national assemblies; and the banning of five out of seven political parties'.[7]

Political Experimentation Process

Pakistan's frequent experimentation with various forms of government reflects her political desperation. The country has variously tried four different types of political systems—parliamentary, presidential, military, and a half-breed between the parliamentary and the presidential system. The Indian Independence Act 1947, established two independent Dominions—India and Pakistan—both with a parliamentary form of government. While India speedily adopted a constitution, Pakistan's effort remained unsuccessful for too long.

There were reasons for the delay. India had a head-start over Pakistan as she inherited an established government with all the paraphernalia of a functioning state. Her electoral mill had groomed the Indian National Congress into a deep-rooted political party with a large reservoir of leadership. It played a long and effective political role in the post-independence India. Prime Minister, Pundit Jawaharlal Nehru, guided his nation's destiny for seventeen years. His wisdom and vision gave stability to India.

On the contrary, Pakistan inherited a country without the infrastructure of a state. The federal government and its institutions did not exist. The immediate influx of refugees from India, and the death of her founding father added to her difficulties. Her problems were aggravated by India's Machiavellian policies. Pakistan's nascent political system suffered a double jeopardy—internal difficulties compounded by the aggressive policies of India. Within one decade (1947-58) her inefficient and quarrelling politicians made a mockery of democracy. This created a vacuum that started a chain reaction.

Presidential Form of Government

General Ayub Khan's Martial Law introduced a presidential form of government under the 1962 Constitution. His motives were considered suspect, and he was accused of desiring a stamp of legitimacy on his personal rule. To be durable and acceptable, a constitution must reflect the aspirations of the people expressed through their chosen representatives. The 1962 Constitution was imposed on the people from the top by a person who had earlier shown the door to a democratic system.

Ayub's 1962 Constitution met its Waterloo and he evinced little faith in it. He rigged his own Presidential election in 1964 and, when forced to resign in 1969, he transferred power to the Army Chief instead of the Speaker of the National Assembly. Street agitation against Ayub caused the collapse of his government. It proved a point that the constitution is too sacred a trust to be made by a single individual. The 1962 Constitution did not directly elect a president on the basis of adult franchise. Instead, Ayub was indirectly elected president by 80,000 Basic Democrats who had themselves been elected earlier on the basis of one man one vote. An indirectly elected President, with the powers of the head of state and the head of government combined in him, was not acceptable to a majority of the Pakistani people.

Military Rule

All four Chief Martial Law Administrators (Ayub, Yahya, Bhutto, and Zia) also wore Presidential hats. This was an administrative, legal and diplomatic requirement as the country had to have a head of state to function. But in the spirit of law their designation was a misnomer. The four Presidents were in reality absolute military rulers who did not derive their authority either from the Constitution, which was abrogated or suspended, or from the Parliament, which did not exist. It was a rule by absolute power that did not allow for any checks and balances.

Quasi-Parliamentary Form

Following a non-party election held in 1985, General Zia's martial law gave birth to a democratic order. He hand-picked Mohammad Khan Junejo as Prime Minister and secured a vote of confidence in his favour from the National Assembly. Junejo, though little known, proved to be an honourable and assertive leader of integrity. He refused to act like a puppet. Zia dismissed him. In the process he, like Ayub Khan, dismantled the system he himself had sought to erect.

With the rebirth of democracy in 1985, the 1973 Constitution was restored but strangely President Zia, in addition to being the Head of State, continued to hold the office of the chief martial law administrator and the chief of the army staff. The critics called it a quasi-democratic order and castigated Prime Minister Junejo for being constitutionally hamstrung.

Constitution-Making Difficulties

The Constituent Assembly, established in 1947 to frame the constitution, took seven years to produce the draft. The ill-fated 1956 Constitution, parliamentary in form, was abrogated two years later. It had compromised the democratic rights of East Pakistan by putting it at par with West Pakistan, despite its larger population. The Parity Formula was assessed differently in the two wings of the country. Generally supported in West Pakistan, it was viewed with reservations in the numerically dominant, economically weak and politically sensitive East Pakistan. President Iskander Mirza lamented that the 1956 Constitution was 'unworkable'.[8] Two points are worth noting. One, it was too early to pass a judgement on a law that did, however, face the guillotine within two years. Secondly, Iskandar Mirza's motive was not above board.

In a parliamentary system, the head of state is a symbol of the nation, and the powers entrusted to him are marginal, largely to be exercised only in an emergency. All powers are exercised by the cabinet through the parliament. The powers of the Indian President are close to that of the President of Pakistan under the 1973 Constitution. The British Sovereign is another example of a parliamentary system, who only performs ceremonial functions and has no executive authority. Division of authority between two independent power centres creates a situation of conflict.

The perceived or real conflicts in the 1956 Constitution prompted Ayub Khan to introduce a presidential form of government. Ayub violated his own constitution in 1969 by asking the Army Chief, General Yahya Khan, to assume control of the country. Ayub's act of nominating his own successor was legally void and morally untenable. Pakistan was back to square one in her search for a constitution. General Yahya Khan abrogated the Constitution and imposed Martial Law.

A greater catastrophe awaited Pakistan. Political alienation in East Pakistan due to denial of due share in power, and misrule by the governments imposed by the distant Centre, bred separatist agitation which was exploited by India through military intervention and aggression to cut Pakistan into two.

The amputation of East Pakistan in December 1971, caused national trauma and created a constitutional vacuum. This difficult situation was inherited by Zulfikar Ali Bhutto, who had earlier himself played the role of political villain. Bhutto was responsible for the interim constitution made in 1972 and replaced by the 1973 Constitution, enacted by the Parliament on the basis of near unanimity of the legislators. Parliamentary in form, the 1973 Constitution was so heavily tilted in favour of the Prime Minister that all the constitutional acts of the President required countersignatures by the Prime Minister to become laws. An omnipotent head of the government and an impotent head of the state were the two most striking features of the 1973 Constitution. The constitutional pendulum swung from one extreme to the other.

Bhutto's rule (1971-77) was a one-person civilian dictatorship. Despite his democratic credentials, he weakened the institutions of the state, converted Pakistan into a serfdom and employed coercive instruments to 'fix up' those who dared to cross his path. The ruling Pakistan People's Party became a cult, and Bhutto an absolute lord of a feudal state. The 1977 elections held under his government were so patently doctored that the people eventually rose in revolt against his high-handed policies. Bhutto destroyed himself.

The 1973 Constitution was put to the test during the country-wide anti-Bhutto agitation in 1977. President Fazal Elahi Chaudhry 'virtually twiddled his thumbs'[9] and helplessly watched the state administration come to a grinding halt. The Constitution did not permit the Head of State to act except on the advice of the Prime Minister. And, Bhutto was too proud a person to compromise his egocentric policies or accept the blame for electoral rigging.

The Gallup polls at the time had predicted an easy victory for Bhutto's Pakistan People's Party in a fairly held election. Bhutto's overkill election strategy boomeranged and the opposition capitalized on the opportunity. The anti-Bhutto agitation soon took a religious turn. The polarization between the Right and the Left paralyzed the country and presented to the military a difficult option—allow a possible civil war or intervene. The Chief of the Army Staff, General Ziaul Haq, who took charge of the country, claimed that the army had been sucked into the political quagmire. His act was upheld by the Supreme Court. Once in the driving seat, General Zia was intoxicated by power.

It was martial law once again. The 1973 Constitution was held in abeyance. Its revival took eight years (1985) and that too with the addition of the Eighth Amendment that included Article 58(2)(b). It empowered the President to dismiss the Prime Minister and the National Assembly if the situation so warranted. The President was also given discretionary powers, besides others, to appoint the services chiefs and the Chairman of the Joint Chiefs of Staff Committee. The enhanced powers of the President created two power centres. The seeds of conflict were planted.

During the period 1985-1996 three successive Presidents invoked Article 58(2)(b) on four different occasions and dismissed four elected Prime Ministers. The repeated use of the President's discretionary powers created uncertainty in the country and started a national debate on whether Article 58(2)(b) was legally valid, politically justified, and institutionally appropriate. The issue was agitated in the Supreme Court of Pakistan under Constitutional Petition No 60/1996. The Supreme Court held that this article had 'in fact shut the door on martial law which had not been imposed since 1977.'[10] The Supreme Court further stated that 'the Eighth Amendment, including Article 58(2)(b), was a valid piece of legislation and it was open to the Parliament to amend it, if so desired.'[11] The controversial parts of the Eighth Amendment were deleted from the statute book by the Parliament by a unanimous vote.

The Political Obstacles

Pakistan's thorny journey through history depicts a panorama of scheming politicians, military chauvinism, bureaucratic arrogance, constitutional pitfalls, feudal lords, and democratic frailty. In this vista the executive excesses, the judicial docility, the legislative feebleness, and the media weaknesses show rather prominently. It does not imply that the progress was minimal. This narrative is not an attempt to prepare a balance sheet of the achievements and disappointments in the last fifty years. The gains were considerable. So were the follies, some serious in nature. Pakistan's geography changed. Who is more blameworthy for her mistakes is a matter of discretion but one conclusion is irrefutable—there is no one completely innocent among Pakistan's power groups. Sadly, since 1947, twenty-nine out of the thirty-eight elected provincial assemblies were prematurely dissolved. During this period, forty-four out of seventy-seven chief ministers were dismissed by the federal government and another thirteen resigned because they failed to win support in the provincial assemblies.

Pakistan took twenty-three years to hold her first national elections, and this too, surprisingly, under a military dictator,

General Yahya Khan. The elections, held in the backdrop of the Six Points Programme, and in the aftermath of the worst cyclone that had hit East Pakistan in her history, were perceived by the people to be fair and free. But they failed to inject political sanity. The post-election period witnessed a fierce struggle for power between two egoistic leaders who precipitated the national collapse. Pakistan was divided in 1971.

Seen with hindsight, democracy made a trying start. The absorption and resettlement of eight million refugees in 1947 was a Herculean task. Jinnah's death, in 1948, was a serious blow to the young state. The people had great faith in Jinnah's ability. However, his exit placed Prime Minister Liaquat Ali Khan at the national centre stage. He tried hard to knit a nation state but, despite his considerable qualities of head and heart, he lacked the charisma and the authority of the Quaid. The Muslim League, facing petty intrigues, lost public contact and regional issues started clouding the national horizon.

Liaquat's assassination in 1951 by a hired Afghan agent was a terrible shock. The nation, stunned by the cruelty, absorbed the shock with commendable courage. This was the beginning of a steep slide. Political minions came to occupy positions of importance. Their minds were unable to address the problems faced by the country.

The national political scene has largely been dominated by the landed aristocracy and the feudal lords in and outside the legislatures. This large and powerful group is opposed to legal, political and agricultural reforms that may weaken its control on the rural areas where seventy per cent of the population lives. So dominant is the influence of this lobby in the legislatures that their agricultural income has remained tax free since 1947. The dichotomy between urban and rural sections of the population is striking.

Pakistan's political parties are also barely democratic. Few have held in-house elections on a regular basis or have only nominally performed the rituals. The country is rich in family-controlled and autocratic parties in which the genes and means take precedence over competence and the accident of birth provides a sure ladder for leadership. 'The feudal system negates the concept of democracy in the same way as the military rule does. Consequently the political system that has taken root in Pakistan is the anti-thesis of democracy. It is feudal in character and practice and democratic in name only.'[12]

In 1947, 'The intelligentsia was westernized, completely urban, partly unemployed, and mostly frustrated.'[13] The situation has not changed much since. Gains and greed dominate the political culture in which moral decline is visible. Political horse trading is a commonly practiced and lucrative business. A search for greener pastures takes precedence over the code of political ethics.

During the period 1985-97, the curse of corruption in the administration, though prevalent previously, became so rampant that the honest few politicians and bureaucrats were laughed at. The policy makers were accused of shady deals and the distinction between public money and private property was lost.

Islam, an enlightened religion, has a remarkable flexibility in happily co-existing with other religions and cultures. A modern and moderate state, Pakistan has consistently abhorred extremism as an instrument of state policy. The country now enjoys freedom of expression. The rightist political parties are vociferous, and they attempt to arouse religious sensitivities on controversial issues. However, their vote-catching ability has never exceeded five per cent in the national and provincial elections.

A corrupt and semi-democratic political environment has co-existed with a disciplined and powerful defence establishment. Bureaucratic role in the administration has been inconsistent. While some excel in professionalism, others bend to the pressures exerted by the ruling political parties. Such weaklings make some worldly gains but impair the institution. Many bureaucrats specialize in the art of survival by changing loyalties at the right time.

The Rise and Fall of the Muslim League

The Muslim League, formed in 1906, was a party of the upper middle class elite and feudal lords. Conservative in outlook, its manifesto was more intellectual than inspirational in content. It was not a party of the masses when Mr Jinnah took charge in the mid-thirties and led it in the 1937 elections.

Jinnah's leadership and the demand for Pakistan (1940) turned the Muslim League into a people's movement. Its popularity surged. The Pakistan Movement turned into a political storm and the Muslim League had a stunning success in the 1945-6 elections. 'It captured a hundred per cent Muslim seats for the Indian Central Legislative Assembly and won 446 out of a total of 495 Muslim seats in the provincial (state) assemblies'.[14] The massive margin of victory, 86.6 per cent of the votes in the Muslim constituencies in the provincial elections, shocked the Congress. Nehru had boasted earlier that, 'There are only two forces in India today, British imperialism and Indian nationalism *as represented by the Congress*'[15] (emphasis added).

The Muslim League's rapid success disguised a weakness. Political parties acquire vitality and experience by the knocks and shocks inherent in an electoral process. The successes and failures in elections enrich the party and make it vibrant. The League's rapid rise to power denied it a grooming and maturing opportunity. Besides, the opposition members in the assemblies were few and weak. The League, 'Began to rule Pakistan by the right of occupation: it was the only party in existence'.[16]

The demand for a homeland was the first phase of the struggle. The emergence of Pakistan, the second phase, required a consolidation effort to transform public expectations into reality. It needed hard and consistent work. The first three years of the League rule were unobjectionable. Thereafter drift ensued. Its doctrine, ideas, and style lost touch with the march of time and complacency gripped its performance.

The Provincial Scene

The Congress ministry in the North-West Frontier Province dug its own grave by declining to honour the national flag. It was dismissed in August 1947. A judicial tribunal found the Chief Minister of Sindh guilty of corruption and maladministration. He was dismissed in 1948. His successor was involved in cases of jobbery and nepotism. Governor's rule was imposed in the province of Sindh.

In 1949, a power tussle in the Punjab led to the dismissal of its ministry, the dissolution of the provincial legislative assembly and the imposition of Governor's rule in the province. Four years later, the anti-Qadiani riots in Punjab created policy differences between the Province and the Centre. Lahore was put under Martial Law. Normalcy instantly returned to the troubled city without firing a shot. But a political price was paid. The politicians had exposed their weakness to the military.

Kalat, a princely state in Balochistan, had acceded to Pakistan at the time of independence. Emboldened by the prevailing unrest in the country, the former ruler demanded the restoration of his state and went ahead to replace the Pakistan flag from the Miri Fort with that of his own emblem. A military flag march in the area restored sanity.

In 1948, some students in East Pakistan demanded that Bengali be declared a national language along with Urdu. In his address to Dhaka University on 24 May 1948, the Quaid-i-Azam said, 'There can be only one lingua franca, that is, the language for inter-communication between the various provinces of the State, and that language should be Urdu and cannot be any other'.[17] The agitation subsided but only temporarily. Bengali is a well developed and rich language and the regional emotions in its favour were high. The language riots that broke out were actively fueled by India. The controversy divided East and West Pakistan on linguistic lines.

The provincial elections for the East Pakistan Legislative Assembly were due in 1953. These were postponed by the Centre by one year because the Muslim League feared an electoral defeat. The Centre's apprehensions were proved right when, in the delayed elections held the following year, the ruling Muslim League was routed—winning only 10 seats in a house of 309.[18] The people's verdict was violated by the bruised power barons at the Centre and East Pakistan was punished for defeating the ruling party. A bureaucrat-turned politician, Iskandar Mirza, was made the Governor of East Pakistan to discipline the province. The imposition of Governor's rule in the province, an undemocratic act, caused alienation and planted the seeds for separation.

In 1955, the East Pakistan Legislative Assembly declared its own Speaker insane and, in a horrifying display of anger, beat to death its Deputy Speaker inside the house.

Intrigues at the Centre

The Quaid-i-Azam was the people's icon not because he was the Governor-General, but because he was the Founding Father of their country. His reverence and eminence in public eyes would not have diminished, even if he had either become the Prime Minister or remained a plain citizen.

Those succeeding Jinnah as Governor-Generals, were primarily respected because of the office held by them. None equalled Jinnah in public esteem. However, they considered themselves taller than their heights. Some violated the Constitution that they had taken oath to protect. Their acts harmed the country.

Governor-General Ghulam Mohammad indulged in arbitrary acts. Differences surfaced between him and Prime Minister Mohammad Ali Bogra. In 1954, a bill was moved in the Constituent Assembly that bound the Governor-General to act on the advice of the Prime Minister.[19] The scheming Governor-General pre-empted the bill. Ghulam Mohammad dismissed the Central Cabinet, dissolved the Constituent Assembly, and declared a state of emergency in the country on the plea that the institutions could no longer function. In October 1954, Bogra formed another cabinet in which the Army Chief, General Mohammad Ayub Khan, was included as Defence Minister. This formally inducted Ayub into national politics on his own terms. He demanded, and retained, the power-wielding post of the Commander-in-Chief.

Ethics and morality were lost in Pakistan's political culture. Legislators changed their loyalties with such gay abandon that between the years 1953 and 1958, seven prime ministers were nominated and removed through palace intrigues. Each of them managed a vote of confidence from the rubber-stamp Constituent Assembly. The drama of musical chairs played in the corridors of power would have been laughable if it had not been so shamelessly pathetic. The political system was further weakened by the creation of the officially sponsored Republican Party.

Extra-Constitutional Measures

Political Synopsis

Pakistan's peculiar geography—two wings separated by 1500 miles of Indian territory—demanded vision and ingenuity from her political leadership. At birth the country faced, among others, five serious problems. First, while East Pakistan had the majority population (54 per cent), West Pakistan enjoyed the monopoly of power. This dichotomy created political and constitutional constraints. Secondly, the massive communal riots and the influx of eight million refugees placed a heavy burden on the meagre resources of the new state. Thirdly, the early death of Mr Jinnah in 1948 and the assassination of Liaquat Ali Khan in 1951, created a leadership vacuum which their political successors failed to fill. The ruling Muslim League got distanced from the people at large. Fourthly, the weakening political control lured the civil and the military bureaucracy into the game of power. And finally, the Kashmir dispute, an unresolved item of the independence agenda, created a conflict of national interests between India and Pakistan that overshadowed their policy options.

At independence, the armed forces inherited the British tradition of non-involvement in politics. They were content to seek career satisfaction in performing their professional role in the defence of the security of the state. After the founding fathers passed away, the military, like senior civil servants, watched the deteriorating politics with increasing concern. Many of the cabinet ministers lacked ability as well as integrity. Few made a contribution to policy making that could earn respect. For years they could not agree on a constitution. Prime Minister Nazimuddin was noble but ineffective. Governor-General Ghulam Mohammad, a civil servant, and his successor, General Iskandar Mirza, also a civil servant, indulged in political intrigues and manipulated politicians to serve their personal interests. The Prime Minister's office became a game of musical chairs for which the tunes were played by the head of state.

The mess civilian rulers and politicians made brought them into popular contempt, undermining the foundation on which democracy stands. As Ayub lamented in 1958, the country had become 'the laughing stock' of Pakistani and foreign observers, President Iskandar Mirza believed that the people needed, 'controlled democracy,'[20] presumably under his own 'control'.

In September 1958 the *de facto* power duo, President Iskandar Mirza and General Ayub Khan, acted in concert to derail the democratic order. The Army Chief, Ayub Khan, was made the Chief Martial Law Administrator. In so doing, Iskandar Mirza ignored the chemistry of power. If his own ambition was high, Ayub loved power no less. Within three weeks Ayub, the king-maker, himself became the king and Iskandar Mirza was forced into exile. With democracy put on the back burner, the Pakistan Army occupied the centre stage of national political power.

So discredited were the politicians, that the public at large heaved a sigh of relief and hailed the imposition of Martial Law. The process of transition was peaceful and smooth. Ayub, a modern and a moderate person, introduced a wide range of reforms that brought economic prosperity to the country.

Ayub decided to use his perch to perpetuate himself in power. The constitution he foisted on the country was praised at first as innovative but soon lost its appeal as it was manipulated by the author to get himself elected as the President. His victory over the revered Mohtarma Fatima Jinnah in the elections of 1964 was widely believed to have been rigged. Besides, he was seen to be preparing the ground for dynastic rule when he encouraged his son to assume a key role in the ruling political party.

In 1965, India and Pakistan blundered into a war on Kashmir. The deadlocked conflict weakened Ayub's grip on the administration. A UN-sponsored cease-fire ended the war, and the Soviet Union-brokered Tashkent Declaration of 1966 restored normalcy between India and Pakistan. Ayub's popularity graph dipped low as the people felt the Declaration was against the national interests of Pakistan. A coronary thrombosis attack in 1968 left Ayub a lame duck President. His protégé, Z. A. Bhutto, exploited his benefactor's waning control on administration to gain power for himself.

Unable to regain control, Ayub decided, in March 1969, to quit power in favour of the Commander-in-Chief of the Pakistan Army, General Yahya Khan. Another view is that Yahya demanded the transfer of authority to him and Ayub was too weak then to resist. This bilateral arrangement was mutually beneficial to both the generals. Ayub Khan ensured his personal safety and Yahya Khan took over the reins of power. Years later, the Supreme Court held the act unconstitutional.

Yahya's Martial Law further weakened the fragile fibre of democracy. His rule gave Pakistan her first general elections in 1970. However, the flawed post-election policy of the government, and the political intrigues of Sheikh Mujib-ur-Rahman of East Pakistan and Zulfikar Ali Bhutto of West Pakistan denied the country a democratic government. The internal security situation in East Pakistan took an ugly turn. Pakistan's follies and the covert and overt aggression committed by India, resulted in the amputation of East Pakistan and the emergence of Bangladesh.

The popular outrage following the 1971 disaster drove Yahya Khan out of power, and the humbled army was pushed out of any political role. With Mr Z.A. Bhutto assuming power as the first civilian Chief Martial Law Administrator of the residual Pakistan, the nation felt it had another chance. Unfortunately, he allowed his dictatorial personal ambitions to overwhelm good judgement. He got the 1973 Constitution framed that he thought would assure him uncontested power for at least fifteen years.

A feudal by birth, a socialist by convenience, and a capitalist at heart, any system that kept Bhutto in the power saddle was considered democratic by him. He was tyrannical in his behaviour to those—politicians, bureaucrats and anyone else—who did not submit to his egotistical preferences. Under his harsh and personal rule all the institutions of the state weakened.

In 1977, he and several other party cohorts got opposition candidates arrested or obstructed to get themselves elected 'unopposed.' In the process he, too, lost legitimacy. The massively rigged elections gave an opening to the people, suffocating under his harsh rule, to revolt against his high-handedness. The opposition parties combined in a protracted agitation against him. Hundreds of people were killed and the economy was 'bled white' as one of his cabinet ministers publicly admitted. Bhutto imposed a mini martial law in parts of the country. It proved counterproductive. Once again the country lay prostate and stood paralyzed. Once again the internal political issues were not settled politically. Once again a political vacuum was created by the politicians that virtually invited the military to fill in. Soldiers indoctrinated to fight the enemy hate to train guns on their compatriots. The armed forces find it easier to dislodge an unpopular leader than to defend him.

General M. Ziaul Haq, the Army chief, imposed martial law in July 1977. His act had the consent of his senior colleagues. Once a charismatic leader, Bhutto was so hated that even the military's draconian act was acclaimed by the public, and the country witnessed scenes of jubilation. Disturbance ended, peace was restored and the paralyzed national life became normal.

On 18 March 1978, Bhutto, and four other co-accused, were sentenced to death by a Full Bench of the Lahore High Court on the charge of conspiracy to murder Nawab Mohammad Ahmad Khan, the father of Bhutto's bitter political opponent, Ahmad

Raza Kasuri. The Supreme Court upheld the sentence on 2 February 1979. Bhutto was executed on 4 April 1979. His execution polarized Pakistan.

Bhutto's death loomed large over the political horizon and affected Zia's options. He knew the danger of jumping off the back of the Martial Law tiger. He wanted public legitimacy for his acts, but without personally participating in an election contest. As his rule prolonged, the extra-constitutional measures came to be seen as maneuvers to maintain himself in power. Nothing brought greater discredit to him than the national referendum in 1984 in which a vote for an Islamic system was equated with endorsement for Zia to remain in power for a further period of five years.

Non-party elections were held countrywide, in February 1985, and Mohammad Khan Junejo became Prime Minister. Democracy was restored but the opposition castigated Junejo for being a quasi-democratic head of the government, even after martial law was lifted in December 1985. Zia twisted the Constitution to dismiss his own nominee, Junejo in May 1988, when, refusing to be a puppet, Junejo asserted his powers, to Zia's chagrin.

General Zia trusted others only to the extent necessary and personally retained the post of the Army Chief, in addition to being the head of state, till he was killed in an aircraft crash in 1988. Three issues dominated the post-Zia era. First, the Eighth Amendment in the 1973 Constitution, and the dismissal of four governments under it. Secondly, the Bhutto phenomenon. And, thirdly, the Zia factor. That the ghosts of Bhutto and Zia have clouded Pakistan's political scene so intensely and for so long, reflects the country's dilemma.

The top leadership of the army was involved in politics during the eight years of Martial Law (1977-85) and three years (1985-88) of partial democracy. Military control on the national policy-making process was complete and perceptible. Zia's grip on the political and the military elements was firm, and the political opposition was too weak and fragmented to pose a threat to his rule. Circumstances favoured Zia and he took advantage of them. These included the Soviet military intervention in Afghanistan, the Iranian revolution, the Iraq-Iran war, India's war hysteria against Pakistan, and the biased and unilateral US tirade against Pakistan's nuclear programme. Domestic factors also favoured Zia. Except for one year, the yields of major crops—wheat, rice and sugarcane—were bumper and the national economy remained within manageable limits.

General Zia's sudden death created a 'power troika' comprising the President, the Prime Minister, and the Chief of Army Staff. The Army Chief was consulted by the other two on matters of substance before taking decisions. General Headquarters became a port of call for the decision makers and even some foreign dignitaries visiting the country. Such acts not only harmed the image of the political masters, but also the military system was violated, as the Chairman of the Joint Chiefs of Staff Committee, senior to the Army Chief, was invariably bypassed.

During this period, some Army Chiefs selectively indulged in politics, in violation of the military norms and the constitution. Their political meddling created an impression that the Army was once again developing political ambitions.

The country remained politically polarized during the period 1988-97. Successive governments lacked a healthy working relationship with the opposition. Such dearth of mutual trust created political instability and retarded the growth of democratic traditions. Corruption became a malignant disease and economic mismanagement was criticized at home and by the international aid giving agencies. Politics became a quick-buck business. The dismissal of four governments in rapid succession exposed the frailty of the democratic institutions. Successive governments sought the support of the Chief of the Army Staff to survive in power.

Military intervention in political affairs is not a new phenomenon in Third World countries. While the reasons for this differ, some factors are common. These are, a low literacy rate, weak democratic institutions, state sponsored repression, corruption, sustained political unrest, internal security problems, lack of accountability, and the high ambition of the military brass. Experience shows that once derailed, a political process takes a long time to be put back on track. The fear syndrome and the dynamics of power come into play. The genetics of military intervention also differ from a bloodbath, to a completely peaceful transition of authority. The psyche of the people, and the country experience come into play. All military coups in Pakistan were peaceful. These were preceded by political chaos that had polarized the country, and the public anticipated that the military would no longer remain a silent spectator.

At various stages and in varying degrees, the Pakistani military has always been a factor in national politics. Some military brass nourished political ambitions. Ayub is an example. On another occasion, the military got sucked into the political whirlwind by the force of circumstances, goaded and abetted by the politicians themselves. Zia is the case in point. On yet another occasion, Ayub did what Yahya wanted him to do, and a deal was made. Power intoxicated all the three commanders. They started riding high and were unwilling to get off the power saddle.

The disengagement process was invariably burdensome. Ayub framed a new constitution but violated it himself. The constitution died its own death when its author lost power. Yahya failed to comprehend that the game was over for him. He floated a draft constitution when East Pakistan was on the verge of collapse. Zia desired to scrap the 1973 Constitution. His military colleagues prevailed on him to retain the document. He agreed, albeit reluctantly, but in the final analysis amended it too liberally, and went ahead to sack a prime minister on the advice of his sycophant advisers.

It is simplistic to judge a dictator by the yardstick of democracy. The military rulers did not topple the civilian governments to demonstrate their love for democracy. Their reasons were different. While some had political ambitions *ab initio*, others were alarmed by threats posed to national security. They believed they could not stay aloof, watching the country erode from within. Whether such acts were legally and morally justified is a valid question for the courts of law to decide. They all claimed to be staunch nationalists. However, repeated military rule has led to a realization within the defence hierarchy that political issues are best settled politically.

A change is discernible. The military has learned that its intervention in civil matters has not helped in finding a durable cure for the ills of the state. Not only do the disadvantages of military action outweigh their gains, but the national image suffers. Furthermore, the professional performance of the military has had a setback.

It is unwise to drag the defence services into the political arena. The two ball games are different. So is the psyche and the suitability of their respective players. Some politicians have had their own agenda in politicizing the armed forces. This is understandable. Also, a couple of military commanders since 1988 misused their position and indulged in political manipulations. Soon, they got exposed. Such acts tarnished their names and harmed military prestige.

By and large, since 1988 the military has slowly receded into the background, and maintains a posture of neutrality and non-interference in political controversies. This discernible change has been publicly applauded by the political leadership. Prime Minister Nawaz Sharif's two acts—the 13th Amendment in the Constitution and the premature retirement of a naval chief in 1997—illustrate the growing political supremacy.

No one can defend, much less justify, unconstitutional and selfish actions whether of civilian or military potentates. It is notable, however, that Ghulam Mohammad, Ayub Khan, Yahya Khan, Z.A. Bhutto, and General Zia all failed to act in accordance with the law and the constitution. They did not use the powers given to them in trust to bring honour to their professions. Why was this so? One has to look for reasons deeper than the surface. Was it lack of experience with democratic politics? Or, was it the social stagnation and decay that overtook the Muslim people after the decline and fall of the Mughal power? What role was played in this decline by the feudal social structure we inherited? Or, were there some flaws of character due to faulty education at homes and in schools? Corruption, nepotism, jobbery, and favouritism were identified by the Quaid-i-Azam in our society. Self-aggrandizement has been a dominant trait of the people in power. Benazir Bhutto and Nawaz Sharif, in their two tenures each as the Prime Ministers, and some of their political cronies, were widely perceived to have accelerated and intensified the debilitation of the state.

Military Sensitivity

Most Pakistani thinkers, scholars, analysts and policy planners perceive a threat to their national security from a numerically superior and hegemonic India. The role played by India against East Pakistan in 1971 revives bitter memories. India desires a subservient Pakistan, and opposes the acquisition of military hardware that this country requires for her legitimate defence needs. India has also repudiated her commitment, made in the UN Security Council, on holding a plebiscite on the Kashmir dispute. This raises doubts about her credibility.

To the Pakistani military, the integrity of the country is sacrosanct and supreme. It firmly believes in what Sir Philips Chetwode once said, 'The safety, honour, and welfare of your country comes first, always, and every time.'

The choice of peace and war is a political decision exercised by the government of the time. In democratic societies, it is not the prerogative of the military to assume this authority or to share it with the government. This is well understood by the defence services and there is no ambiguity on this issue.

Pakistan inherited weak institutions dominated by strong personalities. The self-perpetuation approach of the political leadership further weakened the institutions. Their frailty caused military interventions. This vicious cycle has impaired democratic growth.

The refugee immigrants to Pakistan in 1947 fell into two categories. Those hailing from the Agreed Areas (East Punjab) quickly merged with the people of Pakistan. A second category, from the Non-Agreed Areas, (Urdu speaking from areas other than East Punjab) mostly settled in Sindh. Their leaders faced a difficulty. With their traditional electoral constituencies left behind in India, they did not have safe wards to contest elections, when held. The Constituent Assembly solved this dilemma when it delayed constitution-making and the holding of elections.

Such weaknesses were exploited by the bureaucrats and the military brass. They started dominating the political scene soon after Liaquat Ali Khan's death. Their grip tightened as the political actors on the scene weakened.

It is not comfortable for a small country to co-exist with a large aggressive neighbour. Pakistan has the unenviable position of having three large countries in her neighbourhood—an aggressive erstwhile Soviet Union, a hostile India, and a friendly China. This is a strength as well as a weakness for Pakistan. Her strategic location—close to the Gulf, Central Asia and South Asia—outweighs the disadvantages. Pakistan, dissipating her energy because of internal squabbles, has not taken advantage of her geo-strategic importance.

The inability of the political leaders to check the national downward slide brought the military into the political scene. At times they overplayed the national security concern for genuine and selfish reasons, and portrayed the defence establishment as a 'holy cow'.

Intelligence Agencies and Politics

Pakistan has two federally controlled intelligence agencies. The Intelligence Bureau (IB) covers political intelligence and works under the head of the government. The IB draws its officers from the police departments but the provincial governments are usually reluctant to spare their better trained police officers for federal intelligence work. The IB works in close contact with the Special Branches in all the provinces which are the exclusive domains of the police departments.

The Inter Services Intelligence Directorate (ISI) is the second federally controlled intelligence agency. It largely covers external intelligence. Its manpower needs are met partly from the civil market and partly from the three defence services—army, navy and air force. The ISI operates under the head of the government and maintains a close liaison with the Chief of the Army Staff on matters of professional intelligence.

The tasks of the IB and ISI slightly overlap, but in a democratic rule the dominant intelligence agency for political work is the IB. In practice, this position underwent a change during the 1958, 1969 and 1977 martial laws because the army chiefs found it more convenient to deal with the ISI Directorate.

In 1975, Prime Minister Zulfikar Ali Bhutto created a political cell in the ISI Directorate through an executive order and institutionally tasked it a political role. This act on the one hand showed Bhutto's confidence in the ISI's efficiency, and on the other involved this organization in domestic politics. The successive governments after Bhutto did not change this arrangement.

The intelligence agencies established for the purpose of protecting the State against external aggression and internal subversion were perverted to promote the personal interests of the head of the government of the day. In the process, the institutions were debased and their personnel, selected on the basis of personal loyalty, abused their powers and resources to advance the interests of the rulers as well as their own.

The induction of Soviet military forces in Afghanistan in December 1979 destabilized the area and caused a fundamental change in the regional geopolitical environment. This caused serious concern to Pakistan. The ISI Directorate became the channel for funneling covert support to the Afghan freedom fighters. In due course of time, support to the Afghan Mujahideen from sources other than Pakistan was also handled by the ISI Directorate. During the Zia era (1977-88) the Pakistan Army was not directly involved in the Afghan fighting, although it was generally aware of military developments in this country. Pakistan's Afghan policy was made by a small group, and implemented by the ISI and the ministries concerned, on the orders issued by General Zia. The situation changed on the death of General Zia. In early 1989, Prime Minister Benazir Bhutto directed the Army Chief, General Mirza Aslam Beg, to coordinate the Afghan work handled by the ISI. General Beg developed a taste for political power. In 1990 the Benazir government was dismissed by the President and fresh elections were ordered. Under General Beg's orders the ISI pieced together an anti-Bhutto electoral alliance. This was active politics by a serving military commander. The ISI also received from a Pakistani bank a donation of Rs 140 million and distributed it among political parties before the 1990 elections. The Army Chief was aware of this transaction. The banks do not give a free lunch and for an intelligence agency to accept the huge gift was a serious development. It was illegal, undemocratic, and undignified for the army and for the ISI Directorate to become political puppeteers.

General Beg's political impulse also showed during the Gulf War, causing diplomatic embarrassment to the government. His advocacy of the strategy of defiance by Iraq, whatever it meant, created diplomatic difficulties for Pakistan. That he got away with it, showed the military's clout in domestic affairs.

Non-Military Influencing Factors

The Omnipotent Bureaucracy

The British Raj gave to the subcontinent a distinguished, largely honest, fairly efficient, and a visibly stiff-necked cadre of civil servants that took pride in its professional work and its code of conduct. Corruption was known to exist in the lower tiers of the administration but was trivial in scope and petty in volume. Instances of corruption against the senior bureaucrats were infrequent and frowned at. Conspicuous, though, was the behaviour of these Anglicized Indian civil servants who arrogated to themselves the role of a class superior to the 'uncivilized' native public. A colonial aura had been painstakingly built on the edifice of the 'superiority' of the ruling elite. The system was tailor-made to promote imperial rule. Pakistan inherited a small number of such experienced personnel in the central and the provincial governments.

Experienced individuals were scarce in the political field. Some bureaucrats, therefore, got into political posts and this practice continued for a long while. Some notable bureaucrats-turned politicians included Ghulam Mohammad, Chaudhry Muhammad Ali, and Colonel Iskandar Mirza.

In subsequent years, many more civil servants became politically active and controversial. Aziz Ahmed, Altaf Gauhar, Saied Ahmad Khan, Masood Mahmud, Rao Abdul Rashid, Waqar Ahmad, Agha Shahi, Ghulam Ishaq Khan, A.G.N. Qazi, Roedad Khan, Ijlal Haider Zaidi, Sartaj Aziz, Mahboobul Haq, V. A. Jafri, Salman Farooqi, Ahmad Sadiq, and S. K. Mahmood are some notable examples. The more fertile of these luminaries blossomed in their careers, wielded authority and showed flexibility in their professional conduct. Some civilian as well as military bureaucrats got awarded for service to the chief executive or for sycophancy, and were raised to lucrative political positions.

The bureaucrats in important and high profile assignments came in contact with the policy makers. While some confined themselves to the professional field, others indulged in political work for worldly reasons and caught the eye of the political leadership. In turn, the bureaucrats tightened their grip on the administration.

The bureaucracy is omnipotent and omnipresent in Pakistan. Its hold on the administration is so firm and perennial that nothing moves without its nod of approval. The governments come and go but the real and hidden power lies in the Rules of Business expertly tailored by the bureaucrats, for the bureaucrats, despite a stamp of political approval affixed on them.

Too many discretionary powers are held by too many public servants and ministers. These are interpreted selectively. Many governments have announced a One-Window Operation to promote the growth of industry in the country. The idea remains a fond hope. The power-wielding departments will not close the avenues of corruption. Instead, those trying to break the vicious circle are cleverly accused of violating the Biblical procedure for 'ulterior motives.' Such a corruption-ridden and delay-prone system frightens away foreign investors from Pakistan.

The bureaucrats complain that they lack job security which is exploited by their political masters to extract undue favours and decisions from them. Those who succumb to the pressure, turn into party loyalists to protect their future.

Such an apprehension is a half-truth that reflects only one side of the bureaucratic coin. Barring some exceptions, a vast majority of the civil servants have seldom resisted undue political pressure in their work. In some cases, the bureaucrats become willing instruments of the favour-seeking power barons. A few help themselves as well in the process. Many civil servants have, however, faced punishments under different administrations on charges of corruption, misuse of authority, and possessing wealth beyond their known sources of income. The respect and the honour that the civil servants once enjoyed stands substantially eroded.

Three bureaucrats—Ghulam Mohammad, Iskandar Mirza and Ghulam Ishaq Khan—became the Head of State. This trio had a distinguished career. Ghulam Mohammad was, 'a conservative financier, a strong believer in private enterprise and ruthless in keeping down expenditure.'[21] Iskandar Mirza, a military officer-turned civil servant, was respected for his knowledge and administrative experience. Ghulam Ishaq Khan, a thoroughbred civil servant, was known for his integrity, hard work, and stubbornness. All three brilliant individuals made serious errors in judgement as the Head of State and earned for themselves an unenvious reputation in history.

The reasons for their failure could be many. Were they simply unlucky? If so, the law of averages should have normally worked. Another reason could be that while their bureaucratic background had trained them to synthesize problems, produce option papers and prepare lucidly written summaries, the more complex task of decision-making usually rested with others. Yet another possibility could be that their close advisers misjudged events and got their bosses inextricably involved in political cobwebs.

Notwithstanding their lacklustre performance, it shows that it is seldom simple to govern a complex country like Pakistan. If the bureaucrats failed in this effort, so also did the politicians and the generals.

Judicial Pacifism

The executive branch, the parliament and the judiciary constitute the three co-equal pillars of a democratic state. However, in Pakistan, the executive branch, taking advantage of the Official Secrets Act, the Law of Libel and the coercive instruments of the state, has traditionally dominated the other two. The second pillar of the state—the Parliament—meekly claims undefined privileges, and has generally looked towards the government for a lead. The Committee System, the government-opposition relationship, and the law making performance of Parliament have not been boastful. Most governments have largely ruled through ordinances promulgated by the President.

The Judiciary, the third pillar of the state, has occasionally brandished the whip of contempt proceedings, but has usually been a docile partner playing a low-key role in judicial matters. The subordinate courts have enjoyed some freedom, with some magistrates employed on executive functions. Their judicial performance has neither been envious nor free from allegations and criticism. The 1973 Constitution had fixed a date for the total separation of the judiciary from the executive branch. This was not implemented on one pretext or the other till 1996.

Some judgements given by the Higher Judiciary on important constitutional issues became controversial. The October 1954 dismissal of the central government by Governor-General Ghulam Mohammad was upheld by the Federal Court. It faced criticism on legal and political grounds. So also was the judgement under which the abrogation of the constitution in 1958 was declared legitimate by the court, on the grounds that a 'successful revolution destroys the constitution'.

General Yahya was declared a 'usurper' by the Supreme Court for imposing Martial Law in 1969. This belated judgement was delivered in 1972, after Yahya had already disappeared from the national political scene and had retired from military service following the defeat of East Pakistan. The Martial Law imposed by General Ziaul Haq in 1977 was held valid by the Supreme Court on the doctrine of the 'law of necessity' and he was authorized to amend the constitution.

Pakistan's constitutional history might have been less bumpy if her superior judiciary had interpreted the constitution differently. The country might not have faced subsequent extra constitutional detours if the martial laws of 1953 and 1958 had been struck down. Political streaks running in judicial judgements, not an uncommon phenomenon, have affected the course of Pakistan's history.

The martial laws were not the sole legal and constitutional headaches endured by the country. Three successive presidents since 1985—Zia, Ishaq, and Leghari—have used their discretionary powers under Article 58(2)(b) on four occasions—1988, 1990, 1993, and 1996—to dismiss four prime ministers—Junejo, Benazir, Nawaz Sharif, and Benazir. This started a debate if an elected government can be prematurely dismissed under the law. A noted constitutional expert, Khalid M. Ishaq, writes:

> It is often claimed that whatever mistakes an elected government makes and whatever its other forms of misconduct, it should be allowed to complete its term. This is an absolutely spurious claim. In a democracy no one has a birthright to rule. Nor has any person or group a right to public trust. They get power to take decisions in public interest; vesting of power is justified only so long as their decisions are fair.[22]

Pakistan's higher judiciary now displays a different mood. Since 1996, judicial activism has replaced judicial pacifism. The Benazir government provided an alibi. It packed the higher judiciary with the political loyalists of the ruling Pakistan People's Party. The folly became the beginning of her government's fall. The Supreme Court ruled in March 1996 that the judges could not be appointed to the higher judiciary against the advice of the Chief Justice of Pakistan (for the Supreme Court vacancies) and the Chief Justices of the respective high courts (in respect of elevation to the high courts).

An Analysis of Military Role

Pakistan inherited the British tradition of military forces not engaging themselves in active politics. And yet, barely eleven years after independence, the Pakistani military imposed martial law and subsequently repeated this act more than once. The reasons for this phenomenon are briefly summarized below.

Quick Promotions

The joy of independence came with a bonanza of promotions. Junior officers got too many higher military assignments, at too rapid a pace. The quick promotions denied to the promotees the adequate professional grooming at successive levels in higher command. One case illustrates the point. Ayub Khan, colonel in 1947, became a four-star general in January 1951, to command the Pakistan Army. Such a rapid rise in the professional ladder is unique in peacetime military history.

There was a reason for this phenomena. As a matter of colonial policy, initially the Indian military units only had British officers. The process of inducting Indian officers in the Indian Army was started in 1932 when the first intake of Indian cadets joined the Indian Military Academy. These included a very small number of Muslim cadets, a trend that persisted in the subsequent courses as well. Some of these officers acquired combat experience during World War II, but only at lower levels.

The accident of birth favoured some lucky persons. The bulk of the promotions on independence went to those who had the maximum service at their credit in 1947. In most cases, seniority took precedence over other considerations.

Statistics tell the story. Officers are the backbone of an army. In August 1947, the Pakistan Army inherited only 2310 officers to fill in 4000 vacancies. The rank structure was so unbalanced that only 154 were pre-war regular officers. Another 400 were post-war regulars. The remaining 1934 army officers held emergency commissions and generally lacked command experience. The shortage was telling in the staff-trained officers and those holding higher ranks. The country had inherited only one major-general, two brigadiers and six colonels in 1947. Officers with 8-10 years service commanded units. The brigade commanders had 13-15 years service to their credit and the divisional commanders 17-19 years.

Teething Difficulties

The dawn of independence saw the Pakistan Army in a skeleton form. Only 40 per cent of its share of 150,000 personnel was physically located in the territory of the new state. The balance was either still in India or serving abroad in distant locations, Japan, Hong Kong, South East Asia, West Asia, and North Africa. The state of Pakistan's military hardware, equipment and stores was even worse. The country suddenly got involved in receiving, caring for, and rehabilitating eight million refugees that migrated from India. The army actively participated in this task. The fighting that erupted in the disputed State of Jammu and Kashmir compounded national and military worries. Added to this was the consistently negative role played by India which aimed to cripple Pakistan at birth. The army was thus involved from day-one not only in its own professional reorganization process and defence commitments but also in civil tasks assigned to it by the government. Its dedication and role in the national consolidation effort were widely appreciated and its voice came to be heard.

Cracks in Discipline

'Swift promotions from junior to senior ranks' raised unrealistic 'expectations' and 'perfectly sensible people, Brigadiers and Generals, would go about bemoaning their lot. Each one of them was a Bonaparte, albeit an unhappy one.'[23] So lamented Ayub Khan.

The military culture is built on a moral foundation. Indiscipline can erode this base. An incident took place in 1951. Some 'young Turks'[24] feeling uneasy about the leisurely pace of the government's performance, showed their frustration. They were critical of the government for doing too little too late in handling its responsibilities in general, and the ongoing operations in Kashmir in particular. Emotions got the better of Major-General Akbar Khan, Brigadier Siddique Khan, Colonel Niaz Arbab etc. when they got involved in what came to be called the Rawalpindi Conspiracy case. They were tried in a special tribunal and on conviction given sentences of imprisonment. This unprofessional indulgence and the lenient punishments awarded to them set an unhealthy precedent.

A Taste of Politics

The military's role in civil affairs became conspicuous when General Ayub Khan was included in the federal cabinet in 1954 as a defence minister, while retaining the post of the Army Chief. The cabinet post helped him in acquiring a taste for politics. He was able to judge the political weaknesses from the inside, and plan a military takeover. This set in motion a process that eventually sucked the military into the political quagmire.

Extensions in Service

A military commander, in a democratic country, transfers the baton of his assignment to the next selected incumbent at the end of his fixed tenure. This practice promotes the writ of the political system and rejects the myth of the indispensability of human mortals. This norm was violated. The tenures of the services chiefs were generously extended, presumably to provide stability in the senior rank structure. Such extensions were not without problems. Promotions were denied down the ladder. Besides, the prolonged assignments generated non-professional ideas in the minds of the affected commanders.

The Commander-in-Chief had a term of four years. The first Pakistani incumbent, General Ayub Khan, served in this post for seven and a half years. He upturned the democratic cart. General Muhammad Musa, the second Army Chief, served in this appointment for eight years. Personally loyal to his patron, Musa was incapable of posing a threat to Ayub Khan. The third Army Chief, General Yahya Khan, left behind a shrunken country, beaten in war, a bewildered nation, and an army maimed by the stigma of defeat.

The next Army Chief, General Gul Hassan Khan, had a short tenure of only three months. A personality clash between him and Prime Minister Z.A. Bhutto caused his forced retirement. The new incumbent, General Tikka Khan, was a down-to-earth soldier who joined Bhutto's PPP after his retirement from the army. General Ziaul Haq, the next Army top brass, threw Bhutto out of power in 1977 and remained the Army Chief throughout his unprecedented rule of eleven years until his death.

The grant of extensions to the army chiefs was a political blunder. The country might not have faced the pain of the 1958 Martial Law, if General Ayub Khan had retired from military service in 1955, after completing his full term of four years as the Army Chief. The history of the country might have been differently written.

Civil-Military Relations

The weakening of the political system encouraged some politicians to cultivate senior officers as 'their own men' by showering them with favours. Some weak-kneed officers fell prey to this trap to secure for themselves lucrative assignments and better career opportunities. Their number was small, but the political inroads eroded military discipline.

Self-importance

The military rulers enjoyed a position of authority. The military-martial law relationship was firm and enduring, and the Chief Martial Law Administrators claimed that the military was 'our constituency'. In official work, the writ of the military was always discernible. So was its arrogance.

Martial Law and the Judiciary

In theory, Martial Law and the Judiciary are not the best of friends. Paradoxical as it may appear, in practice, the military governments co-existed with the higher judiciary. It was neither a cosy arrangement nor an antagonistic affair and the mutual working relationship was based on ground realities. The Supreme Court and the High Courts kept functioning and they had the right of judicial review of all cases tried under military courts. The lower civil courts also kept working. The crimes that could be tried in the Military Courts were specified. The system caused occasional pinpricks to both sides.

During the Zia rule, turbulence existed under the surface of apparent calm. Ruling a country, even under usual conditions, is never easy. Pakistan faced an added problem, martial law, and the absence of her Constitution. Ripples of unrest surfaced here and there, between the judicial and the executive branches, but the prompt damage control measures taken by the government usually contained the situation. It was a tight rope walk. The predicament faced by both sides was mutually understood. The supremacy of law was their common desire. The abnormal measures were inescapable because of the peculiar circumstances that prevailed in the country.

Gains and Losses

Unless declared otherwise by the courts, the martial law governments were legal but undemocratic. The martial law administrations had voluntarily introduced a system of checks and balances to prevent administrative excesses. Every martial law initially imposed strict press censorship that was progressively relaxed. The private sector print media progressively became fairly critical of government policies and 'constructive' criticism was well tolerated by the administration. However, it is a matter of regret that Pakistan's electronic media has always remained under government control since 1947. It is overdue for liberation.

Political activity was also filtered through a similar process. Initially, the political parties were either banned or curbs were imposed on their activity. Gradually, such restrictions were removed and political campaigning permitted before the elections were held.

The country made considerable economic progress during the Ayub era. General Zia played a significant role during the Afghan *jihad*. But for the firm posture adopted by the Zia administration, the withdrawal of the Soviet military forces from Afghanistan might have been far more difficult to achieve, if at all. He worked under great pressure exerted by the Soviet Union, and a hostile environment artificially created by the Indian Prime Minister, Indira Gandhi. Zia picked up the game of power politics fast. The diplomatic initiatives taken by his government were timely, well conceived, skillfully planned, and vigorously implemented. During the Zia rule, Pakistan's defence capability improved and her nuclear programme moved towards its ultimate goal.

The losses were no less considerable. Martial law retarded the growth of democracy, weakened the political system, caused constitutional crises, and hindered the development of institutions.

Institutions Weakened

Military rule, a one-person act, is neither designed to promote democracy nor develop institutions. This is unlike a representative government which is perceived to function on the concept of collective responsibility. The institutions of the state weakened under Martial Law. A democratic government may or may not be a good government. But its preference lies in its checks and balances, and in the process of its accountability.

The services chiefs had frequent and direct access to the head of state. They usually discussed their respective problems directly with the President, and in the process bypassed the Ministry of Defence. This not only weakened the system but also prevented an independent and fair scrutiny of the cases by an impartial agency. To skirt the Ministry of Defence was a loss to the country and to the defence services themselves.

Accountability promotes progress. A parliamentary debate on the defence budget, and the questions asked in the assemblies on defence issues like promotion and retirement policies, defence purchases, incidents of indiscipline etc. promote the supremacy of civil rule and help in the detection of errors. The absence of the Parliament precluded such a check. The lacunae gave undue protection to the military, which became over-sensitive to questions asked on defence matters. The military resented the slow decision making process in the civil governments and felt that defence-related cases be addressed on a priority basis.

Internal Security Duties

Law and order is the primary responsibility of the police force and para-military forces. Successive governments politicized the police force by recruiting their political supporters in it. This eroded police impartiality and efficiency. Perforce, army troops were employed on internal security duties for prolonged periods which kept them away from their primary defence-related tasks. Their military training suffered. Besides, the troops were exposed to temptations and local pressures to the detriment of military discipline. The military was extensively used on internal security duties in Balochistan (1973-77), during the Movement for the Restoration of Democracy (1981-84), and during the Muhajir Qaumi Movement agitation in Sindh (1986-97).

National Psyche

Politics without principles and dearth of patience show in Pakistan's political culture. So do her polarization and political instability. The feudal gentry likes democracy from a distance and thinks of the military as a panacea to correct their misdeeds. The army is urged and provoked to end political uncertainty. If it does not agree it is criticized for ignoring national security. The criticism persists if the military intervenes. The growth of democracy is as much a time consuming process, as is the act of depoliticising a military force. There is no push-button solution in either game.

On balance, the military's indulgence in national affairs has weakened not only the country and the political system, but also the military itself. Pakistan's serious security compulsions dictate a full-time commitment from her services chiefs on matters of national defence. The immense additional load of administering the country under martial law greatly over-burdens this heavy schedule. In the process, military work invariably suffers.

The Military's Contribution

The military has invariably acquitted itself with credit during natural calamities and national crises. It has earned the people's gratitude for providing security cover, medical attention, transportation facilities, and humanitarian consideration to the eight million refugees that migrated to Pakistan in 1947. It has provided succour during anti-flood work, disaster relief operations, earthquakes, anti-wild boar operations and droughts etc.

The military plays a silent but a significant role in the national integration effort. Its officers are drawn on a competitive country-wide basis to promote efficiency and national cohesion. The rank and file of all the three defence services are recruited from all parts of the country. It has participated in internal security duties on the orders of the government in areas like Kalat (1958), Bajaur, Balochistan (1973-78), Sindh (1990-97), Swat, MRD Movement in Sindh (1983-85), the Al-Zulfiqar Organization (1981-88), and in unearthing the RAW-aided London Plan in 1984. In recent times, many operations were conducted in the tribal belt against the drug manufactures and the drug trade.

At the international level, the military has actively participated in the United Nations controlled peace-keeping, and peace-enforcing operations in different trouble spots including Angola, Bosnia, Kampuchea, Congo, Eastern Slavonia, Georgia, Haiti, Indonesia, Kuwait, Liberia, Namibia, Rwanda, Sinai, Somalia, Western Slavonia, and Yemen.

The defence services have participated in the national development effort by building roads, airfields, dams, canals and thermal power plants worth about Rs 35 billion. Their contribution in the social sector includes running schools, colleges, hospitals, and in afforestation efforts.

The military's contribution in industry and welfare is noteworthy. The Fauji Foundation, the Army Welfare Trust, Shaheen Foundation and the Bahriya Foundation 'contribute more than two per cent to the country's GNP annually'[25] through taxes.

Military Influence on Decision-making

In a democratic dispensation, the military offers advice on professional matters when ordered by the government. That done, the decisions are taken by the policy-makers, and all concerned, including the military, implement them in letter and in spirit. This system generally worked in the country, except on a few occasions when weak governments found it difficult to ignore military advice.

Challenges to Political Supremacy

Political supremacy suffered for a variety of reasons. These include, the delay in making a constitution and its selective implementation; the weakness of the judicial and the legislative branches; the loopholes in the Political Parties Act; and the continued dominance of the political scene by a coterie of feudal lords. Public awareness of their rights and obligations is low. The accountability process is one-sided and only aims to pressurize the opposition. The political parties create political polarization for self-serving reasons.

The Feudal Curse

Pakistan's feudal elite, dominating the national political scene, is a barrier to progress and change. This group dominates the political parties and has a vast majority in the legislative assemblies. Irrespective of their political divide, the feudal lords act in unison when it comes to protecting the immense powers, privileges and influence exercised by them in the rural areas where 70 per cent of the population lives. They have vigorously resisted the feeble attempts made in the legislatures to carry out land reforms that might loosen their control on the people.

The Moral Decline

An element of double-speak is a part of the political process. So is a degree of corruption at petty levels. In Pakistan, both the menaces have assumed serious proportions. Disinformation and corruption have eroded our political system from within. Moral standards are declining. Politics with low morality has led to anarchy and confusion.

Impartial Bureaucracy

Good governance needs an efficient and impartial bureaucratic cadre that inspires public confidence. Both the standards are on the decline. So also is public confidence in the administration. Pakistan's politicized bureaucracy has lost its old respect and confidence.

Characteristics of Martial Law

Paradoxically, Martial Law was introduced by an elected civilian government when Lahore became its first victim in 1954. It was an immediate success. The politically abetted and the administratively mishandled agitation instantly collapsed, but the surgical cut left behind a permanent scar. The mere arrival of troops on the streets produced a sobering effect and normalcy returned fast. The military did what the civil administration had failed to achieve. However, the ruling elite damaged its own prestige by washing its linen in public. As time passed, a political drift ensued, political fragility increased, low morality promoted corruption and 'palace' intrigues eroded the constitution. The axe fell in 1958, and military rule was imposed. It may be argued that notwithstanding the prevailing political turmoil, Ayub Khan was unjustified in announcing, 'enough is enough. Out you go, in I come.' The legality and the morality of the decision has since been judged by the courts. Ayub claimed to intervene to prevent 'the disintegration of Pakistan from within.'

It is a historic reality that the martial laws imposed by Ayub Khan, Yahya Khan, and Ziaul Haq were initially hailed by a vast majority of the public which was deeply frustrated with the performance of the deposed governments. However, gradually the public reaction took a turn against military rule when their duration exceeded reasonable limits.

Secondly, all the three military coups were bloodless and, by and large, benign in nature—to an extent that a martial law can be benign.

Thirdly, political activity was initially banned by the martial law governments but subsequently permitted to enable the parties to conduct election-related political work. The military rulers were not, *per se*, against the political systems but desired to replace their 'misused and faulty' parts. Their ambitions made them political leaders.

Fourthly, the military rulers preferred a presidential form of government. Ayub introduced one, but the constitution collapsed with him. Yahya Khan's constitutional misfortunes were too obvious to miss. Zia desired a presidential form of government but his military colleagues talked him out of this proposal. Instead, he held party-less general elections which, to his consternation, failed to gain political support of the elected members. These failed experiments raise a query. Why did the military rulers opt for a presidential form of government? There could be three motivating factors. One, they did not wish to reinforce failure by persisting with a system that had repeatedly proved unsuccessful in the country. Two, the presidential system would have removed a major source of corruption by denying executive appointments to the power-seeking parliamentarians. And, finally, military minds are trained to work in an undiluted system of command, which gives timely decisions and abhors compromise on principles.

Fifth, Ayub, Yahya, and Zia succeeded because they had accurately forecast a favourable public reaction to their military takeovers. Their intelligence was good. So also was the timing of their intervention. The secrecy of the plans were maintained and the ousted governments failed to anticipate or prevent military action.

The Pakistan Army, a disciplined professional force, was ably led, and all ranks reposed confidence in the judgement and the skill of their Army Chief. In return, the Army Chiefs had led a well-knit and united Army, and took their senior formation commanders into confidence on their impending plans. The trust was fully honoured.

As against this phenomenon, the coup attempts, and some isolated cases of indiscipline at the lower military levels invariably failed. The leakage always came from within the establishment. The Rawalpindi Conspiracy case (1951), the Attock Conspiracy case (1972), the Tajammal Hussain incidents (1976) and (1981), and the Zaheer-ul-Islam Abbasi case (1996) are examples. This indicates that the Pakistan Army obeyed the Chief of the Army Staff, followed his decisions in letter and spirit, and exposed those who tried to undermine the military and national unity.

Finally, an ostrich-like approach—sweeping one's failings under a carpet—is counterproductive. Instead, we may pick out the skeletons from our dust-filled cupboards to analyze the causes of our past deeds and misdeeds and, thus, learn from our errors. Our open society demands a postmortem of the pleasant and the unpleasant events at the academic, professional, and public levels to record our history, and to evaluate the performance of our history makers. Our expectations might be wanting in some fields, but in many others our achievements are notable. But for the artificial hurdles created by vested interests, our journey to democracy and economic prosperity might have been less arduous.

NOTES

1. *The Partition of the Punjab in 1947*, (privately distributed paper).
2. *Transfer of Power 1942-47*, Vol. X, no. 371.
3. H.M. Seervai, *Partition of India: Legend and Reality*, Emmenem Publications, Bombay, India, 1989, p. 190.
4. Alastair Lamb, *Kashmir—A Disputed Legacy*, Oxford University Press, Karachi, Pakistan, 1942, p. 101.
5. Andrew Roberts, *Eminent Churchillians*, Weidenfeld and Nicolson, The Orion Publishing Group, London, 1994, pp. 100-101.
6. Dr H.L. Saxena, quoted by Alastair Lamb, op.cit., p. 17.
7. Dr Inayatullah, *Dawn*, Karachi, 'Fifty Years of Democracy', 12 April 1997.
8. Mohammad Ayub Khan, *Friends Not Masters*, Oxford University Press, Karachi, Pakistan, 1967, p. 246.
9. General K.M. Arif, *Working With Zia*, Oxford University Press, Karachi, Pakistan, 1995, p. 93.
10. *Dawn*, Karachi, 13 April 1997.
11. Ibid.
12. Javed Hussain, *Dawn*, 'Anatomy of the Crisis Syndrome', 15 May 1997.
13. K.K. Aziz, *Party Politics in Pakistan 1947-1958*, National Commission on Historical and Cultural Research, Islamabad, 1976, p. 228.
14. Chaudhry Muhammad Ali, *The Emergence of Pakistan*, Wajidalis (Pvt) Ltd., Lahore, Pakistan, p. 48.
15. Ibid., p. 29.
16. K.K. Aziz, *Party Politics in Pakistan 1947-1958*, p. 227.
17. Chaudhry Muhammad Ali, *The Emergence of Pakistan*, p. 366.
18. K.K. Aziz, *Party Politics in Pakistan*, 1976, p. 16.
19. Altaf Gauhar, *Ayub Khan*, Sang-e-Meel Publications, Lahore, Pakistan, 1993, p. 92.
20. *Dawn*, Karachi, 31 October 1954.
21. Chaudhry Muhammad Ali, *The Emergence of Pakistan*, p. 361.
22. *Dawn*, 'Demise of Article 58(2)(b)', 22 April 1997.
23. Mohammad Ayub Khan, *Friends Not Masters*, p. 38.
24. Ibid., p. 35.
25. M. Ziauddin, *Dawn*, 28 April 1997.

5

Political Development in Pakistan
Craig Baxter

One hears the term 'failed state' applied to Pakistan, a state that faces numerous problems in development in the political, economic, and social systems and also has international issues that impose themselves on a fragile political system. One method applied by those who study comparative politics to evaluate the progress, or lack of it, of states, is to look at five factors that are the goals of every state. These are state building, nation building, economy building, participation, and distribution. Here, these will be investigated with reference to Pakistan.

State Building

By state building is meant the development of institutions, governmental and non-governmental, that are needed and can be used to meet the other goals that have been mentioned. How quickly have these structures been created or, if they have been inherited, how quickly have they been adapted to meet the new circumstances of independence? How strong are these structures? How well can they be adapted further after independence to meet new or changing goals as the requirements of the citizens change? On the other hand, how permanent are they so that the people can expect change not to be radical, but gradual so that adaptation can take place peacefully, constitutionally, and without violence?

When Pakistan became independent in 1947, it inherited a functioning form of government from British India based on the Government of India Act 1935, as modified by the India Independence Act 1947. There were in place the elements of government that are described as executive or administrative. There existed a civil service that administered governments at the centre and in the provinces, a police force, a military establishment, local governments, and the other essentials necessary to administer this new entity, the state of Pakistan. In many cases these were weak, resulting partly from the shortage of officers on the civil side, as many of those from the subcontinent who had been inducted into the senior civil service were Hindu and opted for India, as did many Muslims whose homes were in India and who chose to remain there. The military did not suffer greatly from a shortage of personnel in either the officer or enlisted ranks except at the highest ranks, but was severely short of equipment as all but one of the regional commands of the British Indian Army had been headquartered in what was now independent India. These personnel shortages would take time to overcome, and in both the civil and military areas many British officers were asked to stay on.

Beside the mere administration of the territory and people of Pakistan was the urgent need to create a basic document in accordance with which the governance of Pakistan would be carried out. The Independence Act of 1947 retained the framework of the Act of 1935, withdrawing British supremacy, but not setting up any clearly defined institution to replace that of the Viceroy/Governor-General. Pakistan thus continued under what was appropriately described as a 'viceregal' system, with ultimate authority vested in one person, whether that person was described as Governor-General, President, Martial Law Administrator, or Prime Minister.

Prior to independence, a Constituent Assembly for (united) India had been formed through indirect elections from the provincial assemblies, which were conducted under the system of separate elections. As the members of the provincial assemblies had been elected in 1945-46 under a restricted franchise and under conditions that had been greatly changed by independence and partition, it can hardly be said that the bodies in Pakistan or in India were truly representative of the people of either country after independence. Further, the death of Muhammad Ali Jinnah in September 1948 deprived the Pakistan Constituent Assembly of leadership it was unable to replace. The lawyer Jinnah, in his earlier experience, had shown his appreciation of the rule of law, although in his leadership of the Muslim League he had shown a tendency toward insisting that his orders be followed without question.[1] He had also shown that those who disagreed with him were likely to be subject to penalties.[2]

There were numerous questions that had to be settled before a Constitution could be enacted for Pakistan—and the Constituent Assembly took its time settling them. Two of particular importance were the extent of provincial powers in a federal system and the place of Islam in the political system.

In the latter, Jinnah's words have allowed no question to be raised about his stand that Pakistan would be a secular and not an Islamic state. His words to the Constituent Assembly[3] on 11 August 1946, are often quoted but have been frequently ignored, especially during the regime of Ziaul Haq. He said: 'You are free; you are free to go to your temples, you are free to go to your mosques or to any other place of worship in this State of Pakistan. You may belong to any religion or caste or creed—that has nothing to do with the business of the State....'[4] It is quite clear that Jinnah wanted a homeland for the Muslims of the subcontinent, at least those who chose to remain in or come to Pakistan, and that his goal was not an Islamic state ruled by the *Shariat* as defined by whatever school of *mullahs* were pleading at the time.

The second question was the relationship between the centre and the provinces. Newly-independent India also faced this question, but India was not burdened with the geographical division of the state as was Pakistan. India's Constitution, as would Pakistan's, would provide for the greatest power to be at the centre.[5] The provinces were given limited powers, and especially, their governments could be dismissed by the centre almost at whim, as occurred early in the North-West Frontier Province (NWFP), and again during the Zulfikar Ali Bhutto regime in Balochistan and the NWFP. The person exercising 'viceregal' authority arrogated the power to dismiss governments at the national and provincial level, a power that was inserted into the Constitution by Ziaul Haq, but used freely almost from the time of independence. When Liaquat Ali Khan was assassinated in 1951, Jinnah's successor as Governor-General, Khwaja Nazimuddin, stepped down from that post to become prime minister. The new Governor-General, Ghulam Muhammad, began almost immediately to exercise powers far in excess of those given to Governor-Generals in the other dominions where parliamentary government was used, and the Governor-Generals had powers that were mainly ceremonial, as in, for example, Canada, Australia, and India.

Ghulam Muhammad dismissed Nazimuddin without permitting him to test his right to remain in office through a vote of confidence in the legislature. Nazimuddin appealed to the Queen, stating that the Governor-General had exceeded his powers, but the Crown did not wish to interfere in the governing of Pakistan.[6] This, however, was merely a warm up for Ghulam Muhammad. When the Muslim League was trounced in the 1954 provincial assembly election in East Pakistan by the United Front of Suhrawardy's Awami League and Fazlul Haq's Krishak Sramik Party (KSP), Ghulam Muhammad did not permit Fazlul Haq to take office as chief minister and imposed central rule on the province in the person of Iskandar Mirza. The will of the people was squelched by this act, although eventually representative rule was established in East Pakistan.

The most egregious of Ghulam Muhammad's enactment of Commodore Vanderbit's statement, 'the people be damned', was his dismissal of the Constituent Assembly. Although the Assembly's representation of the people, if it ever existed, was severely diluted, especially by the trouncing of the Muslim League in East Pakistan, it was the only body at the centre which could make any claim, however tenuous, to represent the people. The litigation that followed this act need not be discussed here although it did lead to the dubious 'doctrine of necessity' that would be a hallmark of Pakistani jurisprudence.[7] A new and indirect election was held for a new Constituent Assembly, one that would be more divided than its predecessor as new parties would be represented (the Awami League and the KSP), and later the Muslim League would divide and some members, egged on by Mirza, by this time Governor-General, would create the new Republican Party.

After more than eight years of debate, a Constitution was finally agreed upon in 1956. This established a parliamentary system, but the method of electing the parliament could not be agreed upon. West Pakistanis insisted on continuing the separate electorate system, although this flew in the face of the desire of Jinnah for a secular state, in which religion would be no business of the state. The East Pakistanis wanted joint electorates. Both the Awami League and the KSP were multi-communal parties, while the Muslim League obviously was not. Awami Leaguers explained that if the Muslims of a constituency evenly divided their votes between the Awami League and the Muslim League in any constituency, the Awami League would win the seat as the non-Muslims would not vote for the Muslim League, of which they could not even become members. The question, of course, became moot as no election was ever held under the 1956 Constitution.

The Constitution included the concept of parity, which meant the East Pakistanis would be under-represented. The more populous east wing would have the same number of seats in parliament as would the less populous west wing. The leader of the East Pakistan group, Suhrawardy, accepted this with the unwritten understanding that efforts would be made to bring the east wing up to parity with the west wing in such areas as economic development and government service.[8]

Elections were to be held in early 1959. The voice of the people would finally be heard through direct elections at the national level. This was not to happen. In two stages in October

1958, the military took over under martial law. General Muhammad Ayub Khan, the commander-in-chief of the army, gained control under martial law. While a number of steps were taken in the economic and social arenas, the concept of freely and directly elected bodies to enact legislation and approve budgets at the national and provincial level was not in the thoughts of Ayub. Earlier, in 1945, he had written a memorandum outlining his concept of a government that would fit the genius of Pakistan.[9]

His ideas included the concept of basic democrats who would perform the roles associated with local government in the subcontinent. They would be directly elected. But they would also serve as an electoral college for higher levels of local government, for the provincial and national assemblies and for the president. In the national assembly and presidential elections, the principle of parity would be upheld, as there would be the same number of basic democrats in each province, who would elect an equal number of members of the national assembly. The system described in the Constitution of 1962 was ostensibly a presidential system, but was actually a continuation of the viceregal system by other means. The powers of the assembly were limited in the crucial area of the budget. Those who were supposed to represent the people were unable to regulate how the country's revenues were to be expended.

Demonstrations and rioting against the Ayub regime began in 1968 as the demand by the people for a free election for a meaningful legislature escalated. Ayub was forced to resign in March 1969, and was replaced by General Agha Muhammad Yahya Khan. Yahya claimed to be a caretaker who would hold an election to choose representatives to a new constituent assembly. He stated that he would have to 'authenticate' any Constitution adopted by the assembly, thereby placing himself above the elected body. Elections were held, and changes in the system were key to the election. The former West Pakistan provinces were restored. Parity was ended and East Pakistan would elect members of the assembly in proportion to its share of the population. The electorates would be joint, as they had been in the polls for Ayub's basic democrats. Political parties were able to campaign freely. This meant that the Awami League was not hindered when it based its campaign on the Six Points of Sheikh Mujibur Rahman. These demanded a high level of autonomy for the east wing and were seen by many as a road to independence for East Pakistan.

It seems that the military leadership expected that there would be no majority in the Assembly and that a multi-party coalition would be needed, and it would produce a compromise constitution. The election results gave the Awami League 160 of 162 seats from East Pakistan and thereby, a majority of the assembly of 300, without winning a seat in the west wing. Bhutto's Pakistan People's Party (PPP) won a majority of seats in the west wing.

It is not necessary here to relate the events that followed the election other than to note that the voice of the people was not followed. The ultimate result was the division of Pakistan and the creation of the new state of Bangladesh.

Bhutto succeeded to power when Yahya resigned the presidency following the defeat in the former East Pakistan. He called those West Pakistanis who had won Constituent Assembly seats in the 1970 election to form a constituent assembly and the parliament for residual Pakistan.[10]

A Constitution was enacted in 1973, and with major modifications remains the constitutional document in Pakistan today. It purported to be a parliamentary Constitution and it gave certain powers to the four provincial governments. But the power of the prime minister became almost absolute and the prescribed method of removing him from office almost impossible. A motion of no confidence must include the name of the successor prime minister. In addition, a member who violated party discipline would lose membership in the assembly.

Two of the provinces, Balochistan and NWFP, had elected non-PPP parties that formed governments in those provinces. As already noted, intolerance by the central government of provincial governments headed by different parties or even individuals who had lost favour with the central government was a long standing pattern. During the first so-called parliamentary government (1947-58) ministries were changed in all three provinces in the west wing by the centre. Now, Bhutto overrode the verdict of the electorate and dismissed governments in Balochistan and NWFP, and, to add insult to injury, banned the National Awami Party and jailed its leaders.

Bhutto also delayed parliamentary elections by decreeing that, although elected in 1970, the parliament did not begin its sittings until 1972 and therefore would expire in 1977. The major opposition parties were able to form an electoral alliance, that is, they put up a single candidate against the PPP candidate and agreed to support that candidate together. The true result of the 1977 election cannot be known as the PPP engaged in substantial rigging of the vote. Most observers appear to agree that the PPP would have won a majority without rigging, but this practice made the margin greater. It also touched off demonstrations and attempts by Bhutto to reach a compromise that would entail a new election. On 5 July 1977, the military took over under the leadership of General Muhammad Ziaul Haq.

Despite Zia's claim to have taken control only to ensure a new, free, and fair election within ninety days, his martial law would remain until after a non-party election in 1985. Governing during this period without the sanction of the people, other than a sham referendum for approval of him and his actions, Zia made a number of changes in the Constitution. Some of these brought in Islamic rules. Another gave the president the right to dismiss the prime minister without the prime minister having been defeated in a vote of confidence in the National Assembly. Zia used this power to dismiss the ministry of Muhammad Khan Junejo in May 1988, and ordered new elections at the national and provincial levels.

The Supreme Court, which had rarely defended the rights of the people as an electorate, stepped in to invalidate several rules that inhibited a free vote by the people. One of the rules overturned was that given by Zia, that elections must be held on a non-party basis. The Court held that the right to form political parties was derivative from the right of free association. From this it followed that a party had the right to use a single, uniform election symbol for all of its candidates. Further, it was held that the right of association was free and that parties could not be required to register before being permitted to contest. The four elections that have been held since these rulings have hardly been examples for a civics class in free and fair elections but they have produced governments with the mandate to rule for good or bad.

The presidential power to remove a prime minister and dissolve the assemblies was used against each of the first three ministries beginning with the Benazir Bhutto ministry elected in 1988. However, the removal of the Nawaz Sharif government in 1993 was set aside by the Supreme Court, although shortly thereafter both the President, Ghulam Ishaq Khan, and the Prime Minister resigned. The second removal of Benazir Bhutto in 1996 was challenged in the Supreme Court but was upheld. The government of Nawaz Sharif in 1997 passed an amendment to the Constitution removing the presidential power to dismiss government. Now the route for constitutional removal of a prime minister will be through a vote of no confidence. My comment about this change notes that the extra-constitutional route of a military coup remains a possibility.

Two non-governmental structures do require some comment here. One of these is political parties. It can be safely said that there are no well organized political parties with the possible exception of the electorally irrelevant Jamaat-i-Islami. The Jamaat is well organized, but throughout Pakistan's electoral history it has attracted very little support unless it has been closely allied with other parties, as in the election in 1990.

At this writing, the Muslim League holds a substantial majority in the National Assembly and the Punjab Provincial Assembly. Historically, the party has never been well organized. Even under Jinnah it was a single-leader party in which he dominated his lieutenants. Jinnah's death weakened the party, and it could only struggle on at the national and provincial level as dissident factions competed and sometimes deserted, as did the Republican Party in the 1950s. In East Pakistan, it all but disappeared with the electoral defeat in 1954.

Ayub's appropriation of the name in the 1960s was simply that, not an adopting of the programmes, if indeed any programmes were identifiable beyond the slogan 'Islam in danger'. Further, Ayub's Convention Muslim League was challenged by some who thought of themselves as the 'original' League and formed the smaller Council Muslim League. Even a former League President, Khan Abdul Qayyum Khan, formed another League and named it after himself. The three Muslim Leagues formed the principal province-wide opposition of the PPP in West Pakistan in 1970. The Leagues languished during the Bhutto period, but allied themselves with the PNA (Pakistan National Alliance) in the 1977 election and the demonstrations that followed. Parties were banned by Zia, but the Junejo government in 1985 allowed parties to re-emerge and the group supporting Junejo took the name Muslim League. It is this group that forms the base of the present Muslim League (despite the existence now of a dissident group that calls itself the Junejo Muslim League). It would be difficult to find a formalized party organization at the provincial or district level even though groups bearing the party's name are in office at the provincial level.

The formation of the PPP under the leadership of Bhutto created another group that was, for all practical purposes, a single-leader party. Bhutto and his allies won a majority of West Pakistan's seats in 1970, but after taking office he deserted many of his original allies and replaced them with others, often from the so-called feudal groups he had opposed.[11] Today, the party, under his daughter, Benazir, can hardly be called a well-organized party. Its electoral performance in 1997 has reduced it, at least temporarily, to a regional party as it won no National Assembly seats from any province other than Sindh. The concept of party organization and democracy that characterized the Congress from the twenties to the sixties has not been followed with the Muslim parties before or after Pakistan's independence.

Regional parties can exercise influence locally, but, at best, can only join coalitions dominated by one or the other of the national parties at the centre. The Muttahida Quami Movement (MQM) is supported only by a substantial portion of the Urdu-speaking descendants of refugees from India and its programme does not permit its expansion to wider groups. The Awami National Party is one that attracts almost exclusively Pathans in NWFP and Balochistan. There are several small Baloch parties that cannot expand beyond Balochistan. The religiously oriented parties, other than the Jamaat, are narrowly based. The Jamiat-ul-Ulema-i-Pakistan (JUP) has a following in the Frontier but this is limited as its programme is based on the Brelvi school of Islam. Even smaller is the Jamiat-ul-Ulema-i-Islam based on the Deobandi school.

A structural operation that has recently been ignored by the government and that is vital to the proper operation of elections, is the taking of the census. There has been no census since 1981, although one was due in 1991. The present government stated that it will hold a census soon, and did so in 1998. The reasons for avoiding a census are two. First, there has been very significant urbanization in Pakistan. A new delimitation of constituencies based on a new census would increase the proportion of urban seats and decrease those allotted to rural areas. This would decrease the power of rural magnates (often called 'feudals') who remain key power brokers and fight to retain privileges including exemption from agricultural income tax. Second, a new census might well increase the voting base of the MQM in Sindh and possibly will show that Sindhi speakers are a minority in the province that bears their name.

The final structure that must be mentioned is the media. There has been a remarkable improvement in the quality of the print media as the controls on the press began to be relaxed towards the end of the Zia regime. When one recalls the dull press of the Ayub period, which with time included the formation of the Press Trust, and the squelching of such newspapers as *The Pakistan Times*, the investigative nature of the present-day press is a welcome change.

The electronic media is a somewhat different story. Pakistan Television is as dreary as it ever was. It remains under control of the government with restrictions on its content. The bright side is the ready availability of satellite television that brings news and entertainment from many places and with varied opinions and outlooks.

Nation Building

The second of the goals of a state is nation building. By this, one means an almost psychological dimension that brings the people resident within the boundaries of a state the feeling that they belong together, that they have common interests that bind them into one nation. These interests may include language and religion, two basic characteristics with which human beings are, in effect, born as they are most often inherited from one's parents. Religion may occasionally change, but a mother tongue is much more difficult to change, even though another language may be added. Other characteristics may include history, mythology or folklore, geographic closeness, economic integration, and even such things as culinary practices. Not all must be present. The Swiss are often cited as a nation that does not share either a common language or a common religion, but yet fiercely consider themselves to be a united nation.

Pakistan has fared very poorly in creating a nation. The most noted failure, of course, was the inability of united Pakistan to create lasting and firm bonds between the two wings. Pakistan was the first state since World War II to divide violently when it lost East Pakistan, now Bangladesh, in 1971. (It has since been joined by Ethiopia which lost Eritrea in 1993.) Some of the causes of discontent in the east wing have been mentioned above with regard to parity in legislatures, the small share of development funds, and representation in the civil and military services. The Six Points of Mujibur Rahman in January 1966 focused on these discontents. The failure to permit the majority to rule after the 1970 election led to the demand for full independence rather than greater autonomy.[12]

The Bangladesh question is now closed, but nation building remains a difficult task for Pakistan. While there is near unanimous adherence to Islam, the country is currently wracked by sectarian conflict between Sunnis and Shias that has led to Draconian anti-terrorism legislation that gives police powers that many fear will be used excessively. During the Bhutto regime, a small group, the Ahmadis, who claim to be Muslims but whose claim is denied by 'mainstream' Muslims, were declared to be non-Muslims. Christians have been harassed, often violently, as shown in Khanewal district in 1997. While the number of Christians and Ahmadis is small, the violence between the Islamic sects is a recognized danger to the peace of the country.[13]

The differences in language have resulted in violence, especially in Sindh. In 1972, the Sindh Assembly refused to follow the other provinces that had voted Urdu as the provincial language and favoured Sindhi as co-equal to Urdu. Protests followed from the *muhajirs*, the refugees from India and their descendants who dominate such cities as Karachi, Hyderabad, and Sukkur. These protests have continued and have led to extreme violence and uncounted dead. The formation of the MQM as a vehicle for protest against the inequities the *muhajirs* believe they suffer, has spawned the violence. Splits in the MQM appear not to have lessened the violence but only to have added violence between the feuding factions.[14] Association of the MQM in a coalition to govern Sindh also causes no apparent decrease in violence, whether the coalition is with the PML or the PPP. The presence of other non-Sindhis in the urban areas such as Pathans, Baloch, Afghans, and Biharis from Bangladesh, many in the lower strata of society, has added more dimensions to the linguistic mix, as each group vies for its place in the life of the urban areas.

Language and ethnic disputes that once were present in Balochistan and NWFP appear to have diminished greatly over the years, although inter-tribal violence is surely not absent. In Balochistan, the Khan of Kalat's independence movement after Pakistan's independence is long since over and the conflict against the central government in the Bhutto period has also ended. Bhutto's violent repression did not work, but Zia's development programme appears to have done much good. The Soviet invasion of Afghanistan appears to have dampened any enthusiasm the Pathans of the Frontier might have had for a Pashtunistan.

Other linguistic demands remain. The Seraiki speakers of southern Punjab and northern Sindh have demanded a separate province, but have done so without extreme violence. The same can be said for the Hindko speakers of the north-eastern reaches of NWFP. A case might be made for the separation of the Pashto-speaking districts of northern Balochistan. In fact, a case might be made for elevating each of the present divisions to provinces on the theory that more provinces will dilute the strength of the Punjab as the majority province in the country.

History is not a unifying factor in Pakistan. Each of the provinces had its own history. Further, the history taught in the schools ignores the pre-Islamic period with the exception of some cursory notice of the Indus Valley Civilization. The Government of Pakistan commissioned British archaeologist Mortimer Wheeler to write a comprehensive history of the territory, now Pakistan, but it too, except for the Indus Valley period, makes it appear that Pakistan's story begins with the arrival of Muhammad Bin Qasim in Sindh in 712 AD.[15] The Chronology in Shahid Javed Burki's *Historical Dictionary of Pakistan* begins with Qasim's arrival, although topics prior to that are included in the dictionary proper.[16]

Economic unity as a factor for nation building can be based on the idea of the unity of the Indus basin. Irrigation works and patterns of trade with Mesopotamia and Central Asia are evident from the archaeological studies of the region. The Mughals, the Sikhs, and the British did much to unify the Indus basin, and it was especially under the British that the integrated irrigation system brought most of what is West Pakistan into a single economic system. Portions of this in the Punjab were lost in the 1947 partition, but the economic damage done then was largely repaired by the Indus basin projects that followed the treaty between India and Pakistan in 1960.[17]

There remains much that needs to be done to integrate Pakistan as a single nation—and much of that will require compromise and education.

Economy Building

It is of importance for any state to take actions that will stimulate growth in the economy. This subject is covered elsewhere in this study of Pakistan's first fifty years, but some comments are necessary in this essay.

Pakistan was once one of the stars of the development league. The creation of institutions such as the Pakistan Industrial Development Corporation in the Ayub period aided the economy. The Ayub period also brought a vast increase in agricultural production through the Indus waters treaty with India, and the international assistance in carrying out the programme of dams and link canals that brought more land under irrigation. This occurred at the same time that new seeds and techniques brought about the green revolution. Government action during that period, while not totally effective, was directed toward economic growth.[18]

The actions of the Bhutto government in nationalizing many areas of industry are generally judged to have caused a setback to economic development.[19] The Bhutto government also nationalized private educational institutions to the detriment of the institutions. The Zia regime reverted to a policy similar to the Ayub government, even though the principle actor in the earlier years was an individual who all but personified the interventionist role of government, Ghulam Ishaq Khan. Some nationalized properties were returned to private ownership.

The PPP, led by Benazir Bhutto, has deserted the socialist policies of her father and his early advisers. The present PML government is self-described as being in favour of a market economy. Some additional and major privatizations have taken place and more are being prepared to take place.[20] None the less many steps, such as agricultural taxation, that should be taken have not been taken, and Pakistan is under heavy pressure from the World Bank and the International Monetary Fund to get its economic and fiscal house in order.[21]

Participation

Elections are the most used measure of participation. Pakistan waited more than twenty-three years to hold its first direct national election. There had been provincial elections in the 1950s in the Punjab, Sindh, NWFP, and East Bengal, but no later ones in these provinces until 1970. Balochistan had the dubious distinction of never having held a direct election until 1970.

Other than the provincial elections in the 1950s, Pakistan held indirect elections during the Ayub regime under the system of basic democrats mentioned above. Ayub at first attempted to avoid a political party system but found that members of the National Assembly elected in 1962 were acting as members of political parties whether Ayub wished them to do so or not. He yielded and gave his assent to the Political Parties Act of 1962. He further entered politics directly by becoming president of the Pakistan Muslim League (Convention).[22]

Ayub had been elected president in 1962 and would be re-elected in 1965 when he was opposed by the candidate of the Combined Opposition Parties, Fatima Jinnah, the sister of Muhammad Ali Jinnah. He defeated Miss Jinnah by a wide margin in West Pakistan but only by a much narrower margin in East Pakistan, a harbinger of things to come.[23] His Convention Muslim League was victorious in the national and provincial assembly elections held in 1965.[24]

The major change in the electoral system came when Yahya decided that elections to the constituent assembly and the provincial assemblies would be held on a direct election basis and that parity between the two wings would be ended. The first decision would allow the voters to choose and would end the influence of the basic democrats, of course, a much smaller group than the electorate at large. The second decision would place Pakistan among the democracies that followed the pattern of one person, one vote. Yahya opened up campaigning by political parties and permitted free reporting of party activities by the press. The run up to the elections can only be described as open. He stated that the elections would be held on 5 October 1970; these were later postponed to 7 December as the result of a cyclone and tidal bore that hit East Pakistan. Yahya did state certain conditions under which the constituent assembly would work when he issued the Legal Framework Order on 30 March 1970.[25] The assembly would have 120 days to enact a Constitution or it would stand dissolved and new elections held. He also reserved the right to authenticate the Constitution for it to become effective. The elections were held and, as already noted, resulted in a majority for the East Pakistan-based Awami League.[26]

The majority of the seats in West Pakistan went to Bhutto's PPP. When Yahya resigned as President, he appointed Bhutto to hold that office. Bhutto convened the National Assembly based on the 1970 election. An election presumably should have been held in 1975, but Bhutto (as noted above) dated the Assembly from 1972 when a new interim Constitution was adopted. An election was called for March 1977. Bhutto may have been surprised that the major opposition parties were able to form the Pakistan National Alliance (PNA) as a joint front to oppose him and the PPP. The announced results gave the PPP a large majority in the National Assembly. The result was rigged. One commentator said, '...rather than helping to establish political accountability and trust in Pakistan's politics, the elections triggered political instability and cynicism.'[27] The PNA-led demonstrations caused Bhutto to offer a new election, but this was rejected. On 5 July 1977, the Chief of Staff of the Pakistan Army, General Muhammad Ziaul Haq, declared martial law and took control of Pakistan.[28]

Elections were promised within ninety days and even the nomination papers were filed. However, this was not to be. Zia declared that 'accountability' must be satisfied before elections could be held. Other dates were suggested but it was not until February 1985 that an election for the national and provincial assemblies was held. Zia decreed that the election would be on a non-party basis like the elections for local bodies in 1987.[29] He also reinstated the system of separate electorates. In the

February 1985 election, a number of members of Zia's cabinet were defeated, perhaps giving an indication that support for Zia was low, even though he had won a referendum in November 1984, which he took as giving him a five year mandate to continue in office. The turnout for the National Assembly poll was 52.93 per cent and for the provincial polls 53.69 per cent, larger than in the last comparable election in 1970.[30] Following the election, and the selection of Junejo as Prime Minister, political parties were formed as noted earlier.

In May 1988, Zia, exercising his powers under the amended Constitution, dismissed Junejo and dissolved the assemblies. New elections were to be held within ninety days of the dissolution. Zia said that a new delimitation of the constituencies was one reason for delay. Another was that August coincided with the Islamic month of mourning, Muharram; and campaigning and voting, he said, should not take place then.[31]

Zia was killed on 17 August 1988, and replaced by acting President, Ghulam Ishaq Khan. The acting President held the election in November 1988, the date that had been set by Zia. As has been mentioned earlier, several of the electoral rules set by Zia were voided by the Supreme Court. Among these was the recognition of political parties and their candidates. The PPP, led by Benazir Bhutto gained a plurality in an election that was judged to be reasonably free of incident. She became Prime Minister in December, ushering in a period of great hope in Pakistan.[32] This hope was not to be justified, in part, at least, as her government did not have a majority sufficient to make major changes.

In August 1990, Ishaq dismissed Benazir's government and appointed a caretaker government headed by Ghulam Mustafa Jatoi, a former member of the PPP who had broken with Benazir. New elections were held in October, with the victory going to Mian Nawaz Sharif and the Islami Jamhuri Ittehad (IJI—Islamic Democratic Alliance). Not untypical of election losers in South Asia, Benazir and the PPP claimed that the elections were rigged. The lead party in the IJI was the Muslim League, of which Junejo was still technically the leader, but because of his illness, Mian Nawaz Sharif was the actual leader. He had been chief minister of the Punjab, first appointed by Zia and later as the result of the 1985 and 1988 elections, after which he became the most powerful leader outside the PPP. The other main member of the IJI was the Jamaat-i-Islami.

Ishaq dismissed Nawaz Sharif in April 1993 and appointed a caretaker government under Balakh Sher Mazari. Nawaz had announced in February that he wished to repeal the amendment that gave the President the power to dismiss the Prime Minister. Ishaq Khan stated that he must preserve the 'safety valve' against the possibility of martial law.[33] Nawaz challenged his dismissal before the Supreme Court, which held that the dismissal was improper and reinstated Nawaz. The conflict between the President and the Prime Minister continued. The army brokered an arrangement under which both Ishaq and Nawaz resigned on 18 July. The Chairman of the Senate, Wasim Sajjad, became acting president and Moeen Qureshi, a retired World Bank official, headed the caretaker government. The election held in October gave a plurality to Benazir and the PPP. With the support of a dissident faction of the PML—the PML (Junejo), a group that had broken from Nawaz Sharif and used the name of the former leader—and several smaller groups and independents, Benazir formed a government. In the election for President, PPP stalwart Farooq Leghari was elected.

Leghari would soon be disillusioned by Benzair. Amid accusations of corruption and other charges, Leghari dismissed Benazir in November 1996 and called upon Meraj Khalid, another one-time PPP leader, to head a new caretaker government. In February 1997, the PML (now divested of its burdensome ally, the Jamaat, in the IJI, which disbanded) won a clear victory with two-third of the seats in the National Assembly and a majority in the Senate. Nawaz Sharif returned as Prime Minister. One of his early decisions was to amend the Constitution so as to eliminate the power of the president to dismiss governments.

Pakistan has since 1985 conducted five elections. It has, with the possible exception of the 1990 election, conducted them in a reasonably free and fair manner. Following the 1997 election, Benazir did not complain of rigging, if for no other reason than that the verdict was so clearly against her and the PPP. One interesting trend has been that the participation in elections has been in a decline. Form the 53.69 per cent in 1985 there has been a steady downward trend with the exception of a slight rise in 1990. The turnout in 1997 was 35.05 per cent.[34] This drop could indicate a lowering of interest in the electoral process or it could simply mean that PPP voters stayed at home in 1997.

Distribution

The final goal of a state is to make the distribution of goods and services more equitable. As with the third point, economy building, distribution is discussed elsewhere in this work as part of the commentary on economics. However, the political system is the part of the state that must make decisions on programmes and funding for the provision of services to the population at large. The World Bank's *World Development Report 1997* is devoted to the topic 'The State in a Changing World'.[35]

In 1994, the latest year for which data are available, Pakistan had a real gross domestic product (GDP) per capita of $2,154 on the purchasing power parity (PPP) basis.[36] With the exception of Sri Lanka, this was the highest in South Asia. However, the distribution of income was greatly stewed so that 11.6 per cent of the population was below the poverty line in the period 1991-5.[37] Data for 1991, show that the highest quintile of the population received 39.7 per cent of income while the lowest quintile received 8.4 per cent.[38] The validity of these data may be questioned as presumably there is considerable unreported income, especially at the higher levels in *black money* and in barter and similar income at the lower levels. One may argue that one way of bringing this skewing into better balance might be to introduce and enforce a strong progressive taxation system and adopt an agricultural income tax.

In many social areas, Pakistan has severely lagged behind. Data which are available but will not be discussed here in detail, indicate the need for greater development in education and health related fields. Pakistan spent 1.8 per cent of GDP on health services (1990), 2.7 per cent on education (1993-4), and 6.5 per cent on defence (1995).[39] Another area which causes harm to the welfare of the population and the preservation of resources is the degradation of the environment, a matter to which little attention is being given.[40]

Conclusion

It has not been intended to give here a catalogue of the faults of Pakistan, but rather to point out areas in which Pakistan can devote its attention as a democratic state that desires to improve the conditions in which all its citizens live. To echo the *World Development Report 1997* prescription, there is much the state can do and must do if the welfare of the people is to be improved. It seems especially appropriate now that a potentially strong government with a working majority in the legislature exists.

NOTES

1. Note, for example, Jinnah's insistence that Sir Sikandar Hayat Khan and Maulvi Fazlul Haq resign from the defence committee established by the viceroy, Linlithgow, in 1939, as they had not taken Jinnah's permission to 'represent' the Muslims.
2. An example of this is Jinnah's dropping of Hussain Shaheed Suhrawardy from the Bengal premiership after independence and replacing him by Khwaja Nazimuddin as Chief Minister of East Bengal.
3. Technically, not the Pakistan Constituent Assembly, but the members of the Indian Constituent Assembly who would formally become members of the Pakistan body on 14 August.
4. Quoted in Stanley Wolpert, *Jinnah of Pakistan* (New York: Oxford University press, 1984), p. 339.

5. Pakistan and India were not confederations of states that had been independent before merging as was that case with Swiss cantons or the American former colonies. In the United States the 'reserved powers' are with the states; in Pakistan and India, with the Centre.
6. Sir Ivor Jennings, *Constitutional Problems in Pakistan* (Cambridge: Cambridge University Press, 1957).
7. See Kamal Azfar, *Pakistan: Political and Constitutional Dilemmas* (Karachi: Pakistan Law House, 1987), chapters 1 and 2.
8. See Craig Baxter, *Bangladesh: From a Nation to a State* (Boulder CO: Westview Press, 1997), chapter 7.
9. The text is contained in Karl von Vorys, *Political Development in Pakistan* (Princeton NJ: Princeton University Press, 1965), pp. 299-306.
10. They were joined by the two non-Awami Leaguers who had won Constituent Assembly seats in East Pakistan. Nurul Amin and Raja Tridev Roy chose to remain in Pakistan.
11. See Craig Baxter, 'The People's Party vs. The Punjab "Feudalists" ', *Journal of Asian and African Studies*, VII: 3-4 (July-October 1973). Also in J. Henry Korson, ed., *Contemporary Problems of Pakistan* (Leiden: Brill, 1974).
12. See Craig Baxter, *Bangladesh: From a Nation to a State* (Boulder CO: Westview Press, 1997), chap. 7.
13. See Mumtaz Ahmad, 'Revivalism, Islamization, Sectarianism, and Violence in Pakistan', in Craig Baxter and Charles H. Kennedy, eds., *Pakistan 1997* (Boulder CO: Westview Press, 1997).
14. Moonis Ahmar, 'Ethnicity and State Power in Pakistan: The Karachi Crisis', *Asian Survey*, XXXVI: 10 (October 1996), pp. 1031-48.
15. Mortimer Wheeler, *5000 Years of Pakistan* (London: C. Johnson, 1950).
16. Shahid Javed Burki, *Historical Dictionary of Pakistan* (Metuchen NJ: Scarecrow Press, 1991) p. xiii. See also Ayesha Jalal, 'Conjuring Pakistan: History as Official Imagining', *International Journal of Middle Eastern Studies*, 27 (1995), pp. 73-89.
17. See Aloys Michel, *The Indus Rivers, Study of the Effects of Partition* (New Haven CT: Yale University Press, 1967).
18. See, for example, Gustav F. Papanek, *Pakistan's Development: Social Goals and Private Incentives* (Cambridge MA: Harvard University Press, 1967) and Stephen R. Lewis, *Economic Policy and Industrial Growth in Pakistan* (London: George Allen and Unwin, 1969).
19. See Shahid Javed Burki, *Pakistan under Bhutto, 1971-1977* (London: Macmillan Press, 1988, second edition), especially chapters 6 and 7.
20. See Robert LaPorte, Jr., and Bashir Ahmed Khan, 'Liberalization of the Economiy Through Privatization: The Case of Pakistan', in Baxter and Kennedy, Pakistan 1997.
21. See Shahid Javed Burki, 'Is Pakistan's Past Relevant for its Economic Future?'. Ibid.

22. See the discussion of this in Lawrence Ziring, *The Ayub Khan Era: Politics in Pakistan, 1958-1969* (Syracuse NY: Syracuse University Press, 1971), pp. 29-34.
23. See Sharif al-Mujahid, 'Pakistan's First Presidential Elections', in *Asian Survey* V: 6 (June 1995), pp. 280-94.
24. The elections were non-party in 1962.
25. The text is contained in *Bangladesh Documents* (New Delhi: Ministry of External Affairs, 1971), pp. 4-65.
26. See Craig Baxter, 'Pakistan Votes—1970', *Asian Survey*, XI: 3 (March 1971), pp. 197-218.
27. Marvin G. Weinbaum, 'The March 1977 Elections in Pakistan: Where Everyone Lost', *Asian Survey,* XVII: 7 (June 1977), p. 599.
28. For a discussion of the events leading to the martial law, see Craig Baxter, 'Restructuring the Pakistan Political System', in Shahid Javed Burki and Craig Baxter, *Pakistan Under the Military: Eleven Years of Ziaul Haq* (Boulder CO: Westview Press, 1991), pp. 27-48. Also see Craig Baxter, 'The United States and Pakistan: The Zia Era and the Afghan Connection', in Daniel Pipes and Adam Garfinkle, *Friendly Tyrants: An American Dilemma* (New York: St. Martin's Press, 1991), pp. 479-506.
29. I observed the local elections in Lahore and noted that the party affiliation of most candidates was known.
30. Craig Baxter, 'Legitimacy for Zia and His Regime?', in Craig Baxter, ed., *Zia's Pakistan: Politics and Stability in a Frontline State,* (Boulder CO: Westview Press, 1985), pp. 113-15.
31. Zia stated this to me when I met him in July 1988.
32. I joined the euphoric welcome with 'A new Pakistan Under a Revised Bhuttoism', *Middle East Insight,* VI:4 (Winter 1989), pp. 23-7, and with an op-ed piece, *Los Angeles Times,* 23 November 1988.
33. Zaffar Abbas, 'The Final Showdown', *Herald,* March 1993, p. 32, quoted in Tahir Amin, 'Pakistan in 1993: Some Dramatic Changes', in *Asia Survey,* XXXIV: 2 (February 1994), p. 192.
34. *Herald,* March 1997, p. 63.
35. World Bank, *World Development Report 1997* (New York, Oxford University Press, 1997) Hereafter WDR, 1997.
36. United Nations Development Programme, *Human Development Report 1997* (New York: Oxford University Press, 1997), p. 165. (Hereafter HDR 1997).
37. WDR 1997, p. 214.
38. WDR 1997, p. 222.
39. HDR 1997, pp. 177, 181 and 189.
40. See Syed Ayub Qutub, 'Pakistan's Environment: Pressures, Status, Impact, and Resources', in Baxter and Kennedy, eds., *Pakistan,* 1997.

6

Development and Significance of Pakistan's Nuclear Capability
Munir Ahmad Khan

Introduction

World public opinion is becoming more and more sensitized against nuclear weapons and the five nuclear powers are facing increasing pressures at home and from the international community to drastically cut down and eliminate nuclear weapons and other weapons of mass destruction. The nuclear weapon states are now beginning to recognize the futility of maintaining their huge nuclear arsenals, which were the pride of the cold war years as symbols of power and prestige. These are now regarded as a liability to be gotten rid off.

This realization has, however, not dawned on South Asia where a nuclear race, reminiscent of the cold war era, appears to be in the making. Some leaders in India and Pakistan still regard nuclear weapons as the hard currency of power and as a means of domination or deterrence. Given the history of conflict and deep-seated mistrust between the two countries, the strongly held views regarding the absolute power of these weapons as final arbiters, and the emotional proclivities of their leaders, the potential nuclearization of these two neighbouring states could pose a real threat to the security and survival of one-fifth of the human race inhabiting South Asia. To understand how the two countries have reached this situation one has to first understand how the nuclear programme evolved in the two countries and the perceptions which have propelled these programmes over the last thirty or more years.

Introduction of Nuclear Technology in South Asia

The history of development of nuclear technology in South Asia goes back to 1948 when India established its Atomic Energy Commission under Dr Bhabha reporting directly to the Indian Prime Minister, Mr Nehru. The Cambridge educated Dr Bhabha had wide contacts in the closely-knit small post-war nuclear community. He was a nationalist who wanted to put India on the world nuclear map to match the West. Towards this end, he laid the foundations of a broad-based nuclear programme making full use of his close relations with key nuclear experts and laboratories in the UK, France, Canada, and Italy. Looking back, it is now clear that right from the beginning, the intent and direction of this programme was towards the acquisition of nuclear capability. India made full use of the ready availability of nuclear technology in the 1950s and 1960s when there were no international safeguard systems to control the flow of nuclear material and technology. The superpowers were busy in developing their nuclear arsenals, and believed that the technical difficulties and financial costs of developing nuclear weapons, together with the secrecy which surrounded their programmes, would constitute insurmountable barriers against proliferation. In 1956, India became the first Asian country to have a research reactor using US supplied enriched uranium. In 1960, India was able to get a 40 MW plutonium production reactor called Canada-India Reactor (CIR), without safeguards. It was supplied under the Colombo Plan by Canada and was originally meant to be a regional facility. In 1964, India completed a reprocessing plant with the assistance of British and American suppliers. With CIR and the reprocessing plant in place India could extract 13 kg of weapons grade plutonium equivalent to two or three bombs per year by the mid 1960s. While this was continuing, India made no secret of its nuclear objectives and repeatedly announced that it could make nuclear weapons within a short time but would not do so. As early as 1957, soon after India had made its first research reactor, the Indian Prime Minister, while in a meeting with General Nichols of Manhattan Project, surprisingly asked Dr Bhabha if he could build an atomic bomb. When Dr Bhabha answered he could do it in a short time, Nehru advised him not to do so until told. This reveals an interesting insight into the Indian nuclear thinking right from the beginning. It is clear that India's pursuit of nuclear capability and acquisition of essential facilities preceded China's nuclear explosion of 1964. But after this explosion, India stepped up its programme and started stockpiling weapons grade plutonium and other materials and equipment.

The development and direction of India's programme started worrying Pakistan in the early 1960s. Pakistan could not ignore India's massive drive down the nuclear road and open claims that India could go nuclear in a year or two. Pakistan started ringing warning bells in many friendly capitals but Canada, United States, or other Western states did not share its concerns. In 1964, during his visit to Pakistan, Dr Glenn Seaboarg, Chairman of the US Atomic Energy Commission, was apprised of the growing nuclear potential of India but he assured Pakistan that India could not go nuclear and Pakistan's fears were not well founded. But this did not allay the apprehension of Pakistan.

After the mid 1960s, the two Superpowers started negotiating the Non-Proliferation Treaty (NPT). Pakistan was concerned about a nuclear threat not only from the acknowledged nuclear states but also from the potential and undeclared nuclear states such as India. Therefore, it cooperated with other countries in sponsoring a UN conference in Geneva in 1967 with the object of seeking security guarantees for non-nuclear weapons states (NNWS) against nuclear attack, threat, or blackmail. The nuclear weapon states refused to offer any credible security guarantees to the non-nuclear states, which further disappointed Pakistan.

India's nuclear programme progressed further with the supply of two power reactors from the USA and two more from Canada. Meanwhile, India continued to stockpile plutonium from its unsafeguarded CIR and reprocessing facilities. In 1971, during the fourth Geneva Conference on the Peaceful Uses of Atomic Energy held in Geneva, India announced its intention to conduct a peaceful nuclear explosion. The major powers took no notice of it, but Pakistan was alarmed and protested to Canada. The Canadian Prime Minister went to India to urge the Indian Prime Minister to respect the undertakings given to Canada that CIR facility would not be used for making a nuclear explosive device. The Indian Prime Minister refused to give any such assurances.

Pakistan's Nuclear Programme—Initial Years

Pakistan established its Atomic Energy Commission in 1958 and installed a US supplied reactor in December 1965, which has remained under IAEA (International Atomic Energy Agency) safeguards. It also ordered the 137 MW nuclear power reactor at Karachi from Canada, which was completed in 1972 and placed under safeguards. Pakistan's infrastructure in the nuclear field was very limited due to the paucity of trained manpower, lack of funds, as well as absence of political support and leadership. While India was rapidly building its nuclear capabilities in the 1960s, the Pakistani programme suffered from bureaucratic red tape and apathy from the establishment. Even President Ayub Khan was never enthusiastic about the national nuclear programme and did not understand its strategic and technological significance. He left it to his Advisers and Secretaries, who had little or no use for it. President Yahya Khan paid no attention to it. The result was that Pakistan failed to acquire nuclear facilities, materials and know-how which were available at low cost and with minimum conditionalities in the 1960s. These missed opportunities cost Pakistan heavily later on.

Role of Zulfikar Ali Bhutto

In the aftermath of the 1971 war with India and the creation of Bangladesh, Pakistan faced serious political and security problems. When Bhutto took over as President, he faced enormous challenges on the political and economic front. He was acutely aware of the fact that the future survival and development of the country depended on the promotion of Science and Technology (S & T) and in neutralizing the emerging nuclear threat from India. Towards this end Bhutto called a meeting of scientists at Multan in January 1972 and announced the establishment of a full-fledged Ministry of Science and Technology. He took charge of the Pakistan Atomic Energy Commission, and asked the author to take over as the Chairman of the Pakistan Atomic Energy Commission. He removed all bureaucratic hurdles and ordered that the necessary funds be made available for the approved projects and programmes of the Commission. By these steps, Bhutto launched the atomic energy programme of Pakistan, and gave it the necessary impetus, and financial and political support which had been lacking so far.

Building the Infrastructure

The first task of the PAEC was to prepare a nuclear plan, build the necessary infrastructure, and develop the required manpower to implement it. The Commission was made autonomous, reporting directly to the Chief Executive. A number of major projects were initiated and feasibility studies for nuclear power projects were begun. Agreements were negotiated with numerous countries for the supply of equipment plants and materials, all under IAEA safeguards. These included a reprocessing plant from France, a fuel fabrication plant from Canada, and a heavy water plant from Germany. Agreements for bilateral cooperation were also signed with such countries as Spain, Italy, and so on. There was a serious shortage of skilled manpower and local training facilities had to be set up. Also, Pakistan's basic industrial infrastructure was also weak and new capabilities had to be developed. All this needed time, effort, and money. However, Pakistan's pursuit of nuclear equipment, technology, and training was soon to run into unexpected trouble.

In order to remove any misgivings about Pakistan's nuclear intent, it was necessary to clarify Pakistan's nuclear policy. In November 1972, at the inauguration of the Karachi Nuclear Power Plant (KANUPP), the President of Pakistan made a formal declaration of Pakistan's Nuclear Policy. He said:

> Pakistan believes in using atomic energy for peaceful purposes and as an instrument for development and progress... The most menacing problem in the sub-continent is that of poverty and misery of its people. Atomic energy should become a symbol of hope rather than fear. For this reason, we would welcome if this entire sub-continent, by the agreement of the countries concerned, could be declared to be a Nuclear Free Zone and the introduction of nuclear weapons banned the same way as the Latin American countries have done.

This declaration still remains the cornerstone of Pakistan's nuclear policy.

Impact of India's Nuclear Explosion

In 1974, India went ahead and exploded a nuclear device. It was a great shock. Although the media around the world expressed indignation, no major power condemned it. France sent its congratulations; USSR seemed to acquiesce, US was restrained in its reaction, and China kept silent. In response to Pakistan's protests, it was told that what had been learned by India could not be unlearned. The US Secretary of State went to India in October 1974 and said that India and USA now shared another 'tradition'.

These developments shocked Pakistan. With the forcible break up of the country in 1971, cut off of all military aid, and now facing a nuclearized neighbour, made Pakistan extremely insecure. Pakistan decided to fight this through political means and took the matter to the United Nations and formally presented a proposal for the establishment of a nuclear free zone in South Asia. Although this proposal was adopted by the majority of the members, the major nuclear weapons states and industrialized countries abstained. The message that we received was that sooner or later India would be admitted to the Nuclear Club as a *de facto* if not *de jure* member. The political leadership at that time realized that Pakistan had to face a *de facto* nuclear India alone, and it had no choice but to acquire essential nuclear technology under safeguards, if possible, without it, if necessary, in order to neutralize India's nuclear edge.

India's nuclear explosion had a profound effect not only on Pakistan but also at the international level. It fuelled the fear of proliferation. The advanced countries, led by the USA, organized the London Suppliers Group (LSG) to restrict the flow of nuclear plants, materials and supplies to those countries which did not subscribe to the NPT or accept full-scope safeguards. Further, it was felt that even though India had managed to escape, all doors should be shut on Pakistan. In other words, Pakistan had to pay the price of India's explosion. Pakistan had been honouring all its safeguards and non-proliferation commitments, and had nothing to do with the non-compliance with any written or unwritten understandings that India had given to Canada, US, and the others not to use the supplied technology equipment and materials for military purposes, including conducting a nuclear explosion.

The result was that Pakistan, from May 1974 on, had to face the full force of increasing restrictions and embargoes placed by the western suppliers. One after the other, the supplier states started cancelling cooperation agreements and supply contracts with Pakistan, even though all these were covered by international safeguards. Canada unilaterally cancelled all agreements with respect to KANNUP, thereby endangering the continued operation and safety of this plant. France, under pressure from the US, also unilaterally abrogated the contract to supply a reprocessing plant, even though Pakistan had concluded a safeguards agreement covering this plant with the IAEA. Other countries followed suit. The result was that Pakistan's difficulties multiplied. It had to resort to acquiring technology and services in the open market at a considerable cost, involving unforeseen difficulties and delays. In spite of all these heavy odds, Pakistan forged ahead with its programme, and continued to build various nuclear facilities including a nuclear fuel and enrichment plant.

US Aid Policy

In April 1979, the United States cut off all aid to Pakistan because of Pakistan's alleged sensitive nuclear programme. In October, a Pakistani delegation went to Washington to discuss Pakistan's economic and security needs, and invited Washington's attention to the growing Soviet military threat in Afghanistan as well as a real nuclear and security threat from India. Pakistan asked for reconsideration of the US attitude and renewal of closer relations with Pakistan. But Pakistan's plea was turned down. In December 1979, the Soviet Union invaded Afghanistan. This led to a dramatic change in the US perception of its strategic interests in the region. After negotiations with Islamabad, Washington decided to resume economic as well as military aid to Pakistan. But the US continued to monitor Pakistan's nuclear programme and demanded assurances that Pakistan would not go nuclear. The Western countries placed strict embargoes on any nuclear cooperation with Pakistan and the indigenous nuclear activites of Pakistan were kept under strict watch.

Pakistan's Non-Proliferation Initiatives

During the 1980s, the United States continued its pressure on Pakistan with regard to the nuclear issue, asking it to sign the NPT unilaterally. Pakistan, on the other hand, argued that nuclear proliferation in South Asia was a regional issue and could not be resolved by singling out Pakistan, because it involved India as well which had already exploded a nuclear device. Pakistan emphasized that both countries should be asked to adhere to the Non-Proliferation Regime simultaneously. In order to demonstrate its non-proliferation credentials, Pakistan tried to initiate a dialogue with India on the nuclear issue and made a number of proposals to India which would require both countries to:

(a) sign the NPT,
(b) accept full-scope safeguards,
(c) allow reciprocal inspection of each other's nuclear facilities,
(d) agree to a bilateral treaty banning nuclear tests,
(e) establish a Nuclear Free Zone in South Asia,
(f) make joint declaration of non-acquisition or manufacture of nuclear weapons, and
(g) convene a UN-sponsored Conference to discuss the nuclear issue in South Asia.

India rejected all these proposals and refused to put forward any proposals of its own to strengthen the Non-Proliferation Regime in South Asia. Pakistan kept the US informed of all these initiatives and the negative response from India. Gradually, the United States began to realize that the nuclear issue in South Asia was, indeed, a regional issue and could not be resolved simply by forcing Pakistan to sign the NPT.

India, on its part, insisted that the nuclear issue was not a regional issue but a global one. For India, the major concern was the existence of nuclear weapons in China and the nuclear stockpiles of the Superpowers. Unless something was done about these two, India would not change its nuclear stance. At the suggestion of the United States, and to respond to these concerns expressed by India, in June 1991, Pakistan proposed a

Five-Nation Conference with the participation of India, Pakistan, China, USA, and Russia to discuss the nuclear issue in South Asia. India did not accept this proposal or change its stance.

The official Indian position was that it did not intend to manufacture nuclear weapons since it had not carried out further nuclear testing after the 1974 nuclear explosion. Yet it was opposed to accepting any non-proliferation initiatives or measures in South Asia, and continued to amass weapon usable fissile material and develop a nuclear delivery system. India says that its nuclear capability is not only a response to Pakistan but it is meant to meet the threat posed by nuclear weapons of China and even Kazakhstan. Hence, its insistence on wider, and even global, disarmament as a pre-condition for giving up its nuclear option. India prefers to hold bilateral discussions with the United States, Russia, and other countries on this matter rather than take part in any multinational conference. Consequently, over the past years, several rounds of discussions have taken place involving India, the United States, Japan, and others on the one hand and Pakistan, the United States, and Japan on the other. However, there have been no direct formal discussions between India and Pakistan on the nuclear problem. There have been some contacts, which have led to an Agreement not to attack each others' nuclear facilities. This Agreement was reached in 1985 and ratified in 1991. In accordance to this, both sides exchange a list of their respective nuclear facilities every year which are supposed to be excluded from any attack in case of hostilities.

As seen from Pakistan's standpoint, India faces no threat from Pakistan whether nuclear or conventional. If India agrees to accept the NPT, Pakistan will automatically do the same. Were this to happen, India, with eight times the population of Pakistan, would still retain overwhelming conventional arms superiority *vis-à-vis* Pakistan. It would appear that it is Pakistan which needs a nuclear deterrent against a far stronger neighbour than vice versa. But India appears to have other objectives. It seeks not only regional dominance, but also wants to be an extra-regional power. For this, it considers the nuclear capability as an essential element to multiply and project its power beyond its borders and extends its sphere of influence. This is why it is developing long range nuclear capable ballistic missiles and building nuclear submarines. If this is, indeed, India's strategic doctrine then it will be on a collision course with many countries outside the region, namely, USA, Japan, China, and Australia, whose vital interests will be adversely affected. Further, it will force India to divert more of its limited economic and technical resources towards building a credible nuclear arsenal which will severly strain its narrow economic base. If India wants to compete in the world market place and meet the basic social and economic needs of its poor at home it requires generous inputs of foreign investment and technology. India will have to decide whether its security and developmental objectives can be met by persisting on the nuclear course or changing this policy.

Pakistan's position on the nuclear issue is very clear. It is ready to sign the NPT, accept full-scope safeguards or subscribe to any other non-proliferation measures, provided the same is applied to India simultaneously. While Pakistan seeks speedy abolition of nuclear weapons all over the world it does not make it a pre-condition for accepting the Non-Proliferation Regime in South Asia provided India accepts the same. India, on the other hand, insists that it cannot be expected to give up the nuclear option unless there is a complete elimination of nuclear weapons by the nuclear powers.

US-Pakistan Nuclear Relations

The 1980-90 decade was a troubled decade between Pakistan and the US as far as the nuclear issue is concerned. Pakistan continued its nuclear programme and refused to sign the NPT or accept full-scope safeguards. The non-proliferation lobby in the USA, particularly the Senate, continued to press the US administration to obtain written assurances from Pakistan with regard to adherence to the non-proliferation regime while Pakistan linked this with getting a similar commitment from

India. However, the Pakistan government gave assurances to the USA that it would not go nuclear or explode a nuclear device or embarrass the US administration. This was not considered to be enough by the US Congress. In 1985 the US Senate passed the Pressler Amendment requiring the President of the USA to certify every year that Pakistan did not possess a nuclear device as a precondition for the continuation of economic cooperation with Pakistan. From the US point of view, this Pressler Amendment was designed to facilitate the continuation of US-Pakistan cooperation with respect to the Afghan war and supply of economic aid to Pakistan but as shown by later developments it proved to be a serious obstacle.

In Febuary 1990, the Soviets withdrew from Afghanistan and the American Congress felt that the US objectives of expelling Soviet troops from Afghanistan had been achieved. Consequently, the pressure on Pakistan with respect to the nuclear issue increased. US demanded immediate capping and rollback of Pakistan's nuclear programme, which Pakistan could not agree to. In September 1990, the US President refused to certify that Pakistan did not possess a nuclear device and all aid to Pakistan was cut off. In subsequent negotiations, Pakistan tried to assure the US that it did not have a nuclear device, would not carry out a nuclear explosion, and would not make weapon grade highly enriched uranium or/transfer nuclear technology to a third country. But these assurances failed to persuade the US Congress. The US President had no power to exercise a waiver with respect to the Pressler Amendment. The result was that US-Pakistan relations worsened. Both countries are acutely aware of the fact that it is in their strategic interest to find a way to restore these relations, particularly in the light of continued fighting in Afghanistan, instability in the Gulf and Central Asia, and need for the US to maintain close relations with its traditional ally in South Asia.

The Pressler Amendment constitutes the greatest impediment in restoring US-Pakistan cooperation. It is widely recognized as a rigid law which has outlived its utility. It was ostensibly designed to cement close security partnership between the two countries, dissuade Pakistan from exercising the nuclear option, and strengthen the prospects of obtaining non-proliferation and stability in the region but has failed to achieve any of these objectives. The US-Pakistan relations are at a new low. The dangers of proliferation have multiplied. Pakistan has now greater incentives to pursue the nuclear option. By refusing to give conventional arms and economic assistance to Pakistan, US policy has upset the delicate power balance in the region and destabilized the security environment. It has left Pakistan with no alternative but to consider exercising nuclear option to ensure its survival. It has encouraged the nuclear hawks in the country. It has given India a veto over US-Pakistan relations, and reduced the options available to the US in playing a positive role to bring peace and development to the region. It has made the emergence of a nuclear race in the subcontinent a real possibility—exactly what the US wanted to discourage. It has also strengthened India's intransigence and given it an overwhelming military supremacy in the area. It is quite clear that the current US policy and legislation on non-proliferation has not succeeded in persuading Pakistan to sign the NPT, accept full-scope safeguards or dismantle or roll back its unsafeguarded nuclear programme. No Government in Pakistan can afford to abandon the nuclear option as long as India continues to pursue one. Therefore, the US, in order to further its non-proliferation objectives and at the same time pursue its strategic interest in the region, has to pursue a more flexible and long-range policy on the nuclear issue *vis-à-vis* Pakistan. Whether the US Administration can persuade the Congress to adopt new legislation on non-proliferation is still an open question and remains to be seen.

The Clinton Administration tried to limit the damage of the Pressler Amendment through the passage of the Brown Amendment which allowed the US to resume limited cooperation with Pakistan in certain areas and find a solution for compensating Pakistan with respect to non-supply of F-16 aircrafts. While the Brown Amendment had some positive impact, it failed to solve the F-16 problem or pave the way for resumption of meaningful cooperation between the two countries. Both Washington and Islamabad have reached the conclusion that the Pressler Amendment is a real impediment in developing a close economic and security relationship sorely needed for regional stability in the area, and a way has to be found to circumvent it.

Is Nuclear Capability Enough for Deterrence?

India and Pakistan are both nuclear capable and can assemble nuclear devices in a short time. Whether they are already weaponized or not is a matter of conjecture. It is very likely that they have not as yet manufactured usable nuclear weapons, deployed them and integrated them into their respective defence strategies. They also do not appear to have developed any nuclear doctrine or established a full-fledged Control, Command and Communication System. The question is 'will a non-weaponized nuclear capability serve as a deterrent and prevent a conventional war in the Subcontinent?' In the opinion of many observers in Pakistan, its nuclear capability has restrained India from attacking Pakistan. In a way, this capability has already acted as a deterrent. This has been corroborated by such eminent Indian military leaders as General Sundarji, who has gone so far as to assert that the 1971 war would not have taken place if Pakistan had nuclear capability at that time. Can we then, by freezing the position at the level of non-weaponized nuclear capability, obtain the advantage of deterrence without incurring the huge cost of building nuclear weapons? This can be worked out only if we can safely make certain assumptions. Both sides have to agree to commit themselves in a verifiable manner that they do not have nuclear weapons and otherwise satisfy each other in this regard. This implies declaration of the existing stocks of fissile material, and placing them under international control. Further, they have to accept safeguards on their respective nuclear facilities capable of producing additional nuclear fissile material. The two countries have to guarantee that neither side has any undeclared nuclear weapons and materials. For nuclear deterrence to work, whether in a weaponized or non-weaponized stage, both sides have to recognize, as a priority, the catastrophic consequences of a nuclear war in the subcontinent in which there can be no winners. The casualties and damage will be too high to be affordable or acceptable. The political, economic and social consequences would be grave, and the countries might even disintegrate. Further, this policy would require a strong centralized Control, Command and Communication System, which at present does not exist in either country. If the two countries weaponize prematurely, the possibility of miscalculation, adventurism and pre-emption is really high and they could slip into nuclear confrontation due to the folly of a few who may act impulsively rather than judiciously.

US Approach to Non-Proliferation in South Asia

There is no doubt that the US is committed to achieving non-proliferation in South Asia. It has finally recognized that it is not a one-country problem but involves two countries, namely, India and Pakistan. Therefore, it is a regional problem. At the same time it realizes that India wants to globalize this issue to gain maximum advantage and delay the emergence of a non-proliferation regime in South Asia as long as possible. The US no longer insists that Pakistan and India should immediately sign the NPT or roll back their nuclear programmes or accept full-scope safeguards. It visualizes a step by step, pragmatic and non-doctrinaire approach to achieve its ultimate objective of non-proliferation in South Asia.

Introduction of Ballistic Missiles

Introduction of ballistic missiles into a region which already has a nuclear capability, will serve to multiply the danger of nuclear confrontation. There is no easy defence possible against guided missiles as they are virtually unstoppable. If these become nuclear-tipped then they are sure to cause incalculable destruction. If either side acquires nuclear missile capability with suitable warheads to match and such missiles are deployed then there might be a strong temptation to go further for a 'killing' first strike in the hope that it could ensure total victory in one go. The situation can be avoided only by taking two essential steps, i.e., non-testing to preclude the development of compact warhead and non-deployment of all nuclear capable launchers.

India has already perfected the *Prithvi* missile with a range of 250 km, which it is ready to deploy. This can bring most Pakistani cities as targets within easy reach. Further, India is rapidly developing the *Agni* missile with a range of 2500 km. *Prithvi* is an immediate and real threat to Pakistan while *Agni* is a potential threat not only within South Asia but also beyond—affecting China, South East Asia, the Middle East, and Central Asia. This will, no doubt, widen the area of concern and potential for confrontation between India and other Asian States. India is also planning to increase the range of *Agni* and develop *Surya* intercontinental missile, which could pose a global challenge to US, Russia, and Western Europe. Pakistan's missile capability is very limited. It is reported to have a few M-11 missiles of less than 300 km range which fall within the MTCR. Pakistan has not tested any longer range missile of its own. This means that it cannot reach targets deep into India from where India could launch *Agni* missiles against Pakistan. If Pakistan feels really threatened it will have to consider speeding up the development of longer range missiles. Thus, the danger of a nuclear arms race could be compounded by a missile race creating a grave security situation in South Asia. Therefore, immediate action on the non-manufacture, non-deployment and non-testing of ballistic missiles in this area is needed.

Nuclear Issue and Domestic Politics

In Pakistan, the nuclear programme enjoys the widest possible public support and the political parties are all in favour of maintaining the nuclear option. Over the last twenty-five years, in spite of many changes, at no stage did any government agree to give up the nuclear option or diminish its support for the national nuclear programme. The nuclear option is regarded as an essential element for national security and survival. Generally speaking most people agree that Pakistan should not sign the NPT or accept any discriminatory conditions *vis-à-vis* India. There are some hard-liners who believe that perhaps we should not give up the nuclear option even if India were to sign the NPT. They argue that Pakistan needs this option against a larger militant and aggressive neighbour, which has not given up the idea of undoing Pakistan. However, various governments have reiterated their willingness to join the Non-Proliferation Regime if India does so. No government in Pakistan can afford to compromise on the nuclear issue and expect to survive. People would just not accept it. No political party in Pakistan can afford to appear to be soft on the nuclear issue. In fact, all political parties want to outbid each other in this regard. The US is beginning to recognize the limitations of any Pakistani government to compromise on the nuclear issue. Contrary to the earlier attempts to force Pakistan to sign the NPT first, the US has realized that any concession from Pakistan can come only in the context of a regional approach. The US has now accepted that non-proliferation in South Asia is a regional issue even though it has a global aspect too. Consequently, the US is not asking Pakistan to roll back or place all its nuclear facilities under international control. At the same time, the continued application of the Pressler Amendment is a serious irritant and regarded as totally unfair and unjust to Pakistan.

Linkage with Kashmir

For Pakistan, the nuclear issue is security-related and its solution lies in the political rather than the technical domain. As long as there is deep mistrust about India's intentions, no progress can be made on this issue. The core problem is that of Kashmir. If it remains unresolved, tension and mistrust will continue. Once it is settled, the atmosphere will dramatically change, enabling the resolution of all issues including nuclear, economic, technical and political cooperation, and so on. The Kashmir conflict is bleeding both countries. It is not only a threat to peace and security in this region but undermines the prospects of economic developments in the whole area. This itself destabilizes the social and political environment and feeds into further deterioration of the security situation by encouraging extremism and violence. An amicable solution of the Kashmir problem is necessary for long term security and stability in South Asia.

Underlying Perceptions of India and Pakistan

Any solution of the outstanding India-Pakistan problem in South Asia will have to take into account the security and political perceptions of the two countries. The smaller states in the subcontinent are deeply distrustful of India's hegemonistic tendencies which has put it at odds with all its neighbours. Obviously all the neighbours of India cannot be wrong on all the issues. India visualizes itself as a successor state to the British Indian Empire with a legitimate sphere of influence extending from Aden to the State of Malacca and encompassing the Indian Ocean as a part of its domain. It wants to be accepted as the dominant and unquestioned regional power so that it can control and influence the defence, security, and political and economic development in the region. It also wants to extend its influence at the international and global levels, with ambitions to become a superpower in the twenty-first century. It considers China as a rival to its ambitions. It also wants to compete with

Japan for influence in Asia. This means that even if Pakistan were to succumb to India it would not make the nuclear issue go away. India's nuclear ambitions are a part of its overall plan to achieve global power status. The possession of nuclear weapons and an associated delivery system are regarded as essential elements for projecting its power beyond its frontiers, outside the region, and at the international level.

It appears that India is on a collision course not only with its smaller neighbours but also with major powers, notably China and Japan in Asia, and USA and Russia outside. In this way, India is not only a regional problem but also a global problem in the making. Pakistan on the other hand is a smaller country, which is struggling economically, technologically and politically, is much weaker and poses no threat to India. Pakistan knows its limitations. Its primary concern is its security, development, and survival. It has no ambition to become a leader of the Muslim world, sponsor an alliance with the Central Asian Muslim Republics, annexe any territory or pose a credible challenge to India. Therefore, it is far more anxious and reasonable in trying to resolve the nuclear and Kashmir issue than India. It has always responded positively to any proposal for making South Asia a nuclear free zone or strengthening non-proliferation regime in the area. It perceives a real threat from India and is anxious to take all political and defensive measures to blunt this threat. The continuing erosion of its defensive capability as compared with the increasing military might of India, is a source of great worry and anxiety for Pakistan and compels it to retain its nuclear option as long as India retains it.

Differences and Similarities between Indian and Pakistani Nuclear Stands

There are some similarities as well as wide differences between the views of India and Pakistan on nuclear non-proliferation and disarmament issues. Both countries regard the NPT as discriminatory and subscribe to the goal of complete nuclear disarmament. However, while paying lip service to these views India seems to have its own nuclear agenda. It uses the slogan of complete nuclear disarmament as a cover for continuing its pursuit of nuclear and missile capability. Although it proposed the cessation of all nuclear testing as far back as the mid 1950s, when the CTBT was being negotiated in Geneva, and voted upon it in the UN General Assembly, it has refused to support it. It insisted on retaining its nuclear option to test, and linked its adherence to CTBT to the nuclear powers first agreeing to a fixed time-frame for complete disarmament, which obviously is not realistic. Further, it refuses to have meaningful discussion on Fissile Cut Off Treaty (FMTC) using the same arguments because it wants to continue amassing weapon grade material for its future nuclear stockpile. It has also ruled out the signing of NPT in the foreseeable future.

Pakistan, on the other hand, is willing to sign the NPT inspite of its shortcomings and defects, if India agrees to do so, and thereby advance the cause of non-proliferation in South Asia. Even though, unlike India, Pakistan has not carried out a nuclear test and finds CTBT still deficient in certain respects, it voted for the CTBT and is ready to subscribe to it provided India does the same. As far as the FMTC is concerned, Pakistan is willing to accept it in principle. In fact, it is known to have voluntarily frozen the production of weapon grade fissile material several years ago. India has not reciprocated. There are many in Pakistan who feel that the US and others have not appreciated this voluntary freeze. Pakistan is participating at the discussions in Geneva with the hope that a formal treaty can be negotiated on a non-discriminatory basis. Pakistan has also proposed that South Asia should get rid of all ballistic missiles and become a zero ballistic missile zone. India opposes this. In fact India has stepped up its missile testing, production, and deployment programme particularly with respect to *Prithvi* which has already been inducted into its defence forces and aimed against targets in Pakistan.

From the foregoing it is clear that India is not at present willing to subscribe to any non-proliferation regime either in the nuclear or missile fields. This attitude will inevitably lead the two countries into a costly and dangerous arms race with grave consequences for peace and security in the region.

Confidence-Building Measures

In spite of all the intractable problems between India and Pakistan, certain measures can be taken for reducing tensions between the two countries and improving the overall security climate to gain time for resolution of the key issues:
i) The first step should be a dialogue between India and Pakistan to discuss all outstanding issues. The fact that no comprehensive and meaningful dialogue has been held between the two sides, is in itself, an indication of deep-seated mistrust and lack of communication between the two sides. In the long run, the two countries will have to sit together and face each other across the negotiating table, and settle their differences to find a lasting solution to all their problems, including Kashmir. It is only recently that the two countries have started talking to each other, and meetings have been held at the level of Foreign Secretaries and even the Prime Ministers have met. This is a step in the right direction. However, judging from the statements from both sides, no progress has been made towards resolving the major issues.
ii) In order to make such a dialogue productive some outside friendly party, particularly the US, could play a constructive role behind the scenes to bring about a real compromise between the two sides. The US, as a sole super power, can and should take some positive initiatives in this regard because it alone enjoys the necessary political and economic leverage over both countries.
iii) Pakistan, at the suggestion of the US, put forward the idea of holding a 5-power conference to discuss the nuclear issue as far back as 1991. China was included to accommodate the Indian

viewpoint. The US and ex-USSR (Russia) were included to take care of Indian global concerns. India rejected this proposal. Later, the US advanced the idea of a 9-power conference including UK, France, Germany, and also Japan. India again turned it down. Basically, India fears that in 5 or 9-power conference it would not be able to defend its stand on many of the issues and would become isolated. Hence, it wants to enter into separate bilateral discussions with all these countries and circumvent the main issue. It seems that India is now running out of excuses as far as multilateral or bilateral discussions are concerned. The international community, in order to bring India to the conference table, should keep up pressure. It desperately needs foreign investment and dual-purpose modern technology to build its economy and thereby compete in the world market place with better products. A concerted approach by the major economic powers would certainly go a long way to bring India around.

iv) Although official negotiations and discussions between India and Pakistan have been generally difficult and so far non-productive, the unofficial and informal meetings between the scholars, experts and opinion makers of the two countries have provided excellent opportunities for free and frank exchange of views at different levels and have been conducted in a more relaxed manner. This is, indeed, a very valuable communication link and should be strengthened and broadened. In the long run, the unofficial dialogues may provide some constructive ideas as was the experience in US-Soviet relations.

v) On the nuclear side, informal contacts have played their role in paving the way for an Agreement leading to 'no attack on each others' nuclear facilities'. This idea was officially endorsed in 1985 but negotiations of the Agreement and ratification of the text took another six years.

vi) Another idea which has been put forward by India visualizes a bilateral Agreement of 'no first use of nuclear weapons'. Pakistan has already proposed that both sides should foreswear the possession of nuclear weapons and make a joint declaration that they will neither manufacture nor deploy nuclear weapons on their soil. India has rejected this. Pakistan believes that any Agreement on 'no first use' would implicitly accept and legitimize the possession of nuclear weapons by the two sides. Since these weapons are not to be used, why possess them in the first instance? In the view of Pakistan, primary emphasis should be on non-possession and non-weaponization rather than non-use after manufacture.

It should be remembered that nuclear capability or nuclear weapons are not the root cause of the problems between India and Pakistan. They are by-products of mutual mistrust and suspicion. The basic issues are political and security related. Unless these issues, the foremost being the Kashmir issue, are resolved there will be only limited progress in the nuclear or other domains.

7

The Nuclear Subcontinent: Political and Economic Realities

Walid Iqbal

India's Explosive Gamble

When India shattered a global moratorium on nuclear testing by conducting five detonations on 11 and 13 May 1998, immediate world reaction was not just that of surprise but also of disbelief; almost no one expected India to take this seemingly unwise and reckless step. Echoing this reaction, US Senator Jesse Helms, the Chairman of the Senate Foreign Relations Committee, opined, 'The Indian government has not shot itself in the foot—it has most likely shot itself in the head'.[1] In its Editorial Comment, *The New York Times* observed, 'India faces a ruinous cutoff in foreign aid, a self-defeating arms race with Pakistan, and isolation even from friends'.[2]

However, at ground zero of the detonations were Indian leaders possessing a different world view—notwithstanding their chaotic coalition government and an increasingly polarized population. At the helm of a country with an ancient civilization, with a land mass jutting thousands of miles into the Indian Ocean, with the second largest population on this planet, and said to be the largest democracy in the world, they were driven by 'aspirations and ambitions to become a major world power'.[3]

Thus, in that eventful week in mid-May, as the fine print of events was examined minutely and hard facts were assessed more objectively, there was something that emerged as a bigger surprise than the tests themselves. It was how apparently well informed analysts around the world had allowed themselves to be convinced that the Indian government would never take this step. It was how all and sundry were deluded into thinking that the highly unlikely nuclear testing would turn India into a pariah state like Iraq, bury it under the weight of economic sanctions and result in its expulsion from the community of civilized nations.

On part of the Indian strategists, it was a well thought out and meticulously planned move. It is clear that they had assessed beforehand all possible sanction scenarios. They went ahead with their plan, and the best case scenario performed like clockwork—internationally as well as domestically. While planning their move, Indians drew great strength from the fact that for decades their economy remained introverted, with minimal links with foreign banks and companies due to near isolationist industrial policies. It was only in 1991 that they opened their doors to the outside world. In addition, the sheer size of the Indian economy—its output in goods and services totalled $350 billion in fiscal year 1996—provided an ample cushion. The system could sustain the harshest of sanctions with appropriate ease. Foreign investors would suffer more than a local populace accustomed to poverty and a political leadership used to austere lifestyles. In any event, the harshest of sanctions were never imposed.

Apart from economic indicators, the record of history itself provided ample evidence to Indian planners in pre-assessing the impact of a new round of nuclear tests in the Pokhran desert after a silence of more than twenty years—Pokhran II as the testing exercise came to be known. Enough writing was left on the wall by Pokhran I in 1974. The Indians set the stage for an action replay in 1998 and succeeded to the hilt. The rest of the world ought to have been on constant notice—Pokhran I was just a wake up call. Like volcanic eruptions, twenty-four years fall short of a millisecond in the life of nuclear detonations. Bhabani Sen Gupta had warned the world at that time:

What the international community must ask of India now is a formal commitment to the UN Security Council that it will never undertake the manufacture of nuclear weapons and that such commitment be written into the Indian Constitution through an amendment sponsored by the government. The two measures alone can reassure the world that India will not use its nuclear capability for destructive purposes. If Mrs Gandhi refuses to take them (a mere undertaking to the Security Council will not be enough simply because it is not enforceable), she will have betrayed, or confirmed, what many suspect to be India's true nuclear ambition.[4]

India's economic situation in 1974—much worse than it is now—never deterred it from going ahead. Following the 1973 oil shock and a general recession in the country, India was in a desperate position. Consumption of food, edible oil and clothing had declined, industrial production was stagnant, more than seventy per cent of the population was illiterate and about seventy-five per cent of university graduates unemployed.[5] Nevertheless, international reaction was considered irrelevant by Indian planners. This furnished sufficient guidelines towards the implementation of Pokhran II. Pokhran I drew sharp reactions only from Canada. Japan and USA. The significant sanctions following Pokhran II have come from the same countries. This was not too difficult to calculate in advance.

Canada had not bought the Indian story in 1974 despite Mrs Gandhi's emphatic statements that her country's atomic projects were peaceful: to extract metal ores, build canals, create harbours, and open natural gas reserves. The Canadians had been key foreign donors in the construction and development of India's two atomic reactors at Trombay and in the Rajasthan desert. This co-operation originated in a 1956 agreement between Prime Ministers Louis St. Laurent and Jawaharlal Nehru. In 1968, Canada signed the world-wide treaty to prevent the spread of nuclear weapons. The attention of the Indian government was drawn to Canada's responsibility under the agreement to contain development of nuclear devices, and India was expected to adhere to necessary safeguards. This position was reaffirmed by Prime Minister Pierre Trudeau in an exchange of letters with Mrs Gandhi in 1971; Canada believed that there is no such thing as a 'peaceful' nuclear explosion.[6] Feeling deceived and betrayed by the Indian government in 1974, Canada suspended its aid to the Indian atomic energy programme. Food and agricultural aid remained unaffected. Given this background, Canada's suspension of aid to India in 1998 was only a natural and logical consequence of Pokhran II.

Japan's angry reaction to Pokhran II was as foreseeable as ever in the given scenario. The only victim of nuclear attack, Japan is acutely aware of its role as a front line state in the global efforts to halt the spread of nuclear weapons. It immediately cancelled $30 million of annual grant aid to India, and took another two days to 'suspend' the major part of Japanese aid—being loans amounting to $1 billion. It may be noted that 'suspension' is a temporary measure different from cancellation. It leaves room for 'restoration' at any expedient time. It is also worthy of mention that in 1996 Japan imposed sanctions on China for testing nuclear weapons. These sanctions primarily involved cancellation of grants. For equality of treatment between India and China, it seems highly likely that Japan will restore its loans to India in the not too distant future. Therefore, despite Pokhran II, the major portion of Japanese aid to India is likely to remain unaffected.

If the US government had a choice, India would have gotten away with Pokhran II with a verbal reprimand even milder than a slap on the wrist. The immediate US reaction to Pokhran I were strong words to the effect that India, while neglecting its starving masses, had squandered great talent and resources on its hunger for power. A short while later, the US resumed aid to India (which stood suspended since the 1965 Indo-Pak war) and started a $75 million assistance programme. This situation had altered in 1998, but only slightly. The only reason why the US could not take the same liberty in 1998 was the enactment of the Nuclear Proliferation Prevention Act of 1994. This law makes it mandatory for the US government to impose certain sanctions on any state that detonates a nuclear device after 30 April 1994.[7] This does not, however, mean that the US possesses no leeway whatsoever in diluting the effect of this law to the extent that sanctions become merely symbolic. An examination of the key aspects of this law provides an array of possibilities.

The statutory provision mandating sanctions is general in nature and furnishes overall guidelines only. Details of sanctions are always contained in sanction regulations whose articulation is a matter of executive discretion. Past experience suggests that there are sometimes lengthy delays in the issuance of such regulations (the US government took exactly one year in issuing the Burmese Sanction Regulations). Even while confining itself to the general dictates of the statute, the executive branch has significant latitude in constructing these regulations since it is the first time sanctions are being imposed under this 1994 law. It is evident that Indian strategists not only assessed carefully the purview of the sanctions law but also followed it up post-Pokhran II with hectic lobbying in Washington DC, attempting to seek the mildest impact possible.

In all, four sub-sections of the sanctions provision concern the US government directly. These call for termination of assistance to India (except humanitarian, food, and agricultural assistance); termination of sales of defence and defence related goods and services and cancellation of related export licenses; termination of all foreign military financing; and prohibition of export of specific goods and technology whose export requires licensing by the Commerce Department. Since it is the former Soviet Union and not the US on which India has historically relied for such assistance, the impact of these direct sanctions is expected to be under $100 million annually. Also, until further specification is provided, it is not clear which exports will be prevented and which licenses terminated.

The remaining three sub-sections of the said law involve indirect action on part of the US government, i.e., through other agencies and institutions. Firstly, the sanctions direct the US government to 'deny' to India 'any credit, credit guarantees or other financial assistance by any department, agency or instrumentality of the United States government.' This essentially concerns loans, political risk insurance and other guarantees extended by the US Export-Import Bank (Eximbank) and Overseas Private Investment Corporation (OPIC). Before Pokhran II, Eximbank had about $500 million in existing loans and loan guarantees and OPIC provided about $750 million in loans and insurance related to India.[8] The sanctions law does not address the question of how, or if, existing loans or credits will be affected. It is highly likely that, following past patterns, the sanction regulations permit the performance of contracts that predate the imposition of sanctions.

Even otherwise the impact of sanctions on Eximbank and OPIC activity came across as more detrimental to US business interests than to the Indian economy. The US aircraft manufacturer Boeing was given an order for ten 373s by Jet Airways Limited, India's largest private sector airline. The deal was announced in 1996, and valued at $486 million, and it relied largely on Eximbank financing. Three of the planes had been delivered before the nuclear tests. Eximbank also agreed to finance a $500 million contract awarded in April 1998 to Hughes Network Systems (a subsidiary of General Motors) to build a huge wireless telephone system. These deals found cover under the 'existing contract' principle. So did deals of total value greater than $3 billion where OPIC had lent support to companies like Enron, Motorola, US West and Bechtel.

A major deal still in the negotiations phase, however, had to be scrapped—the planned purchase of eighteen planes by Air India from Boeing. The American behemoth lost a $2 billion contract. India lost nothing. The ultimate gainer is expected to be Boeing's European rival Airbus Industrie since France and the rest of Europe did not impose, but in fact opposed, any sanctions against India.

Secondly, the sanctions prohibit 'any United States bank from making any loan or providing any credit to the government' of India, except 'for the purposes of purchasing food or other agricultural commodities'. This sub-section has various cracks through which the punitive impact of sanctions can leak.

The law does not define 'government' of India—the detailed sanctions will do so. It is not known whether this term will include any political subdivisions, agencies or instrumentalities of the government, as well as any entities associated with, owned, controlled, or acting directly or indirectly on behalf of the government of India. Therefore, it is quite likely that US banks' dealings with Indian banks and major state owned enterprises will remain unaffected. The term 'United States bank' is also not defined in the law. It is quite possible that foreign branches, subsidiaries organized under foreign laws and foreign-incorporated, and controlled subsidiaries would not be deemed 'US banks'. This could totally nullify the punitive impact of this sanctions provision. The terms 'loan' and 'credit' are also not defined. Until detailed regulations appear, it is totally unclear whether the actual scope of the sanctions extends to overdrafts, currency swaps, purchase of debt securities, standby letters of credit and drawdowns on existing lines of credit.

Finally, the US government is required to oppose the 'extension of any loan or financial or technical assistance' to India by any international financial institution. This provision has zero impact if taken on face value. In essence, all the US government can really do is cause delay in or to vote against disbursement of loans or other assistance to India by the World Bank, International Development Agency (IDA), and the International Monetary Fund (IMF). The US has a voting power of 17.03 per cent in the World Bank, 15.29 per cent in IDA, and 17.78 per cent in the IMF.[9]

As regards the IMF, India has about $26 billion in foreign exchange reserves and is in no need of assistance. As regards the World Bank and IDA, the extent to which the US government can persuade G-8 countries to vote against India is now well-known. In any event, World Bank and IDA operate by consensus, and matters are never actually voted upon. At best after Pokhran II, the US used its muscle to 'delay the vote on' (by no means a 'cancellation' of) $865 million in loans to the highway and power sectors of India. If push came to shove, the maximum vote the US can muster in collaboration with Japan, Canada, and a handful of other countries strongly opposed to India, will not be more than forty per cent—well short of a majority. Being the World Bank's third largest borrower at present, its support is important to India. The country's planners had carefully assessed this scenario before Pokhran I as well as Pokhran II. The World Bank meeting for loans to India scheduled for 30 June and 1 July 1998 was not cancelled because of any sanctions requirements. By sheer coincidence, the venue of the meeting was in Japan, who refused to play the host after Pokhran II due to obvious reasons. The World Bank has subsequently clarified that its lending policies to India shall remain unaffected. Ironically, Pokhran I was timed three weeks before the 1974 meeting of the World Bank aid to India Consortium in Paris.[10] The blast had no impact on that meeting or on the World Bank's subsequent assistance to India, except that the disbursement of loans saw an insignificant delay.

Diplomatic manoeuvering on part of India and the Clinton administration's measured response have provided instructive hints on the direction that the detailed regulations concerning US sanctions against India would most likely take.

Indian leaders exercised caution and tact in the immediate aftermath of the tests. During the solitary week that their 'defiant' step was the focus of world attention, not a single aggressive statement was issued. Prime Minister Vajpayee's initial press conference was hurried, brief and confined to technical details. No media questions were entertained. The transcript of the press conference was attached to identical letters dispatched by Vajpayee to all G-8 leaders including President Clinton, explaining India's 'deteriorating security environment' and 'the rationale for these tests'. Without naming his two 'bitter' neighbours, the Indian PM dilated upon China's overt nuclear ability, its concealed assistance to Pakistan and the 'unremitting terrorism' sponsored by the latter in the Punjab and Kashmir. Seeking 'understanding for our concern for India's security' the PM closed with 'my highest consideration for your country and yourself'.

President Clinton was as firm but as tactful in his response—criticizing India, and complimenting it, in almost the same breath. A 'terrible mistake', he noted, by a 'perfectly wonderful country'. Feeling that India may have been driven by a self-esteem problem and felt 'underappreciated' as a world power, the President concluded, 'Well, I think they've been underappreciated in the world and in the United States itself'.[12] Chancellor Kohl stood by Mr Clinton's side as the President made these observations during his sanctions announcement outside the Sans Souci Palace in Potsdam. Such was the disunity between the US and its allies that the Chancellor felt it unnecessary to announce his sanctions at the same time. His only statement 'Germany would make it very clear that it was the wrong decision for the Indians to take.'[13]

Curiously, German sanctions did not end up being as firm as its leader's statement. Germany 'called off' aid talks with India supposed to be held the following week in Bonn. A 'portion' of new development aid for India amounting to $168 million was 'put on hold' and it was said that 'no talks will take place any time soon'.[14] The rest of the allies were stunningly uncooperative. The French government criticized American sanctions against India and emphasized that it did not 'encourage the Americans to pursue sanctions, this is not the way to discourage India'.[15] Derek Fatchett, the British State Minister for Foreign and Commonwealth Affairs, stressed that his government was firmly opposed to the idea of sanctions as they would amount to 'punishing the poorest and the ordinary people of India for a decision taken by their government'.[16] The office of the European Union was critical of the reckless testing, but stopped short of announcing any penalties.

The closure of the chapter on sanctions saw Sweden announce a 'curtailment' of three-year aid agreement with India worth $118 million that commenced in 1997, but said it would re-negotiate after six months, and Denmark froze its $28 million aid package to India. Nothing of significance happened at the UN level, barring an expression of 'deep regret' by its Chief Kofi Annan—reminiscent of the 'serious concern' shown by Kurt Waldheim in 1974.[17]

The combined short term impact of the 'world-wide' government sanctions against India is expected to be less than $1 billion. This amounts to about one day's output of the Indian economy and is outstripped by private portfolio investments in India which total about $9 billion. Markets are known to have short memories. In the longer term, the impact of these symbolic sanctions will be reduced to nothing. 'Peanuts' is perhaps an overstatement.

Amongst the nuclear club, China came forward with the expected response of a concerned neighbour. Britain, France and Russia showed indifference to the prospects of a new member. In essence, the US stood alone in guarding this nuclear oligopoly advocating that 'a sixth wrong cannot make a right'. Ironically, the US itself has carried out more than 1000 nuclear tests and continues to test on an ongoing basis through sub-critical explosions, hydronuclear experiments and super computer simulations. Only recently, the Clinton administration declared that the US would maintain its nuclear weapons for an indefinite period.

A shift of analysis from the international arena to the Indian domestic scene provides a somewhat different picture. With the benefit of hindsight, the international reaction to the tests could be termed as unsurprising. Paradoxically, it is the domestic impact of the pestilential explosions which is likely to be unpredictable. Pokhran I proved to be a massive short term success in 1974, boosting the sagging morale of an impoverished nation and catapulting a weakened Mrs Gandhi into a crest of popularity. 'It's one of the most heartening bit of news in recent years,' acknowledged L.K. Advani,[18] then leader of the opposition and President of the right wing Jan Sangh Party; presently the Home Minister of India known for his volley of threats directed at Pakistan following Pokhran II, 'to roll back its anti-India policy and vacate Azad Kashmir'.[19]

Such was the support from urban intellectuals that within a week following the blast, Indian newspapers started writing scathing editorials, attacking Western critics as 'ridiculous', 'ignorant', 'difficult to understand', 'silly', and 'irrational'.[20]

Duly encouraged, Mrs Gandhi complained in an interview with *Newsweek* that the developed world was treating India as 'a favourite and convenient whipping boy'.[21] In the same week, a strengthened Indian government was able to crush a twenty-day-old railway union strike which had caused a national loss estimated between $1.5 and 2 billion. Mrs Gandhi had afforded the risk of imprisoning nearly 35,000 railway workers who were demanding a uniform wage policy.[22] But the real blow that brought the striking workers to their knees was the arrest of their leader—a tough 43-year-old Bombay socialist and former seminarian called George Fernendes—presently the hawkish Defence Minister of India.

The jubilation, however, was short lived. As the excitement died down and the Indian population woke up yet again to the day to day misery of their struggle, Pokhran I became a thing of the past. Within thirteen months, Mrs Gandhi's popularity took such a nosedive that she had to declare an emergency, suspending civil rights and losing the ensuing electoral battle in 1977.

The domestic political impact of Pokhran II, at least initially, was overwhelmingly positive. But the nature and duration of the euphoria sounded questionable. Although opinion polls showed that ninety per cent of the Indian people initially supported the tests, it is not necessary that this would translate into BJP (Bharatiya Janata Party) votes ensuring an outright majority in the next elections. Much depends on when new elections are held and how effectively the BJP can sustain any popularity ensuing from the nuclear tests given India's fragile and unwieldy politico-economic system.

Sadly, India seems to have undergone an ideological metamorphosis. Her celebrated conception of non-violence appears to have died with its self-proclaimed founder decades ago. Now we see that weapons of mass destruction have become 'a national matter, not a partisan one, on which every Indian stands united'.[23] In the limelight now is the Bombay toughie Bal Thackeray, roaring about Pokhran II from his ideological temple of Hitler worship, 'we have to prove that we are not eunuchs'.[24] Like a ribbon on this violent present to the world are the words of Tushar Gandhi, the great-grandson of the apostle of Indian non-violence; 'I am proud that it was done by India and the Indians'.[25] Thus wrote Arundhati Roy:

> All in all, I think it is fair to say that we're the hypocrites. We're the ones who've abandoned what was arguably a moral position, i.e.: *We have the technology, we can make bombs if we want to, but we won't. We don't believe in them*...Once again we are pitifully behind the times—not just scientifically and technologically (ignore the hollow claims), but more pertinently in our ability to grasp the true nature of nuclear weapons. Our comprehension of the Horror Department is hopelessly obsolete...[26]

Pakistan Evens the Score

Pakistan has been continuously aware of India's nuclear ambition. In 1969, prior to becoming Prime Minister, Zulfikar Ali Bhutto had observed:

> It appears that she [India] is determined to proceed with her plans to detonate a nuclear bomb. If Pakistan restricts or suspends her nuclear programme, it would not only enable India to blackmail Pakistan with her nuclear advantage, but would impose a crippling limitation on the development of Pakistan's science and technology. Our problem, in its essence is to obtain such a weapon in time before the crisis begins. If India builds the bomb, we will eat grass or leaves, we will go hungry. But we will get one of our own. We have no alternative.[27]

Predictably, Pokhran I was termed by Prime Minister Bhutto in 1974 as 'a fateful development' and a threat directed towards Pakistan. While noting that nuclear weapons were different from other military hardware and worked as 'a means of pressure against non-nuclear countries', Bhutto emphatically declared, 'Pakistan is determined not to be intimidated'.[28] Accordingly, Bhutto is unquestionably acknowledged as the leader who sowed the 'first real seeds of Pakistan's nuclear programme' on 31 July 1976.[29] That date marks the formation of the Engineering and Research Laboratories (now A.Q. Khan Research Laboratories) in Kahuta near Islamabad. This was established as an autonomous organization, aimed to provide a uranium enrichment plant that could arm Pakistan with nuclear capability. General Ziaul Haq, who succeeded Bhutto and also became known as his arch foe, is nevertheless accredited for pursuing the nuclear programme through its crucial phase with equal zeal and persistence. The rest is history.

While India has always aspired to assert its dominance, enlarge its defence perimeter, become the policeman of South Asia and be recognized as a major world power, Pakistan's agenda on security 'can be summed up in five words: survival in a hostile environment'.[30] Bowing before Indian dominance is wholly unacceptable, and Pakistan has always maintained its defensive arsenal at a level sufficient to protect its independence and sovereignty.

Following the Indian nuclear tests, the government of Pakistan was under immense pressure at two different levels—at the international level not to conduct its own tests, and at the domestic level to do so without any delay. US President Bill Clinton and British Prime Minister Tony Blair held several telephone conversations with Prime Minister Nawaz Sharif, discouraging a tit for tat response to the Indian tests. The Japanese Prime Minister sent a message of restraint through his Ambassador in Islamabad. It was evident that the rest of the world was spending more time and energy on discouraging Pakistan from testing rather than condemning India for the tests already conducted. At the same time, as days of Pakistan's inaction turned into weeks, public pressure from within Pakistan began mounting—editorial columns in daily newspapers continuously and unanimously pressed for the tests and right wing religious parties threatened to take to the streets.

New Delhi's well planned action at Pokhran provided Pakistan with some simple but important lessons. Firstly, in this day and age a nuclear detonation in South Asia is of limited media value. Information technology has become too advanced and the world has become too volatile a place for any major event to gain prominence for more than a few days—the Indian tests did not figure anywhere in the international headlines four days after Pokhran II.

Secondly, even though all calculations predicted Pakistan's ultimate economic doom, the risk of testing was worth taking. It is a preliminary and fundamental principle of success that one who takes the greatest risk reaps the greatest benefit. The biggest advantage of taking the risk was the handing down of a *fait accompli*. No amount of sanctions could then turn back the clock of time. The US government may have promised great benefits in exchange for nuclear restraint, they may have promised the respect and gratitude of the rest of the world, but no promise could have guaranteed Pakistan's security the way an open declaration of a nuclear capability could. Leave aside security, the US could not even guarantee how Congress would vote on a bill to repeal the Pressler Amendment. Besides, release of the twenty-eight F-16s held up at that time due to this Pakistan specific law would have been hopelessly inadequate in combating the quantum leap taken by India. Accepting injections of economic aid in exchange for nuclear restraint or bowing to international pressure in the face of threatened sanctions was always thought of as a sign of ultimate weakness, but the debate was confined to Pakistan's power elite. Following Pokhran II it became a major national issue:

> Weakness and appeasement invite trouble. Nations that compromise their security under what they believe to be high moral principles invariably put their security in jeopardy. Running after mirages invites destruction.[31]

In fact, it was the country's nuclear programme itself which had always been subject to the harshest international sanctions. Yet, it enabled 'a country that could not make sewing needles or even ordinary durable metaled roads...to conduct uranium enrichment using centrifuge technology':[32]

When a comprehensive account of Pakistan's nuclear programme is written, a word of gratitude should be expressed for those countries which closed the tap of nuclear technology on Pakistan. It created a realization in the policy-makers and the scientists at home that all substitutes to self-sufficiency were transitory and unreliable. Dependence on external crutches breeds internal lethargy and provides a mirage of security. When attention was focused on achieving indigenous capability, gradually light started appearing at the end of the research tunnel.[33]

Thirdly, no sanctions are permanent in nature. Geopolitical and economic realities force developed nations to change their stance from time to time. There was no better example of this for Pakistan than the virtual isolation faced by the US in its attempts to isolate India. US law also called for sanctions to be imposed to isolate Iran, but under pressure from the European Union it had to back down. Just two weeks after the Indian tests, the US was forced to waive sanctions against French, Russian and Malaysian energy companies doing business in Iran despite laws requiring imposition of penalties against any company investing more than $20 million in the Iranian oil and gas industry. Also, Pakistani policy-makers must have considered the possibility that the 1994 law, under which the US imposed sanctions against India, could have been used against Pakistan even if no Pakistani tests were conducted. Detonation by a non-nuclear state after 30 April 1994 is but one of the actions that can invite the sanctions. The law can also operate against a country if the President 'determines' it to be a non-nuclear state which has 'received' a 'nuclear explosive device' after 30 April 1994. US experts could have made out a case against Pakistan at will, and this was well known to all concerned.

Having weighed all options, Pakistan finally conducted its own round of nuclear tests on 28 and 30 May at a guardedly constructed testing site in Chaghai, a remote hilly region in the southwest of Pakistan near the border with Afghanistan and Iran. 'Today we have evened the score with India', said Prime Minister Nawaz Sharif in a televised address in Urdu, '...Today,

God has given us the opportunity to take critical steps for the country's defence. We have become a nuclear power'.[34]

These unpleasant yet unavoidable tremors set off in the Chaghai hills were greeted by swift action on part of the developed West. No time was wasted in slapping on the threatened sanctions. Predictably, these sanctions followed the same pattern as those imposed against India. The figures that came to light immediately after the Chaghai tests showed that their impact on Pakistan would be disturbing, but not alarming.

Starting with US bilateral aid, Pakistan, unlike India, had been subject to US sanctions since 1990. Thus, as a result of the post-Pokhran II US sanctions, India lost about $120 million of soft aid annually. Post-Chaghai Pakistan lost nothing. Throughout the 1990s, India received massive US Eximbank guarantees, yielding about $10 billion in foreign private investment. By contrast, US Eximbank got re-involved in Pakistan only in late 1997 (after the partial lifting of the Pressler sanctions), and the total amount of US private investment in the country was less than $400 million.[35]

On the other hand, Japan has been the biggest aid donor to both Pakistan as well as India. On a pattern identical to the sanctions imposed against India, Japan's response to the Chaghai blasts consisted of cancellation of $40 million in grants and a 'halt' in new loans amounting to about $230 million. The German punishment for Pakistan was also similar to that meted out to India—'cancellation of planned discussions' scheduled for June 1998 concerning new development aid worth $45 million. Canada put relations with both India and Pakistan on hold, without specifying any amounts, and promised to announce further measures. In the same vein, Australia suspended military links with both New Delhi and Islamabad and blocked all assistance except relief aid. Britain, France, Russia and China ruled out sanctions, but competed in their selection of words to characterize the tests, coming up with 'condemn', 'deplore', 'regret' and 'abhor'.[36]

At the end of the day, Pakistan attained more than just nuclear parity with India—it also attained a dubious parity of sanctions.

For once, no one could complain: the industrialized west operated as neutral umpire in the Chaghai-Pokhran sanctions match.

But disparity continues to exist in the impact, not the imposition of sanctions. The blame for this lies squarely on Pakistan's successive governments and their economic planners, who for decades have squandered and mismanaged the country's resources. In the sanctions context, India is now perceived as a rich country with poor people; Pakistan, a poor country with rich people.

According to latest figures Pakistan's per capita income of $480 per annum surpasses that of India by $100 since the latter's population is seven times larger but gross national product only five and a half times greater than Pakistan. However, Pakistan annually receives close to $900 million in net official development assistance, constituting 1.4 per cent of GNP, 6 per cent of Federal Government expenditure and amounting to $7 in aid per capita. In contrast, India receives twice as much in aid but depends on it less than half as much as Pakistan (the $1.9 billion official aid to India forms 0.6 per cent of GNP, 3.3 per cent of Central Government expenditure and amounts to $2 per capita).[37] In addition, Pakistan's foreign exchange reserve hovering around $1 billion, are enough to pay for about six weeks of imports. India's reserves, totaling about $26 billion, are enough for a year's worth of imports. It was not surprising then that the Indian government brushed off the idea of sanctions since it could sustain the shock whereas the Pakistan government issued cautious statements like 'the nature and duration of the sanctions' will dictate their impact on the economy, and then panicked in face of the aftermath.

More significantly, as fuller implications of the sanctions process continued to sink in, the great economic powers were faced with a dilemma. Given the global economic landscape, they were being forced to decide whether their foreign policies will be driven by commercial interests or by 'moral' concerns. The emerging scenario suggests that the former is taking precedence.

As far as the US is concerned, the policy of engagement rather than punishment is widely gaining support. Economic sanctions are a preferred apparatus of Congress to shape foreign policy. On the other hand, the Administration contends that sanctions are becoming counterproductive and weaken its ability to manage the affairs of the state. Particularly, unilateral penalties such as those imposed on India and Pakistan which primarily hurt US companies and make them wary of entering new markets. The general terms of the 1994 sanctions law are also quite inflexible. The President can interpret and apply, but cannot waive its provisions—only Congress can do so through an amendment. During the thirty days after 15 May, the White House was flooded with calls not from the press corps but from corporate America—frantic companies including Boeing, Goldman, Sachs & Co. and IBM wanting to know the implications of the two rounds of sanctions. These influential companies, among others, have worked hard to make inroads into the subcontinent and would not like to see it all come to naught, especially since most of the other Asian economies lie in tatters.

Moreover, President Clinton's much publicized visit to China in late June, was a disappointment in the business context as major US corporations returned with far less than expected. In all, eleven deals were signed by American companies including Boeing, General Electric, IBM, Cargill and Hewlett-Packard, adding up to about $1.6 billion.[38] By contrast, just one planned deal that Boeing lost in India due to imposition of sanctions was worth $2 billion.

The farm lobby in the US is another story. What used to be a minor detail in US-Pakistan trade statistics has suddenly become an observable fact. As sanctions proceeded to cut off wheat credits guaranteed by the US and extended to farmers, it transpired that Pakistan is the third largest importer of US wheat and, if lost to Canada or Australia, these sales could never be recovered. In particular, the wheat-rich state of Washington sends Pakistan 37 per cent of its produce each year, worth about $500 million. It was not surprising that the bill to amend the sanctions law was introduced in each house by lawmakers from Washington state—Senator Patty Murray, a Democrat, and Representative George R. Nethercutt, a Republican—both of whom were up for re-election in November 1998.[39]

Apart from commercial interests, the tide of public opinion in the US is also heavily in favour of a reduction or lifting of sanctions against India and Pakistan in exchange for commitments to end testing and to refrain from weaponization and sharing their nuclear knowhow with other countries. Editorial comments in all leading newspapers and statements of eminent scholars and analysts have consistently referred to sanctions as a 'blunt weapon' that is rarely known to work. Some have even gone to the extent of acknowledging that by supporting Pakistan to the hilt in the 1980s and then taking the 180 degree turn after 1990, the US itself was responsible for weakening the country. 'Our own policy, which denied them a credible conventional capability, has in a way forced them to rely more on the nuclear deterrent', said Nicholas Platt, former US Ambassador to Pakistan, in an interview with *The New York Times*.[40] Robert Oakley—another former Ambassador—concurred, 'For eight years Pakistan has been deprived of everything, and therefore we severely weakened their conventional military capability, which was predicated on the use of American equipment. We certainly weakened their confidence in the United States.'[41]

Finally, the US is also coming to terms with the fact that there is a wide philosophical gulf between itself and its allies on the issue of economic sanctions. Dictated by commercial competitiveness and need for cash (cash strapped Russia brazenly sold two nuclear power-plants to India in June 1998 and has been negotiating the sale of SU-30 fighter bombers), almost all G-8 trading partners have avoided the path of punishment. After bullying the allies into a one-off postponement of World Bank loans to India and an IMF tranche to Pakistan, the US effort seems to have run out of steam. The approval of a World Bank loan package involving education, health, irrigation, and village roads to the Andhra Pradesh government in mid-June 1998 and a wider US interpretation of 'basic human needs' speaks for itself. Furthermore, the delay Pakistan has been encountering in the disbursement of the much needed IMF credits has more to do with merit and less to do with sanctions—the sanctions only exacerbate the situation where a poorly managed economy shows weak fundamentals in face of strict IMF conditionalities.

Unlike the US which has been booming for the last six years, the Japanese economy is in the grip of a recession. In the last eight years, its stock market has tumbled upto 60 per cent and its currency has lost 43 per cent of its value since the 1995 high point. More importantly, its banking sector is in shambles and buried under bad debts from a property market that has cascaded 90 per cent to a high of 370 per cent.[42] Pakistan owes about $2 billion in loans to Japan, and Japan's exports to Pakistan are twice as much as its imports. As the saying goes, if you owe $2 to the bank, you should be an anxious person; but if you owe $2 billion, it is your creditor who would be losing his sleep. A crippled, insolvent, bankrupt Pakistan is the last thing Japan would want to see. It would be sooner rather than later that Japan modifies its sanctions position.

What the Future Holds

Against the political and economic backdrop of a nuclear subcontinent, the US has now entered into a bilateral dialogue—on the one hand with India and on the other with Pakistan—persuading the two States to become signatories to the Comprehensive Nuclear Test Ban Treaty (CTBT). Talks have so far been inconclusive but are said to be moving in a positive direction. India has continued to maintain the posture that the international non-proliferation regime is discriminatory—it is agreeable to becoming a CTBT signatory if certain conditions are met, essentially related to India begin recognized as a nuclear power.

Pakistan, which in the past was agreeable to sign the CTBT on the condition that India sign as well, has now shifted its position. The post-testing scenario has brought the country to the verge of bankruptcy, not because of sanctions *per se*, but the government's panic response thereto—an incoherent foreign exchange policy which has shattered public confidence, diminished the moral authority of the government, and dried up the country's hard currency reserves in the face of a tremendous foreign debt burden.

Seeking US support for a major economic bailout, Pakistan is said to be ready to sign the CTBT without any preconditions, because arguably its national interests will not be compromised 'as it will relieve Pakistan from US pressure and put India on the spot'.[43] The US, on the other hand, has presented Pakistan with a four point agenda, asking the government to: (a) participate positively in negotiations on the Fissile Materials Control Treaty (FMCT); (b) commit to sign and accede to the CTBT: (c) exercise restraint on the deployment of ballistic missiles; and (d) formalize the commitment not to export nuclear and missile technology.[44] It is too early to predict what the final outcome of these negotiations will be, but it is hoped that it will promote global disarmament and make the world, particularly the subcontinent, a less dangerous place to live in without compromising the national security and economic stability of the two nations who celebrated their golden jubilees with a display of nuclear fireworks.

NOTES

1. *The New York Times*, 15 May 1998.
2. *The New York Times*, 13 May 1998.
3. Lt-General (Retired) Kamal Matinuddin, 'Nuclearisation of South Asia: Implications and Prospects', *Regional Studies* (Institute of Regional Studies, Islamabad), Vol. XVI. No. 3 (Summer 1998), p. 10.
4. *The New York Times*, 30 May 1974 (Letter to the Editors).
5. As reported in *The New York Times*, 20 May 1974.
6. As reported in *The New York Times*, 21 May 1974.

7. In relevant part, Section 826-a of the Nuclear Proliferation Prevention Act, 1994.
8. *The New York Times*, 14 May 1998.
9. *The World Bank Annual Report, 1997; IDA Special Purpose Financial Statements, 1997* and *IMF Publications*, 8 April 1998.
10. *The New York Times*, 21 May 1974.
11. Letter reproduced in *The New York Times*, 13 May 1998.
12. *The New York Times*, 14 May 1998.
13. Ibid.
14. Ibid.
15. Ibid.
16. Ibid.
17. *The Dawn*, 12 May 1998 and *The New York Times*, 21 May 1971.
18. *The New York Times*, 20 May 1974.
19. Matinuddin, *Nuclearisation of South Asia*, p. 30.
20. As reported by *The New York Times*, 26 May 1974.
21. As reported by *The New York Times*, 28 May 1974.
22. *The New York Times*, 28 May 1974.
23. Sonia Gandhi, as quoted by *The New York Times*, 16 May 1998.
24. As quoted by *The New York Times*, 13 May 1998.
25. Ibid.
26. Arundhati Roy, 'The End of Imagination', *Frontline* Vol. 15. No. 16 (1-14 August 1998).
27. Dr Abdul Qadeer Khan, 'Dr A.Q. Khan Research Laboratories Kahuta: Twenty Years of Excellence and National Service', in Hussain and Kamran (eds.) p. 212.
28. *The New York Times*, 20 May 1974.
29. Dr Abdul Qadeer Khan, 'Dr A.Q. Khan Research Laboratories' in Hussain and Kamran (eds.) *Dr A.Q. Khan on Science and Education*, (Sang-e-Meel Publications, Lahore, 1997), p. 211.
30. Matinuddin, *Nuclearisation of South Asia*, p. 12.
31. General (Retired) K.M. Arif, *Working with Zia: Pakistan's Power Politics 1977-78*, (Oxford University Press, Karachi, 1996) p. 378.
32. Dr Abdul Qadeer Khan, 'Pakistan's Nuclear Programme: Capabilities and Potentials of Kahuta Project' in S. Shabbir Hussain and Mujahid Kamran, (eds). pp. 113-23.
33. Arif, *Working with Zia*, p. 370.
34. As reported in *The New York Times*, 29 May 1998.
35. Azhar Abbas, 'Where Do We Go form Here?' *Herald*, Volume 29, 6 November (June 1998) p. 33.
36. *The New York Times*, 29 May 1998.
37. *The New York Times*, 29 May 1998.
38. *The New York Times*, 30 May 1998.
39. *The New York Times*, 15 June 1998.

40. *The New York Times*, 1 June 1998.
41. *The New York Times*, 29 May 1998.
42. *The New York Times*, 27 June 1998.
43. Azim M. Mian, 'Pakistan Ready to Unilaterally Sign CTBT', *The News*, 28 August 1998.
44. Maleeha Lodhi, 'Testing Times for Pakistan's Nuclear Diplomacy', *The News*, 30 July 1998.

8

Pakistan's Economy: Achievements, Progress, Constraints, and Prospects

Robert E. Looney

Introduction

Since independence, Pakistan can look back on fifty years of steady, sometimes spectacular economic advance. Pakistan's growth has been the fastest in South Asia. The gross national product has increased on average by over 5 per cent a year since 1947. Pakistan started behind India at the time of independence, but its income per capita is now 75 per cent higher. In spite of high population growth, per capita income has more than trebled in the past two decades.

Still, despite these accomplishments there is growing dissatisfaction with the country's economic performance. Here the main shortcomings often cited include: (a) large budgetary and balance of payments deficits, (b) increasing inflationary pressures, (c) population explosion and rising unemployment, (d) physical infrastructural constraints, and (e) inadequate human resource development.[1]

Pakistan's golden jubilee presents an opportune time to examine the country's economic performance during the last fifty years. How far has the economy progressed and at what cost? Is progress sustainable? What are the main limitations associated with the country's development model? Is Pakistan on the verge of becoming an Asian Tiger? Ultimately, one has to address the question posed by Mahbubul Haq 'Why are its people so poor when the economy has made such rapid progress?'[2] Perhaps a related question is whether and to what extent democracy can be sustained in light of the massive economic and social difficulties the country currently faces.[3]

Overview

Pakistan's economic history is a classic case of half empty or half full. The Gross National Product (GNP) and per capita income have increased substantially during the last fifty years. Between 1960 and 1980, Pakistan's real GNP increased by 250 per cent. This translates into an average annual increase of 4.07 per cent. Again, between 1980 and 1997 Pakistan's Real GNP went up by 179 per cent or an average annual increase of 5.88 per cent. Thus, the country's GNP increased in real terms by about 430 per cent during the period averaging 4.77 per cent. However, real GNP per capita increased only by about 125 per cent due to the massive increase in the country's population from 43 million in 1960 to approximately 135 million in 1997.

The marked increase in Pakistan's GNP during the last fifty years was made possible through substantial increase in agricultural and industrial output.[4] Production of all the major agricultural crops registered impressive increases during the last five decades. Production of wheat went up from 3.9 million tons in 1960 to 16.4 million in 1997. Production of rice rose from about one million tons in 1960 to an estimated 4.3 million in 1997. Production of cotton moved up from 1.7 billion bales to 9.4 billion, while production of sugarcane increased from 10.7 million tons to 42 million tons during the above period.

As far as the manufacturing sector is concerned, Pakistan started almost from scratch. At the time of establishment of Pakistan, there were only one or two textile mills and cement plants in the country. During the last fifty years, not only have hundreds of textile mills been established, but food industries including vegetable ghee and sugar mills, cigarette manufacturing units, cement plants, and fertilizer factories have also been established in the country. The production of vegetable ghee rose from 17,000 tons in 1956 to 717,000 tons in 1997. Production of sugar went up from 81,000 tons in 1956 to about 2.5 million tons in 1997, whereas, production of cement increased from 732,000 tons in 1956 to 9.6 million tons in 1997.

Apart from the above-mentioned industries of a basic nature, Pakistan is entering the era of engineering and automotive industry, electrical and mechanical goods industry, steel, shipbuilding, and pharmaceutical industry. Presently, the manufacturing sector accounts a share of 18 per cent in the country's Gross Domestic Product (GDP) and this share may go up further when the engineering, automobile and other value added industries make a headway in the coming years.

For many, the increase in Pakistan's GNP and per capita income resulting from the development of the country's agricultural and manufacturing sectors translates into improved living standards. The number of motor cars, jeeps and station wagons registered in Pakistan increased from 15,849 in 1950 to 923,577 in 1995. The number of telephone connections went up from 60,000 in 1960 to 2.4 million in 1997, whereas the availability of television sets increased from 92,000 in 1970 to 2.7 million in 1996.

On the negative side, it is clear that the country has achieved too little and what has been accomplished has been done at a very high cost. Despite the substantial increase in the production of major agricultural crops, the country has still not been able to achieve food self-sufficiency and has to spend about $2 billion annually on the import of wheat, edible oil, and the like. As far as manufacturing is concerned, the country has yet to make a real breakthrough in engineering and other value added industries and is heavily dependent on imports to meet its requirements of machinery, electrical and mechanical goods, transport equipment, steel, and chemicals.

It is due to this fact that Pakistan's annual imports ($11.5 to $12 billion) exceed its annual exports (8.5 billion on average) by about $3 billion to 4 or 3.5 billion. As a result, Pakistan's external debt has mounted to an alarming $32 billion and in addition there is an internal debt of Rs 1000 billion. Because of such a heavy debt liability, the allocation for debt servicing alone (Rs 249 billion) in the federal budget for 1997-98 constituted nearly 45 per cent of the total outlay and the government had to cut down on its vital defence and development budgets in real terms.

Unfortunately, it seems that after fifty years of independence and economic planning, the country's fortunes still depend in a large part on the country's cotton crop. More than half of the country's exports still consist of cotton products, mainly textiles and related materials. In the past three years, successive crop failures have increased the price of cotton in the domestic market and eroded the profits of the textiles sector. Export growth has been slow and both the international trade and current account deficits have swelled.

Even more importantly, the country has failed to develop its human capital. In this regard Pakistan's economic growth is a puzzle because there is scant evidence that this economic advance has affected the lives of ordinary people. Indices of poverty and deprivation are so widespread and so stark that many sceptics have begun to doubt the reality of economic growth itself. The simple explanation is in fact that growth has taken place but the prosperity it has produced has been very unevenly distributed.

- In 1960 about 19 million people lived below the poverty line in Pakistan. By 1980 the number of people defined by the government as absolutely poor had grown to 34 million.
- Poverty then fell by 10 million during the 1980s thanks to a bonanza of external remittances, largely from Pakistani workers in the Middle East.
- But poverty has started increasing again alarmingly. In just five years between 1990 and 1995 the number of absolute poor rose from 24 million to 42 million.[5]

Summing up, the country appears to be at the crossroads. The predicament facing the government at the moment is that it can neither repay all of its debt and get out of the debt trap nor is it left with enough money after making budget allocations for defence and debt servicing so as to spend on the development of the physical and social infrastructure.

The present Government is trying hard to retire part of the external and internal debt by speeding up its privatization programme. Simultaneously, the authorities have announced an economic reform package to boost the GDP growth rate and exports in the shortest possible time. One thing is clear. Whether the country will be able to revive its growth and retain the hope of becoming an Asian Tiger will depend largely on the goodwill of the International Monetary Fund and the country's major creditors.

Patterns of Economic Growth and Development

To gain a sense of how the country got in its current predicament, the following sections trace the economic history of the country. In particular, we are interested in determining the factors that appear to have been responsible for periods of high growth as well as those associated with periods of relative decline. Based on this analysis, several scenarios are developed for the period up to the year 2000.

Pre-Ayub Years (1947-57)
Pakistan's initial economic conditions could not have been much less favourable for supporting rapid economic growth and development. The parts of India that became Pakistan in 1947 were for the most part the outlying areas situated on the boundaries of the subcontinent. No real industries existed. The major sources of wealth were the Jute Crop in East Pakistan and Cotton in the Punjab. Agrarian relations in the Punjab were predominantly feudal, with tenant cultivators tilling the land, while land ownership resided with big landlords who exercised

complete social domination in their estates. Both the system of land tenure and the level of agricultural technology worked against productivity. Thus, the fertile plains of the Punjab could hardly produce surpluses large enough to aid in the establishment of an industrial base. In fact the main source of surplus for investment for the new state was the jute crop in the East. During the fifties the export of raw jute provided the major source of foreign exchange earnings for Pakistan. In sum Pakistan began its economic development in an environment of:

- Pre-industrial institutions
- Low productivity
- Non-existence of an established manufacturing industry
- Uneven regional development
- High population growth.[6]

Despite these limitations, several key economic developments took place (Fig. 1) during this period:

- The most notable economic accomplishment was the rapid expansion of large-scale manufacturing. Although the average growth rate of 19.1 per cent per annum must be interpreted with caution because of the very small base from which the economy started, the achievements in the manufacturing sector were impressive and laid the foundation of a consumer goods industry. However there was a significant slowing down in growth during the last three years—1955 to 1957.
- Throughout the period the dominant sector of the economy, agriculture, stagnated, and its growth was in fact even less than the growth in population, so that the per capita consumption of food grain declined and in many cases had to be supplemented through food imports.
- Because of little growth in the agricultural sector, the small share of manufacturing and the high growth rate of the population, the overall per capita income did not increase during this period.

Figure 1
Pakistan, Patterns of Growth and Collapse, 1947-1969

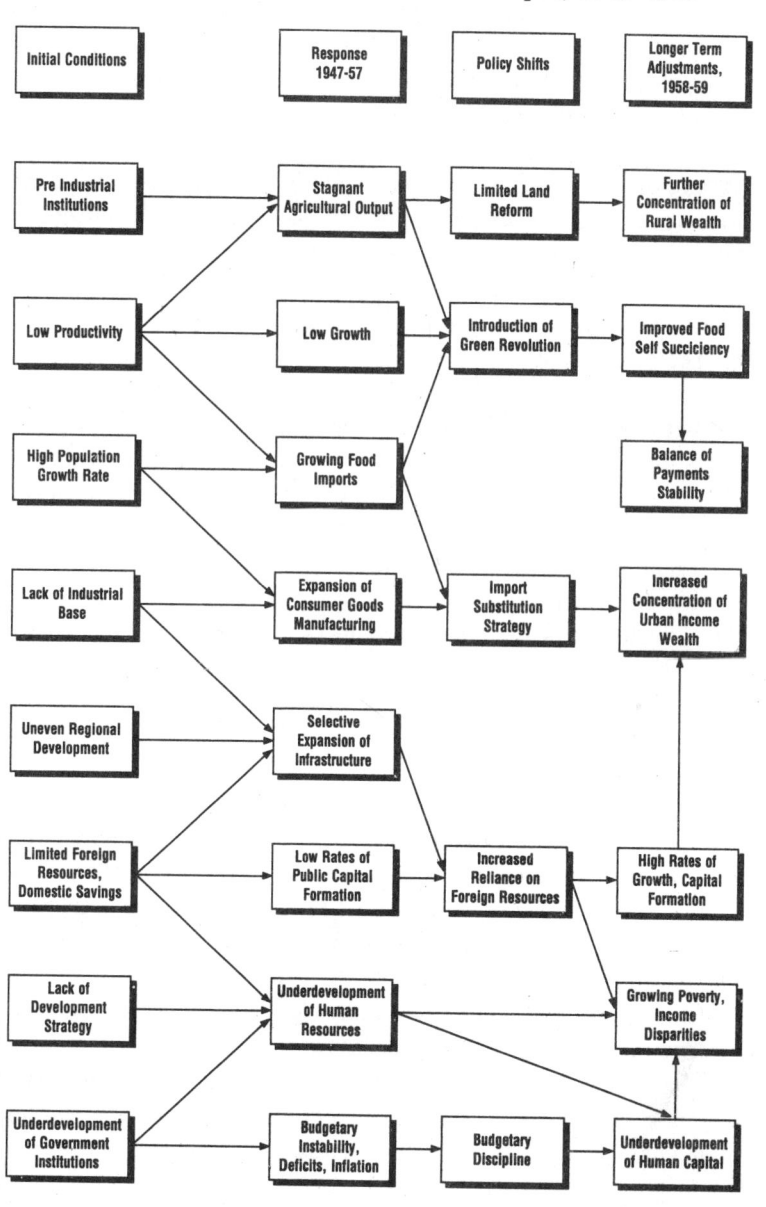

- There were, however, other important achievements which tend to be overlooked. The settlement of seven million refugees, the setting up of the administrative machinery of government, the establishment of vital economic institutions like the State Bank, and other financial institutions were all achieved with considerable success during this period.[7]

An examination of the patterns of public and private investment does reveal the initial development of what were to become several of the country's long-term development priorities:

- Investment in the industrial sector dominated the private sector investment.
- Investment in the agricultural sector was minimal compared with that in industry.
- Significant improvements were made in infrastructure development especially in the transport and communication sector. There was also substantial private sector investment in housing which was undertaken mainly by the higher income groups.
- Investment in the social sectors, i.e., education and health, were minimal and these sectors had a very low priority in the total development expenditure.[8]

Ayub Administration (1958-69)

This was a period of rapid economic growth averaging 5.4 per cent annually. Given the rate of population growth this translated into an increase of per capita incomes of 3.5 per cent. Large-scale manufacturing grew at almost 17 per cent annually. During this period, the Green Revolution provided a major stimulus to the agricultural sector.

There is considerable controversy regarding overall economic performance during this period.[9] For some, the sixties were a time of considerable economic success. Those who take this position usually point to various economic indicators to prove their case. Their usual defence is that the resulting economic problems and tensions were either exaggerated or were a 'cost' one had to bear for rapid economic development.

For others, the growth performance was exaggerated. Even worse, they argue, this period of rapid economic growth generated a great deal of economic tensions: Regional and class inequalities increased, while large segments of the population experienced falling standard of living. The concentration of incomes was particularly disturbing.[10] Twenty-two families owned 66 per cent of industry, 97 per cent of the insurance sector, and 80 per cent of banking. Only 0.1 per cent of landlords owned 500 acres or more, yet they owned 15 per cent of the country's total land.

While the matter is controversial there is no doubt these patterns contributed to the social and political unrest which, in the winter of 1968, led to the downfall of Ayub's government. On the other hand, there is general agreement that this period in the country's economic history was characterized by sound economic management. In contrast to the fifties and seventies, the economy was subject to some kind of overall economic discipline within the frameworks provide by the Second and Third Five-Year plans. There was considerable monetary discipline and budget deficits were kept at a minimum. There was overall price stability, although several years did have relatively steep increases in price. Significant steps were taken to increase exports and in the case of manufactured goods, there were substantial gains. The government machinery of economic controls over prices, imports, and industrial investment were steadily dismantled and greater use was made of market forces.

Bhutto Administration (1971-77)

The regime of Zufikar Ali Bhutto was given the mandate to eradicate the class structures that economic growth had produced. Economic growth during this period was 4.3 per cent per year. Large-scale manufacturing declined substantially growing at a rate of less than 3 per cent annually compared with growth rates that exceeded 10 per cent in the 1960s. There was a decline in per capita agricultural production. Industry and educational institutions were nationalized, the efficiency of industry declined and people became disenchanted with the economy. The main events of this period are outlined in Figure 2.

This period represents a marked shift in the country's pattern of savings and investment.

- During the fifties the level of investment had been low and its peak in 1954-5 was only around 8 per cent of Gross Domestic Product. It had, however, increased considerably over the earlier years of the fifties when it had started from a low of 4.6 per cent.
- Investment was mainly undertaken by the private sector with the public sector contributing only about 30 per cent to the total fixed investment in 1954-5.
- In the earlier years of the fifties almost all of the investment was financed by domestic savings and in 1954-5 foreign resource flows were only one per cent of GNP.
- In the Ayub years the situation changed dramatically with an almost doubling of the investment level between 1959-60 and 1964-5. Coinciding with this increase was a large inflow of foreign resources. These increased from 5.4 per cent of the GNP in 1959-60 to 8.9 per cent in 1964-5.
- Gross Domestic savings also experienced a substantial increase from 6.0 to 12.2 per cent of GNP.
- After 1964-5 the level of investment began to decline and it was 15.6 per cent in 1969-70 compared to 21.2 per cent in 1964-5. This was also associated with a substantial decline in foreign resource inflows which, by the end of the sixties, were only 3.1 per cent of the Gross National Product.
- Gross Domestic savings stagnated at the same level as in 1964-5.
- The division between public and private investment increased substantially in favour of the private sector whose share in the total investment increased from 38.8 per cent in 1959-60 to over 50 per cent in the sixties.

Figure 2
Pakistan, Transition Policies Under Z.A. Bhutto, 1972-1977

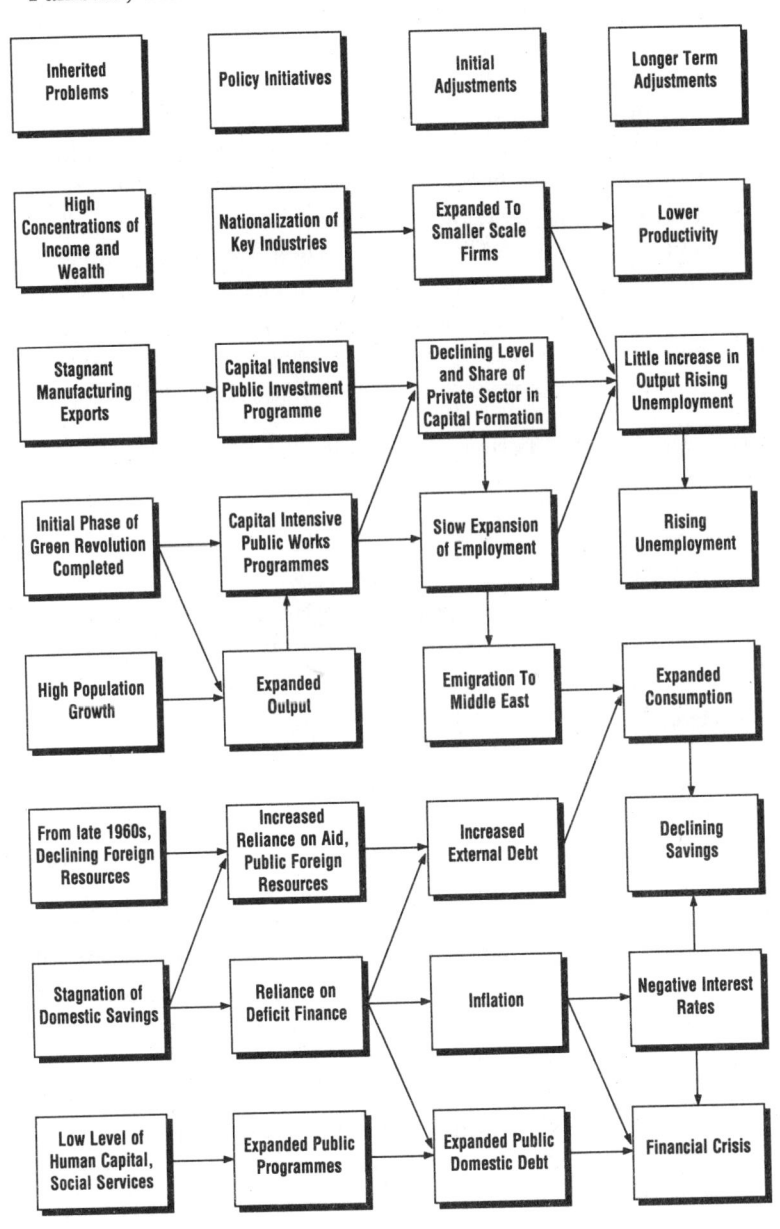

Inherited Problems	Policy Initiatives	Initial Adjustments	Longer Term Adjustments
High Concentrations of Income and Wealth	Nationalization of Key Industries	Expanded To Smaller Scale Firms	Lower Productivity
Stagnant Manufacturing Exports	Capital Intensive Public Investment Programme	Declining Level and Share of Private Sector in Capital Formation	Little Increase in Output Rising Unemployment
Initial Phase of Green Revolution Completed	Capital Intensive Public Works Programmes	Slow Expansion of Employment	Rising Unemployment
High Population Growth	Expanded Output	Emigration To Middle East	Expanded Consumption
From late 1960s, Declining Foreign Resources	Increased Reliance on Aid, Public Foreign Resources	Increased External Debt	Declining Savings
Stagnation of Domestic Savings	Reliance on Deficit Finance	Inflation	Negative Interest Rates
Low Level of Human Capital, Social Services	Expanded Public Programmes	Expanded Public Domestic Debt	Financial Crisis

- The decline in the level of gross fixed investment, which had started in the late sixties continued in the early seventies until about 1972-3 after which it began to improve. By 1976-7 it had reached 17.7 per cent of GDP.
- The increase in investment also coincided as it had done in the sixties with large increases in foreign resource inflows which were now at a higher level than they had been in the 1960s, averaging about 10 per cent of GNP.
- The important difference between the sixties and the seventies: the share of private investment in total investment declined drastically and in the seventies, public investment contributed about 70 per cent of the total. The situation was now almost the reverse of what it had been in the fifties.

Summing up this period is difficult, but several main failure patterns stand out:

- The administration's economic and social development programmes were over-ambitious with costs far exceeding the availability of domestic and foreign resources. By relying on deficit financing to meet the country's resource gap and by furthering inflation it squeezed the middle classes and they finally revolted against the regime.
- Critical to success of the government's strategy was the achievement of high growth rates of agriculture and industry to cushion the long gestation of public sector programmes. The failures of these sectors meant that there was very little growth of output from 1974-5 to 1976-7.
- The government's programmes failed to generate much employment because the bulk of investment was in capital-intensive projects. However the employment situation was considerably improved by the large-scale emigration of the industrial labour force to the Middle East.
- The government failed to establish the ideology of state capitalism which it had initiated through the process of nationalization. It failed to establish a working relationship with the big monopoly houses which refused to invest throughout the period and preferred to invest abroad.

- The government exceeded its original policy of nationalization and began to nationalize industries other than those which had originally motivated the reform. This was especially true of the smaller units in the agro-based industries.[11]

The result of the lack of private capital formation during this period was that the economy became caught in a double squeeze. High oil prices and increase in remittances from workers abroad led to inflationary pressures and with the private sector not investing, more funds were diverted towards consumption which further increased the demand pressures on the economy.

Zia Administration (1977-88)

As Burki has observed, an interesting pattern that emerges when one looks at the economy is that Pakistan has generally not been in step with the other developing economies.[12] This suggests that economic policy rather than external environment has played a much more significant role in shaping the course of development. Successive governments seldom pursued the same set of objectives and seldom emphasized the same sectors of the economy. Consequently, there were sharp fluctuations in sectoral fortunes. Light manufacturing was the sector favoured by the governments of the early 1950s, to be replaced by agriculture in the 1960s.

Although the Bhutto government was interested in increasing output, neither agriculture nor industry received sufficient attention to meet that objective. In the concluding years of the 1970s and early 1980s the government turned its attention once again to the development of the agricultural sector with a subsequent improvement in that sector's fortunes (see table 1). In general:

- Pakistan has a service sector that is relatively large given its income and an industrial sector that is underdeveloped for its stage of development.

- With regards to demand, as noted, the country's levels of savings and investment are considerably below the norm for low-income countries.
- While public consumption and exports are more or less in line with countries of similar income levels, private consumption is considerably above the average for this group.

Economic growth accelerated under Zia. The average annual GDP growth rate was 6.3 per cent during 1978-83. The manufacturing growth rate was 9 per cent, substantially above the 3.8 per cent average during 1972-8. All sectors except services and construction showed improved growth performance and from 1982-8 the economy grew at an even better pace: the GDP at an annual rate of 6.6 per cent and large-scale manufacturing at an average annual rate of 16.6 per cent. The economy clearly started to revitalize after the Bhutto government was overthrown.

Another economically and politically significant event was the flow of people to West Asia to find jobs. Approximately ten million people, 11 per cent of the total population benefited directly from this exodus. Rough estimates are that from 1975 to 1985, Pakistan received a total of $25 billion in remittances from the workers in the Middle East, a good proportion of which went to the poorer segments of the population.[13]

Another cause of the impressive growth during the Zia era was the large amount of foreign assistance coming to Pakistan in connection with the Soviet invasion of Afghanistan. Assistance from the United States after 1982 totaled around $5 billion, making Pakistan the third largest recipient of US aid in the 1980s.

Perhaps because of the acceleration in capital inflows the government did not pursue any major initiatives in promoting exports. Instead, the high level of imports was fueled largely by the fortuitous increase in remittances and foreign aid.

Table 1
Comparative Evolution of the Structure of the Pakistani Economy

	1960	1965	1980	1990	1995
Composition of Output					
Agriculture					
Pakistan	46	40	30	26	26
Low Income	49	41	34	31	25
Middle Income	24	19	15	12	11
Industry					
Pakistan	16	20	15	25	24
Low Income	26	26	35	36	38
Middle Income	30	34	40	37	35
Services					
Pakistan	38	40	44	49	50
Low Income	25	32	29	35	35
Middle Income	46	46	45	50	52
Structure of Demand					
Public Consumption					
Pakistan	11	11	11	15	12
Low Income	8	9	11	11	12
Middle Income	11	11	14	14	14
Private Consumption					
Pakistan	84	76	83	73	73
Low Income	78	74	68	61	59
Middle Income	70	67	64	62	59
Gross Domestic Investment					
Pakistan	12	21	18	19	19
Low Income	19	19	25	31	32
Middle Income	20	21	27	23	25
Gross Domestic Savings					
Pakistan	5	13	6	12	16
Low Income	18	18	22	28	30
Middle Income	19	22	25	24	25
Exports					
Pakistan	8	8	13	16	16
Low Income	7	8	9	18	19
Middle Income	17	17	25	28	24

Source: World Bank, World Development Report, various issues.

All in all, however, the eleven years of General Zia's rule represent an extraordinary missed economic opportunity (Figure 3). Just when generous levels of western aid were forthcoming, inflows of remittances from overseas Pakistani workers were also peaking. Between 1975 and 1985 Pakistan received $25 billion in remittances. Failure of the government to mobilize and direct a large share of these funds into infrastructure investment and improvements in education and health care meant that a unique set of fortuitous factors yielded to durable economic dividends. Lack of investment in the infrastructure in rapidly growing cities like Karachi sowed the seeds for crime, violence and ethnic tensions.[14]

Despite its rapid growth the economy showed an increasing number of structural weaknesses toward the end of the Zia Administration. These included: (1) heavy regulation of economic activity through price control, industrial licensing, and Government ownership; (2) a trade regime that provided a high level of protection and created distortions, thus inhibiting competitiveness and export growth; (3) a weak public resource position due to a narrow and inelastic revenue base, high consumption expenditure, particularly defence, and inadequate development expenditure, resulting in an excessive budget deficit; (4) an inefficient financial sector with mostly public ownership, directed credit, and weak commercial banks; and (5) a high and growing debt service burden resulting from the country's heavy reliance on external borrowing to finance its economic growth in the 1980s.

The main reason many of these problems did not come to a head until the late 1980s was that the real interest rates on both external and domestic debt were substantially negative during the 1970s. Mainly because of this factor, debt to GDP ratios continued to decline even though Pakistan ran substantial fiscal and current account deficits in the 1970s.[15]

However, real interest rates began turning positive during the 1980s. This development had an adverse impact on Pakistan's debt situation. Consequently, the interest burden of the domestic and external debt began increasing significantly in the 1980s into the 1990s.

Figure 3
Pakistan's Economy Under Zia (1977-1988)

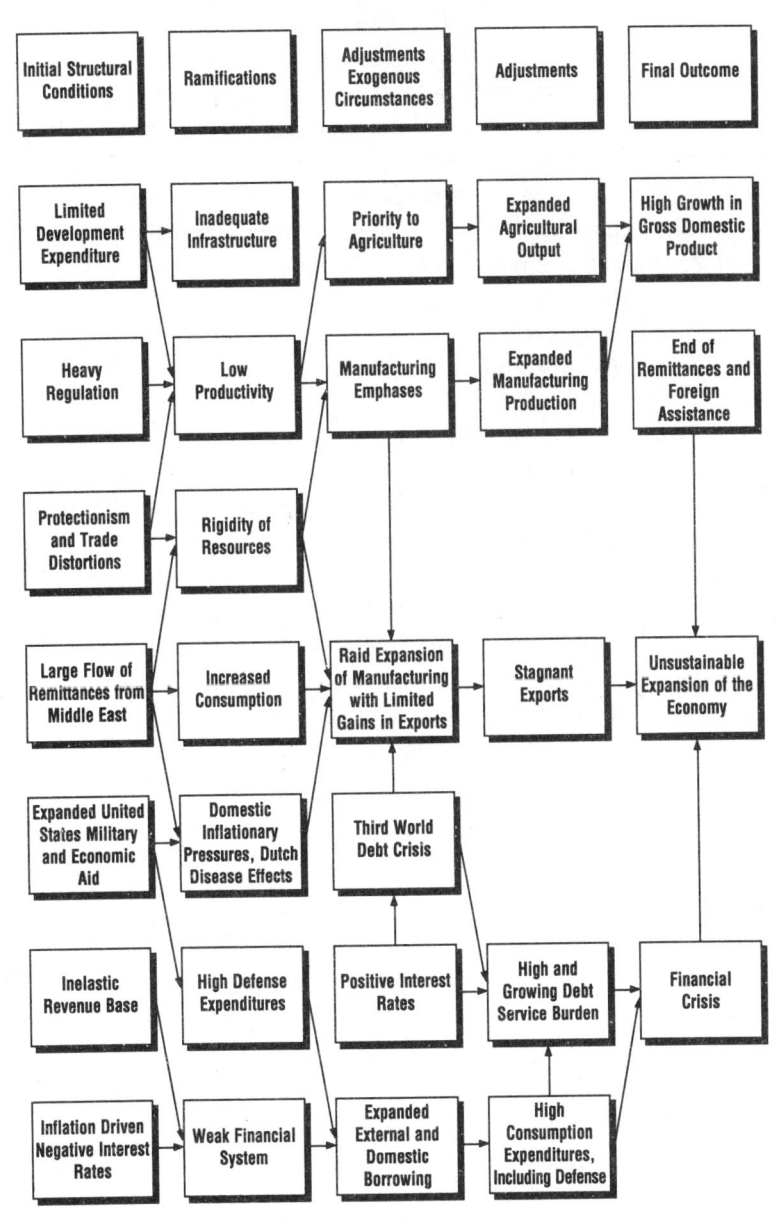

The Post-Zia Years

In this setting of runaway deficits and a resource crunch, democracy was re-born after General Zia's death in a plane crash in 1988. The return to an uncharted democracy coincided with the end of the cold war and the resultant diminution of Pakistan's strategic value in the eyes of its allies. Compounding the adjustment was the suspension in the 1990s of US military and economic aid on the grounds of Pakistan's continued pursuit of nuclear capability to match India's.[16] In a 1991 study, Khiliji and Zampelli anticipated that the termination of US assistance would significantly reduce private consumption and investment opportunities thus affecting adversely the country's standard of living and private capital formation.[17] Their forecasts have been largely borne out (Figure 4).

As an aftermath of the continuing resource scarcities that began to plague the country in the late 1980s, the government entered into agreements with the World Bank in the early 1980s and the IMF in the later part of the decade. The major emphasis of these agreements rested on the correction of prices and deregulation of trade. However latter agreements became all-inclusive as they involved structural and fiscal reform for deficit reduction, extensive trade liberalization and policy measures for reducing price distortions, deregulating production and investment for promoting efficiency of the system.[18]

Adjusting to new global realities while coping with the country's legacy of living beyond its means was not easy. For both Benazir Bhutto and Nawaz Sharif, a daunting challenge has been to deal with the political consequences of undertaking austerity.

The Benazir Bhutto Government (1988-90)

The first Benazir Bhutto government was of the democratic-distributive kind, emphasizing the socio-economic aspects of democracy. Unlike her father's policies of nationalization and public sector expansion, Benazir attempted to bring the private sector to the forefront of economy in Pakistan.[19] The economy, however, proved difficult to stimulate. The Bhutto Administration

Figure 4
Pakistan's Economy Under Zia (1977-1988)

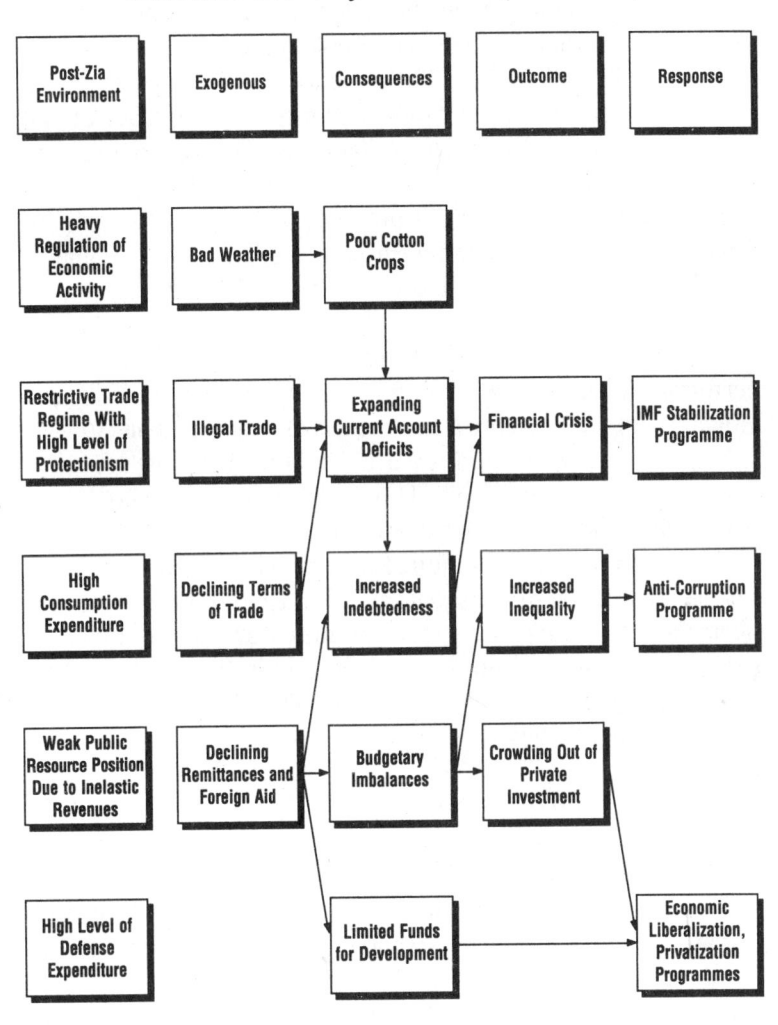

inherited a deal negotiated by the Zia regime in accordance with economy-restricting guidelines under which Pakistan received $1.169 billion from the IMF and World Bank.

Toward the end of the 1988 financial year, the deteriorating resources position caused a financial crisis. The budget deficit reached 8.5 per cent of GDP, inflation accelerated, the current account deficit doubled to 4.3 per cent of GNP, the external debt service ratio reached 28 per cent of export earnings, and foreign exchange reserves fell in half to $438 million, equal to less than three weeks of imports.

The economy's performance during this period was largely constrained by the crisis it had inherited. The macro-economic performance during 1989-90 was slow and uneven. In 1989, the Government implemented the measures envisaged mostly on schedule and achieved improvements in a number of macroeconomic indicators. However, exogenous shocks, in particular floods and a deterioration in the country's terms of trade took their toll and required an extension of the target date for the completion of the programme. In 1990, serious slippages occurred in implementing reform measures in the financial sector, in containing liquidity growth, and in fiscal policy. As a result, the reform programme was substantially off-track at the end of the second year.

Nawaz Sharif Administration (1990-93)
The Sharif administration's primary interest was in the economy. However, growth declined somewhat from the Zia years, averaging at 4.9 per cent during the 1990-1994 period. Privatization and increased exports were the primary focus of the government with a fairly dramatic shift in output towards the export sector. Under this administration numerous measures were enacted to expedite the pace of growth through privatization. Sharif privatized some government institutions by providing incentives to foreign investment. His reforms opened several industries to private enterprise and his government offered liberal tax and tariff incentives to new industries.[20] It also liberalized foreign exchange, opened export trade to foreign

firms, and returned almost all industrial units and financial institutions to the private sector.[21]

In large part, the economy slowed down because foreign channels of funding had gradually dried up. Foreign aid dwindled in the post-cold war era and remittances from expatriate Pakistanis fell as the Gulf boom of the 1970s and eighties came to an end. Unfortunately, private foreign direct investment has not picked up the slack. The strategy of Sharif's government has been to offset this reality with the potential for economic stimulus, often linked to the increased economic freedom associated with his reform programme.

Clearly, this approach is consistent with the growing literature stressing the association between economic freedom and economic performance. For example in *Economic Freedom of the World, 1975-1995* Gwartney, Lawson, and Block show a strong direct connection between economic freedom and economic well-being.[22] From the standpoint of basic economic theory, this result is entirely understandable: restrictions on economic freedom cause inefficiency and result in sub-optimal levels of utility, personal income and the like.

A short, reasonably accurate definition of economic freedom is that it exists when persons and their rightfully-owned property (that is 'thing' acquired without the use of force, fraud, or theft) are protected from assault by others. An individual's private ownership right includes the right to trade or give rightfully acquired property to another. It is asserted throughout by Gwartney *et al.* that protection from invasion by others and freedom of exchange are the cornerstone of economic freedom. Economic freedom can thus be distinguished from political freedom which focuses on political and civil liberties.

For our purposes, the main issues are: What gains have been made to date and in what areas? How has progress in the country compared to that attained in other parts of the world? What are the implications for the country's future growth?[23]

In the Gwartney study, 102 countries were rated on each of the main areas of economic freedom on a scale of 0-10, in which zero means that a country is completely unfree and ten means it is completely free. Such scores were given for 1974, 1980, 1985, 1990 and 1993-5 (depending on the latest figures available).

Having obtained such ratings, however, a major problem remains in the construction of some sort of aggregate summary index. Do all of the measures matter equally? Any method is inherently arbitrary. The authors used three methods: (1) with each component having an equal impact (Ie); (2) with weights determined by a survey (Is1) of 'knowledgeable people', defined as economists familiar with the problem; and (3) with weights derived from a survey (Is2) of experts on specific countries.

While Gwartney *et al.* feel (2) above is the best measure, one can easily make the case that a more objective measure might provide additional, if not necessary superior insights. The factor analysis developed below is one such measures. Using the three summary measures, together with the four broad components of economic freedom one can trace Pakistan's progress in recent years (Table 2).

Pakistan's summary economic freedom rating (Is1) improved from a very low 2.3 in 1975 to 5.4 in 1993-5. Most of the improvement came in the 1990s. In terms of the ranking, Pakistan moved from 93rd in 1975 to 50th in the mid-1990s. The improvement in the country's economic freedom rating can be attributed to a few components in the index. First, top marginal tax rates have been reduced from 61 per cent in 1975 (and 60 per cent in 1985) to the current 38 per cent. A significant liberalization of the exchange-rate system has reduced the black market exchange rate premium from a high of 27 per cent in 1980 to zero (and a rating of 10) in 1993-94. Some of the increase in the summary rating for 1993-95 may reflect the fact that the Taxes on International Trade (Iva) datum was not available for Pakistan in that year. In all the previous periods, this component received a zero rating. Its absence in the most recent period may have artificially inflated the summary rating slightly.

Table 2
Pakistan: Economic Freedom Ratings, Components and Summary Indexes

Components of Economic Freedom	1975	1980	1985	1990	1993-5
Money and Inflation	**1.9**	**3.6**	**4.8**	**6.1**	**5.8**
1. Annual Money Growth (last 5 years)	4	2	7	5	5
2. Inflation Variability (last 5 years)	2	9	8	8	7
3. Ownership of Foreign Currency	0	0	0	10	10
4. Maint. of Bank Account Abroad	0	0	0	0	0
Government Operations	**4.9**	**5.2**	**5.2**	**4.8**	**4.6**
1. Government Consumption (%GDP)	8	8	7	5	7
2. Government Enterprises	2	2	2	4	4
3. Price Controls	–	–	–	–	4
4. Entry into Business	–	–	–	–	5
5. Legal System	–	–	–	–	0
6. Avoidance of Neg. Interest Rates	–	6	8	6	8
Taking	**0.8**	**3.8**	**3.0**	**4.5**	**6.1**
Transfers and Subsidies (%GDP)	.	.	.	.	.
Marginal Tax Rates (Top Rate)	1	2	1	3	5
Conscription	0	10	10	10	10
International Sector	**2.3**	**2.0**	**3.0**	**2.3**	**6.1**
Taxes on International Trade (Avg.)	0	0	0	0	.
Black Market Exchange Rates (Prem.)	4	3	6	4	10
Size of Trade Sector (%GDP)	4	4	5	4	6
Capital Transactions with Foreigners	2	2	2	2	2
Summary Ratings					
Ie	2.4	3.6	4.2	4.5	5.3
Is1	2.3	3.5	3.9	4.2	5.4
Is2	1.9	3.2	4	4.3	5.0

Source: Gwartney, 1996, p. 186.

Summing up, it is clear there has been a slight move toward economic liberalization in Pakistan over the last two decades. This improvement has allowed Pakistan to report modest, if unremarkable, annual growth of per capita GDP of approximately 2.5 per cent. For Pakistan to make the move into the modern market economy like Malaysia, Thailand, and Singapore, it must improve its regulatory environment that restricts citizens from holding bank accounts abroad, restricts prices and market entry, fails to treat equally before the law, and interferes with the capital transactions with foreigners.

As noted above, this theory suggests that a sustained increase in economic freedom will enhance growth, while a decline will retard it. Thus one would expect countries with an expanding amount of economic freedom to have high growth rates than those with a contracting amount of freedom. However, as Gwartney and associates stress, the immediate impact of a change in economic freedom is likely to be small.[24] The reason is simple, there will be a large gap between the time when institutional arrangements and policies become more consistent with economic freedom and when they begin to exert their primary impact on economic growth. Clearly, however, through economic reform, the government is laying the foundation for the restoration of strong economic expansion.

Benazir Bhutto (1993-97)
Benazir Bhutto's second administration took office in October 1993. That government continued and reinforced the country's economic reform programme. The second Bhutto administration has been widely criticized for mismanagement of the economy.[25] Until her last week in office, she refused to name a finance minister, keeping the crucial powers of the purse for herself and her husband. She relied on an economic aide whose economic data proved so unreliable that, just before Ms Bhutto fell, the International Monetary Fund threatened to walk out of emergency loan talks with Pakistan unless he was replaced. Without a credible economic team, Ms Bhutto ran up huge budget deficits, inflation soared, and the IMF halted its loans to

the country. There was general fear that the economy was collapsing.

In the weeks before Ms Bhutto's ouster, Pakistan's foreign exchange reserves fell to just $600 million, or less than the cost of three weeks' imports. At the same time, the country was facing debt repayments of some $900 million in the latter part of 1996, a burden it couldn't possibly bear without fresh loans from foreign banks.

Nawaz Sharif (1997-99)
At the time Nawaz Sharif assumed power for the second time, Pakistan's economy had seldom before faced such a gloomy outlook. At the start of the new financial year in July, many analysts were forecasting that the country would for the first time default on its $39 billion foreign debt (largely due in December). Unexpected help from the IMF has averted that crisis, but the need for expanding and accelerating the reform programme remains urgent:[26]

- Servicing the burden of foreign and domestic debt during the current financial year (1997-8) is expected to absorb more than 40 per cent of budgetary expenditure, the largest proportion ever devoted to debt servicing.
- An increasingly heavy debt burden has hardly been helped by meager economic growth. For the year ending in June 1996, the economy grew by only 3.1 per cent. In a country where annual population growth is at least 3 per cent, that effectively amounts to a standstill.
- Other economic indicators were also bad. Large-scale manufacturing contracted for the first time in over fifty years, while agriculture, which is the backbone of the economy and responsible for almost a quarter of GDP, grew only 0.7 per cent.
- Pakistan's worsening international trade performance is among the most visible symbols of its economic malaise. The trade deficit for the year that ended in June hit a record high of $3.37 billion, up from $3.1 billion the previous year.

Yet the government has slashed personal taxes from a range of 10 to 35 per cent to one of 5 to 20 per cent and announced reductions of between 3 and 8 per cent in corporate tax rates. The measures have been accompanied by cuts in imports tariffs of up to 20 per cent lowering the top rate to 45 per cent. The cuts are part of Nawaz Sharif's strategy to encourage more people to pay taxes. Inadequate systems of collection and inspection mean that currently only one million Pakistanis— less than one per cent of the 130 million population are tax payers.

Many businessmen have acclaimed the tax cuts on the grounds that they will help to improve Pakistan's investment climate and restore a battered confidence in the country. Mr Sharif's reforms are beginning to pay off with help from the IMF, which is in the process of considering a request for $1.6 billion medium-term loan due for disbursement over the next three years.

Pakistan desperately needs the Fund's support to overcome its short-term debt repayment crunch. With foreign banks taking the lead from an IMF programme and offering new credits in Pakistan, Mr Sharif would then be able to survive the tough year head. Sharif hopes to use such a window of opportunity to launch some of the biggest economic changes ever undertaken in Pakistan, including large-scale reform and privatization of the public sector. In addition, exporters have also been offered a number of incentives. This is a high-risk strategy that will most likely encounter a number of difficulties, most notably the risk that government revenues will fall short of expectations in spite of the tax breaks. The IMF has been promised a budget deficit of 5 per cent of GDP this year, down 6.1 per cent from last year. But many argue that large scale tax evasion is a deep rooted cultural problem in Pakistan and it is unrealisitc to expect an end to this phenomenon.[27]

On the other hand, the country's recent tax reforms may help to reduce the size of the underground or 'black economy' hence improving tax collection. In Pakistan's case the black economy consists of:

- The Illegal Economy: This consists of economic activities which are anti-social in nature. Here the most common type of underground activity is drug trafficking.
- The Unreported Economy: The unreported economy comprises those activities that circumvent or evade the payment of taxes. It includes income which should be reported to the authorities but is not.
- The Unrecorded Economy: This area includes those activities which are concerned with the problems relating to the rules and regulations of the reporting requirements of statistical agencies. It includes that income which should be recorded in the national accounts but is not included.
- The Informal Economy: This comprises those activities that entail a cost but are excluded from the benefits and rights of the formal activities. They are illegal but not anti-social.[28]

Ahmed's findings suggest that the share of the black economy was high during the sixties and eighties which can be attributed to high taxes and regulations imposed by the government. In the late eighties the black economy had started to fall mainly because of the lowering of direct taxes (personal income tax and the corporate tax) levied. However, the black economy still stands at about one-third of the GDP. Ahmed estimates that the revenue loss due to the presence of the black economy was between Rs40 to Rs45 billion in 1989-90. The implication is that substantial revenue gains can be realized by reducing the extent of tax evasion in the economy.

The illicit flow of consumer goods across Pakistan's leaky borders—chiefly from Afghanistan, has already ruined some domestic manufacturing industries. Industrialists say smuggling is a strong contributor to Pakistan's poor recent economic performance. Foreign direct investment in 1996, for instance, fell to $540 million from $1.1 billion a year earlier, while manufacturing output contracted by 1.4 per cent for the first time in the country's fifty-year history.[29]

Summary

Summing up, the country's growth experience suggests some important macro-economic patterns and relationships that will be instrumental in affecting the country's future economic health:

- Highest growth (averaging 6.72 per cent per annum) occurred during the 1980s. This was also the period of highest annual savings and the smallest resource gap (difference between savings and investment).
- Also during this period, Net Factor Payments, consisting largely of remittances, were by far their highest. This influx of funds allowed the country to have the highest ratio of imports to production (Gross Domestic Product) in its history.
- The lowest growth (averaging 3.69 per cent per annum) occurred during the 1970s. During this period, investment's share of GDP reached a low of 16.4 per cent, with savings only slightly above the low period of the 1960s.
- In terms of trends, savings have gradually increased over time from a low of 12.69 per cent of GDP to 17.17 per cent in the 1980s, only to decline slightly to 17.18 per cent in the 1990s.
- Disregarding its decline in the 1970s, investment has also shown improvement over time, increasing from 16.83 per cent in the 1960s to 19.49 per cent in the 1990s. It should be noted however that both figures are very low by international standards, with the average saving and investment rates averaging in the mid-twenties for low-income countries and in the twenties for the South-East Asian Tigers.
- The country has gradually become integrated into the world economy as evidenced by exports nearly doubling their share of GDP (from 8.69 per cent in the 1960s to 16.31 per cent in the 1990s). Imports have shown a similar steady increase over time averaging 12.9 per cent in the 1960s and 19.98 per cent in the 1990s.

As noted above, the different economic priorities and policies of various administrations (Table 3) have no doubt modified this pattern of economic performance (Table 4):

- The Bhutto regime of the 1970s experienced the lowest savings and investment rates, with the average rate of growth of 4.3 per cent per annum only slightly above that of the 1960s.
- On the surface, economic performance was by far the best during the Zia regime, averaging over six and one-half per cent. However, a closer examination shows that this period was not characterized by a significant improvement in exports. Instead, the high level of imports was fueled largely by the fortuitous increase in remittances.
- The composition of consumption is consistent with this assessment. During the Zia administration, consumption was at an all time high, increasing to slightly over 90 per cent of GDP. Despite a period of relative peace with India, defence expenditures also reached a high of 6.75 per cent of GDP during the Zia years, with government expenditures increasing (19.54 per cent of GDP vs. 16.73 per cent) over that of the previous socialist regime.
- The figures on the composition of consumption also suggest that whatever gains the country had made in increasing savings had come about through the fall in private consumption. Public consumption actually increased over time (from 9.59 per cent of GDP during the Ayub years to nearly 14 per cent in the post-Zia period). Correspondingly, private consumption had fallen from slightly over 78 per cent during Ayub's regime to 71 per cent in the post-Zia era.
- A more ominous trend is the general tendency for increased government expenditures to outrun revenue collection. Expenditures increased from 15.56 per cent of GDP during the Ayub regime to 23.87 per cent in the post-Zia period. Correspondingly, revenues increased at a slower pace (from 12.69 per cent to 18.367 per cent), resulting in expanding the deficit from 2.87 per cent to 5.51 per cent.

Table 3
Economic Performance Since Independence: Summary

Government	Strength	Weakness	Distinguishing Aspects
Pre-Ayub (1947-57)	Rapid Expansion Large-Scale Manufacturing	Agricultural Stagnation	Neglect of Social Sectors
Ayub (1958-69)	Budgetary Stability	Limited Social Progress	Inward-Oriented High Growth
Z. Bhutto (1971-77)	Equity Concerns	Economic Decline Low Saving Rates	Nationalizations Private Sector Insecurity
Zia (1977-88)	High Growth	Limited Reforms Unsustainable Policies	High Remittances/ Foreign Assistance
B. Bhutto (1988-90)	Attempt at Stabilization	Sluggish Growth	Democratic Distribution
Sharif (1990-93)	Privatization	Budget Stabilization	Economic Liberalization
B. Bhutto (1993-97)	Continuation of Reforms	Budget Stabilization	Economic Mismanagement

- Unfortunately, constant data on the composition of savings was not developed until the early 1970s. Still, the observed patterns reinforce those noted earlier. In particular, whatever success the country has had in increasing savings must be attributed exclusively to the private sector. Savings from this source increased from 8.64 per cent during the Bhutto regime of the seventies to 12.79 per cent under Zia and up to 13.72 per cent in the post-Zia period. The corresponding figures for the public sector are 0.41, 1.80 and -0.25 per cent.
- It is interesting to note that public investment has not changed much over time, increasing from 9.05 per cent of GDP during Zulfikar Ali Bhutto's regime to 9.85 per cent

Table 4
Pakistan: Macro-economic Patterns by Administration, 1960–95

Year	GDP	Savings	Invest	Gap	Exports	Imports	NFP	CurrAcc	Defen	Fiscal Bal
1960		9.17	16.32	-7.15	8.74	13.11	0.13		4.36	-3.98
1961	0.00	12.22	16.18	-3.96	8.65	12.28	0.17		4.15	-4.26
1962	6.03	11.67	16.32	-4.65	9.91	13.85	0.32		3.73	-4.81
1963	7.68	12.09	19.12	-7.03	9.24	15.04	0.44		3.80	-2.69
1964	5.26	11.93	19.03	-7.10	9.05	17.04	0.40		3.99	-1.59
1965	3.66	14.75	16.98	-2.22	8.81	12.03	2.47		6.19	-1.86
1966	7.26	15.44	16.41	-0.97	8.26	13.14	2.95		6.84	-5.58
1967	-4.34	13.65	16.08	-2.44	8.75	11.17	0.25		5.58	-1.47
1968	5.07	13.06	16.11	-3.05	7.88	10.96	0.02		5.22	-1.80
1969	5.39	12.93	15.80	-2.87	7.62	10.35	0.13		5.42	-0.68
Ayub	4.00	12.69	16.83	-4.14	8.69	12.90	0.49		4.93	-2.87
1970	2.47	13.06	15.80	-2.74	7.62	10.35	0.00	-7.03	6.23	0.22
1971	0.76	13.02	15.64	-2.62	7.76	10.54	0.16	-5.63	6.86	-1.28
1972	0.56	12.88	14.17	-1.30	7.25	8.75	0.18	-3.06	7.55	-3.20
1973	6.61	14.16	12.93	1.23	14.89	14.36	0.69	-1.96	7.02	-4.29
1974	5.72	10.35	13.37	-3.02	13.77	17.50	0.71	-6.23	6.83	-3.14
1975	4.52	9.29	16.23	-6.93	11.57	20.50	1.02	-10.36	6.69	-4.69
1976	4.67	14.83	18.22	-3.39	10.51	18.06	2.26	-7.09	6.14	-3.52
1977	3.74	14.42	19.27	-4.85	9.34	17.86	3.66	-7.01	6.04	-2.75
Bhutto	4.30	12.65	15.70	-3.05	11.22	16.17	1.42	-5.95	6.71	-3.60
1978	7.85	15.74	17.86	-2.12	9.43	18.48	6.88	-3.37	5.82	-3.19
1979	4.91	14.71	17.88	-3.16	11.03	21.80	7.45	-5.65	6.20	-3.45
1980	8.58	15.80	18.48	-2.68	12.57	23.27	7.79	-4.80	6.22	-1.27
1981	7.00	17.43	18.76	-1.33	12.84	22.33	8.16	-3.65	6.37	-2.89
1982	6.52	15.36	19.45	-4.09	10.28	21.33	7.89	-5.00	7.05	-1.55
1983	6.77	19.28	18.79	0.49	12.18	22.51	10.81	-1.78	7.39	-3.52
1984	5.15	17.14	18.27	-1.13	11.40	21.97	9.43	-3.20	7.31	-2.76
1985	7.55	14.41	18.32	-3.91	10.57	22.60	8.11	-5.41	6.76	-3.66
1986	5.51	18.99	18.76	0.23	12.29	20.11	8.04	-3.92	6.92	-3.24
1987	6.47	20.21	19.13	1.08	13.81	19.09	6.35	-2.18	7.21	-3.04
1988	7.61	16.75	18.01	-1.26	13.86	19.43	4.31	-4.37	6.96	-5.67
Zia	6.72	16.89	18.52	-1.63	11.84	21.17	7.75	-3.94	6.75	-3.11
1989	4.99	16.28	18.93	-2.65	14.07	20.35	3.64	-4.18	6.64	-6.25
1990	4.41	17.79	18.93	-1.14	14.79	20.24	4.31	-4.73	6.86	-3.30
1991	5.46	19.73	18.96	0.78	16.93	18.49	2.34	-4.76	6.33	-6.54
1992	7.83	18.03	20.15	-2.12	17.27	20.42	1.04	-2.75	6.26	-6.42
1993	1.91	15.35	20.70	-5.35	16.20	22.30	0.74	-7.12	6.52	-6.54
1994	3.77	16.50	19.52	-3.02	16.25	19.00	0.26	-3.78	6.00	-5.72
1995	4.48	16.55	18.71	-2.15	16.41	19.40	0.81		5.46	-3.81
Post Zia	4.69	17.18	19.41	-2.24	15.99	20.03	1.88	-4.66	6.29	-5.51

Compiled from International Monetary Fund, International Financial Statistics, All non-GDP variables defined as shares of GDP.

under Zia, falling to 8.62 per cent in the post-Zia regimes. Contrary to popular opinion, private investment as a share of GDP was slightly higher under Bhutto (7.56 per cent) than under Zia (7.51 per cent). This index increased fairly dramatically to 9.26 per cent during the post-Zia years.
- As noted, aid and remittances have fallen off considerably in recent years. Remittances reached a high of 45 per cent of gross domestic investment under Zia. In the post-Zia years this figure has averaged only 21.44 per cent.
- Increased current account deficits in an environment of falling aid and remittances have resulted in a fairly dramatic expansion in the country's external debt. Already fairly high by low and middle income country standards, Pakistan's external debt servicing as a share of exports increased from 18.3 per cent in 1980 to 22.8 per cent in 1990 and 35.3 per cent by 1995. The corresponding figures for low income countries were 9.6, 20.1, and 15.4 per cent.

Empirical Relationships

Several studies have attempted to quantify these relationships and in particular those factors that have contributed to the country's pattern of expansion (Figure 5).

Source of Growth
With regards to the sources of growth:

1. Physical capital accumulation played a very important role in Pakistan's growth performance—overall and in the manufacturing sector. The fixed investment rate grew steadily during the 1970s and then stabilized at around 17 per cent of GDP in the mid-1980s. This allowed the capital stock, economy-wide and in the manufacturing sector, to expand fairly rapidly which in turn supported a substantial increase in the capital labour ratios and labour productivity.

2. Accumulation of labour also played a significant role in overall economic growth, although the statistical significance of labour in explaining growth in the manufacturing sector came out as rather low. The relatively weaker statistical significance of the labour coefficient, especially in the manufacturing growth equation, reflects the growing capital intensity of production. But it is also an indication that population growth may be too rapid, particularly with Pakistan's very low skills level. The increase in capital intensity could be the effect of two forces at work. First, Pakistan's macro-economic policies have generally favoured greater capital intensity of production, resulting from under-priced capital imports due to overvalued exchange rate (well into the mid-1980s), low interest rates and other incentives. Second, external migration of skilled and semi-skilled labour in the 1970s and early 1980s that tended to raise real wages.
3. Greater trade liberalization, as measured by the increase in the ratio of total value of exports and imports to GDP had a strong positive impact on Pakistan's growth performance. Again, however, that statistical significance of trade policy surprisingly was reduced in the case of the manufacturing sector. Nevertheless, the strong positive role of greater trade openness suggests that Pakistan needs to continue with further trade reforms to enhance competition and economic efficiency.
4. The structural change variable included capturing the impact of the change in the policy regime in Pakistan from the interventionist policy regime of the 1972-78 period to the market-oriented economy since 1978, camp up with a significant coefficient in the case of both aggregate and manufacturing sector growth equation. This result is explained by the major improvement in efficiency resulting from the reduction in controls and bureaucratic interventions. Estimates of total factor productivity (TFP) confirm this finding as well—TFP change was negative in first period as compared with the positive contribution of TFP change to

growth in the later period. Once again, this reinforces the importance of further progress with economic liberalization.[30]

Unfortunately, as noted above, savings and investment rates in Pakistan are unusually low, averaging annually 14.8 per cent and 19.6 per cent of Gross National Product during the five years 1995-96.[31] At these low rates of savings and investment, it would not be possible to support future economic growth of 7 per cent a year. Seven per cent growth is socially necessary, in view of the country's neglected infrastructure system and low levels of investment in social sectors. Efforts to maintain a high rate of growth without mobilizing more national savings would result in a rapid accumulation of non-concessional external debt with serious consequences for the balance of payments position of the country in the not too distant future.

Various reasons have been put forward to explain Pakistan's poor savings performance. These include the existence of a large, unorganized underground or 'black' economy whose savings are not captured in official statistics; a feudal outlook characterized by wasteful expenditure; conspicuous consumption and ostentatious living; a development strategy which has emphasized the production of consumer goods; rates of inflation higher than the rate of return on savings; a high population growth rate with a resulting high dependency ratio; the low level of per capita income; and deficiencies in the methods used to prepare official statistics of savings.[32]

The most frequently cited reason, however, is culturally induced bias in favour of consumption.[33] But while such a bias would affect the propensity to save, it cannot by itself explain all aspects of Pakistan's savings performance and by constantly citing this factor, the importance of other determinants tends to be either disregarded or discouraged. Empirical evidence has shown that inadequate returns on financial savings and unequal and inefficient distribution of credit have exercised an inhibiting impact on the process of savings and investment. Admittedly the real rate of return is not the only determinant of savings, but the evidence suggests that it is a far more important factor than often acknowledged by policy makers.[34]

The savings/investment relationships are clearly the crucial factors affecting the country's economic destiny at this point in time.

Macroeconomic Linkages
Because of the importance of defence expenditures in the government's budget, any discussion of macroeconomic patterns and linkages would be incomplete without the explicit introduction of this variable.[35] Here the main linkages between defence expenditures and economic activity are assumed to be both direct (as with Keynesian demand creation) and indirect (through possible deficit-induced crowding out of private activity and/or diversion of private savings to the public sector. Concerning the more important individual equations:[36]

- **Gross Domestic Product** is affected mainly by expansion in the private and public stocks of capital, employment and military expenditures. Here it should be noted that the links between GDP and non-defence expenditures were not statistically significant.
- **Employment** increases with an expanded population together with increments to the stock of public infrastructure.
- **Defence** expenditures expand in line with the general size of the economy. However, allocations to the military compete with infrastructure for funding. In addition, expanded levels of foreign borrowing in the previous year constrain allocations to the military. The same is also true for increased levels of indebtedness to the international institutions.
- **Non-defence public expenditures** also expanded in line with GDP. However, allocations to this category were reduced by short run increases in the defence budget.
- **Gross National Savings** expand with the general growth of the economy. However, these funds are pre-empted

(or crowded out) by the current fiscal deficit, as well as the deficit in the previous year.
* **Private investment in large-scale manufacturing** followed a lag adjustment pattern whereby investment in any one year was undertaken to bridge the gap between investor's optimal and actual capital stocks. The optimal level of private investment was in turn influenced by defence expenditures and ability to attract foreign funding. Again, however, this category of private investment was crowded out by the fiscal deficit.
* **Private investment in non-manufacturing activities** expanded with the total size of the economy and availability of savings. In contrast to investment in manufacturing however, this type of investment was discouraged by expanded defence expenditures.
* **Government credit** from the monetary system was also related to past deficits and short run movements in defence expenditures.
* **Inflation** is largely a function of expanded credit to the public sector, together with movements in the international price level.
* **Public borrowing in the domestic markets** was largely a function of the fiscal deficit. However, the authorities' ability to borrow internationally reduced some of the pressures on the domestic capital markets.
* **Public borrowing in the foreign capital markets** was also largely a function of the fiscal deficit. Again, however, increase in defence expenditures *ceteris paribus* reduced the amount of funding from this source.

In summary, the model captures the fundamental dilemma facing Pakistani policy-makers. Looked at in isolation, defence expenditures have tended to positively influence the economy. However, if these expenditures are funded with increased level of deficit financing, the subsequent crowding out of private investment may actually result not only in increased inflation, but, more importantly, in a net negative impact on the economy.

The inability of non-defence expenditures other than infrastructure to impact positively on the economy has only compounded this dilemma. In any case, the concern of external creditors over the country's high defence burden will in all likelihood increasingly constrain allocations to the military.

Prospects for the Future

Realistically Pakistan's fiscal options for the foreseeable future are likely to be narrowly constrained by the International Monetary Fund (IMF), with the most recent package, anticipated at around $1.6 billion, to be approved before the end of October 1977.[37] It should, however, be noted that the past record of IMF programmes in the country has not been good, with bad feelings occurring on both sides.[38] During the past decade Pakistan has entered into six IMF programmes, but each was aborted mid-term when the country failed to meet its key conditions. Part of the problem has been widespread tax evasion which has led revenues to trail behind collection targets, with the budget deficit staying above estimates.[39] Clearly, to restore a stable growth path, the country will have to chart out medium-term objectives that are realistic and consistent.

Policy Constraints and Objectives

As a starting point, the macroeconomic relationships outlined above were used to assess the extent to which the following set of objectives are attainable over the period to the year 2000 and under what conditions. These include:

1. A stable rate of GDP growth of between 6.0 per cent and 7.0 per cent per annum—this is in line with the average rate of growth since 1976.
2. Employment growth of 2.8 per cent to 3.1 per cent—around the rate of growth of population and consistent with past rates of job creation.
3. Inflation, 5 per cent or lower—somewhat below the historical range of 7-8 per cent.

Figure 5
Pakistan: Source of Growth and Constraint

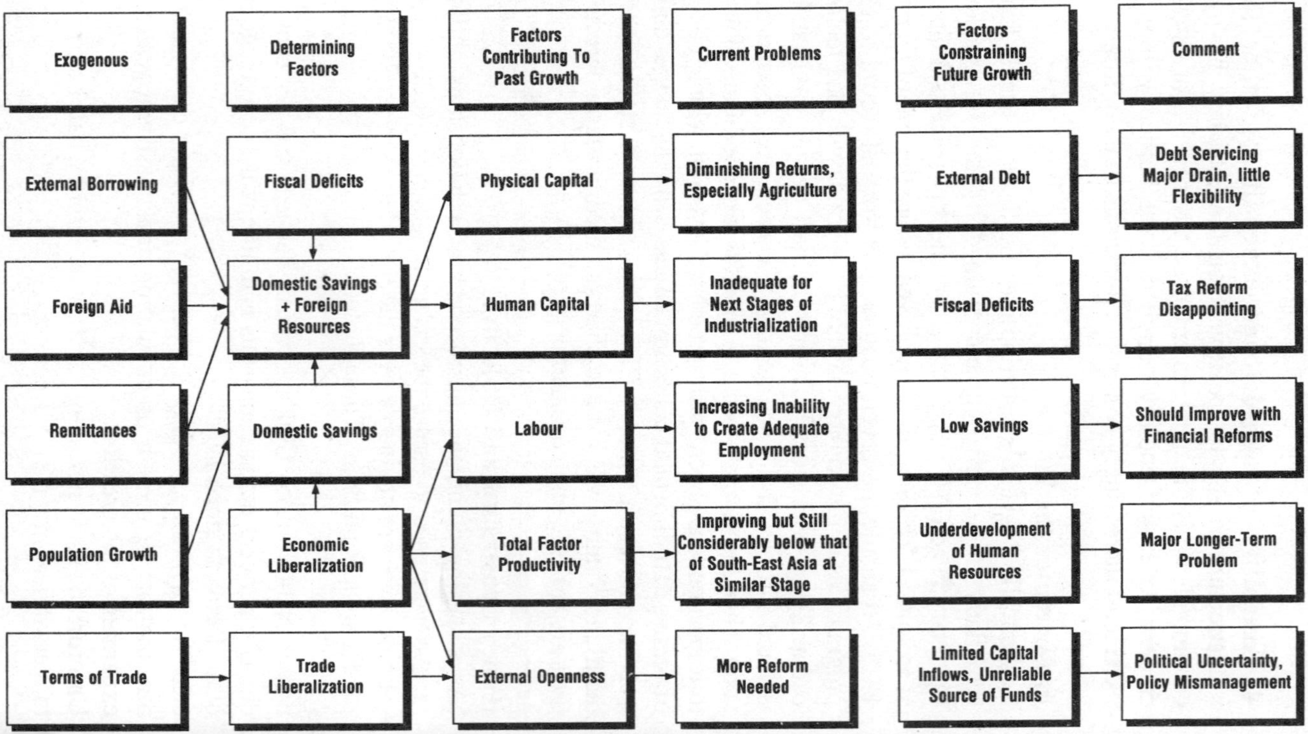

Exogenous	Determining Factors	Factors Contributing To Past Growth	Current Problems	Factors Constraining Future Growth	Comment
External Borrowing	Fiscal Deficits	Physical Capital	Diminishing Returns, Especially Agriculture	External Debt	Debt Servicing Major Drain, little Flexibility
Foreign Aid	Domestic Savings + Foreign Resources	Human Capital	Inadequate for Next Stages of Industrialization	Fiscal Deficits	Tax Reform Disappointing
Remittances	Domestic Savings	Labour	Increasing Inability to Create Adequate Employment	Low Savings	Should Improve with Financial Reforms
Population Growth	Economic Liberalization	Total Factor Productivity	Improving but Still Considerably below that of South-East Asia at Similar Stage	Underdevelopment of Human Resources	Major Longer-Term Problem
Terms of Trade	Trade Liberalization	External Openness	More Reform Needed	Limited Capital Inflows, Unreliable Source of Funds	Political Uncertainty, Policy Mismanagement

4. Foreign borrowing to expand at a rate slower than the general expansion in economic activity; this is, around 5 per cent or less.
5. Defence expenditure to decline to around 4-5 per cent of GDP—down from the 6-7 per cent range in the late 1980s and early 1990s.
6. Government deficits to fall to 3-4 per cent of GDP-down from the 6 per cent figure reached in the early 1990s.
7. A general expansion in the share of savings in GDP up toward the range of 18-20 per cent—typical values for countries at Pakistan's stage of development.
8. An expanded share of private investment in GDP.

Policy Simulations

Using a policy oriented macroeconomic model of the economy, several policy packages were examined in terms of their ability to improve the country's economic fortunes. The main findings of these simulations are summarized in Figure 6.

In summing up, the fiscal pattern that developed in Pakistan during the 1980s and extending into the 1990s is not sustainable. Over-expansion in expenditures, both for defence and non-defence purposes, together with sluggish revenues and excessive foreign borrowing have created a situation in which growth will be increasingly constrained by debt servicing, inflation, and shortages of domestic savings for private investors.

However, given the complex nature of defence expenditures in both stimulating and suppressing growth, budgetary reductions in this are by themselves unlikely to improve the country's economic performance. In fact, rapid reductions in defence are likely to impair the situation even further. On the other hand, modest efforts in tax reform are by far the most effective means for restoring fiscal stability.[40] The optimal policy mix is one of tax reform together with defence expenditures expansion that is constrained in the 2.5 per cent range. Unforeseen events aside, this package would enable the country to meet the goals established by itself and its major creditors in restoring a rapid, self-sustaining growth in an environment characterized by a declining defence burden.

Implications
The results summarized above are suggestive of the country's future macroeconomic environment. They show that the country has, through fiscal reforms, the potential of sustaining a relatively high rate of economic expansion throughout the 1990s. Combining the fiscal simulations summarized above with an (admittedly subjective) estimate of their likely occurrence, the country has, in most likelihood, a probability of around 40 per cent of sustaining a strong economic expansion through the remainder of the 1990s (Figure 6).

A broader issue is whether this expansion is broad-based enough and sustainable to the point that the country might evolve into a dynamic South Asian Tiger. The Japanese like to compare Asia's economic development to a formation of flying geese with Japan, whose economic miracle started in the 1950s, at its head. Japan was followed by Hong Kong, South Korea, Singapore, and Taiwan. In the 1970s, Indonesia, Malaysia, and Thailand joined the flock. In the 1980s came China. An obvious question is whether the latter 1990s will see some of the countries of South Asia join the flock.[41]

In this regard, the present Southeast Asian Tigers have a number of characteristics that set them apart from Pakistan and most other developing countries. These include the following:

1. More rapid output and productivity growth in agriculture.
2. Higher rates of growth of manufactured exports.
3. Earlier and steeper declines in fertility.
4. Higher growth rates of physical capital supported by higher rates of domestic savings.
5. Higher initial levels of growth rates of human capital.
6. Generally higher rates of productivity growth.
7. Declining income inequality and reduced poverty.

Figure 6
Pakistan: Fiscal Options and Prospects to the Year 2000

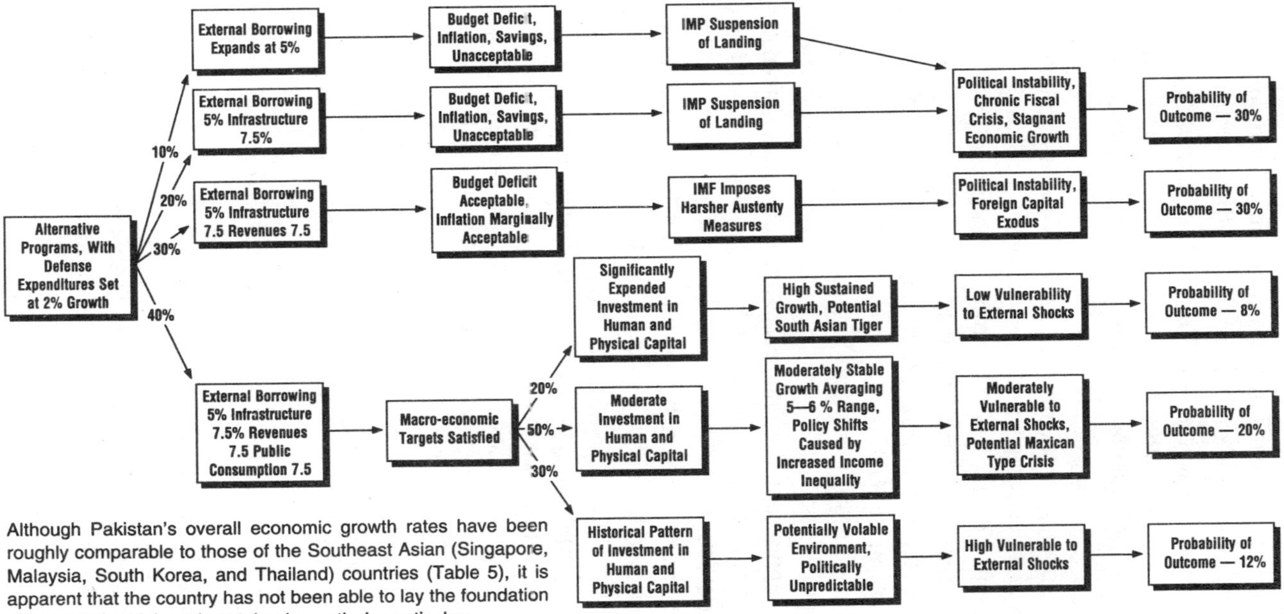

Although Pakistan's overall economic growth rates have been roughly comparable to those of the Southeast Asian (Singapore, Malaysia, South Korea, and Thailand) countries (Table 5), it is apparent that the country has not been able to lay the foundation necessary for high and sustained growth. In particular:

1. The country's savings rate is one of the lowest in the world.
2. Export performance has been erratic.

Although Pakistan's overall economic growth rates have been roughly comparable to those of the Southeast Asian (Singapore, Malaysia, South Korea, and Thailand) countries (Table 5), it is apparent that the country has not been able to lay the foundation necessary for high and sustained growth. In particular:

1. The country's savings rate is one of the lowest in the world.
2. Export performance has been erratic.
3. Manufacturing has not shown an ability to grow at a faster rate than the overall economy.
4. Government consumption accounts for a relatively high share of the GDP.
5. The country's population growth rate remains relatively high.
6. As opposed to the Southeast Asian countries, Pakistan would be beginning its phase of high growth with an extremely high debt ratio.
7. By most measures, Pakistan's military expenditures are considerably above those in Southeast Asia.

Most important, the country has seriously neglected the development of human capital. The country's literacy rate of 38 per cent is one of the lowest in the world. Educational facilities are unevenly distributed and generally favour urban areas. Mortality and life expectancy indicators are similarly disappointing for a country of Pakistan's economic standing. Health coverage is limited, and heavily focused on urban areas and hospital-based curative care. The data paint a stark picture:[42]

- Two-thirds of Pakistan's adult population and over three-quarters of adult women are illiterate.
- Basic health facilities are not available to over half the population.
- Sixty-seven million people lack access to safe drinking water while eighty-nine million are without elementary sanitation facilities.
- A quarter of newborn babies are malnourished.

Table 5
International Comparison of Economic and Social Performance

Measure	Total	SE. Asia	S. Asia	Pakistan
Economic Performance (% Growth)				
Gross Domestic Product, 1970-80	4.9	8.2	4.1	4.9
Gross Domestic Product, 1980-91	2.8	7.5	5.2	6.1
Investment, 1970-80	6.5	10.5	7.3	3.7
Investment, 1980-91	0.3	7.8	4.0	5.6
Exports, 1970-80	4.0	7.9	2.3	0.7
Exports, 1980-91	4.7	10.7	7.9	9.9
Government Expenditures, 1970-79	8.1	9.4	5.9	7.4
Government Expenditures, 1981-91	0.8	4.9	5.0	7.0
Population, 1970-80	2.6	2.	2.4	3.1
Population, 1980-91	2.5	1.8	2.2	3.1
Economic Structure (% GDP)				
Investment, 1970	21.7	28.0	17.3	16.0
Investment, 1991	20.5	37.8	20.7	19.0
Savings, 1970	18.6	20.3	13.7	9.0
Saving, 1991	14.0	36.3	14.7	12.0
Private Consumption, 1970	69.1	67.8	76.0	81.0
Private Consumption, 1991	72.2	52.5	73.7	75.0
Exports, 1970	22.7	43.3	12.3	8.0
Exports, 1991	28.5	83.3	17.7	16.0
Resource Balance, 1970	-2.7	-7.5	-3.7	-7.0
Resource Balance, 1991	-6.8	-1.5	-6.0	-7.0
Government Consumption, 1970	13.8	12.3	10.3	10.0
Government Consumption, 1991	13.9	11.5	11.7	13.0
Manufacturing, 1970	14.2	17.3	16.0	16.0
Manufacturing, 1991	15.2	28.0	16.3	17.0
Infrastructure Investment (% Growth)				
Paved Roads, 1970-80	8.6	8.5	5.6	4.4
Paved Roads, 1980-90	3.0	4.8	5.3	8.6
Irrigated Land, 1970-80	4.5	2.5	1.6	1.3
Irrigated Land, 1980-90	2.4	1.5	1.0	1.5
Electric Generating Capacity, 1970-80	8.9	11.8	6.6	8.3
Electric Generating Capacity, 1980-90	6.2	7.9	10.1	10.0

Table 5 (continued)
International Comparison of Economic and Social Performance

Measure	Total	SE. Asia	S. Asia	Pakistan
Debt (%)				
External Debt/Exports 1980	152.4	90.7	156.1	208.8
External Debt/Exports 1991	392.3	65.4	250.4	244.9
External Debt/GDP 1980	40.9	34.2	33.5	42.4
External Debt/GDP 1991	82.5	33.7	50.7	50.1
Debt Service/Exports, 1980	17.3	15.0	13.1	17.9
Debt Service/Exports, 1991	21.0	9.5	21.9	21.1
Military (Average % Share)				
Defence Expend/Budget, 1970-80	15.2	22.0	17.7	29.5
Defence Expend/Budget, 1980-91	16.1	18.9	17.0	26.2
Arms Imports/Total Imp., 1970-80	8.5	2.4	5.3	8.5
Arms Imports/Total Imp., 1980-91	17.7	1.3	6.9	6.9
Defence Expend/GDP, 1970-80	5.6	9.1	7.0	6.1
Defence Expend/GDP, 1980-91	5.6	9.1	7.0	6.1
Armed Forces/1000 Pop., 1970-80	7.1	10.8	3.3	6.5
Armed Forces/1000 Pop., 1980-91	8.0	12.2	3.4	6.3
Social				
Population per Physician, 1970	15470.4	4047.5	5033.3	4310.0
Population per Physician, 1990	10570.2	2472.5	2700.0	2940.0
Life Expectancy (years) 1991	60.4	71.0	63.3	59.0
Illiteracy (%) 1991	37.4	11.0	43.0	65.0
Malnourishment (%), 1991	25.4	25.0	51.0	57.0
Education (% Relevant Age Group in School)				
Primary School, 1970	71.9	94.5	70.7	40.0
Primary School, 1990	87.5	99.0	80.3	37.0
Secondary School, 1970	20.8	34.8	28.7	13.0
Secondary School, 1990	39.8	61.0	46.7	22.0
Tertiary School, 1970	8.1	11.0	4.5	4.0
Tertiary School, 1970	10.8	17.5	3.5	3.0
Primary Pupil/Teacher Ratio, 1970	38.5	38.3	41.0	41.0
Primary Pupil/Teacher Ratio, 1990	35.4	25.0	51.0	41.0

Sources: Economic/Social, World Bank, Military, United States Arms Control and Disarmament Agency.

The unequal distribution of human capital in turn has created an income distribution much more unequal than found in Southeast Asia. Most analysts feel that the success of the Southeast Asian economies is linked to their initial, equitable distribution of income and assets.

Given the budgetary constraints that the government is likely to be faced with during the remainder of the decade, it is difficult to see how the country could significantly improve its social infrastructure. Without these human assets and capabilities, the country will be unable to achieve the productivity increases necessary to transform itself, certainly in the near future, along the lines of the Southeast Asian model.

Conclusions

It is remarkable that despite a troubled and crisis prone political history, Pakistan has managed to make significant strides in several spheres, including rapid economic growth, and industrial development. Much of this has occurred despite and not due to official policy or action, encouraging the belief among most Pakistanis that less government is the key to a better future.[43]

Returning to the questions posed at the start of this paper, while it is unlikely that the country will become a South Asia Tiger in the near future, one cannot rule this out in the longer term. Human capital deficiencies aside, in many respects Pakistan is better positioned now to move ahead with rapid economic development. If the Cold War's end forced difficult adjustments, it also opened new opportunities. Its situation next to the newly independent and resource-rich region of Central Asia means that Pakistan could become of central importance to this area.[44]

The majority of the country's population remains poor no doubt, largely because of limited economic freedom. Government controls restricting access to opportunity, together with a budgetary process dominated by the country's elite and biased against human capital development, have prevented the spread of economic prosperity to the mass of the population.

Less certain is the extent to which democracy can be sustained in light of the massive economic, and social difficulties the country currently faces. If the current government can press ahead with broad based reforms that provide more economic freedom in the longer run prospects for democracy may improve.[45] Robert Barro has examined the links between economic freedom, development and democracy.[46] His findings suggest that:

- The favourable elements for growth include small distortions of market prices, an inclination and ability of the government to maintain the rule of law, high levels of health and education, low government spending on consumption, and a low fertility rate. If these variables and the level of pre-capita income are held constant, the overall effect of more democracy on the growth rate is moderately negative.
- There is some indication that more democracy raises growth when political freedom is low, but depresses growth once a moderate amount of freedom has been attained.
- There is a stronger linkage between economic development and the propensity to experience democracy. Specifically non-democratic countries that have achieved high standards of living—measured by real per capital GDP, life expectancy and schooling—tend to become more democratic over time. Examples include, Chile, South Korea, and Taiwan.
- Conversely, democratic countries with low standards of living tend to lose political rights. Examples include the newly independent African states in the 1970s.

In Pakistan's case, high growth during the Zia years may have contributed to the desire for greater participation. In turn, no doubt this led to improved democracy under Benazir Bhutto and greater economic freedom under Nawaz Sharif. Improving the position and efficiency of the private sector offers a major opportunity to encourage that segment of the economy to expand its saving and investment. In addition, finding a greater role for the private sector in the politics of the country will broaden the state's legitimacy.

NOTES

1. A.A. Khan, 'Pakistan's Development Record: Achievements and Failures.' *The News*, 15 September (1997).
2. M. ul-Haq, 'The Poverty Puzzle.' *The Financial Times*, 14 August (1997a): p. 10.
3. M. Monshipouri and Amjad Samuel. 'Development and Democracy in Pakistan: Tenuous of Plausible Nexus?' *Asian Survey*, 35, November (1995); pp. 973-989.
4. A. Ahmad, 'The Dream of Economic Self-Reliance.' *The News*, 8 September (1997).
5. M. ul-Haq, 'The Poverty Puzzle.' *The Financial Times*, 14 August (1997a): p. 10.
6. A.A.M. Dhakan, 'Fifty years of Economic Development in Pakistan' *Economic Review* 27, No. 11 (1996): pp. 17-19.
7. V. Ahmed and Rashid Amjad, *The Management of Pakistan's Economy: 1947-82*. Karachi: Oxford University Press, 1984.
8. Ibid., p. 75.
9. Ibid., p. 77.
10. Omar Noman, *Pakistan: A Political and Economic History Since 1947*. London: Kegan Paul International, 1988.
11. Ahmed, op.cit., p. 98.
12. S.J. Burki, *Pakistan: The Continuing Search for Nationhood*. Second ed. Boulder, Colorado: Westview Press, 1991, p. 116.
13. S.J. Burki, 'Pakistan Under Zia, 1977-1988'. *Asian Survey*, October 1988, p. 1093.
14. M. Lodhi, 'Fifty Years of Independence: Belief in Potential Remains'. *The Financial Times*, 12 August 1997, p. 10.
15. S. Ahmed, 'Explaining Pakistan's High Growth Performance Over the Past Two Decades: Can It Be Sustained?' Washington: The World Bank, 1994.
16. M. Lodhi, 'Fifty Years of Independence: Belief in Potential Remains'. *The Financial Times*, 12 August 1997, p. 10.
17. N.M. Khilji and Ernest M. Zampelli, 'The Effect of US Assistance on Public and Private Expenditures in Pakistan: 1960-1988'. *The Pakistan Development Review* 30, no. 4 Part 2 (1991): 1169-1184.
18. M.H. Chaudhry. 'Economic Liberalization of Pakistan's Economy: Trends and Repercussions.' *Contemporary South Asia* 4, No. 2 (1995): pp. 187-192.
19. M. Monshipouri and Amjad Samuel, 'Development and Democracy in Pakistan: Tenuous of Plausible Nexus?' *Asian Survey* 35, November 1995: p. 982.

20. R.E. Looney, 'An Assessment at Pakistan's Attempts at Economic Reform.' *Journal of South Asian and Middle Eastern Studies*, XV, no. 3 (1992): pp. 1-28.
21. R.E. Looney, 'Financial Innovations in an Islamic Setting: The Case of Pakistan' *Journal of South Asian and Middle Eastern Studies*, XIX, no. 4, (1996): pp. 1-30.
22. J. Gwartney, R. Lawson, and W. Block *Economic Freedom of the World: 1975-1995*. Washington, DC: Cato Institute, 1996.
23. R.E. Looney, 'Pakistan's Progress Towards Economic Freedom' *Contemporary South Asia*, 6, no. 1 (1997): pp. 79-100.
24. J. Gwartney, R. Lawson, and W. Block *Economic Freedom of the World: 1975-1995*. Washington, DC: Cato Institute, 1996.
25. P. Waldman, 'Bhutto Undone By Pride, Sick Economy', *The Wall Street Journal*, 20 November (1996): A15.
26. F. Bokhari, 'Mr. Sharif's Fiscal Gamble,' *The Financial Times*, 12 August (1997): p. 10.
27. Ibid.
28. M. Ahmed and Qazi M. Ahmed, 'Estimation of the Black Economy of Pakistan Through the Monetary Approach,' *The Pakistan Development Review*, 34, no. 4 Part II (1995): pp. 791-807.
29. M. Nicholson, 'Scourage of Pakistan's Manufacturers,' *Financial Times*, 5 August (1997): p. 5.
30. S. Ahmed, 'Explaining Pakistan's High Growth Performance over the Past Two Decades: Can it be Sustained?' Washington: The World Bank, 1994.
31. A.A. Khan, 'Pakistan's Development Record: Achievements and failures'. *The News*, 15 September 1997.
32. A.A. Khan, 'Pakistan's Development Record: Achievements and failures'. *The News*, 15 September 1997.
33. A.A. Khan, 'Pakistan's Development Record: Achievements and failures'. *The News*, 15 September 1997.
34. A.H. Khan, 'Budgetary Deficit: Options and Limitations'. *PIDE Tidings* 1, no. 3 (1988): 19-22.
35. R.E. Looney, 'Budgetary Dilemmas in Pakistan: Costs and Benefits of Sustained Defence Expenditures,' *Asian Survey*, XXXIV, No. 5 (1994a): pp. 417-429.
36. R.E. Looney 'Pakistan Defence Expenditures and the Macroeconomy: Alternative Strategies to the year 2000,' *Contemporary South Asia*, 4, No. 3 (1995): pp. 331-356.
37. A.A. Khan, 'Current Economic Trends and Prospects: Pakistan on the path of recovery'. *The News*, 6 October (1997a)
38. M. Ijaz, 'The IMF's Recipe fro Disaster,' *The Wall Street Journal*, 10 June (1996).

39. F. Bokhari, 'Pakistan: Imminent Deal with IMF on $1.6bn Loan,' *The Financial Times*, 25 July (1997a).
40. A.H. Khan, 'Budgetary Deficit: Options and Limitations,' *PIDE Tidings* 1, no. 3 (1989): pp. 19-22.
41. J. Williamson, 'The Next Miracle Region Could Be South Asia', *International Herald Tribune*, 9 October (1997).
42. M. ul-Haq, 'The Poverty Puzzle.' *The Financial Times*, 14 August (1997a): p. 10.
43. M. Lodhi, 'Fifty Years of Independence: Belief in Potential Remains'. *The Financial Times*, 12 August 1997, p. 10.
44. M. Lodhi, 'Fifty Years of Independence: Belief in Potential Remains'. *The Financial Times*, 12 August 1997, p. 10.
45. R.E. Messick, 'Economic Freedom Around the World'. *The Wall Street Journal*, 6 May 1996.
46. Robert Barro, 'Economic Growth in a Cross Section of Countries'. *Quarterly Journal of Economics* (1991), pp. 407-43.

9

The Sunni-Shia Conflict in Pakistan
Anwar H. Syed

Muslims, who number more than one billion in the world, are divided into numerous sects and sub-sects. If one were to look for something roughly comparable, the Shia-Sunni split within Islam might be seen as corresponding to the Catholic-Protestant divide in Christendom. The latter have fought extended wars in Europe and, in more recent times, they have been fighting one another for several decades in Northern Ireland. The Shia and the Sunni have been fighting, even if intermittently, since shortly after the death of Muhammad (PBUH), the Prophet of Islam.[1]

The Sunni and Shia Profiles

The Sunni and the Shia agree that there is no God other than Allah, that Muhammad (PBUH) was His prophet, and that he was the last of the prophets. But, in some ways, this is where they begin to part company. Some of their rituals and doctrines are different, but not all of them are offensive enough to the other side to cause conflict. The Shia may think that the Sunnis are misinformed, or misguided, but there is little in the Sunni belief or practice which is really offensive, or infuriating, to the Shia. The Sunnis object to the Shia doctrines, beliefs, and practices in varying degrees, and some of these are infuriating to them. The Sunnis form the vast majority in the Muslim world; the Shia are a minority except in Iran, Iraq, and Bahrain. In Pakistan they constitute about 20 per cent of the population.

In the literal sense, *Shia* means a partisan. But in popular Muslim usage it refers to those who were, and are, the partisans of Ali ibne Abu Talib, the Prophet's (PBUH) cousin and the husband of his daughter, Fatima. They uphold his claim to leadership and rulership over the Muslim community following the Prophet's (PBUH) death in 632. This is the focal point of their belief system. The Sunnis regard Ali as the last of the four righteous caliphs who succeeded the Prophet (PBUH), but not as significantly more righteous than his predecessors. More of this a little later.

The Sunnis are divided into numerous sub-sects, depending partly on which one of the four schools of law (founded by Abu Hanifa, Malik, Hunbal, and Shafai) they accept. A few of the Sunnis in Pakistan are Wahabis, who do not subscribe to any of these schools. These are 'non-conformists,' inclined to be purists, with their own rules of guidance. Then there are the more numerous neo-Wahabis, called the 'Deobandis.' They follow Abu Hanifa's fiqh. Beyond that they believe that no one, not even the Prophet (PBUH), can intercede with God on any person's behalf. The great majority of the Pakistani Sunni are Hanafis in the 'Barelvi' tradition, believing in the efficacy of intermediaries between man and God. They venerate *'pirs,' 'faqirs,'* and *'sufis'*; go to their *'dargahs'* and mausoleums, to pray for favours they seek from God. Of the Sunni groups in Pakistan, the Wahabis and the Deobandis are the ones more intensely opposed to the Shia beliefs and practices.

Sunni Reactions to the Shia Doctrine and Practice

Let me now turn to the Shia doctrines, beliefs, and rituals.[2] My purpose here is not to examine their theological correctness but to indicate how strongly the Sunnis object to them. The Shia believe that after the Prophet's (PBUH) death, the office of interpreting the true faith, and that of rulership, belonged to his 'house' *(ahl-e-bait)*, which consisted of Ali and his descendants through Fatima, for the next eleven generations. Ali and his eleven descendants were *imams*, each of them appointed by his predecessor by God's grace, free of sin and incapable of error. Leaders they were of those who followed them, but rulers they were not, except Ali for about five years and his son, Hasan, for six months. That they did not rule means only that those who became rulers were illegitimate. The twelfth of these imams, popularly known as Mehdi, ascended to heaven when he was a child and there he will remain until shortly before the Day of Judgment when he will return to set the world right. In the Shia belief these twelve imams partook of the qualities (though not the substance) of God, and were divinely inspired in whatever they said and did. The Sunnis honour the Shia imams, respect some of them as great scholars, but object to the attribution of infallibility to them. This is more troublesome to the Wahabis and the Deobandis than to the Barelvis who, on their own part, attribute an exalted spiritual status to a variety of 'saints.'

Since the 'imams', including Mehdi, are gone, their right to be rulers is no longer an issue of any practical significance. The Shia believe that in Mehdi's absence all actual governments are essentially illegitimate. Muslims may remain aloof from them, obey them if they must, but they may also resist impious and unjust rulers when such a course of action is open. These propositions need not trouble the Sunnis. Aloofness from the government of the day, or obeying it if one must, have firm foundings in the writings and personal conduct of Sunni jurists and scholars (Abu Hanifa and Malik for aloofness; Ghazali for obedience). Sunni doctrine, especially that of Imam Hunbal, also upholds resistance to unjust rulers.[3] In this connection, the present position of the Shia ulema in Iran should not be overlooked. It is that since they know the mind of the 'hidden imam' (Mehdi), a government directed and supervised by them is legitimate.

Most of the Shia imams were killed, and their followers endured intense persecution, notably during the Abbasid rule. They developed a doctrine, called *taqiyya* (dissimulation), which meant that it was permissible to hide the fact of their being Shia if the profession of their true faith was liable to bring them grievous harm. The Sunnis are likely to regard *taqiyya* merely as sanctioned dissimulation. But it should be noted that in the Sunni theory itself the jurists have upheld the 'doctrine of necessity,' meaning that 'necessity' makes lawful that which is otherwise forbidden. A well-known affirmation of a Sunni moralist and poet, Sheikh Sa'di, has it that *darogh-e-maslahat amez beh az rasti-e-shar angez* (an untrue statement which is expedient is better than a truth that provokes mischief and conflict). More recently, Ayatollah Khomeini in Iran forbade *taqiyya* because the Shia were in no danger from any non-Shia force in that country. In Pakistan, the Shia are not resorting to *taqiyya* in spite of the hostility they encounter. They are openly declaring themselves to be what they are. *Taqiyya*, then, is not really an issue in the Sunni-Shia conflict in Pakistan.

The Shia allow *mut'a* which is a marriage for a specific duration determined by the mutual consent of the parties. The man pays the woman the 'dower,' agreed upon between them, before the marriage is consummated. Theoretically, the duration of the marriage could be an hour or even less. If any children result from the relationship, they are legitimate and entitled to inherit from the father. The Shia maintain that the *mut'a* is a facility which the Prophct (PBUH) had allowed, and that Omar (the second righteous caliph) forbade it, which he had no right to do. The Sunnis ridicule the *mut'a*, regarding it merely as a legalization of sexual promiscuity. It should, however, be noted that in the 'regular' Sunni or Shia marriage, the man can divorce his wife within hours (even minutes) of having contracted it. In any case, the Shia in Pakistan do not normally have *mut'a* marriages. The Shia belief in the efficacy of *mut'a* then is also not an active contributor to the Shia-Sunni conflict in Pakistan.

The Sunnis allege that the Shia affirmation of faith (the *kalima*) is different from that of their own, that the Shia, after affirming the unity of God and the prophethood of Muhammad (PBUH), add that Ali ibne Abu Talib was God's friend, that the Prophet (PBUH) had left (or wanted to leave) a will in his favour, and that, rightfully, he should have been the Prophet's immediate successor. The Shia in Pakistan do not make this affirmation publicly but it is possible that some of them do so privately. The Sunnis allege also that the Shia question the Quran's authenticity. But there is no Shia version of the Quran; the existing version is all that they, like the Sunnis, have. They are said to believe that, beyond their 'external' or apparent meanings, the verses of the Quran have hidden meanings, which their imams knew, and which refer to the exalted status of Ali and Fatima and their descendants. The Sunnis regard this belief as calculated to distort the Quranic text. But the Shia in Pakistan have not produced any *tafsir* (exegesis) of the Quran along the alleged lines, which means that this, too, is not a vital issue in the Shia-Sunni relations in the country.

On a theoretical level the Sunnis maintain that doctrinal issues can be settled through a consensus of the community. This is called *ijma*. In actual practice, it refers to consensus of the *ulema* of the medieval period. In recent history no doctrinal issue has been settled through resort to public discussion. The Shia regard their imams as the authoritative interpreters of such issues as may arise. The chain of the imams ended with the disappearance of Mehdi more than eleven hundred years ago. But the Shia allow *ijtehad* (innovative reinterpretations), on the part of their higher-ranking ulema (*mujtahids*), while the door to *ijtehad* among the Sunnis has virtually been closed since the tenth century. However as far as I know, the Shia have not used *ijtehad* to revise any of their known doctrines or even practices. Many Sunnis believe in predestination', while the Shia assert the freedom of human choice. The Shia-Sunni differences on these points—*ijtehad*, and predestination—are minor, without any significant, practical consequences, and they cannot be regarded as reasons for their conflict.

I now come to a set of Shia practices to which the Sunnis object rather strongly and a set of Shia beliefs which they regard as intolerable. Husain, the third Shia imam, the younger son of Ali ibne Abu Talib and a grandson of the Prophet (PBUH), declined to give allegiance to Yazid who had become the ruler, following the death of his father, Muawiya (who had waged war against Ali and become 'Caliph' following Ali's assassination in AD 661). Husain and a small band of his family members and followers were killed by Yazid's army in a brutal manner at Karbala (Iraq) in AD 680. The Shia, and many Sunnis (especially the Barelvis), condemn the slaughter at Karbala, but the Shia mourn it every year during the month of Muharram. They hold gatherings, narrate various heart-rending versions of the event, weep and wail, and beat their breasts. They call it *matam*, or *azadari*. They go out in processions, doing *matam*, surrounding a decorated horse, that symbolizes the horse that Husain had ridden to battle, and carrying replicas of his tomb. They regard all of these activities as purifying acts of devotion.[4] The Sunnis see them as heretic deviations from the correct path, bordering upon idolatry.

The Central Issue in the Shia-Sunni Conflict

The Shia-Sunni difference over certain issues of political theory and interpretation of early Muslim history (especially from the Prophet's (PBUH) death in AD 632 to the assassination of Ali in AD 661) constitutes the most potent reason for their tension and conflict. The Sunnis regard the first four rulers, following the Prophet's (PBUH) death (Abu Bakr, Omar bin Khattab, Osman bin Affan, and Ali ibne Abu Talib), as not only legitimate but as 'pious' and 'righteous' caliphs, worthy of great reverence. As stated above, the Shia consider Ali ibne Abu Talib alone to have been a legitimate ruler and treat his three predecessors as usurpers. They believe also that these first three caliphs were not really true to the Prophet (PBUH) and his mission. Allegedy they speak ill of them in various other ways in their own gatherings and some of them use insulting vocabulary in referring to them. The Sunnis find these Shia attitudes and interpretations to be intolerably offensive.

The Sunnis consider all Muslims who knew the Prophet (PBUH) personally, and sat with him from time to time, as his 'companions' (*sahaba*) and worthy of reverence. They include in this group even individuals who later made war against Ali—

for instance, Talha bin Abdullah, Zubair bin Awan, and Muawiya bin Abu Sufyan. They refer to Muawiya as *hazrat* (a prefix denoting veneration) in spite of the fact that effectively, he did away with the caliphate and instituted hereditary monarchy. The more militant Sunnis are respectful even toward Yazid whose men had perpetrated the slaughter at Karbala. Needless to say, the Sunni expression of reverence for the enemies of Ali and his family is irritating to the Shia.

How have the Shia derived their belief that rulership belonged to the *ahl-e-bait*, house of the Prophet (PBUH) and their interpretation that the first three caliphs were usurpers? It may be surprising to many Sunnis that these ideas have come directly from the pronouncements of Ali ibne Abu Talib. In some of the sermons he delivered after becoming the caliph, he spoke of the exalted status of the members of the Prophet's (PBUH) 'house,' the *ahl-e-bait*.[5] They, he maintained, were the ones in whom God had placed His trust; they were the preservers, protectors, and authentic interpretaters of His word. The Prophet (PBUH) had willed that they should succeed him in leadership and rulership, and that none of his followers and 'companions' could be placed in comparison with them. In a celebrated *khutba* (sermon), called *Shiqshiqiya*, he spoke of his own qualifications for succeeding the Prophet (PBUH) as the Muslim community's leader and ruler. He observed that his predecessors had deprived him of the caliphate, even while knowing that he alone was entitled to this office, and that his wisdom, knowledge, and virtue were unsurpassed. Their usurpation of his right had been painful to him, but he decided to endure it patiently instead of resisting it. Then he went on to criticize his predecessors' style of rule. Abu Bakr was prone to 'faults and failures', and he often needed the advice of others to compensate for his own shortcomings. Yet, he thought himself to be wise enough to appoint Omar as his successor. These first two caliphs (Abu Bakr and Omar) 'misused public funds, ruled arbitrarily,' and weakened the state and religion. Before he died, Omar appointed a committee of six persons (including Ali) to choose the next caliph from amongst themselves. According to Ali, several members of this committee had been his rivals or even enemies, and they chose Osman bin Affan to be the third caliph. Osman treated the caliphate like a 'private grazing field'; he and his relatives 'plundered' the community's wealth in a 'reckless and gluttonous' fashion.

Next to God and the Prophet (PBUH), Ali ibne Abu Talib occupies a central place in the Shia belief system. It is clear from the sermons to which I have referred above that he did not think well of his predecessors. What are the Shia then to do? They cannot applaud the first three caliphs if Ali, their ideal, thought of them as usurpers and plunderers. This might pose a problem for the Sunnis also. They regard Ali as one of the four 'righteous' caliphs. How would they deal with his denunciation of his predecessors? They might deny the authenticity of the pronouncements attributed to Ali and collected in a volume called *Nahj-al-Balagha*. To the best of my knowledge, they have never done so, which may be because most of them have never read it. Alternatively, they might say that they were 'neutral' in the political rivalries that developed between Ali and others.

The Shia-Sunni Conflict: A Brief Review

The Shia-Sunni conflict is almost as old as Islam itself. Within months of Ali's accession to the caliphate, his opponents, led by one of the Prophet's wives (Ayesha, daughter of Abu Bakr), waged war against him (in what is known as *Jang-e-Jamal* or the Battle of the Camel, denoting the camel that Ayesha rode). Then, Muawiya, who had been the governor of Syria for more than twenty years, declined to accept Ali as a legitimate caliph and fought him at a place called 'Safeen.' His son, Yazid, authorized the slaughter at Karbala to which I have already referred. During the Umayyad and Abbasid rule (661-750, and 750-1258), the Shia were persecuted and many thousands of them were killed, mostly in Iraq. From time to time, they revolted, notably in southern Iraq and Iran. At the beginning of the sixteenth century, when the Safvids made Shiaism the state religion in Iran, Shah Ismail ordered the killing of some 20,000 Sunnis in Azerbaijan to which Sultan Salim, the Ottoman emperor, responded by killing an equal, or even a larger, number of the Shia in eastern Anatolia. At about the same time, the Hazaras (a Shia tribe) in Central Asia were massacred and such that remained were expelled. In our own time, the war which Iraq imposed upon Iran (1980-1988), with the help of Saudi Arabia and Kuwait, may be seen as an instance of a most brutal conflict between the Sunni and the Shia regimes.

In the Arab world, in Anatolia, in Iran, Central Asia, and Afghanistan, Muslims predominated. When they were not fighting non-Muslim foes, they might have tended to vent their aggression against sects and factions within their own community. But such was not the case in the Indian subcontinent where Muslims faced a much larger Hindu population. From about the end of the twelfth century, when Qutb-ud-Din Aibak became the resident Muslim ruler in northern India until the coming of British rule, Shia-Sunni tension remained at a low level, with the exception of Aurangzeb, an orthodox Sunni who oppressed the Shia and spent many years fighting the Shia rulers of Golkanda and Bijapur in the Deccan yet, generally the Muslim kings did not take much interest in sectarian differences within the Muslim community. The British, being Christian, were also not interested in them. Moreover, they wanted to keep order in the country and did what they could to control sectarian conflict.[6] The same might be said of the essentially secular-minded governments in Pakistan from 1947 to the beginning of Ziaul Haq's rule in 1977.

During British rule, and during the first thirty years after independence in Pakistan, one did occasionally hear of a Shia-Sunni riot (*fasad*) but, generally speaking, the two groups lived peacefully together in the same neighbourhoods. They might go to their own separate mosques and practice their respective rituals, but the fact that one man was a Shia, and another a Sunni, did not come in the way of their friendship. Certainly, they did not fear one another.

Shia-Sunni Conflict: Recent and Current

But during the last fifteen years or so, Shia and Sunni 'activists' and 'militants,' categories that were not known before, have been killing one another, assassinating each other's leaders, and bombing each other's mosques. These killings and bombings have taken place periodically in Karachi, in the Parachinar area of the North West Frontier Province, and more frequently in the Punjab. According to one report, 469 persons were killed and 2258 wounded in sectarian violence in the Punjab alone during the last ten years. Referring to the same province, another report places the number of persons killed in sectarian violence during the first six months of 1997 at 110. It appears that many more Shia, than Sunnis, are being killed. In addition to laymen and bystanders, who are hit when a bomb explodes or when someone opens indiscriminate fire in a public place, religious leaders, notables in Shia and Sunni organizations, merchants, professional men (doctors and lawyers), and high-ranking government officials are being targeted. Husain al-Husaini, head of a major Shia organization, Ziaur Rehman Farooqi (a top Deobandi leader), and senior civil servants on both sides have been killed.[7]

This is not the way it used to be until sometime after Ziaul Haq's coming to power. From the day he seized the government (5 July 1977), he began to say that the obligative for the creation of Pakistan could not be fulfilled unless it became an Islamic state, that is, a state in which Islamic law and injunctions (the *shariah*) were implemented. In February 1979 he declared that the Hanafi fiqh would be enforced in the country. Then he issued an ordinance for enforcing the Islamic penalties for certain violations (theft, adultery, fornication). The following year (June 1980), he levied certain Islamic taxes (*zakat* and *ushr*). Then he went on to establish a Shariat Court and authorized it to annul any law of Pakistan which it deemed to be repugnant to the *shariah*. He appointed some notables of the Islamic parties as ministers in his government, and placed many of them as members of a consultative assembly (called the Majlis-e-Shura).

These developments alarmed the Shia. They subscribed to their own Fiqh-e-Jafariya, not to the Fiqh of Abu Hanifa, and had their own interpretations of Islamic taxes and penalties. They established an organization, called the Tehrike-e-Nifaz-e-Fiqh-e-Jafariya (Movement for the Enforcement of the Jafari Fiqh) to demand that the Shia in Pakistan be allowed to follow their own fiqh. In 1980 the TNFJ (which is now called TJP) sponsored an agitation to get exemption from the payment of the Islamic taxes (*zakat* and *ushr*). Ziaul Haq eventually relented, exempted the Shia community from paying zakat and ushr, and declared also that they would not be governed by any fiqh other than their own. This gave the TJP a sense of efficacy.[8]

But Ziaul Haq's concession to the Shia may have caused resentment among certain Sunni elements (especially the Deobandis) who regard the Shia as misguided, and feel that concessions to them are unjustified. In 1985, they formed an organization of their own, called Sipah-e-Sahaba, Pakistan (the Pakistan army of the Prophet's companions), with the mission of defending the companions' honour against Shia attacks.

Both the TJP and the SSP have officially dissociated themselves from acts of violence. But the militants in each organization, considering the 'parent' to be much too tame, have made factions of their own. Riaz Basra and some of his associates in the SSP organized the Lashkar-e-Jhangvi (meaning Jhangvi's army, named after Haq Nawaz of Jhang, an SSP leader who was assassinated a few years ago). The more militant Shia in the TJP formed Sipah-e-Muhammad, Pakistan (meaning the army of Muhammad [PBUH]). The Lashkar and the SMP are the main Sunni and Shia organizations engaged in sectarian violence. While the parent organizations do not formally approve of their offsprings' activities, they do not actively oppose or condemn the same. This may partly be due to their fear of the more militant faction leaders. Recently, when Murid Abbas Yazdani, the SMP 'commander,' signed an agreement with his SSP counterparts, saying that belief in the righteousness of the first four caliphs was a part of the Islamic faith, the organization split and a group, led by Ghulam Raza Naqvi, killed Yazdani.[9]

The Lashkar was formed because Riaz Basra felt that the SSP leaders were not hard enough in their opposition to the Shia.

While the Lashkar and the SMP have access to several thousand trained militants, the terrorists—or, let us say, the killers—in the two organizations are said to number only a couple of hundred. Most of them have had a few years of education in a *deeni madrasah* (seminary). Many of them, especially the ones in the Lashkar have had military training and experience in the use of weapons in Afghanistan and Kashmir. They work under the direction of 'co-ordinators,' who obey their respective 'commanders.' The co-ordinator calls a certain 'worker' in his organization on a mobile telephone, which the police cannot trace, and arranges a meeting. He tells this 'worker' about the person to be killed, takes him to the neighbourhood where the intended victim lives, and arranges their next meeting. In the meantime, the 'worker' studies the neighbourhood and watches the intended victim's movements and routines. On the appointed day, the co-ordinator meets him, delivers appropriate weapons to him, and provides transportation. After the 'worker' has done his work (killed the intended victim), he meets the co-ordinator at an appointed place, returns the weapons that were given to him, and then goes to hide for a time in a *madrasah* or a mosque.[10] These 'workers' are quite convinced of the righteousness of their own 'cause,' and they are equally convinced that their victims are the enemies of Islam. On each side the top-ranking leaders are somewhat more literate. Ghulam Raza Naqvi (the SMP commander), for instance, graduated from a high school, obtained a bachelor's degree as a private candidate, attended a madrassah is Qum (Iran) and, upon returning to Pakistan, served as a *Khateeb* (deliverer of sermons) in an important mosque in Jhang.[11]

Saudi Arabia and Iran fund many of the Sunni and Shia madrasahs in Pakistan. These madrasahs have spread even to smaller towns and they enroll more students than the public elementary and middle schools do. They teach theology, but many of them also teach their students to disapprove of sects other than their own, and give them some military training.

A further word about the rivalry between Iran and Saudi Arabia may be appropriate here. Many Pakistani observers interpret the Shia-Sunni conflict as a 'proxy' war between the Saudi and the Iranian governments waged on their soil. In this connection, it may be well to recall that, soon after taking power, Ayatollah Khomeini invited the Muslim peoples throughout the world to overthrow their respective governments because they were un-Islamic. The government of Iran has, however, said that it will not use force to bring about a change of regime in another Muslim country. On the other hand, Saudi Arabia provided much of the funding (many billions of dollars) for Saddam Husain's war against Iran which went on for eight years. Some observers view it as a Saudi Arabian war against Iran in which the Saudis spent treasure and the Iraqis shed blood.[12]

While Saudi Arabia and Iran may be funding the *madrasahs*, there is no hard evidence that they also fund the Lashkar and the SMP. It is likely that these organizations get their money locally, especially from small and middle-ranking merchants and shopkeepers. When short of funds, they resort to bank robberies, dacoities, kidnapping for ransom, and extortion. They do not think twice about the legality of these activities, because the law is that of a state which they deem to be un-Islamic, and, in their thinking, their acts are calculated to serve the Lord's purposes.

Prospects of Controlling the Conflict

What are the central and the provincial governments doing to curb sectarian violence? They condemn it and vow to eradicate it, as they vow to eradicate many other evils and disorders. Shahbaz Sharif, the chief minister of the Punjab, recently described the *madrasahs* as 'dens' where 'terrorists' were sheltered, and promised to restrain and control them.[13] But it is not at all clear how he intended to accomplish this goal. The great majority of the Sunni and Shia in Pakistan are moderate people. They are not inclined to be unfriendly, much less to lay hands of violence upon one another. At the same time, this is the proverbial 'silent' majority, not organized to stop the militants. The government is afraid that the militants might mobilize large enough crowds to appear on the streets to challenge its authority, as they had done in 1953 and, again, in 1973, while agitating against the Ahmadis. The more militant among the Sipah-e-Sahaba shout that the Shia are *kafir* (non-believers), and that they should be placed outside the pale of Islam. The Shia, more numerous than the Ahmadis, but fearful of being marginalized in the country the way the Ahmadis have been, are assertive and ready to resist the Deobandi attack. The government, both at the centre and in the Punjab, has been inviting the two sides to a 'dialogue' to resolve their differences. But for those who feel passionately about their beliefs, the Shia-Sunni differences are not resolvable.

The bureaucracy, including the police, is also afraid of the harm that might come to its members if they act forcefully to curb the militants. In 1996, the commissioner of Sargodha, a Shia, was assassinated. In early 1997, a secretary to the Punjab provincial government, a Sunni, was killed. Ashraf Marath, a senior police officer, was killed by the Lashkar's agents, even though he was a fellow-Sunni, because he insisted upon pursuing the killers of seven persons at the Iranian cultural centre in Multan. Newspapers have published reports of police officers sending apologies to the militant sectarian captains for having dared to investigate them, with promises to leave them alone in the future. Riaz Basra, head of the Lashkar, escaped from police custody in 1994, allegedly with the assistance of two members of the provincial assembly who then sheltered him. He is in 'hiding,' but continues to direct the Lashkar and feels free to communicate with journalists at will. Ghulam Raza Naqvi, head of the Shia 'Sipah-e-Muhammad,' has been in police custody since December 1996, but apparently the numerous allegations against him are not being investigated with any seriousness or vigour.[14]

The latest reports seem to suggest that the government, and the police, may have recovered their nerve and resolve to some degree. The Punjab police has recently arrested about ten Lashkar militants. Actually, hundreds of sectarian militants have been arrested in recent months, but their arrests have not reduced sectarian violence to any significant degree. Even in 1998 one sees reports of sectarian killings in the Punjab almost every day.

In considering what might be done to curb sectarian violence, one must inevitably ask why it has mounted to the scale that it has during the last twenty years. One can speculate and suggest probabilities, which is what I propose to do, but I have no firm explanation. Several aspects of this issue are worthy of attention.

First, consider that until 1979, when the Shia clergy seized power in Iran, and barring a fifteen-year period in Muslim Spain several hundred years ago, never in Muslim history have the *ulema* (Islamic scholars) been rulers. In medieval Islam, and in the Indian subcontinent until the establishment of British rule, they occupied places of honour and enjoyed a reasonably good living. They acted as judges, jurists, teachers and professors, administrators of trusts and endowments, advisers to rulers, and declarers of the correct Islamic position on points at issue. They have these roles and privileges in Saudi Arabia and in the Persian Gulf Emirates even now. In India, they lost these roles and positions during British rule. They would like to recapture them. Successive governments in Pakistan, and that of Ziaul Haq more than any other, have professed their intention of Islamizing the country and enlivened the ulema's hope of regaining the role they once had. That the ulema have taken power in Iran, and that the 'Taliban' (many of whom attended the madrasahs run by Pakistani Islamic parties) are ruling much of Afghanistan, may have intensified the ulema's feeling that they should have a directing role in the governance of Pakistan.

But which of the ulema would have such a role and the rewards that come with it? The Shia ulema, being the spokesmen of a minority, cannot expect to be dominant. They would, therefore, like to have their own separate domains and offices in legislation, the courts, schools and colleges, and their share of jobs and public funds. When the SSP militants shout that the Shia are *Kafir,* that they should be declared a non-Muslim minority, and that Pakistan should be made a Sunni (Hanafi) state, they are in effect saying that the Shia should not have any share of authority and power in the 'Islamic' republic of Pakistan.

One way of dealing with this situation might be for the state to declare that it is each individual Muslim's own responsibility to earn eternal bliss in the hereafter, and that it is none of the state's business to ensure that he will obtain it. The state may be sympathetic to his goal but its achievement is still his own personal responsibility. In making public policy, and in defining the 'good society,' the state may be guided by Islamic values and principles, as determined by the people's representatives, but it will not enforce the Islamic law beyond personal affairs (marriage, divorce, inheritance) with regard to which Muslims have traditionally been free to follow the school (*fiqh*) of their choice. Let the ulema go out and preach, bring Islamic insights and wisdom to bear upon issues of public policy, and let these be debated in the legislatures. If they want to be rulers, let them contest elections.

But beyond a small minority, where in Pakistan is the receptivity to this course of action? I doubt that the politicians' promises of 'Islamization,' even if they were neither given nor taken seriously, can be withdrawn openly and formally. The people of Pakistan have consistently rebuffed the ulema's quest for power in successive elections. But many of them will still come out on the streets to disrupt public order if the ulema can tell them that their government has rejected the Islamic way.

With specific reference to the Shia-Sunni conflict, it is the Shia denunciation of some of the Prophet's companions (the *sahaba*), and especially that of the first three 'righteous' caliphs, that infuriates the Sunnis. Some of the recently arrested SSP militants have told police investigators that they become inflamed, and lose control, when they hear or read the Shia insults. Could the Shia be persuaded to stop this practice? The difficulty here is that although Ali ibne Abu Talib did not actively oppose his predecessors while they ruled, he did condemn them after they were gone. The Shia might ponder the fact that when he remained quiet in the earlier period he did so in order not to divide the community. They might do the same: practicing *taqiyya*, which is allowed to them, they might choose to tone down their disapproval of the first three caliphs and others who had opposed Ali. Alternatively, they might undertake *ijtehad* and, following Ayatollah Khomeini, decide that, in the larger interest of Muslim unity, denunciations of those who had opposed Ali fourteen hundred years ago shall now cease, because they serve no useful purpose.

But I see no signs of movement in any of these directions. Belief in Ali's entitlement to leadership and rulership has been a part of the Shia faith all along. The Sunnis have always honoured the four righteous caliphs, but belief in their righteousness has now been made a part of their faith. As noted above, when Murid Abbas Yazdani, the SMP commander, agreed to this proposition, the more militant of his Shia associates killed him.

The Shia-Sunni conflict might also be related to a general spread of violence, and an overall decline of civility, in the political culture of Pakistan and many other countries. Since the end of the Second World war, hardly a year has passed when a civil war was not taking place somewhere in the world. Millions of people have been killed in these wars. The incidence of terrorism has increased manifold during the last half century. In Pakistan itself, it is not just the Shia and the Sunni who are killing one another. Bombs explode for no apparent reason; mass murders and gang rapes happen with an unprecedented frequency. In ethnic conflicts, the Urdu-speaking *muhajirs*, Sindhis, Punjabis, Pathans, and Balochis have killed one another in great numbers and with unspeakable brutality. Almost every day muhajir militants kill fellow muhajirs belonging to a rival faction in the city of Karachi.

In the same connection, consider the astounding plan of Qazi Husain Ahmad, head of the Jamaat-e-Islami, to raise an army of five million to surround the National Assembly in Islamabad, make its members prisoners in the building, and thus force the government to surrender authority to the invaders. The Jamaat-e-Islami does not have a single representative in the National Assembly at this time. It has no mandate from the people to exercise power. But regardless of the people's wishes in the matter, it wants to take power, by recourse to violence if necessary.

One might return to James Madison's observation in the Federalist Number 10 that 'so strong is the propensity of mankind to fall into mutual animosities, that where no substantial occasion presents itself, the most frivolous and fanciful distinctions have been sufficient to kindle their unfriendly passions and excite their most violent conflicts.'[15] But one should recall also his insight that while conflict cannot be abolished, it can be managed and controlled. At this time, it is hard to say how soon the Pakistani polity can gather the requisite resources in wit and managerial capacity to control the currently rampant disorder and violence in society.

NOTES

1. This essay is based on my reading of Muslim history, personal observation, and conversations with Sunni and Shia friends over the last many years. Reference to published sources will be provided when it appears to me to be essential.
2. For a Sunni account of the Shia doctrines and beliefs, see Fazlur Rahman, *Islam*, Chicago: University of Chicago Press, 1979, pp. 170-175. A Shia version of the same may be seen in Syed Mohsin Naqvi, *Defending the Shia Faith*, Princeton, NJ: Mohsina Memorial Foundation, 1997.
3. Anwar Syed, *Pakistan: Islam, Politics, and National Solidarity*, New York: Praeger, 1982, chapter 2.
4. An excellent account of *matam*, *azadari*, and the Shia gatherings (*majalis*) during the month of Muharram may be seen in David Pinault, *The Shiites: Ritual and Popular Piety in a Muslim Community*, New York: St. Martin's Press, 1992, pp. 99-114 and *passim*. The author is describing the Shia community's practices in Hyderabad (India) but these are essentially the same as those of the Shia communities in the cities of Pakistan.
5. The sermons to which I have referred are Numbers 5, 6, and 7 in *Nahjul Balagha*. I have consulted an English translation (Syed Mohammad Askari Jaferey, Elmhurt, NY: *Tehrike Tarseele Quran, 1981*). I have also seen an Urdu translation which says substantially the same thing.

6. During much of the British rule, the conflict in Muharram took place, more often, between the Shia and the Hindus, and it seems that in these conflicts the Sunnis sided with the Shia. See Pinault, *The Shiites*, chapter 7.
7. See *Herald* (Karachi), June 1997, pp. 58-59, for facts and figures of those killed in sectarian violence in the Punjab. Also see Adnan Adil's reports in the Lahore weekly, *The Friday Times* (TFT), March 21-27, May 2-8, and May 9-15, 1997. Reports and editorials on the subject have appeared in *The Nation* (Lahore) on a continuing basis during the last several months.
8. For a good account of the beginning, and further development of the TNJP, see Afak Hayder. 'The Politicization of the Shias: the Development of the Tehrik-e-Nifaz-Fiqh-e-Jafaria in Pakistan,' in Charles H. Kennedy, ed., *Pakistan 1992,* Boulder, Col: Westview Press, 1993, chapter 5.
9. Zaigham Khan's report in *Herald*, June 1997, pp. 50-57.
10. Adnan Adil's report in TFT, July 18-24, 1997.
11. See profiles of Naqvi, Basra, and several other sectarian militants in *Herald*, June 1997, pp. 60-61.
12. James A. Bill & Robert Springborg, *Politics in the Middle East*, Glenview, Ill: Scott Foresman, 1990, pp. 385, 388.
13. *The Nation* (Lahore), 21 July 1997. Chaudhury Pervez Elahi, Speaker of the Punjab Assembly, said the same thing the day before. (*The Nation*, 20 July 1997).
14. See Adnan Adil's reports in *TFT* referred to earlier.
15. Alexander Hamilton, James Madison, and John Jay, *The Federalist Papers* (originally published in New York newspapers during 1787-1788 and subsequently collected in a volume.) Many editions.

10

The Sipah-e-Sahaba Pakistan
Afak Haydar

Introduction

This chapter has two main theses:

That the Muslims of the South Asian subcontinent,[1] in recent times, for a variety of reasons, have had a more pluralistic and ecumenical societal attitude than the Muslims of many Muslim majority countries, such as contemporary Saudi Arabia or Iran; and,

That the divisiveness prevalent in Pakistan, on grounds of differences in jurisprudence (*fiqh*) may be attributed to the rise of the Sipah-e-Sahaba Pakistan (SSP) and the Tehrike-e-Nifaz-e-Fiqh Jafaria (TNFJ). This chapter is concerned with the birth, and the aims and objectives of the SSP.

The birth of the SSP may be attributed to a combination of four different events that occurred at the same time in one location. These factors are:

- The rise to power of General Ziaul Haq; and his slogan of Nizam-e-Mustafa;
- The revolution in Iran and its impact on Pakistan;
- The socio-political environment of the city and district of Jhang, in the Punjab; and,
- The life and death of Maulana Haq Nawaz Jhangvi.

South Asia: A Pluralistic Muslim Community

Traditionally, the Muslims of the subcontinent have had a pluralistic societal attitude. It is true that they have had religious divides: principally Shias and Sunnis, but all communities have lived peacefully with all other communities.

The Shias of the subcontinent are primarily *Athana-Ashari*; there are some Ismailis also. The Sunnis, mostly of the Hanafi persuasion, are divided into Deobandis, Barelvis, Ahl-e-Hadith, etc.

Historically, except for rare communal or sectarian disturbances, the Shias and the Sunnis lived in peace, with others and with each other. They lived and raised their families in the same village; they lived as neighbours in the same *mohalla*; they attended each others' joyous and not-so-joyous ceremonies (weddings, *iftars, bismillah*, funerals); they attended the same secular schools; they even inter-married. It was not very unusual to find a large family (*kunbah*) with both Shias and Sunnis as part of the familial group.

Muslims of all persuasions, various schools of jurisprudence of Shias, including the *Athna Ashari*, the Ismailis, and the Bohras, and practically all schools of jurisprudence of the Sunnis, even the Ahmadis (who in British India were treated as Muslims; it was not until 1973 that they were declared non-Muslims in Pakistan), worked together for the creation of Pakistan.[3] They worked together in Pakistan in various fields of life, in the public services, in the armed services, in academic institutions, in business, in industry, in the public sector, and in the private sector from 1947 to 1977.

The first major religion based crisis occurred in 1953, when ulema (religious scholars) belonging to different schools of jurisprudence launched a campaign to have the Ahmadis (also known as Qadianis) declared non-Muslims and to have them removed from all strategic and major public offices. The Government of Prime Minister Khawaja Nazimuddin (October 1951 to October 1954) refused to accede to the demand; civil strife and disturbances ensued. An inquiry commission was appointed.[4]

The Politicization of the Sectarian Divide: The Birth of the Sipah-e-Sahaba Pakistan

The Rise to Power and the Rule of General Ziaul Haq

Things changed drastically after the take-over of the government by General Ziaul Haq, Chief of the Army Staff, on 5 July 1977. General Zia was not the first absolute ruler in the history of Pakistan. Governor-General Ghulam Mohammad (1951-56) had exercised absolute power. General, later Field Marshal, Ayub Khan (1958-69), had ruled as a military dictator.

General Zia introduced a new factor in the political life of Pakistan: Islam

It is true that Pakistan was sought and obtained in the name of Islam. But, the founder himself had made no secret of his desire and determination to establish a secular, and not a theocratic, state, where the Muslims would have the right and the opportunity to lead their lives according to the injunctions of Islam; equally important, others would be free to follow the dictates of their own religious convictions.

The governments that followed the Quaid-i-Azam, dictatorial or otherwise, remained secular, inclining more towards separation than fusion of religion and state. Was the Quaid-e-Azam a secularist for philosophical reasons, who did not want politics and religion to mix? Or, was he a practical politician, who recognized the difficulty (the impossibility?) of establishing a state based on Islam, because the question would be: whose interpretation of Islam?

But, General Zia raised the slogan of Nizam-e-Mustafa. His desire was to establish an Islamic order and an Islamic society in Pakistan. General Zia knew very well that he was creating a division in the community, a Shia-Sunni divide. He may even have *wanted* to create the division, knowing that it would permit him to prolong his rule.[5]

What contributed to this Shia-Sunni divide?

This author believes that General Zia's Islamization of the laws in Pakistan contributed greatly to the development of this divide, and to the politicization of the Shia-Sunni rift in Pakistan. General Zia tried to Islamize the laws; to impose Nizam-e-Mustafa, meaning the system of government as practised by the Prophet of Islam (PBUH) and his four righteous caliphs. As early as the fall of 1977, Maulana Kausar Niazi, a former minister in the cabinet, had warned General Zia that Nizam-e-Mustafa may be a good slogan but it will result in sectarianism.[6] It is easy to say that the country should have an Islamic system of government. The big question is: whose interpretation of Islam?

In 1979, General Zia introduced the Hudood ordinances and the ordinance for the collection of *ushr* and *zakat*.[7] The Shias objected to the ushr and zakat ordinances. They said that their *fiqh* does not require them to pay ushr, and does not allow them to pay zakat to a state agency. Eventually, General Zia had to accede to the request of the Shias for exemption from the payment of ushr and zakat.[8]

The ordinances remain on the statute book; ushr and zakat are collected by the state; no hands have been cut for theft; the society has not been Islamized by the Islamization of the laws. It remains the same as before, with the changes that would have come with time, anyway. But irreparable damage has been done. The Shia-Sunni divide is deep, and seems to be widening rather than narrowing.

The Revolution in Iran and its Impact on Pakistan

The second factor that contributed to the widening of the Shia-Sunni rift was the Iranian revolution of 1979. The seemingly invincible regime of Mohammad Raza Shah, the Shehanshah (emperor) of Iran, who had recently celebrated with pride 2500 years of Iranian monarchy, was overthrown by a coalition of merchants, Marxists, intellectuals, and other anti-Shah elements of Iran, all led by an Ayatollah—a religious leader.

The leader of the Iranian revolution, Ayatollah Ruhullah Khomeini, labelled the revolution as an Islamic revolution, not as an Iranian revolution, or as a Shia revolution. It was hailed as a triumph of Islamic forces over secular forces, not only in Iran, but also in Pakistan and other Muslim countries.[9] Their slogan was:

Neither Oriental nor Occidental—Islamic and only Islamic.
Neither Shia nor Sunni—Islamic and only Islamic.[10]

This author has traced the gradual politicization of the Shias in Pakistan in another essay;[11] it is not necessary to recount the details here.[11] But, it must be emphasized that up to 1983 the principal Shia organization (The Tehrik-e-Nifaz-e-Fiqh-e-Jafaria: TNFJ), established in 1979 to protest the imposition of the *Hudood* ordinances in Pakistan, remained an apolitical organization. Its primary goal was to protect the religious rights of the Shias; the rights to *azadari*, the right to use of Shia *waqf* (trust) funds on Shia religious activities; and, the right to have Shia *fiqh* taught to Shia children if any *fiqh* was taught in public schools. The TNFJ had no political agenda. Mufti Jafar Husain was the leader of the TNFJ. On his death in August 1983, Allama Arif Husain Al-Husaini, a young, relatively unknown cleric, a graduate of Shia seminaries in Iran and Iraq, and a disciple of Khomeini, was elected as the President of the TNFJ.[12]

The Socio-Political Environment of Jhang

Jhang is an administrative district of the province of the Punjab. According to scholars, the politics of Jhang, as that of the rest of the country, particularly of the rural areas, is controlled by the landlords. In Jhang it has revolved around three lineages: the Siyals, the Rajooas, and the Shah Jeewana. Most of the landlords in Jhang happen to be Syed and Shia.[13] Most of the population, rural and urban, is non-Syed and Sunni.

It will not be untrue to state that the majority of the District, like the majority of the nation as a whole, do not have a leadership role in the affairs of the area because of the hold of the landlords.

Was this a usurpation of the rights of the Sunnis by the Shias or was this a usurpation of the rights of the poor masses by the rich landlords? For ages the situation had been perceived as a struggle between the poor, landless masses and the rich landlords; their respective sects were not relevant.

The Life and Death of Maulana Jhangvi[14]

The Anjuman Sipah-e-Sahaba, later named the Sipah-e-Sahaba Pakistan (SSP) was formed by the late Maulana Haq Nawaz Jhangvi, a young Sunni cleric, primarily because of his dislike for the Shias and Shia doctrines and *fiqh* and because of the socio-political environment of his native Jhang, and not so much because of his dislike for the contents of the Iranian revolution. He wanted to dispel the belief, based on what he termed Iranian state propaganda, that the Iranian revolution was indeed an Islamic revolution. He wanted to publicize the revolution as a Shia revolution, with no relevance to Pakistan and its Sunni majority.[15] The life (and death) of Maulana Haq Nawaz Jhangvi played a very important role in the creation and continuance of the SSP in Pakistan.

Maulana Jhangvi was born in a large family in 1952 in a rural community located at the confluence of the Rivers Chenab and Jhelum in District Jhang of the Punjab. After completing primary education from the village 'middle' school, he was placed on the religious education track; he learnt the Quran by heart; he learnt how to recite the Quran; he studied *tafseer, hadith, fiqh*, (Quranic exegesis, sayings of Prophet Muhammad (PBUH), and Islamic Jurisprudence), history, literature, philosophy, logic, etc. at the religious *madrasah* (school) in Kabirwala, District Multan. (This is the standard curriculum at Islamic religious institutions in Pakistan.) By the time he was nineteen, he had successfully completed the courses of study at the religious *madrasah* and had also learned the art of *manazra*: polemics, disputation.

It must be reiterated that a vast majority of the Shias and the Sunnis in the subcontinent live in an environment of understanding, peace, and harmony. There are certain elements amongst the ulema of the two groups who have sought and encouraged a confrontational dialogue (*manazra*) with each other. Some of the religious schools (*madrasahs*), both Shia and Sunni, teach not only *tafseer, hadith*, and *fiqh*, but also the art and science of *manazra*, disputatious debate (with ulema of the other fiqh).

Maulana Jhangvi studied *manazra* under distinguished scholars of his time in this field, and mastered the art. He started his professional career in 1972, at the age of 20, as a teacher in a 'religious school'. In 1973, he became the 'preacher' (*khateeb*) in a mosque in his native Jhang. According to Maulana Farooqi, Maulana Jhangvi soon became a popular *khateeb*, not only for the rural masses from neighbouring villages but also for the ulema of various mosques in town, who would come to his mosque to listen to his lecture after having led prayers in their own mosques. In his public lectures, Maulana Jhangvi discussed *tauheed* and *risalat* (the unity of God and the concept of prophethood, culminating in Prophet Mohammad (PBUH), the two most important elements of Islamic theology and culture. But, according to Maulana Farooqi, he soon realized that the most important matter for the people in his area to understand and accept was the importance and relevance of the *Sahaba* (the companions) of the Prophet (PBUH).

Muslim society gives a very special and distinguished status to the companions of the Prophet: those who accepted Islam and remained with the Prophet (PBUH) during the twenty-three years of his life after his announcement of his prophethood. It must be remembered that the source of most *ahadith* (documented traditions, statements, actions) of the Prophet were his companions.

The major area of doctrinal difference between the Shias and the Sunnis in Islam is the succession to the Prophet (PBUH): should he have been succeeded by a *Khalifa* (caliph), elected, selected, nominated, and appointed by the people or, should the Prophet have been succeeded by an Imam, appointed by him (the Prophet) under Divine instructions?

The Prophet (PBUH), was succeeded by Abu Bakr (RA) who was selected by the people.

The Sunnis accept this as legitimate; the Shias accept the historical fact that Abu Bakr, Omar, Osman, and Ali (RA) succeeded the Prophet (and, each other) but they do not accept the legitimacy of this succession. One of the major issues of conflict between the two sects is the acceptance of the legitimacy of the caliphate of the first three caliphs Abu Bakr, Omar, and Osman (RA). The Shias would not want to accept the legitimacy of the caliphate of the fourth caliph, as well. But, he happens to be their first Imam so, they usually refer to his caliphate as his *Khilafat-e-Zahiri* (the temporal caliphate).

However what causes offence to the Sunnis is not so much that shia religious diction does not accept the legitimacy of the first three Caliphs, but that the Shias denounce the three caliphs for 'usurpation' of the rights of Ali.

Maulana Jhangvi decided to focus in his lectures on the role of the *sahaba*. This action was motivated not only by his religious and spiritual desires but also by his understanding of the local politico-economic conditions of Jhang. According to his biographer, Maulana Farooqi:

> The reason for Maulana *Shaheed* [the martyred Maulana] giving attention to this issue was the special religious and political conditions prevailing in Jhang. All major landlords in the district were followers of the Shia belief and the Sunnis were being suppressed under their [the Shias'] repression. *Tabarrabazi* [calling names] was done on the *Sahaba* openly.[16]

Focusing in his lectures on the *sahaba* would rally the Sunni majority, and help break the grip that the Shia landlords had on the politico-economic structures of the community. In short, it was, for him, spiritually fulfilling and politically rewarding.

Maulana Jhangvi reacted to the Shia-Sunni conflicts in the late 1960s and the 1970s. There were some disturbances in the area involving the Shia and the Sunnis, resulting in some deaths. The environment was charged with sectarianism. The main manifestations of the Shia-Sunni conflict was the calling names of *sahaba* by the Shias and the singing of praises of the *sahaba* by the Sunnis.

Maulana Jhangvi cashed in on these conflicts to promote his views. According to Maulana Farooqi, Maulana Jhangvi invited Sunni ulema belonging to different schools of thought (Deobandi, Barelvi, and Ahl-e-Hadith) to sink their 'peripheral' differences and to unite to fight against the 'great and most dangerous challenge posed by the Shia'. He was successful in setting up a committee of two ulema from each school of thought; the committee was titled Tahaffuz-e-Namoos-e-Sahaba (The Committee to Protect the Sanctity of the Sahaba). The Committee worked against Shiaism for a couple of years, within the city, or at most within the district. Maulana Jhangvi's efforts to fight Shiaism were not as successful as he wanted them to be. According to his biographer, Maulana Farooqi, Maulana Jhangvi noticed that after the revolution in Iran, Iranian literature about Shiaism, with *tabbarra* (on the *sahaba*) was inundating Pakistan. He started to speak out against the Iranian revolution and the Khomeinite views (Shiaism), and was arrested under Martial Law regulations. Maulana Jhangvi was now convinced that he needed to establish a youth organization to fight Shiaism.

He launched the Sipah-e-Sahaba Pakistan (SSP) on 6 September 1985, from his own mosque; it grew into, according to Maulana Farooqi, 'the largest' religious organization of the country. The SSP achieved its first major success when the Shias of Jhang entered into an agreement with the SSP to desist from *tabbarra* during the Moharram commemorations in 1986. Many Sunni (SSP) leaders who were placed under detention by the Government, some for implication in a murder case, were released.

Maulana Jhangvi became the object of cases filed against him for disturbing peace, inciting religious sectarian tension, and possible implication in criminal activities. Despite these obstacles, the Maulana continued to work for his mission which consisted of developing national sentiments against the Shias.

During the summer of 1987, followers of two Sunni sects in Jhang had a disagreement; the brawl ended in the deaths of two persons belonging to the Barelvi fiqh. Maulana Jhangvi and his senior associates and office-bearers of the SSP were implicated in criminal cases, including conspiracy to murder. Ten of the twelve persons arrested, including Maulana Jhangvi, were released on bail; two spent more than three years in jail before being released, after the two sects settled their disputes without a court trial.

According to his biographer and successor, as leader of the SSP, Maulana Jhangvi was the target of two unsuccessful assassination attempts: first on 10 October 1989 and second on 25 January 1990. The report filed with the police alleged that several Shia persons, including a member of the Punjab Provincial Assembly (Mr Ghulam Abbas Najafi), a member of the National Assembly (Begum Syeda Abida Hussain), and the leader of the Tehrik-e-Nifaz-e-Fiqh-e-Jafaria, Maulana Sajid Naqvi, were implicated in the attempt to murder their opponents. No action was taken against any one of them.

Maulana Jhangvi was shot and killed at the doorsteps of his house on 22 February 1990.

According to his biographer, his main contributions may be summarized as:

—Protest against the dictatorial regime of Ayub Khan (1969);
—Participation, at the local level in Jhang in the Tehrik-e-Khatm-e-Nubbuwwat (Movement to acknowledge the End of Prophethood [with Prophet Muhammad (PBUH)]) (1974);
—Participation, at the local level, in the Tehrik-e-Nizam-e-Mustafa (during the Bhutto regime) (1974);
—Initiation of public praise of the Sahaba, as an instrument of anti-Shiaism (1985 onwards); and,
—Establishment of the Sipah-e-Sahaba Pakistan (1985).

The Demands of the Sipah-e-Sahaba Pakistan

The SSP has articulated certain demands. They are listed below, with some comments by this author about each of these.[17]

Revival of the System of Khilafat-e-Rashida

The first four caliphs of Islam are designated as the *Khulafa-e-Rashideen*, the righteous caliphs. They succeeded the Prophet (PBUH) (and, each other); they were all *mohajirs* (fellow immigrants with the Prophet who migrated to Medina from Mecca); they were all related to the Prophet (the first two were also his fathers-in-law; the third and fourth were sons-in-law, the fourth also being a first cousin); they were persons of impeccable character and irreproachable integrity. The religion and its domains expanded enormously during their rule from North Africa to South Asia. They collected and published a version of the Quran, which is universally accepted by all Muslims. The Quran had not been collected during the Prophet's own lifetime, and, they accomplished all this, and much more, with flawless honesty, immaculate integrity, total dedication and steadfast devotion. The Muslims look back at the period of twenty-nine years of the four righteous caliphs as the Golden Era, second only to the era of the Prophet himself.

Political leaders of all persuasions in Pakistan and in other Muslim lands have invoked the name of the Khulafa-e-Rashideen whenever they have found it profitable to do so; just as they have invoked the name of Islam, whenever it has suited their needs and political agendas.

To Get Pakistan Declared as a Sunni State

The second aim of the SSP as articulated in the brochure is to get Pakistan declared a Sunni State. Maulana Farooqi states:

> Christianity in England is divided into two sects, i.e. Catholics and Protestants, but as Protestant are in majority, Public Law is framed on the basis of their beliefs. Although Queen Elizabeth subscribes to the Catholic faith yet she has to abide by the Public Law representing the Protestants' majority.[18]

Apart from the factual error of the Queen being stated to be a Catholic, there is also an error of interpretation. (The Queen is not only a Protestant; she is also the Head of the Church of England.) A similar error was made by Maulana Farooqi during an interview with this author on 15 May 1995, when he stated that although John Major, then Prime Minister of England, was a Catholic, he was obliged to enforce the Protestant laws because the majority of the people of the UK are Protestant. The Maulana also referred to fundamental laws, that jurists call constitutional laws, pertaining to the exercise of the sovereign power of society (for example, laws pertaining to election of public officials), as personal laws. It may be stated that jurists refer to laws pertaining to marriage, divorce, inheritance, etc., as personal laws or family laws, as contra-distinguished from public laws.[19] The Maulana said that the SSP demands that the public laws of Pakistan should be according to the Sunni *fiqh*.

We know that although the Queen is head of the Church of England and is designated as the Defender of the Faith there is no mixing of church and state in England besides this symbolic position of the Queen. Public Law is made not on the basis of Protestant belief but on the basis of public opinion. The country is ruled by the Parliament; the Parliament is controlled by the majority party; and political parties are based on political ideologies (conservative, liberal etc.) and not on religious beliefs.

During the interview with this author on 13 May 1995, Maulana Farooqi said that Sunnis constitute 35 per cent of the total population of Iran but a Sunni cannot be elected as a Member of Parliament or as President of Iran; therefore, Pakistan should have a similar law that no Shia should be eligible for election to positions of power.

It is important to recall that Pakistan was created by the Muslims of the subcontinent working together, not as Shias and Sunnis, not as Hanafis and Shafaiees, Malikis, or Hunbalis, but as Muslims. The Shias included the Ismailis, the Bohras, and the *Athna Asharis*; the Sunnis included various schools of *fiqh*, various jurisprudence and shades of beliefs: Deobandi, Barelvi, and Ahl-e-Hadith. It included all Muslims of the subcontinent. To declare Pakistan a Sunni, Hanafi state would be a betrayal of the non-Hanafis who helped create Pakistan.

The Days Commemorating the Anniversaries of the Khulafa-e-Rashideen (RA) be Observed as Public Holidays

It is really unfortunate that the days commemorating the death anniversaries of the *Khulafa-e-Rashideen* (RA) are not observed as public holidays in Pakistan.

The late Maulana reiterated this demand of the SSP during the 1995 interview with this author. He said that Pakistan observes two days of public holiday to commemorate the martyrdom of Imam Husain, on 9 and 10 Moharram, each year. It should similarly, observe at least one day of holiday to commemorate the death anniversaries of Hazrat Abu Bakr, Omar, Osman, and Ali, the four *Khulafa-e-Rashideen*.

It may be pointed out that Imam Husain was the son of Hazrat Ali and Hazrat Fatima (and, the grandson of the Prophet [PBUH]). Yazid Ibn Muawiya led a life in defiance of the dictates of Islam, therefore, when he demanded allegiance from Imam Husain, Imam Husain refused. Yazid arranged for Imam Husain and his family and friends to be brutally massacred in Karbala, Iraq. Imam Husain is treated with reverence by all Muslims; he is a very great religious figure and is accepted as an Imam of the Shia.

Shia Mourning Processions Run Contrary to Shia Religion Itself.

The Shias of the subcontinent take out processions to commemorate and mourn the tragic events of Karbala in Iraq, in 61 AH (C. CE 680), where Husain, the younger grandson of the Prophet (PBUH) and his family and friends were brutally massacred by the forces of Yazid ibn Muawiya, who had inherited the caliphate from his father, Muawiya ibn Abu Sufyan.

In many communities in the subcontinent, including the hometowns of this author, Budaun and Lucknow, both in the UP, the Moharram processions were taken out not only by Shias but also by Sunnis. The nature and format of the processions were different in different communities, and different for the Shias and the Sunnis. The SSP alleges that 'every year, when some Shias publicly assail the *sahaba karam* with invectives, emotions burst into fierce clashes which claim the lives of so many'.

The Activities of the Iranian Cultural Centres and Sipah-e-Sahaba

The Government of Iran has opened a number of cultural centres in Pakistan; six, according to the SSP brochure. These are located in Hyderabad, Karachi, Lahore, Multan, Peshawar, and Rawalpindi. The SSP alleges that these centres are run not as cultural centres or as institutions to teach the Persian language to interested Pakistanis, but to supply sophisticated arms and ammunition to Shia agents of Iran engaged in terrorism in Pakistan who also propagate objectionable Shia literature. Every year, lacs of rupees are provided to promote Shia educational centres,...[20] and to train Shia *Zakireen* (preachers).

Death Penalty for the Impudent Maligning Sahaba-e-Karam, Khulafa-e-Rashideen and Ahl-e-Bait Uzzam as Kafirs

The brochure states[21]

> Sipah-e-Sahaba stands for striking at the root of the trouble by enacting a law to give death penalty to those who are found guilty of maligning verbally or in writing the revered elders in Islam as *Kafir*.
>
> Besides, those who use offensive language or castigate these personalities be flogged or imprisoned.

This author believes that using abusive and offensive language for anyone is reprehensible; nobody should be allowed to indulge in such practice.

To Secure Legislation Declaring Them [Shias] as Kafir[22]

The inside back cover of the brochure from which the demands of the SSP have been taken, carries the title:

Goals it Pursues and Stragegy it Adopts

One of the goals is stated to be 'to prove and expose the *Kufr* of Shias and secure legislation declaring them as *Kafir*.'

A *Kafir*, by definition, is a non-believer: a non-believer in the unity of God; in the concept of prophethood and the long line of prophets culminating in Prophet Muhammad (PBUH); and in the life hereafter. The Shias believe in the unity of God; they believe in prophethood; and, they believe in the life hereafter.

Shaikh Mohammad Shaltoot, Rector, Al-Azhar University Cairo, Egypt, in his *fatwa* dated 17 Rabi-ul-Awwal 1378 AH[23] has categorically stated that it is all right for Muslims to follow the Shia school of jurisprudence. He accepts Shias as Muslims.[24]

It may be noted that Pakistan is the first Muslim country in modern history to declare a group (Ahmadis) that says La-ilaha il-lallah; Muhammadur-rasul-allah; translation: (There is no deity but Allah, and Muhammad is His last Prophet) as *Kafirs*, non-believers.

During the interview with this author on 13 May 1995, Maulana Farooqi reiterated this demand of the SSP: to get Shias declared by the Government of Pakistan as *Kafirs*, as non-believers, as non-Muslim. He directed this author's attention to a chapter titled 'Shia key Kufriya Aqaid'[25] (The Heretic Beliefs of the Shias) in his compilation titled *Tareekhi Dastawez: Shia Musalman Ya Kafir: Faisla Aap Kareyn.*

On 15 August 1997, this author met with Maulana Mohammad Nasser Saghaya Biria, the Resident Alim (Scholar) of the Islamic Education Center, Houston, Texas, Maulana Biria is a Shia *Mujtahid* (Scholar) and is originally from Iran.[26] This author raised questions about beliefs attributed to the Shias in the chapter cited above.

Question: Do the Shias believe that the Quran is complete as revealed to the Prophet (PBUH)?

Answer: All current Shia *ulema* (scholars) believe that the Quran is the same as revealed to the Prophet (PBUH) and there has been no *tahreef* (Change).

Question: The SSP says that Shias believe that certain *Ayahs* (verses of the Quran) had names of Ali and *Ahl-e-bait* (family of the Prophet (PBUH)), which have been deleted from the text as we have it today.

Answer: These may have been the beliefs of the Akhbari sect; these are not our beliefs.

Question: The SSP says that the Shias believe that anyone who does not believe in the superiority of Hazrat Ali over all others after the Prophet (PBUH) is *Kafir*. True?

Answer: The word *kafir* does not mean non-believer, non-Muslim; it means a person who denies the superiority of Ali over all others except the Prophet (PBUH).

Question: The SSP says that Shias believe that the Imam can declare anything that is *halal* to be *haram* and vice versa. True?

Answer: Just as a *Mujtahid* can. (It must be noted that in Shia *fiqh* a *Mujtahid Marja-e-taqleed* [a scholar who is accepted by the Shia community as being capable of issuing such fatwa] can issue a *fatwa* declaring items to be *halal* or *haram*.)

Question: The SSP says that Shias believe that when the twelfth Imam returns to earth and establishes his reign, he will bring back Bibi Ayesha (wife of the Prophet [PBUH] who led armed forces against Ali at the Battle of the Camel and will punish her.

Answer: We do not believe this. Please recall that when Bibi Ayesha led the enemy forces against Ali, who was then the (fourth) caliph, he killed the camel on which Bibi Ayesha was riding and asked her half-brother Mohammad to escort her, with proper respect, back to her tent at the battlefield.

Question: The SSP says that Shias believe that the first two caliphs deserve to be and are in the worst part of hell. True?

Answer: No, we do not believe this. Please remember that just as there are *ahadith* in the reliable Sunnis books that most Sunnis may not believe in, Shias also have, in their otherwise reliable books, items attributed to the Imams that we do not believe in; these narratives have been received through weak and unsupported sources.

Maulana Biria wanted this author to quote him saying:

> That there are some undeniable differences [between the Shias and the Sunnis]; some beliefs are shocking to each other. But as long as we believe in Allah and the Quran, and the Qibla, we would be all together. We are all Muslims. Those who wish to divide us are enemies of Islam and the Muslim *ummah* (nation). We should emphasize what is common amongst us, specially today, when the Muslim world is threatened by the material values of the Western culture.

This author had a very delightful and enlightening interview with Maulana Biria and is eternally grateful to him for his time and scholarly discourse.

Conclusion

The following points may be concluded from the above discussion:

1. That the Muslim community in South Asia has been an ecumenical community, accommodating differences of religious belief among its members. Shias and Sunnis have lived peacefully and amicably with each other; they lived as neighbours without declaring each other *kafirs*; they even inter-married.

2. The revolution in Iran politicized the Shias of Pakistan. (The TNFJ came under the leadership of a Shia cleric, educated and trained in Iran.).

   The religious elements of Muslims in general, and the Shias in particular, felt 'powerful' since a very powerful Shah of Iran, backed by the West, had been overthrown by a coalition of various elements led by a cleric.

3. While the Muslims of Pakistan were relishing and applauding the revolution in Iran, General Zia raised the slogan of Nizam-e-Mustafa in Pakistan.

   The Shias looked at Islamization in Pakistan as a threat to their Shiaism, to their *fiqh Hudood* ordinances: Shias believe that the penalty for theft is the disambiguation of fingers and not the hand. These is no provision for *ushr* in Shias' fiqh, and Zakat is not paid to the government.

4. The socio-political environment of the district and city of Jhang provided the perfect breeding ground for the rhetoric of the late Maulana Haq Nawaz Jhangvi, a relatively less known Sunni preacher.

5. The socio-political life of Jhang is dominated by Syed landlord families that are also Shia.

6. The late Maulana Jhangvi termed the domination of life in Jhang by the landlords, who happened to be Syed and Shia as Shia domination of the Sunni majority.

7. Maulana Jhangvi, while in his early twenties, started the Sipah-e-Sahaba Pakistan (SSP), as an anti-Shia and anti-Shiaism association.

8. The late Maulana Jhangvi's rhetoric brought him national acclaim and generated anti-Shia sentiment amongst many people in Pakistan.

9. His assassination made him a hero, a martyr. He was succeeded by his lieutenant, the late Maulana Zia-ur-Rehman Farooqi, as the leader of the SSP. Maulana Farooqi declared that his mission was to have the Shias declared as *kafirs* (non-believers).

10. Shia scholars contacted by this author have said that the allegations made by the late Maulana Farooqi about Shia beliefs are not true; Shias do not hold those beliefs.

11. One Shia scholar, Iranian by descent and educated in Iran, said that Shias are Muslims; Shias treat followers of all other schools of jurisprudence (*fiqh*) as Muslims; and that Shias and Sunnis should emphasize what is common among them rather than what is different.

NOTES

1. We will use the term subcontinent to refer to the South Asian subcontinent, comprising Bangladesh, India, and Pakistan. A country will be named when the reference is intended to be made to a specific country.
2. Some scholars maintain that Islam has always shown an enumenical attitude as far as intra-Islam groups are concerned: as long as the believers believe in the fundamentals of Islam (unity of God, concept of prophethood culminating in the Prophet Muhammad [PBUH] and the Day of Judgement and a life hereafter), Islam and Muslims have tolerated different schools of interpretations (*fiqh*). See, Moosa Khan Jalalzai, *73 Firqe Kaisay Baney: Tareekh-e-Islam* [How Were the 73 Sects Formed: History of Islam] (in Urdu), Lahore [Pakistan]: Fiction House, 1996, p. 130.
3. For an excellent description of the role of the Shias of British India in the struggle for creation of Pakistan, please see Mohammad Wasi Khan, *Tashkheel-e-Pakistan men Shian-e-Ali Ka Kirdar* [The Role of the Shias in the Creation of Pakistan] (in Urdu), Volumes I and II, Karachi [Pakistan], Idara-e-Mehfil-e-Haidari, 1982 and 1983, respectively.

   The Ahmadis (also known as the Qadianis) are followers of Mirza Ghulam Ahmad (1840-1908) of Qadiyan; they accept Mirza Ghulam Ahmad as a prophet. Muslims believe that Prophet Muhammad Ibn Abdullah (569-632) was the last prophet and there can be no true prophet after Muhammad [PBUH]. In 1973, the Ahmadis were declared a non-Muslim minority in Pakistan, by constitutional amendment. See Craig Baxter, et al. *Government and Politics in South Asia*, Boulder, Co: Westview Press, 1987. p. 176.
4. Government of the Punjab, Report of the Court of Inquiry Constituted Under the Punjab Act II of 1954 to Enquire into the Punjab Disturbances of 1953, Lahore [Pakistan] Government Printing Press, 1954. This report will hereinafter be referred to as the Munir Commission Report, 1953.

5. See Azhar Suhail, *General Zia Key Giyarah Saal* [Eleven years of General Zia] (in Urdu), Lahore [Pakistan]: Feroze Sons, 1982, p. 14.
6. Suhail, Gen. Zia, p. 51.
7. These ordinances, collectively known as the Hudood Ordinances or the Hudood Laws, are:
   Prohibition Enforcement of Hadd) Order, 1979;
   The Offence of Zina (Enforcement of Hadd) Ordinance, 1979;
   The Offences Against Property (Enforcement of Hadd) Ordinance, 1979; and,
   The Offence of Qazf (Enforcement of Hadd) Ordinance, 1979.
   These may be found in Hamid Ali (ed.), *Combined Set of Islamic Laws, 1979* (rev. ed.), Karachi [Pakistan]: The Ideal Publishers, 1988.
8. See Afak Haydar, 'The Politicization of the Shias and the Development of the Tehrik-e-Nifaz-e-Fiqh Jafaria' in Charles Kennedy, Pakistan: 1992, Boulder, Co: Westview Press, 1993.
   This will hereafter be cited as Haydar, TNFJ, followed by the page number.

   Also see Afak Haydar, 'From the Anglo-Muhammadan Law to the Shariah: The Pakistan Experiment,' *Journal of South Asian and Middle Eastern Studies*. Vol. X, no. 4, (Summer 1987), pp. 33-50.

   This will hereafter be cited as Haydar, From Am-Law to the Shariah, followed by the page number.
9. Abu Rehan Zia-ur-Rehman Farooqi, *What is Sipah-e-Sahaba: What it Aims At: Introduction, Aims, and Objectives* [This is a 24-page brochure in English, given to this author by the late Maulana Zia-ur-Rehman Farooqi, the brochure's author, and then patron-in-chief of the Sipah-e-Sahaba, in the town of Samundri, District Faisalabad, Pakistan during an interview on 13 May 1995.] No publication data, pp. 2-3.
   This publication will hereafter be cited as Farooqi, what is..., followed by the page number.
10. See, Farooqi, *What is...*, p. 3.
11. Haydar, TNFJ, p. 83.
12. Suhail, Gen. Zia, p. 51.
13. The term Syed, in Pakistan, refers to persons who trace their lineage to Prophet Muhammad [PBUH] through his daughter Hazrat Fatima, who was married to Hazrat Ali (RA), a cousin of the Prophet [PBUH], the fourth caliph, and the first Imam of the Shias. Also see Vakil Anjum, *Siyasat Key Firaun: Punjab Key Jagirdaron Key Urooj aur Zawal ki Kahani* (in Urdu) [The Pharaos of Politics: The Story of the Rise and Fall of the Jagirdars (landlords) of the Punjab], pp. 305-324. This chapter is titled 'The Siyal, The Rajooa, and the Syeds of Jhang.'
14. See Abu Rehan Zia-ur-Rehman Farooqi, *Amir-e-Azimat Maulana Haq Nawaz Shaheed Ki Jadd-o-Jihad* [The Struggle of Amir-e-Azimat Haq

Nawaz, the Martyr], Faisalabad, Pakistan: Idara-e-Al-Ma'arif, 1994; it is a brief biography of Maulana Jhangvi;
This publication hereafter will be cited as Farooqi, *Biography*, followed by the page number.
15. Farooqi, *Biography*, p. 12. This biographical sketch of Maulana Jhangvi is based on the brief biography written by Maulana Farooqi.
16. Farooqi, *Biography*, pp. 12-13.

The phrase *tabbarra-bazi* needs an explanation for those who may not be familiar with the Shia-Sunni conflict and its manifestations in the subcontinent. The Shias believe, that Ali's right to succeed Prophet Muhammad [PBUH] was usurped by the first three caliphs: Abu Bakr, Omar, and Osman (RA). The Shias, as an article of their faith, want to 'dissociate' themselves with those who usurped Hazrat Ali's (and, according to the Shias, the rights of the Prophet's only surviving daughter, Hazrat Fatima, who was married to Hazrat Ali. This dissociation sometimes is carried to the extreme and many uneducated Shias use invective, denunciatory and abusive language for the first three caliphs and many others, including some *Sahaba-e-Karam* (the holy companions of the Prophet). In an authoritative book titled *Tohfat-ul-Awam Maqbool Jadeed* (The Accepted and Latest Gift for the People) (in Urdu), published according to the *fatawa* of three different ayatollahs, who were recognized, in their own time, as the *maraja-e-taqleed* (the sources for following by the Shia masses) (Ayatollahs Tabatabai, Khomeini, and Al-Khoiee) and authenticated by two other scholars (Allama Syed Ali Naqvi Al-Naqvi and Maulana Syed Mohammad Jafar, and edited by Maulana Syed Manzoor Husain Naqvi, (Lahore, Pakistan: Iftikhar Book Depot, nd.)

The following statement is given under the section Furoo-e-Deen:

furro-e-Deen   Usool-e-Deen

(fundamentals of religion), that is, the roots of religion have been described above. Now, the Furoo-e-Deen, that is the branches of religion are described.

According to some theologians, there are four additional Furoo-e-Deen. And these are:......and tenth tabbarra that is maintaining animosity and distance with enemies of God, His Prophet, and the Ahl-e-bait (AS) (the family of the Prophet).

This author believes, as a Shia Athna Ashari, that this belief may be acceptable to all Muslims: maintain a distance and animosity with the enemies of Allah and His Prophet, and his family; but the practice of using abusive language for the Prophet's companions, including the first three caliphs, is totally uncalled for, unnecessary, irresponsible, and un-Islamic. It is not and should not be treated as a universal Shia practice, or Shia belief.

17. These demands of the SSP are taken from Farooqi, *What is...*
18. Farooqi, *What is...*, p. 15
19. George Whitecross Paton, *A Text-book of Jurisprudence* (third ed., edited by David P. Denham). Oxford: Oxford University Press, 1964.
20. Farooqi, *What is...*, p. 20.
21. Farooqi, *What is...*, p. 21.
22. Farooqi, *What is...*, Inside back cover.
23. Ayatollah Shaikh Mohammad Husain, *Asl-ish-Shiatae-was-Usooleha* (in Arabic) translated in Urdu by Allama Syed Ibn-e-Hasan Najafi, *Asl-o-Usool-e-Shia*, Karachi, Pakistan: Idara-e-Tammuddin-e-Islam, 1986, pp. 128-154.
24. A photocopy of the *fatwa* is reproduced in the fortnightly Al-Muntazar: Shariat Bill Number, *Volume 28-29, number 24 and 1 [respectively], February 05-20, 1987, Lahore [Pakistan]: Al Muntazar office, 1987,* pp. 43-45.

The question asked of Professor Shaltoot and his response are translated below:

> Some people believe that: it is obligatory on a Muslim to follow one of four well-known schools of jurisprudence (Hanafi, Shafaie, Hambali, Maliki) if he wants to perform his religious obligations and his inter-personal relations properly. These four schools of jurisprudence do not include the Shia *Athna Ashari* nor the Shia Zaidis. Do you also disapprove of following the Shia *Athna-Ashari fiqh*, as described above?

His response was as follows:

> Islam does not require its followers to follow a particular school of *fiqh*. On the contrary, every Muslim is free to follow a *fiqh* that is based on proper narrations and whose religious commands (rituals) are recorded in its books. A person who used to follow a *fiqh* is free to change his *fiqh* and start leading his life according to some other *fiqh*. This is not wrong.
>
> According to Islamic jurisprudence it is just as valid to follow the Jafari *fiqh*, which is commonly known as Shia Imami Athna-Ashari, as to follow the other *fiqh* of Ahl-e-Sunant.
>
> All Muslims must understand this truth and should not be prejudiced against other schools of *fiqh* because God's religion and *Shariat* (jurisprudence) are not subordinate to a particular school of thought. All followers of different *fiqh* have attempted to understand *Deen* (Religion) in their own ways; all these attempts are accepted by God. A person who has not achieved the status of *ijtehad* [ability to discover laws and issue religious edicts] and research is free to follow the orders of a *faqeeh* or *mujtahid* and act to his *fatwa*, in regards to prayers or inter-personal relations.

25. *Tareekhi Dastawez: Shia Musalman Ya Kafir: Faisla Aap kareyn* (in Urdu) (Historical Document: Shias: Muslim or Kafir: You Decide), Jhang [Pakistan]: Shoba-e-Nashr-o-Isha'at Sipah-e-Sahab Pakistan, Markazi Daftar Jame Masjid Haq Nawaz Shaheed, pp. 52-59.
26. Interview with Maulana Muhammad Nasser Saghaye Biria, Resident Alim (Scholar) at the Islamic Education Center, Houston, Texas on 15 August 1997. The author took notes of the comments made by Maulana Biria. Remarks attributed to Maulana Biria have been reviewed and approved by him.

11

A Ride on the Roller Coaster: US-Pakistan Relations 1947-1997
Dennis Kux

On 14 August 1947, President Harry S. Truman and Secretary of State George C. Marshall warmly welcomed the birth of Pakistan. Few, if any, US officials imagined that the new nation would become a close partner of the United States. In the summer of 1947, as the battle lines of the cold war were hardening, South Asia lay outside the struggle with the Soviet Union and was not an area of priority foreign policy concern in Washington. The United States anticipated that Britain would continue to play a dominant role in relations with the two successor states to the Raj.

As Pakistan struggled to cope with the tidal wave of Muslim refugees and the daunting challenge of setting up a new government from scratch, foreign policy—except for relations with India—was not a top concern for Governor-General Mohammed Ali Jinnah and his colleagues. But, with the UN General Assembly scheduled for the fall, the Cabinet discussed instructions for the delegation on 9 September. Stressing that his country should lean toward the West, Jinnah told the Cabinet, 'Pakistan was a democracy and communism did not flourish in the soil of Islam. It was clear therefore that our interests lay more with the two great democratic countries, namely, the UK and the USA rather than with Russia.'[1]

Although Pakistan perceived America as a potential source of financial support, the new government revealed its ignorance of Washington realities by seeking a mammoth $2 billion military and economic assistance programme, in effect, asking the United States to underwrite Pakistan's development and security. Surprised, US officials flatly turned down the request. In the end, Pakistan received $10 million from war relief funds.[2]

Like Britain, the United States hoped that India and Pakistan would cooperate in defence and security matters. It quickly became clear that this was not to be. After the anguish of partition, the two countries started fighting over the fate of the princely state of Jammu and Kashmir. When India took the issue to the UN Security Council in January 1948, the State Department initially rebuffed British pressure to take the lead in trying to resolve the dispute.[3] As the United Nations deliberated the Kashmir problem during 1948, the United States, nonetheless, began to play an increasingly important role. At first, Americans found little to choose between Indian and Pakistani positions. Ambassador Klahr Huddle, the senior American representative on the UN Commission on India and Pakistan, described India's Prime Minister Nehru and Pakistan's Foreign Minister Zafrullah Khan as equally uncooperative.[4]

This view gradually changed. After Pakistan accepted and India rejected President Harry Truman's August 1949 proposal that the two countries mediate their differences over plebiscite arrangements, Washington began to perceive Pakistan as the more cooperative party. Karachi's westward-leaning foreign policy was more agreeable to Americans than India's preachy neutralism. Good personal relations with Pakistani officials and troubled dealings with Indians further enhanced Pakistan's standing.

After Jinnah's death, his successors, Prime Ministers Liaquat Ali Khan and Khwaja Nazimuddin, maintained an anti-Communist foreign policy, but were unwilling to commit Pakistan unequivocally to the Western camp without a security guarantee against India. When Washington refused to provide this, Karachi decided against sending troops to Korea in 1950, and again in 1951, even though Pakistan politically supported the UN cause.[5]

Nor was the United States, despite good feelings about Pakistan, willing to respond positively to repeated requests for military assistance. Even though senior Truman administration officials thought Pakistani troops could bolster the defence of the Middle East against the Communist threat, they did not want to enter into a security arrangement that might embroil the United States in Pakistan's disputes with India.[6] Secretary of State Dean Acheson recalled that the Pakistanis 'were always asking us for arms and I was always holding them off.'[7]

Eisenhower: The US-Pakistan Alliance

This situation changed in 1953. In Washington in January, Republican Dwight D. Eisenhower moved into the White House and named John Foster Dulles, who favoured extending the system of anti-Communist security pacts, as his Secretary of State. In Karachi in April, autocratic Punjabi Governor-General Ghulam Mohammed fired Bengali Prime Minister Khwaja Nazimuddin in what amounted to a 'constitutional coup.' After Nazimuddin's ouster, effective power passed from the politicians to the West Pakistani dominated civil service and military. Unlike Liaquat and Nazimuddin, the new leadership was eager to join the Western camp in return for American arms aid even without a firm US security guarantee against India.

In May 1953, Secretary Dulles visited New Delhi and Karachi. He departed from South Asia with a positive impression of Pakistan's anti-Communism and a negative view of India's neutralism. Briefing the National Security Council (NSC) after returning home, Dulles said he was 'immensely impressed by the martial and religious qualities of the Pakistanis' and characterized India's Pandit Nehru as 'an utterly impractical statesman.'[8] In closed session testimony before the Foreign Affairs Committee of the House of Representatives, Dulles glowed about the Pakistanis, 'I believe those fellows are going to fight any Communist invasion with their bare fists if they have to.'[9]

In a 1 June radio and television broadcast, Dulles publicly floated the idea of a northern tier security pact as a means of strengthening the Middle East against the Communist threat. Instead of a security organization with largely Arab membership—as the British earlier envisaged—Dulles spoke of a defensive arc of states stretching from Turkey to Pakistan.[10] Given other foreign policy concerns, Washington was in no hurry to push the northern tier concept.

For the Pakistanis, however, it was different, especially for General Ayub Khan, the Army commander and Defence Minister. Because of weak finances and the lack of other plausible foreign help, US assistance was the only feasible way Ayub could modernize Pakistan's ill-equipped armed forces. The tall, handsome, England-trained General Ayub proved an effective salesman in Washington, stressing Pakistan's anti-Communist credentials, playing up the utility of the Pakistan Army in the defence of the Middle East, and playing down the impact that US arms for Pakistan would have on India.

Following press leaks from Karachi, India's Prime Minister Nehru reacted strongly, warning both Pakistan and the United States against entering into a security arrangement. As a result, when Dulles formally put the issue to President Eisenhower, the Secretary focused more on the consequences of backing down in the face of Nehru's strident and public opposition than on the benefits of military ties with Pakistan.[11] Eisenhower's approval set in motion a contrived arrangement under which Washington responded positively to Karachi's request for arms on 24 February 1954, after Pakistan and Turkey had concluded a bilateral security pact.

Later in 1954, the United States and the British took the lead in creating a Southeast Asia defence organization (SEATO). Although Dulles was not eager to have Pakistan join, Foreign Minister Zafrullah Khan participated in the pact negotiations. Zafrullah tried but failed to gain agreement that SEATO would cover aggression from all quarters, not just from the Communists.[12] When Prime Minister Bogra met Dulles in Washington in October 1954, the Secretary again refused to agree that the SEATO umbrella include an attack by India against Pakistan.[13] An ambivalent Pakistani cabinet formally ratified SEATO membership in January 1955.

Later in 1955, the northern tier defence arrangement took concrete form. Iraq, Britain and Iran joined the Turkish-Pakistan security accord which became the Baghdad Pact. Although the concept was an American policy initiative, Washington ironically did not become a full member of the Baghdad Pact. It feared that this step would intensify friction with Nasser's Egypt, a bitter rival of Iraq, and could trigger Congressional pressure for a parallel US security pact with Israel. Pakistan was initially reluctant to join, but agreed after the Turks and Iraqis convinced Ayub Khan, by then a major political force, that membership would entail no new security obligations.[14] Even though Pakistan thus became America's 'most allied ally,' motives for entering into the security relationship differed. Washington realized that Karachi desired to strengthen its defences against India, but concluded 'that the importance of bringing in Pakistan on the defence of the Middle East is greater than the importance of preserving pleasant relations with Mr Nehru.'[15]

The United States soon stunned Ayub and his colleagues by advising that military aid would not amount to more than a token $30 million. Unlike the Pakistanis, the Americans conceived of the alliances as primarily political-psychological ventures to bolster shaky governments against the Communists and did not envisage major military assistance commitments.[16] In the face of Pakistani pressure tactics and threats, Washington gradually gave ground. In the fall of 1954, the Administration agreed to a substantial military aid package, involving US financial support to equip four infantry and one and one-half armour divisions, six air force squadrons and to provide twelve naval vessels. The Defence Department put a $171 million price tag on the programme.[17]

The Pakistanis did not stay happy for long. After it became apparent that the Pentagon had badly underestimated costs, a testy argument ensued whether the agreed force levels or the $171 million ceiling would govern the programme. Once more,

Washington ceded to the Pakistanis, showing rather vividly how the weaker partner in an alliance can twist the tail of the stronger. The revised estimate for the programme was put at $301 million.[18] In 1956, a new study boosted the figure to $505 million or almost three times the original estimate.[19]

To compound Washington's unhappiness, America's new ally suffered from chronic political instability and severe economic problems, requiring substantial American economic aid. When the NSC reviewed South Asia policy in January 1957, an exasperated President Eisenhower criticized 'our tendency to rush out and seek allies' as not very sensible. The President continued: 'In point of fact we were doing practically nothing for Pakistan except in the form of military aid. This was the worst kind of a plan and decision we could have made. It was a terrible error, but now we seem hopelessly involved in it.'[20]

The Eisenhower administration felt a good deal better after Pakistan agreed that the Central Intelligence Agency (CIA) could use the Peshawar air force base for flights of the top secret U-2 aircraft over the Soviet Union and also approved setting up a US communications intelligence listening post at Badaber near Peshawar. Pakistan became an important link in the global chain of American intelligence gathering facilities. The United States received a tangible quid pro quo for its arms aid.

Although American economic help was providing a vital boost to Pakistan's faltering economy, the alliance was not popular politically in Karachi. Pakistan took India's shrill opposition in stride, but was upset by the loss of friends in the Muslim Middle East and elsewhere in the Afro-Asian world. America also disappointed its ally by refusing to support Pakistan's position fully on the Kashmir issue even though the Soviet Union took advantage of events to back India to the hilt. Apart from the Pakistan economy, the main gainer from the relationship was the military. Thanks to substantial amounts of US equipment and training, the Pakistan army and air force became a modern force that provided the country a genuine deterrent against the threat perceived from India.

On 6 October 1958 after the domestic political situation deteriorated badly, President Iskander Mirza[21] carried out an oft-threatened takeover of power, brushing aside US advice that he not do so.[22] Three weeks later, Army Chief Ayub Khan ousted Mirza to become President and Chief Martial Law Administrator. The Ayub regime soon won applause from Washington by its promising efforts to improve the economy, to reduce corruption and to introduce moderate reforms.

In March 1959, the United States signed a bilateral defence accord with Pakistan (and Iran). Designed to provide reassurance after Iraq's 1958 revolution broke up the Baghdad Pact (then replaced by the Central Treaty Organization—CENTO), the bilateral agreement promised US action in the event of external aggression. Careful drafting, however, limited the US commitment to an attack by Communist powers. Although this lawyer-like restriction satisfied Dulles's desire not to commit the United States to support Pakistan against India, it later caused major grief. Pakistanis either failed to understand or simply ignored the restrictive character of the 1959 security agreement.

But these differences lay in the future. In December 1959, a smiling Dwight Eisenhower enjoyed a hugely successful visit to Pakistan (and India). As Eisenhower's term drew toward its end, the bilateral relationship seemed on solid ground. The only serious upset during 1960 arose after the Soviets shot down a CIA U-2 spy plane that had taken off from Peshawar. Ayub's private reaction was to shrug his shoulders.[23] In public, however, he assured his countrymen after the Soviets threatened Pakistan that they would not stand alone in a crisis. The episode stirred doubts about the wisdom of Pakistan's total identification with the United States. As the U-2 incident showed, this involved risks as well as benefits.[24]

Kennedy: The Alliance Starts to Come Apart

When John F. Kennedy succeeded Eisenhower, Pakistanis worried that Washington would shift the focus of South Asia policy to India. As Senator, Kennedy had urged a major increase in economic assistance for India and criticized the emphasis that the Republicans placed on military aid to developing countries. Although the new Administration quickly boosted aid to India to $1 billion annually, it was slow to consider an increase in assistance for Pakistan. Troubled by this and reports of possible military aid to India, Ayub had extensive talks with Kennedy during a successful state visit to Washington in July 1961. Even though JFK refused Ayub's request to use American aid as a lever to force Indian concessions on Kashmir, he promised to consult with Pakistan should he consider military assistance to India.[25]

Despite the fact that Kennedy remained sceptical about the value of security arrangements with Pakistan, he did not want to lose a cold war ally. His policy goal was to improve relations with India without impairing US-Pakistan ties. Events would soon show how difficult this would be. In October 1962, after suffering a serious military setback in fighting with the Chinese over disputed frontiers, India turned to Washington for military help. Kennedy's response was positive and rapid.

It was, in fact, so rapid that he did not fulfil his commitment to consult Ayub before taking a decision. Although Pakistani objections would not have swayed Washington, Kennedy's failure to keep his promise deeply angered Ayub. An official US assurance of help in the event of an Indian attack, conveyed in a 5 November 1962 *aide mémoire*, did not allay Pakistan's objections to American arms aid for India.[26]

The two leaders saw the Sino-Indian conflict very differently. For Kennedy, bolstering India with military aid against China fit naturally into the US cold war strategy of containing Communism. Although Kennedy regarded China as the major US foe in Asia, Beijing's clash with New Delhi made China a potential partner for Pakistan in keeping with the adage, 'The enemy of my enemy is my friend.' Ayub, who did not believe China intended a major attack against India, feared the Indians would use American arms aid against Pakistan. After China offered a generous settlement during late 1962 border negotiations and made other gestures of friendship, a Sino-Pakistan entente began to take shape. Washington was not pleased.

Under Western pressure, Prime Minister Nehru had agreed to negotiations on Kashmir that began in December 1962. From the start, the impact of Pakistan's *rapprochement* with China and signs that Nehru was not serious clouded the discussions. After six rounds, the talks ended in failure in May 1963. Despite the failure of the Kashmir talks and strenuous Pakistani objections, Kennedy was determined to proceed with long-term military help for India.

When bilateral tensions mounted, including signs Pakistan might curtail US use of the intelligence base, Kennedy sent Under Secretary of State George Ball to confer with Ayub in September 1963. Their extensive discussions laid bare the depth of US-Pakistani disagreement. Even though Ayub said that he did not want to lose US friendship or assistance, he claimed that US military aid to India hurt Pakistan's security and was forcing him to try to reduce the threat from other neighbours through improved relations with China and, if possible, the Soviet Union.[27] Ball left Pakistan in a pessimistic mood, predicting a further Pakistani shift toward neutralism, a decline in US influence and the end to the alliance.[28] Kennedy himself accurately summed up the policy dilemma in a 12 September 1963 press conference 'Everything we give to India adversely affects the balance of power with Pakistan....we are dealing with a very complicated problem because the hostility between them is so great,' the President stated.[29]

Johnson: Texas-Style Arm Twisting

Lyndon Johnson, who became President after Kennedy's assassination, was less at ease in foreign affairs and more prone to use Texas-style arm twisting. Nor did Johnson have Kennedy's nuanced understanding of the security problem US arms aid to India was causing Pakistan. The new President bluntly warned Foreign Minister Zulfikar Ali Bhutto after Kennedy's funeral that Pakistan's growing ties with Communist China could threaten US friendship.[30] In December 1963, when General Maxwell Taylor, Chief of the Joint Chiefs of Staff visited Pakistan, President Ayub again stressed that US arms aid for India was endangering his country's security. Taylor's oral assurances—similar to those offered by Ball and other US officials—that Pakistan could count on American help should India attack failed to satisfy Ayub.[31]

In May 1964, after protracted review, Johnson approved a long-term military aid package for India. Even though Washington refused the Indians supersonic F-104s to match F-104s earlier supplied to the Pakistanis, Karachi reacted with official outrage. When Ayub and Bhutto intemperately attacked US policy in public statements,[32] an angry Johnson instructed Ambassador Walter McConaughy to tell Ayub he was hurt by the harsh criticism. The President further ordered the envoy to stress continuing opposition to Pakistan's *rapprochement* with China and disagreement that US arms aid to India was hurting Pakistan's interests.[33]

In 1965, after Johnson and Ayub won re-election, their differences sharpened. As he had told Ball, Ayub sought to establish good relations with two former adversaries—China and the Soviet Union—while at the same time maintaining friendly relations with the United States. Johnson's aim was to make sure that Ayub understood he could not count on US aid if he continued to ignore its views on China. Ayub's high-wire traverse of the 'triangular tightrope' started well with a successful March 1965 visit to Beijing and a more restrained, although useful, April 1965 trip to Moscow. But then, in mid-April, Johnson upset Ayub's diplomatic trapeze act. He abruptly and impolitely put off the Pakistani president's visit to Washington at the last minute. Two months later, Johnson upped the pressure, forcing postponement of a World Bank Pakistan consortium meeting through his refusal to make a US aid pledge pending discussion 'of certain other problems' (i.e. Pakistan's relations with China).[34]

A proud Ayub refused to bend to Johnson's pressure tactics. Relations went into a deep freeze. Just at this point, the usually cautious Pakistani president approved a plan urged by Foreign Minister Bhutto and other hawks to foment an insurrection in the Indian-held part of Kashmir. Operation Gibraltar, as the plan was called, backfired badly. After the Indians rounded up infiltrators, Ayub raised the stakes by launching a large-scale military attack in southern Kashmir. In turn, India responded by attacking across the international boundary near Lahore. On 6 September 1965, the two countries were at war.

President Johnson refused to intervene directly, backing efforts of UN Secretary General U Thant to halt the fighting. He brushed aside Pakistan's call that he implement assurances of American help against an Indian attack, noting that Pakistani incursions in Kashmir had triggered the crisis.[35] Instead, Johnson suspended economic and military aid to Pakistan (and also India). Since Ayub's military depended entirely on US supplies, this action hit Pakistan far harder than India.

Backing even further away from direct involvement in South Asia, Johnson supported Soviet efforts to mediate a peace settlement at Tashkent after India and Pakistan agreed to a cease-fire—an astounding turnaround after a decade of American anxiety about Soviet activity in the subcontinent. When Ayub came to Washington in December 1965, LBJ was full of flowery praise but, in effect, drove the final nail in the coffin of the old US-Pakistan relationship.

Increasingly preoccupied with the Vietnam war, Washington had limited time for South Asia and was weary of trying unsuccessfully to reduce India-Pakistan tensions. Although Johnson agreed to resume substantial economic aid, he refused to renew military aid for Pakistan. For their part, Pakistanis were bitter about US policy during the 1965 war. Bhutto, whom Ayub fired as foreign minister in 1966, voiced this anger in speeches charging American betrayal of Pakistan and also blasting Ayub for agreeing to the status quo ante at Tashkent.

For a while, Ayub rode out the storm. China filled America's place as the main arms supplier. Washington was continuing large-scale economic aid. Patient diplomacy with Moscow began to pay off with increased economic aid and, in 1968, agreement to provide military hardware. The quid pro quo for Soviet arms was Ayub's decision not to renew the lease for the US intelligence base at Badaber which shut down the following year.

But after Ayub fell seriously ill, domestic opposition began to undermine his position. East Pakistanis, angry over their second class status, and West Pakistanis, disgruntled over the lack of democracy and unequal sharing of the fruits of economic growth, took to the streets in increasing numbers. By the end of 1968, Ayub was beginning to totter. Finally, after failing to reach agreement with opposition political leaders, a sad Ayub relinquished power in March 1969 to Army Chief General Mohammed Yahya Khan.

Nixon: The Tilt

Even though Richard Nixon, a longtime friend of Pakistan, became President in January 1969, he did not noticeably alter US South Asia policy. His administration remained content to focus on economic aid and to steer clear of security commitments. Still, in order to make a gesture toward Pakistan, in October 1970 Nixon approved a 'one-time exception' to the restrictive arms supply policy. This action allowed Pakistan to purchase some $50 million worth of armoured personnel carriers and combat aircraft. More important, when Nixon visited Pakistan in August 1969, he asked Yahya Khan to tell the Chinese Communists of his desire to normalize relations. Pakistan's friendship with China, a vice under Kennedy and Johnson, became a virtue under Nixon. Although the White House used parallel channels to communicate with Beijing, Pakistan became the key intermediary when Yahya Khan was asked in April 1971 to arrange Henry Kissinger's secret visit to China.

This dramatic diplomatic manoeuver coincided with Pakistan's gravest, and ultimately fatal, political crisis. December 1970 elections gave East Pakistan's Awami League an absolute majority in the constituent assembly. After the elections, Yahya, Bhutto, whose Pakistan People's Party (PPP) had won a majority of seats in the west, and Awami League leader Mujibur Rahman failed to agree on the extent of East Pakistan autonomy. Believing the use of force would 'fix' things, Yahya Khan on 26 March 1971 outlawed the Awami League and ordered the Pakistan army to crush East Pakistani resistance.

As the world gradually became aware of the Pakistan military's brutal repression of the Bengalis, Nixon refused any public censure of Yahya. His silence sparked widespread criticism from Americans who believed Washington, on moral grounds, should speak out. Neither the public nor any but a handful of key aides, not including the Secretary of State, were aware of the proposed opening to China and of Pakistan's key role in the process. After Kissinger's visit was publicly announced in July 1971, Nixon continued the 'tilt.' Perceiving events in East Pakistan not as a regional crisis but as part of a global struggle between the Soviet Union, China and the United States and their surrogates—India and Pakistan—the White House wanted to protect the opening to China by demonstrating to Beijing that America would be faithful to its friends and those of China (i.e. Pakistan) even under unpopular circumstances.[36]

With millions of Bengali refugees flooding into India, the threat of an India-Pakistan war mounted. Although the United States prodded Yahya to reach a political settlement, American diplomacy failed to budge him on the key requirement—that Yahya negotiate with Awami League leader Mujibur Rahman, then jailed for treason.[37] As Mrs Gandhi upped the military pressure against East Pakistan, Yahya committed his final blunder on 3 December 1971, attacking India in the west.[38] The third India-Pakistan War was under way.

In the United Nations, Soviet vetoes blocked Security Council action, but the General Assembly overwhelmingly called for a cease-fire. The United States condemned India as the main aggressor. Badly outnumbered, Pakistan forces in the east fell back toward Dhaka. Nixon and Kissinger—almost alone in the US administration—believed that India also planned to launch a major attack against West Pakistan and despatched the aircraft carrier *Enterprise* toward the Bay of Bengal as a warning signal. On 17 December, Pakistani troops surrendered in the east. On 19 December the war in the west ended after Yahya accepted Mrs Gandhi's cease-fire offer.

Although Nixon and Kissinger's handling of the crisis stirred passion among Americans (and Indians), it had scant effect on either Pakistani or Indian actions. Yahya's mistaken belief that he could 'fix' things by the use of force caused the East Pakistan tragedy. His blunder presented India, as K. Subrahmanyam put it, 'an opportunity the like of which will never come again.'[39]

Zulfikar Ali Bhutto achieved his ambition to become leader of Pakistan after a discredited Yahya relinquished power. As Bhutto strove to restore confidence to his demoralized and shrunken country, he received sympathy and generous economic aid from America, but no weapons. Congressional opinion remained too critical of Pakistan's actions in 1971 and Nixon's handling of the crisis to permit an early easing of the restrictions on arms transfers.

In the meanwhile, Bhutto reoriented Pakistan's foreign policy. He pulled out of SEATO, maintained only a nominal membership in CENTO, and stressed ties to the Middle East and Islamic world. In 1974, he proudly hosted the second meeting of the Organization of Islamic Conference (OIC) in Lahore. That same year, 1974, saw Gerald Ford become President after the Watergate crisis forced Nixon to resign. In February 1975, Ford lifted restrictions against arms transfers to Pakistan, but did not resume grant military aid or credits.

About this time, a new problem arose—American nonproliferation policy opposition to Pakistan's quest for a nuclear weapons capability. After the United States realized in late 1974 that Pakistan was seeking a nuclear device, Kissinger tried hard but unsuccessfully to convince Bhutto to drop the effort. Pakistan's leader firmly believed that his country needed the nuclear option to offset India's military superiority, especially after New Delhi exploded its own nuclear device in May 1974.[40]

Carter: Nuclear Sanctions and Afghanistan

In March 1977, Bhutto won re-election handily, too handily in fact. Opposition protests over vote rigging soon shook his hold on power. Reverting to US bashing, a cornered Bhutto shrilly charged that Washington was out to get him.[41] In July 1977, the Pakistani military ousted Bhutto and Army commander Ziaul Haq imposed martial law. In September, after failing to convince Zia to drop the nuclear option, President Jimmy Carter suspended US aid pursuant to an amendment which barred assistance to countries, like Pakistan, that were importing equipment for nuclear reprocessing.[42]

A year later, Washington briefly resumed aid after the French, who were supplying the reprocessing equipment, pulled out. Sanctions were, however, reimposed after Washington learned that Pakistan was pursuing a second track toward a nuclear device, one based on the uranium enrichment process.[43] When queried about nuclear activities, Pakistani officials routinely insisted the programme was peaceful and not directed toward developing nuclear weapons. For example, Zia told *Newsweek*, 'It's pure fiction. We don't want to make a bomb.'[44]

Bilateral relations hit their low point on 21 November 1979. Agitated by reports that the United States was involved in the sacrilege against the Muslim holy place at Mecca, an enraged student mob set fire to the American Embassy in Islamabad. Four died and 137 other employees, trapped inside, nearly suffocated before the mob dispersed. When Pakistani authorities were slow to respond, an angry Jimmy Carter had a 'very impassioned' telephone conversation with President Zia.[45]

Five weeks later, after the Red Army invaded Afghanistan, the US attitude fundamentally changed. Carter once more called

Zia, but his tone and message were radically different. The United States, he said, reaffirmed the 1959 bilateral security agreement against Communist attack.[46] Pakistan had become a 'frontline' state.

Washington subordinated restraining Pakistan's nuclear programme to seeking Zia's cooperation against the Soviets in Afghanistan. Zbigniew Brzezinski, Carter's national security adviser, flew to Islamabad to woo the Pakistani dictator with $400 million worth of economic and military assistance. 'Peanuts,' was Zia's undiplomatic response. According to then Foreign Minister Agha Shahi, the Pakistanis judged the American offer too small to offset the trouble its acceptance could cause with the Soviets.[47]

Reagan: A Meeting of Minds against the Evil Empire

After Ronald Reagan became President, a satisfactory arrangement with Pakistan ranked high on his national security agenda. When the Administration proposed a five-year $3.5 billion assistance package, Zia did not consider it 'peanuts.' Washington and Islamabad soon established a close partnership to oppose the Soviet presence in Afghanistan. Unlike the 1950s, there was no formal alliance. Pakistan remained a member of the Non-Aligned Movement, which it had joined in 1979 after quitting CENTO.

The Pakistanis took the lead in mobilizing diplomatic pressure, especially among Muslim countries, against the Soviets. Year after year, Moscow found itself roundly criticized in UN General Assembly resolutions. The United States cleverly stayed in the background so that the issue could be mainly framed in terms of opposition to Soviet occupation of a non-aligned Muslim state.[48] Although the United Nations initiated peace negotiations in Geneva, the talks at first made little progress. Even as the US-Pakistan partnership flourished, the nuclear issue lurked below the surface. Zia's denials that

Pakistan was trying to develop nuclear weapons kept colliding with intelligence reports of Pakistani progress toward a nuclear device. There were also embarrassing arrests of Pakistanis seeking illegally to export sensitive nuclear equipment from various countries, including the United States. A shrewd judge of how far he could push the Americans, Zia believed that as long as the war in Afghanistan continued—neither he nor Washington expected an early end—the US government would find some way to avoid imposing sanctions provided Pakistan did not explode a device.[49]

In 1985, growing Congressional concern about the nuclear programme forced the Reagan administration to accept a new amendment in order to gain approval for a multi-year renewal of Pakistan aid. The amendment, introduced by Senator Larry Pressler (Rep-S. Dakota), called for an annual presidential certification that Pakistan did not possess a nuclear device for aid to continue. Quite apart from Zia's pledges, the requirement seemed safe enough given what US intelligence knew of the state of the nuclear programme.

In 1986-87, the Geneva negotiations unexpectedly became serious after Soviet leader Gorbachev decided to withdraw Soviet Russian troops from Afghanistan. In April 1988, agreement was reached on a timetable for the departure of the Red Army. In 1988-89, as the Red Army was withdrawing from Afghanistan, the Iron Curtain in Eastern Europe crumbled. The Berlin Wall came down and Germany was reunified. The Cold War ended. Meanwhile in Pakistan, in August 1988, an unexplained airplane crash killed Zia as well as US Ambassador Arnold Raphel. Free elections then brought to power Benazir Bhutto, the daughter of Zulfiqar Ali Bhutto, the man Zia had hanged in 1979. In Washington, Vice President George Bush won the November 1988 elections to succeed Ronald Reagan.

Bush: The Pressler Axe Falls

The departure of the Red Army from Afghanistan and the end of the Cold War altered the policy dynamics on the nuclear issue. With Pakistani cooperation no longer essential, pressure to impose Pressler sanctions from nonproliferation policy supporters became much stronger. The Bush administration certified in 1989 that Pakistan did not possess a nuclear device, although it was not an easy decision.[50]

But the fair weather did not last long. During a fresh India-Pakistan war scare in early 1990, US intelligence concluded that Islamabad had taken the final step toward a device, machining the nuclear cores. American officials warned that Washington would impose Pressler amendment sanctions unless Pakistan rolled the programme back. The ruling—and squabbling—troika of President Ghulam Ishaq Khan, Chief of Army Staff Mirza Aslam Beg and Prime Minister Benazir Bhutto, took no action, hoping that Washington would not cut off aid.[51] In August 1990, President Khan dismissed Bhutto and called for new elections. About this time, President Bush decided he could not issue the necessary certificate.

After October 1, 1990 passed, Pressler sanctions went into effect. Pakistan lost $564 million worth of assistance slated for the fiscal year 1991. The stunned reaction in Islamabad was one of deep anger. 'With the Afghan War over, the United States no longer needs Pakistan. You Americans have discarded us like a piece of used Kleenex,' Pakistanis commented bitterly.[52] During the remainder of the Bush administration, diplomatic discussions about lifting sanctions continued. Pakistan's willingness to freeze the nuclear programme was not, however, sufficient to meet US demands that Islamabad destroy its existing capability.[53]

As if nuclear sanctions were not enough, the Bush administration threatened to put Pakistan on the 'terrorist state' list after the ISI actively supported the armed struggle of young Kashmiris against Indian rule that began in the late 1980s. In the end, the government of Nawaz Sharif, who succeeded

Benazir in late 1990, took sufficient steps to avoid having Pakistan placed in the company of Libya, Iran, North Korea, etc.[54] In the process, the Afghan War partnership lay in shambles. For Washington, yesterday's partner became today's troublemaker. For Islamabad, the Americans had once more proven their fickleness and inconstancy. Although Pakistani public opinion and a robustly free press roundly excoriated the United States, officials and political leaders, whether Bhutto or Nawaz Sharif, did not believe it was in Pakistan's interest to stir additional trouble with the world's sole superpower. They hoped that somehow their country could regain favour with the Americans. In 1995, Benazir, who had returned to power after squabbling Prime Minister Sharif and President Khan both resigned under Army pressure, enjoyed another successful US visit. On this occasion, President Bill Clinton agreed to support an amendment to ease Pressler sanctions and to sell elsewhere F-16s aircraft Pakistan had purchased, but had not received, so Islamabad could be repaid. 'I don't think it's right for us to keep the money and the equipment,' Clinton declared.[55] In the Congress, Senator Hank Brown (Rep.-Colorado) introduced an amendment to permit economic aid and military training, but not military assistance. After a hard battle, which heavily engaged Pakistani-American and Indian-American ethnic lobbies, the Brown amendment carried by a 55-45 vote.

Bilateral relations once more warmed. Pakistan saw the Clinton administration's action as an effort to make amends for sanctions and vindication of their criticism of the Pressler amendment. The fact that Assistant Secretary of State for South Asia, Robin Raphel became embroiled in public argument with the Indians was a further plus. Still, the bilateral relationship remained relatively thin in terms of substance. In line with Clinton administration support for 'enlarging democracy,' Washington applauded Islamabad's efforts to institutionalize representative government, but offered little more than nice words to help the Pakistanis deal with their mounting economic woes. Narcotics—a continuing US concern—became a further bilateral burden. Because of Pakistan's lack of zeal in pursuing anti-drug measures, presidential waivers were needed in 1996 and 1997 to avoid new sanctions. Pakistan's support for the Islamic fundamentalist Taliban movement in civil war-racked Afghanistan posed an additional friction.

Despite these difficulties, the public rhetoric about relations was positive as Pakistan celebrated its 50th anniversary in Washington. Secretary of State Madeleine Albright stated that America 'continued to view Pakistan as a key partner in advancing peace and prosperity in South Asia.' Pakistan's Ambassador Riaz Khokar declared that US-Pakistan friendship 'has endured the test of time.'[56] Plans were afoot for visits to Pakistan by the Secretary of State, the first since 1983, and by the President, the first since 1969.

A Half Century of Volatile Relations

If plotted on a graph, the curve of fifty years of the US-Pakistan relationship would show a series of sharp and uneven fluctuations:
— Three high points: The alliance years of the 1950s, the Nixon-Ford years, and the Afghan war partnership during the 1980s;
— Three low points: The mid-1960s disputes, the troubles over nuclear matters in the late 1970s, and again after 1990; and
— Two periods of friendly but not very substantive relations: The Truman presidency and the past several years.

Pakistan's policy toward the United States has been the more consistent factor, and the US stance toward Pakistan the more volatile. From its first days in 1947, Pakistan has sought external support, especially from America, to lessen its sense of insecurity against India. US interest in Pakistan has, however, varied widely over the years, largely as a function of how Pakistan, at any given moment, fit into US global policies.

Although intermittent, America's involvement has had a considerable impact on Pakistan. Some historians blame the failure of democratic institutions in the 1950s on US arms aid.[57] The author disagrees. The disintegration of the Muslim League in the 1950s, the poor quality of political leadership after the death of Jinnah and Liaquat, and the anti-democratic orientation of key figures, such as Ghulam Mohammed and Iskander Mirza, appear far more important factors than the inflow of US arms in explaining the failure of parliamentary rule to take root. Had Eisenhower maintained Truman's policy of not entering into a security arrangement with Pakistan, the author finds it hard to believe that political developments in Karachi would have unfolded very differently.

The arms aid relationship, nonetheless, significantly strengthened Pakistan's military. By providing a secure and substantial source of funds outside the regular budget process, the United States helped create larger and more capable armed forces than Pakistan could have afforded on its own. This capability provided Pakistan a far greater sense of security against India. When coupled with India's poor performance in the 1962 Sino-India war and in the April 1965 Rann of Kutch skirmishing, it also contributed to the sense of overconfidence that led to Ayub's disastrous green light for Operation Gibraltar.

After the Red Army moved into Afghanistan, Washington turned the military (and economic) aid spigot back on. This decision clearly bolstered the position of unpopular military dictator Ziaul Haq. Even though renewed US arms aid benefitted the Pakistan military, Zia failed to use the opportunity to build up the country's defence industrial capacity to reduce dependence on foreign supplies. The supply of covert arms for the Afghan resistance movement, mainly financed by the United States and Saudi Arabia, has also had a significant negative spill-over effect on Pakistan. The enormous influx of weapons has significantly contributed to the serious and unsettling increase in violence in recent years in Pakistan.

Economic assistance has been less controversial. In the 1950s, US aid was a life saver for the floundering economy. In the 1960s, together with Ayub's pro-market policies, American help—about one-half of foreign assistance inflows—helped advance Pakistan to the edge of self-sustaining growth. Although US economic assistance during the Afghan War period was larger in absolute terms, it had a much smaller impact given the growth of the Pakistan economy and the expanded role of other foreign lenders.

Given the volatile history of the relationship, the relatively positive current atmospherics are perhaps somewhat surprising. Part of the explanation lies in Pakistan's desire to put the best face on ties with the United States, seeing no advantage in stressing the negative *vis-à-vis* the sole super power. Pakistan also benefits from a residue of goodwill in Washington, especially in the Pentagon and the intelligence community, where there are fond memories of days of closer cooperation.

Pakistanis claim that America has been an unreliable friend. Although the charge is not without justification, the explanation lies less in US insincerity than in the absence of continuing common security interests.[58] Although genuinely anti-Communist in the 1950s, Pakistan's leaders were not seriously concerned about the threat of Communist aggression and used the alliance mainly as a means to strengthen the country against India. Except for Nixon's 'tilt' in 1971, however, Washington has never been willing to side with Pakistan against India. The United States has generally sought friendly relations with both countries, an approach that has often ended up pleasing neither. In the 1980s, Islamabad and Washington shared a strong desire to combat the Soviet presence in Afghanistan. Once the war was won, they shared few other important security interests and had significant differences. Although the imposition of Pressler amendment sanctions was hardly a pleasant way to say 'thank you' to a former close partner, Washington had little legal choice and had clearly warned Islamabad in 1989 and 1990 of the dangers it was running. Forced to choose between continued US security and economic aid or a nuclear capability, Pakistan chose to forego US assistance.

Summing Up

Over the past half century, the relationship between the United States and Pakistan has had almost as many ups and downs as a ride on a roller coaster. At times, the two countries have been close partners and allies. Occasionally, they have had sharp differences. And at other times, including the present, the relationship has been friendly but substantively thin.

Fifty years after Pakistan gained its independence, the situation is not unlike the state of affairs that prevailed during the Truman years. Although the United States wishes Pakistan well, it does not perceive major interests and does not wish to take sides in the Kashmir dispute with India. As Pakistan begins its second half century, the relationship with the United States has, to a considerable degree, come full circle.

NOTES

1. Minutes of Pakistan Cabinet Meeting, 9 September 1947, CF/47, National Documentation Centre, Islamabad.
2. Pakistan Embassy memorandum to Assistant Secretary of State for Economic Affairs Willard Thorp, October 1947, Department of State Records, National Archives (DSR, NA); *Foreign Relations of the United States (FRUS), 1947, Vol. III*, pp. 172-74, Memorandum from the Acting Secretary of State to the Pakistan Ambassador, 17 December 1947.
3. *FRUS, 1948, Vol. V, Pt. 1*, pp. 276-68, Memorandum of meeting of British officials with Acting Secretary Robert Lovett, 10 January 1948; British Mission to the UN telegram to the Foreign Office, 13 January 1948, FO 371/69706, Public Record Office, London.
4. *FRUS, 1948, Vol. V., Part 1*, pp. 349-53, 358, 362-65, Embassy Karachi (Huddle) telegrams to State Department, 15 July and 10 August 1948; Embassy New Delhi (Huddle) telegrams to State Department, 19, 21, 27 July and 16 August 1948.
5. Embassy Karachi despatches 287 and 424, 11 August and 6 September 1950 and Embassy Karachi telegram to the State Department, 30 August 1950, DSR, NA; *FRUS, 1951, Vol. VI, Pt. 2*, pp. 2203-06, State Department telegrams to Embassy Karachi, 11 and 14 May 1951 and Embassy Karachi telegram to the State Department, 15 May 1951.
6. Interview with Ambassador George McGhee, 17 March 1995.

7. Selig Harrison, 'Pakistan and the United States,' *New Republic*, 10 August 1959, p. 14.
8. *FRUS, 1952-54, Vol. IX*, pp. 379-83, Minutes of 1 June 1953 NSC meeting.
9. US House Committee on Foreign Affairs, *Selected Executive Sessions Hearings, 10*, p. 96. Testimony by John Foster Dulles, 2 June 1953.
10. *Department of State Bulletin*, 15 June 1953, p. 835. Text of 1 June radio and television address by Secretary Dulles.
11. See Dennis Kux, *Estranged Democracies, India and the United States, 1941-1991* (Washington: National Defence University Press, 1993) pp. 108-115 for fuller discussion of events.
12. Interview with Ambassador Agha Hilaly, 30 January 1996. Hilaly served as Zafrullah's deputy during the SEATO negotiations.
13. *FRUS, 1952-54, Vol. XI, Pt. 2*, pp. 1868-68, Memorandum reporting the meeting between Secretary Dulles and Prime Minister Bogra, 18 October 1954.
14. Farooq Naseem Bajwa, *Pakistan and the West, 1947-1957* (Karachi: Oxford University Press, 1996), pp. 140-41 and 144-48.
15. *New York Times*, 14 February 1954.
16. Interview with Ambassador Henry Byroade, 5 May 1990.
17. *FRUS, 1952-54, Vol. XI, Pt. 2*, pp. 1860, 1864, 1868-71. State Department Memorandum of conversation with Ambassador Amjad Ali, 6 August 1954; Embassy Karachi telegram to State Department, 17 August 1954; State Department memorandum reporting meeting between Secretary Dulles and Prime Minister Bogra, 18 October 1954; and State Department telegram to Embassy Karachi, 22 October 1954, summarizing talks with Pakistanis. State Department Aide Memoire on talks with Pakistan and briefing memo for President Eisenhower's meeting with Prime Minister Bogra, Whitman File, Dwight D. Eisenhower Library (DDEL), Abilene, Kansas.
18. Memorandum for JCS Chairman Admiral Radford from Maj. Gen. Robert Cannon, 31 August 1955, DDEL; *FRUS, 1955-57, Vol. VIII*, pp. 445-46, 450-52, 454-56; Consulate General Lahore to State Department, 4 October 1955, reporting talk with General Ayub Khan; letter from Assistant Secretary of Defence Gray to Under Secretary of State Hoover, 5 December 1955; and Embassy Karachi telegram to the State Department, 19 January 1956.
19. Report of Military Assistance Study Committee headed by Under Secretary of State Herbert Prochnow, DDEL.
20. *FRUS, 1955-57, VIII*, pp. 25-26, Report of the 3 January 1957 NSC meeting.
21. A former British Raj political officer, Mirza had open contempt for Pakistan's politicians and did not believe the country was ready for democracy. After he succeeded an ailing Ghulam Mohammed in 1955,

Mirza's manipulative tactics were an important factor in undermining political stability.

22. *FRUS, 1958-60, Vol. XV*, pp. 666-67, State Department telegram to Embassy Karachi, 6 October 1958.
23. Interview with senior US intelligence officer who was dealing with the U-2 at the time, 12 June 1997.
24. *Dawn*, 18 May 1960 and *New York Times*, 27 June 1960.
25. *FRUS, 1961-93, Vol. IX*, pp. 68-74.
26. Ibid., p. 372. Text of *aide memoire* given to Ayub can be found in Embassy Karachi airgram 883, 23 February 1963.
27. Ibid., pp. 661-68, Embassy Tehran telegram to the State Department, 5 September 1963, reporting Ball's wrap-up meeting with Ayub.
28. Ibid., pp. 671-74, Embassy Lisbon telegram to the State Department, 6 September 1963, providing Ball's assessment of his talks.
29. *New York Times*, 13 September 1963 for transcript of Kennedy press conference.
30. State Department telegram to Embassy Karachi, 2 December 1963, reporting Johnson's talk with Bhutto, Lyndon B. Johnson Library (LBJL), Austin, Texas.
31. Memorandum of conversation between Taylor and Ayub, 20 December 1963, LBJL.
32. *Daily Mail* (London), 23 June 1964 for Ayub interview and Embassy Karachi telegram to State Department, also 23 June 1964 reporting Bhutto National Assembly speech.
33. State Department telegram to Embassy Karachi, 29 July 1964, providing instructions for McConaughy's meeting with Ayub, LBJL.
34. State Department telegram to Embassy Karachi, 30 June 1965 and Harold H. Saunders, 'Narrative and Guide to the Documents, NSC Histories', p. 6, LBJL.
35. State Department telegrams to Embassy Karachi, 2 and 4 September, 1965, LBJL; for a Pakistani report of McConaughy-Bhutto 9 September 1965 meeting, see Farhat Mahmud, *History of US-Pakistan Relations* (Lahore: Vanguard, 1991), pp. 282-91. See also Sir Morrice James, *Pakistan Chronicle* (Karachi: Oxford University Press, 1993), p. 140.
36. Interview with Harold H. Saunders, 26 April 1991. Saunders was dealing with South Asia on the NSC staff in 1971.
37. Interview with Ambassador Sultan Mohammed Khan, 6 July 1995; Leo Rose and Richard Sisson, *War and Secession: India, Pakistan and the Creation of Bangladesh* (Berkeley: University of California Press, 1990), pp. 173-74 and 193-94.
38. In late November, Indian forces occupied East Pakistan territory to mount pressure on Pakistani strong points near the border. D-Day for a full-scale invasion was December 6, but when Yahya attacked in the West, India was spared the onus of striking first (Rose and Sisson, *War and Secession*, pp. 213-14).

39. *National Herald* (New Delhi), 5 April 1971, article by well-known Indian security analyst K. Subrahmanyam.
40. *New York Times*, 10 August 1976; interview with Ambassador Robert Oakley, 15 June 1995. Oakley, an NSC staff member at the time, accompanied Kissinger on his August trip to Pakistan.
41. *New York Times*, 27 April and 6 May 1977 and *Washington Post*, 29 April and 8 May 1977.
42. Steve Weisman and Herbert Korsney, *The Islamic Bomb* (New York: Times Books, 1981) p. 168.
43. Interview with Ambassador Jane Coon, then Deputy Assistant Secretary of State for South Asia.
44. *Newsweek*, 14 January 1980.
45. Interview with Thomas P. Thornton, 21 September 1995. Thornton was then handling South Asia on the NSC staff.
46. Ibid.
47. Interview with Ambassador Agha Shahi, 31 December 1995.
48. Ibid.
49. Interview with Lt. Gen. (Rtd) Syed Refaqat, formerly Zia's principal staff officer, 16 February 1996 and former Foreign Minister Yakub Khan, 19 January 1996.
50. Interviews with Ambassador Robert Oakley, 15 June 1995, and Richard Haass, 27 April 1997. Haass was dealing with South Asia as an NSC staff member in the Bush administration.
51. Interview with Ambassador Oakley, 15 June 1995.
52. The author heard this comment frequently during an extended stay in Pakistan, November 1995-April 1996.
53. Interview with Ambassador Akram Zaki, 10 March 1996. Zaki was Pakistan Foreign Ministry Secretary General; *Washington Post*, 7 and 14 June 1991; *The Nation* (Islamabad), 25 November 1992; Interview with Ambassador Abida Hussain, 11 March 1966.
54. Interview with Ambassadors Abida Hussain, 11 March 1996, and Nicholas Platt, 9 February 1995.
55. *Washington Post*, 23 March 1995.
56. *India Abroad*, 22 August 1997.
57. See for example, Robert J. McMahon, *The Cold War on the Periphery* (New York: Columbia University Press, 1994) and Ayesha Jalal, *The State of Martial Rule: The Origins of Pakistan's Political Economy of Defence* (Cambridge: Cambridge University Press, 1990).
58. At one point in the Bhutto-Kissinger meeting in Lahore, Kissinger commented, '...as for our relations, I've never raised the question about sincerity. I don't think it has meaning for nations. I assume a nation does something for its own interest. The question is whether there is compatibility.' (Memorandum of conversation of Kissinger-Bhutto meeting, 9 August 1976, Lahore, Pakistan, DSR.)

12

Pakistan's Relations with the Soviet Union and Russia
Hafeez Malik

Pakistan's graph of fifty years of its relations (1947-1997) first with the Soviet Union, and then with Russia (1991-), the successor state, shows no highs, but a series of lows, reflecting a calculated disregard for the geostrategic imperatives of Eurasia. An attempt is made here to highlight some of the significant 'lows', including: (1) the early options for some strategic decisions; (2) the crisis of Bangladesh; (3) attempts at bilateralism; and (4) the Soviet debacle over Afghanistan. Finally, an analytical word or two are added about Pakistan-Russian relations to cover the period of 1991-98.

Pakistan's leadership made some basic strategic decisions at its inception in 1947 in regard to its relations with the United States and the Soviet Union. This option was available as the Cold War had just set in, and the two superpowers were prepared to reward the newly emerging states, if they committed themselves to support their designs to establish a post World War II balance of power system. The rewards were offered in the form of economic and military aid, which the fledgling new states so desperately needed. The psychological comfort or a sense of security came in the form of different grades of an alliance with a superpower.

Pakistan's Early Options and Some Strategic Decisions

The cold war was not merely a struggle for power, but a sustained effort to create a global equilibrium—where both the Soviet Union and the United States wanted it to tilt in their favour. Centered in Europe, the previous system of the balance of power, which had been structured in 1815 at the end of the Napoleonic wars, had seen Britain playing the role of a balancer between major powers, including France, Prussia/Germany, Austro-Hungarian Empire, and Russia. The United States was then viewed as a regionally dominant power in the Americas, and this position the United States had claimed by virtue of the proclamation of the Monroe Doctrine in 1823. World War II thrust the United States from the position of a regional hegemony to a global power and eliminated the role of a 'balancer', and projected the Soviet Union as a competitive superpower with global aspirations.

In the previous balance of power system (1815-1939/45), the 55 major, secondary, and small states of Europe, functioned diplomatically in a homogenous cultural environment of Europe, which was the product of Greco-Roman legacy and Christianity, that in turn spawned the Renaissance and scientific-industrial revolution. The countries of Asia, the Middle East and Africa were their colonial and imperial possessions, and played no role in the Europe-centered balance of power system. The bipolar new system not only became truly global in scope, including cultural and religious diversity, but witnessed major discordant ideological notes, which turned the United States and the Soviet Union into 'enemies', rather than 'rivals' playing by the rules of the same old game of the balance of power.

Highly prosperous and economically super developed, having suffered no destruction on its own soil, the United States competed with the Soviet Union from a position of strength and projected itself with grand claims that: (1) as an engine of development, capitalism is superior to the Soviet Union's socialism-communism, which is Godless, totalitarian, and oppressive of the individual initiative and personality; (2) multi-party democratic system disallowed dictatorship of one party rule; (3) independence of the judiciary guaranteed the exercise of individual freedoms, including the freedom of speech, assembly and religion; and (4) the basic human rights must not be abridged or cast aside for any state reason.

The Soviet Union, on the other hand, not only established communist parties in third world countries, which invariably toed the Soviet foreign policy line, but also projected Communism as a shortcut to industrial development. Since European capitalism had enriched itself at the expense of the Third World economies, the Soviet model of 'socialism' retained a substantial attraction for the underdeveloped countries. Especially the Soviet claim that the newly independent states' feudal economies could bypass capitalism (entailing glaring economic inequalities) to socialism (meaning industrial development and economic equality) under Soviet patronage carried an irresistable appeal. The relative backwardness of the Soviet economy, however, remained a less attractive feature, and indeed a handicap for Soviet diplomacy. Consequently, throughout the Cold War, the Soviet Union could extend economic and military aid only to a few strategically important countries.

In 1947, Pakistan's economic survival was exceptionally uncertain, and relations with India were plagued by disputes over the distribution of British India's economic assets and military hardware, and the territorial claims over the princely states of Junagadh, Mongrol, Manavadar, and Kashmir. The first three states had acceded to Pakistan, but India gobbled them up, claiming that their Muslim rulers had no right to disregard the wishes of their Hindu population to remain with India. When Kashmir's Hindu ruler overlooked the preference of 85 per cent Muslim population of the state for Pakistan, India championed the Hindu ruler's right to do so, which led to the first India-Pakistan War in 1948.

Pakistan's public opinion in the 1940s and early 1950s considered the danger of invasion by the Soviet Union as remote, compared to the high probability of Indian aggression. Internally, the Communist Party of Pakistan (CPP) was structurally weak, and had no following, with the exception of some notable poets and litterateurs, who were organized in the All-Pakistan Progressive Writers' Association. Ideologically, Pakistanis did not consider Communism or Marxism subversive of Islam, or an instrument of Soviet cultural imperialism. Speaking (1956) in the National Assembly, a religiously conservative politician of substantial political reputation in the Punjab, Mian Abdul Bari, dismissed the ideological challenges of the Soviet Union.[1]

Even before the creation of Pakistan, the leaders of the National Movement saw 'the conflict between the great powers mainly as a background to [their] national struggle'. Speaking in 1946, Firoz Khan Noon, who later in December 1957 became the Prime Minister of Pakistan, articulated a highly pragmatic approach toward the major powers, and the All-India National Congress. He stated: 'If Hindus [i.e., the Congress Party] give us Pakistan and freedom, then the Hindus are our best friends. If the British give it to us then the British are our best friends. But if neither will give to us, then Russia is our best friend.'[2]

This pragmatic approach was extended into the period of independence by none other than Jinnah himself, who instead of turning to the Soviet Union, looked to the United States to strengthen Pakistan's economic and military capabilities. Ravaged by World War II, the Soviet economic capabilities, especially from 1945 to 1950, were considered to be exceptionally limited, and the Soviet Union was engaged in repairing the damage done to its economy.

In 1948, Nicholas A. Voznesensky, Deputy Prime Minister of the Soviet Union, revealed in a published book, *Soviet Economy During the Second World War* (Moscow: 1948), the statistical evidence of the destruction of the Soviet economy, which also demonstrated Soviet industrial, and hence, military weakness. Despite Voznesensky's repeated homage to Stalin's leadership of the Soviet economy, and the conduct of war, his book was condemned for its un-Marxist approach. First dismissed from all of his offices, Voznesensky was then ordered to be shot in 1950. Voznesensky's execution certainly did not enhance Soviet reputation for military or economic power, which might have further encouraged the Pakistani leaders to court the United States. In the late 1940s, the United States contributed 50 per cent of the World Gross National Product (GNP), while even in the 1970s, the Soviet Union and East European socialist states had lagged behind the United States.

Jinnah's approach thus to the United States was determined by these equally pressing problems, which included: (1) primarily the hostility of India and, to a lesser degree, the antagonism of Afghanistan; (2) the lack of economic resources for industrial development and the refugees' resettlement in Pakistan; (3) exceptionally inadequate military capability, which exposed Pakistan to India's hegemony. Initially opposing the creation of Pakistan, when Britain presented the Cabinet Mission Plan in May 1946 for preserving the territorial unity of India, the United States shifted its support to Pakistan when this plan collapsed.

Exactly thirty-seven days before the establishment of Pakistan, the United States had officially determined to have the 'friendliest relations with Pakistan'.

Secretary of State, George C. Marshall, informed Jinnah through a cable on 7 July 1947 to US Ambassador Henry F. Grady at New Delhi that the US would soon have an ambassador accredited to Pakistan, and sent messages of good wishes to the Pakistan Constituent Assembly when it convened. There is some evidence to demonstrate that the US recognized the strategic importance of Pakistan, and even at this early stage of US-Pakistan relations, the US extended parity of esteem to India and Pakistan, despite disparity in their size, population and material resources. This policy was maintained until 1971, when Pakistan suffered a major defeat in Bangladesh, and East Bengal was severed from Jinnah's original Pakistan.

Encouraged by American goodwill, Jinnah made a bold bid for US economic and military support. Almost one month after the creation of Pakistan, Jinnah sent, in October 1947, a special secret emissary, Mir Laik Ali (of Hyderabad), to Washington in order to negotiate with the State Department two separate aid programmes. The first was to be a short-term loan package of $45 million to resettle Muslim refugees in Pakistan. The second loan envisaged US aid for the next five years for the purchase of military hardware: (1) Army - $170 million to provide for a regular army of 100,000; (2) Air Force - $75 million to purchase 12 fighter squadrons (150 planes); (3) Navy - $60 million to purchase 4 light cruisers, 16 destroyers, 4 corvettes, 12 coast guard gunboats, and 3 submarines.[3]

This request was shot down in December 1947 when war over Kashmir had erupted. Moreover, the United States was not yet ready to replace British influence in South Asia and the Middle East. In order to deal with former British 'possessions' in these regions, the USA had arranged four extensive assessments—the first three under the Democratic Administration, and the fourth under the Republican—in 1947, 1950, 1952 and 1954 in Washington. Pakistan's approach to the United States can be evaluated only against the background of those strategic assessments.

After each assessment, Pakistan's strategic significance as a state closer to Soviet Central Asia, was progressively highlighted; and finally, Afghanistan was considered to be of no great strategic importance to the global strategy of the United States.[4] Consequently, on 19 May 1954, under President Eisenhower, the USA signed the Mutual Assistance Agreement, and Pakistan joined the South-East Asia Treaty Organization (SEATO) in September 1954, and the Baghdad Pact in April 1955—subsequently called, in July 1958, the Central Treaty Organization (CENTO)—linking Pakistan with Turkey and Iran.

Thus, the two significant legs of Pakistan's alliance triad were structured.

China, the third leg of Pakistan's alliance triad, was most receptive to Pakistan's diplomatic overtures, despite her Treaty of Friendship, Alliance and Mutual Assistance (1950) with the Soviet Union, which was stipulated to last for thirty years. China's policy toward Pakistan was governed by three strategic considerations: (1) the Islamic factor; (2) relations with India; and (3) the Sino-Soviet split.

Clearly, the Islamic factor recognized the strategic importance of Pakistan's northern boundaries which are contiguous with Xinjiang. Covering one-sixth of the surface of the Peoples Republic of China, Xinjiang is the largest Muslim minority area. Consequently, a very substantial understanding of each other's motives was reached by the PRC and Pakistan at the Bandung Conference in April 1955. To highlight the Islamic factor, Premier Zhou Enlai had brought to Bandung a Muslim Imam (prayer leader) from Xinjiang. Introducing him to the 22 nation Asian-African Conference, Zhou stated: 'We Communists are atheists, but we respect all those who have religious beliefs ... There are in China not only seven million Communists, but also tens of millions of Muslims [etc.] ... Here in the Chinese delegation, there is a pious Imam of the Islamic faith.'[5]

Muhammad Ali, the Prime Minister of Pakistan, Zhou pointed out, had assured him that (1) Pakistan's membership in SEATO was not against China; (2) Pakistan had no fear China would commit aggression against her; (3) should the US take aggressive action under SEATO or launch a global war, Pakistan would not be involved in it. Then he added: 'We have achieved a mutual understanding.' Clearly the PRC was prepared to accept that Pakistan's participation in western-sponsored alliances was motivated by a desire to strengthen her defence capability in regard to India, while the US motivation was to contain Soviet influence in South Asia.

The parameters of Soviet-Pakistan relations were thus determined by Pakistan's security concerns about India and her desperate economic situation, and not by any ideological bias against the Soviet Union. After all, China was, and still is, ideologically a socialist/communist state which has become a close strategic partner of Pakistan. But once Pakistan was ensconced in the embrace of US-China partnership, Pakistan found that room for interaction with the Soviet Union had shrunk still further.

Pakistan's leadership was never quite comfortable with the avowedly anti-Soviet orientation of the Baghdad Pact, CENTO, and SEATO, because, in their perception, threats to Pakistan's security emanated from India. Consequently, Pakistan endeavored to add the dimension of security *vis-à-vis* India to the structure of US-sponsored alliance. Eventually, Pakistan came to believe erroneously that the United States had given firm assurances of support to Pakistan against 'Indian aggression'. Henry Kissinger has pointed out that 'over the decades of our relationship with Pakistan, there had grown up a complex body of communications by the Kennedy and Johnson Administrations, going beyond the 1959 pact, some verbal, some in writing, whose plain import was that the United States would come to Pakistan's assistance if she was attacked by India.'[6] (Consequently, Pakistan had invoked the Executive Agreement of 1959, when the Indian forces attacked East Pakistan across the international border in 1971.)

From 1947 to 1960, Pakistan basked in the favours of US diplomacy, so that no real initiative was left to Soviet foreign policy for influencing Pakistan's policymakers in the Soviet direction or steering Pakistan's policy towards non-alignment. Ruefully, this lack of initiative was forthrightly admitted by the Soviet Union in an *aide-memoire* to the government of Pakistan (GOP) in 1958: 'The Soviet Government is compelled to note with regret that for reasons beyond its control, the relations between the USSR and Pakistan leave much to be desired...'[7]

Establishment of Diplomatic Relations

Despite Pakistan's steady tilt towards the United States, the Soviet Union endeavored to establish with Pakistan normal and friendly relations during 1947-54. Stalin's government even indicated a preference for Pakistan over India; because foreign capital, mostly British, was dominant in most branches of the Indian economy, and Moscow perceived the Nehru government and the Congress Party as representatives 'of the interests of the Indian, and first of all, the Hindu, bourgeoisie'.[8] Moreover, India retained in 1947 Lord Mountbatten as the Governor-General of independent India, while Jinnah had spurned Mountbatten, and himself become the Head of Pakistan. To the ideological eyes of Stalin it meant something. No wonder that Stalin did not bother to meet even once India's first Ambassador, Madam Vijyalakshmi Pandit, one of Nehru's well-known sisters.[9]

To the chagrin of the Soviet leaders, Pakistan's government under Jinnah, informed Moscow on 21 August 1947 that Britain would represent Pakistan's interests in the Soviet Union. How did this decision serve Pakistan's interests in Moscow? The Soviet analysts saw in the GOP's policy, and Pakistan's public opinion, a big gap, because they thought that Pakistanis not only shared religious ties with Soviet Central Asia, but retained a consciousness of ethnic and historic relations with Central Asian nationalities. Moreover, Pakistanis appreciated with deep sympathy Central Asia's agricultural and industrial development, which took place in conditions 'which were very similar to Pakistan's [under-developed] conditions.'[10] In other words, the GOP was maintaining social and economic distance between Pakistan and the USSR against the 'natural' and historical inclination of its own people.

Despite Pakistan's less than enthusiastic attitude toward the Soviet Union, Stalin's government made friendly overtures to Pakistan, and in fact, invited Prime Minister Liaquat Ali Khan to visit the Soviet Union at a time when the two states had not exchanged ambassadors, and their embassies did not exist in each other's capitals. A.G. Stetsenko, the first Soviet Ambassador, arrived in Karachi on 18 March 1950, almost three years after the birth of Pakistan. Returning from the 1949 Commonwealth Prime Ministers' Conference, Liaquat visited Tehran from 14 to 18 May at the Shah's invitation. In an informal conversation with the Soviet Charge d'Affaires at a reception, Liaquat expressed his desire to visit the Soviet Union. In the first week of June, Stalin sent the formal letter of invitation to Liaquat, which he accepted on 8 June 1949.[11]

A cultured man, Liaquat breached the well-established traditions of diplomatic protocol in exploiting Stalin's invitation of 8 June 1949 to wangle an invitation from President Harry S. Truman on 6 December 1949. Causing an affront to the dignity of the Soviet Union, Liaquat never visited the Soviet Union; instead he visited the United States during 3-30 May 1950, and then, adding insult to injury, spent several leisurely days in Canada. This calculated disregard for the international norms of civility, and a deliberate affront to Stalin, was uncalled for. Liaquat's visit to both superpowers would have enhanced his personal stature as a statesman, and would not have precluded him from cultivating close military and economic relations with the United States, which was unquestionably his major political objective.

As an ideological state the Soviet Union attempted to articulate its policies in Pakistan through the Communist Party of Pakistan (CPP) and All-Pakistan Progressive Writers' Association (PPWA). From 1947 to 1954 the CPP operated as a technically legal party, and enjoyed limited popularity in Pakistan, since it had supported the creation of Pakistan in 1945-7. In March 1951, Liaquat accused the CPP of having conspired to overthrow his government with the aid of certain military officers of Pakistan, and with the knowledge and support of a certain foreign country—an unmistakable reference to the Soviet Union. Consequently, Sajjad Zaheer, Secretary-General of the CPP, and Faiz Ahmad Faiz, well-known poet and an activist in the PPWA, were arrested and tried along with Major-General Akbar Khan, the Chief of Staff of the Pakistan Army, and other military officers. The trial resulted in the conviction of all the accused persons in January 1953. In July 1954, the CPP was banned, and in 1958 the PPWA was destroyed when its centre of activities—the Progressive Papers Ltd—was forcibly occupied by the Army in the dead of night.[12]

The banning of the CPP occurred in the same year (1954) when President Eisenhower authorized the Military Assistance Program for Pakistan. To the Soviet Union, the GOP's actions amounted to hostility toward the leftist wing in Pakistan, and hostility toward the Soviet Union. Consequently, the Soviet Union adopted a policy towards Pakistan that included (1) routinely warning her when hostile actions emanated from Pakistan; (2) offering friendly and beneficial technical assistance and trade relations to her, and then (3) supporting diplomatically India in her disputes with Pakistan over Kashmir; and simultaneously, (4) encouraging Afghanistan in its irredentist claims of Pashtunistan. This policy was designed to convince Pakistan that while her western supporters could provide her with economic and military aid, they could not contribute towards the solution of territorial disputes to Pakistan's total or partial satisfaction. The USSR Council of Ministers officially adopted this policy, which was published in *Pravda* on 7 February 1956: (1) 'The USSR subscribed to the view' of cooperation between states of different social systems; (2) viewed negatively the military blocs to which Pakistan belonged; (3) the USSR wanted to widen relations with Pakistan on the basis of peaceful co-existence, in order to (4) give Pakistan technical assistance without any strings attached, and (5) to share with Pakistan knowledge about the use of nuclear energy for peaceful purposes. It was only in February 1957 that the USSR exercised her first veto to defeat a Security Council Resolution authorizing UN force to facilitate demilitarization in Kashmir.

Open Skies, U-2, and Blow to Pakistan's Troubled Relations with the USSR

During President Eisenhower's administration, a highly confidential report of the Quantico Panel, 10 June 1955, organized by Governor Rockefeller, had argued that the US enjoyed as of 1955, a significant military advantage over the Soviet Union. The gap was narrowing and might close by 1960 if the present trends continued. US officials were convinced that serious arms control required reliable means for mutual inspection.

To enhance US aerial capability, the proposal to allow mutual aerial inspection was presented by President Eisenhower at the general Summit on 21 July 1955, but was rejected by Nikita Khrushchev. Subsequently, the US decided to engage unilaterally in the aerial inspection of the USSR with the U-2.[13] On 1 May 1960, the U-2 was shot down over the Soviet Union, after it took off for a 3788-mile spy flight from Peshawar.

In 1957, the U-2 operation in West Germany was phased down; and was then shifted to Pakistan. When the USA approached Pakistan, the Pakistani leaders complained about the current rate of US military assistance. In January 1957, Eisenhower approved a three-year increase; and in 1958 final arrangements were made with General Ayub Khan for flying the U-2 from Lahore and Peshawar. In 1959 Ayub Khan signed a ten-year lease for an American intelligence base at Peshawar.

From Peshawar, the U-2's chartered flight was over Afghanistan to Soviet Central Asia—Dushambe-Tyuratam (cosmodrome)—and over Russia to Chelyabinsk-Sverdlovsk-Kirov-Plesetsk-Archangel-Kandalaksha-Murmansk, and over the Barents Sea to Bodo in Norway. The U-2 searched 'for targets, including energy installations along the Trans-Siberian Railway and a large down-range radar array that was a terminal site for missile firings from Kapustin yar ... information was gathered to learn of Soviet nuclear test explosions, their location, force and pullout'. The U-2 flights from Peshawar had continued for almost three years.

Khrushchev, who attended a reception at Czechoslovakia's embassy on 9 May 1960 in Moscow, cornered Ambassador Salman Ali of Pakistan, and bluntly told him: 'Peshawar has been marked on our map. In the future, if any American plane is allowed to use Peshawar as a base of operations against the Soviet Union, we will retaliate immediately...[we] will have to aim our rockets at your bases as well.'[14] Remarkably, Khrushchev had provided two days earlier an escape route to Pakistan. Delivering an address to the Supreme Soviet 7 May 1960, he stated:

> We warn those countries that make their territory available for launching planes with anti-Soviet intentions: Do not play with fire, gentlemen...[However], if these governments did not know—and I allow in this case they were not informed—they should have known

what the American military was doing on their territory against the Soviet Union.[15]

When the news was brought to President Ayub Khan on 1 May that the U-2 had been shot down over Soviet territory, his reaction was: 'So what.'[16] Soon, however, sober thoughts prevailed, when the incident was underlined by three probabilities: (1) that such an incident could touch off a war; (2) Pakistan would be a prime target for the Soviet Union in case of such a war; and (3) that the Soviet Union very nearly touched Pakistan's northern border at the trijunction of Hunza, the Wakhan Corridor, and Xinjiang, while her patron, the United States, was almost 10,000 miles away. Taking the escape route provided by Khruschev, Ayub ordered an inquiry to ascertain the facts 'if the U-2 plane had actually taken off from Peshawar.'[17] Since 1947, for the first time, the GOP made a realistic assessment of the dangers inherent in ignoring her relations with the USSR; a sense of realism began to develop in Soviet-Pakistan relations.

From Confrontation to Realistic Relationship (1960-70)

Barely three months after the U-2 incident, the USSR made an offer to Pakistan to help in exploiting Pakistan's mineral resources, particularly oil, after the Soviet Ambassador Michael Kapitsa had assured Pakistan that her alliances with the West would not be regarded as an obstacle in its economic and cultural links with the Soviet Union. Clearly, the Soviet gesture was a recognition of Pakistan's strategic position in Southwest Asia, constituting a buffer zone (along with Afghanistan) between Soviet Central Asia and India.

Moreover, the USSR attempted to convince Pakistan that its economic problems were primarily caused by 'the blessings of SEATO and CENTO'. According to Soviet projection, these problems included: (1) population explosion by 13 million between 1951 and 1959, while agricultural production remained low; (2) the first five-year plan could not be fulfilled due to shortage of resources; (3) the taxation rate had increased annually; (4) the cost of essential goods and foodstuff had increased by 4-5 times; (5) even President Ayub admitted in December 1961 that no significant economic improvement could be foreseen within the next 25-30 years. This was due mainly during the last ten years to military expenses, which were one and a half times more than the funds allocated for the development of industry and other productive segments of economy.[18] Consequently, the Soviet advice to Pakistan was to seek Soviet aid, and withdraw from the burdensome military pacts.

In addition to the U-2 incident, two further developments— including the 1962 Sino-Indian conflict (when both the USSR and the US supported India), and the 1965 Indo-Pakistan war over Kashmir—strengthened pragmatic and realistic aspects of Soviet-Pakistan relations. Internally, in order to strengthen his cabinet, Ayub Khan appointed Z.A. Bhutto his foreign minister. Bhutto injected dynamic, diplomatic thinking in Pakistan's foreign policy planning and led Ayub to substantially improve Pakistan's relations with the USSR and China.

Ayub now forthrightly admitted that 'we were deprived of the opportunity to understand the Soviet Union earlier,' because of Pakistan's commitment to the United States. Consequently, he sent his foreign minister, Z.A. Bhutto, to visit the Soviet Union in January 1965, and when on 3-11 April, Ayub Khan made his first visit to the Soviet Union, both sides agreed on several issues: (1) trade agreement for (1965-7) commodity exchange, and the delivery of equipment to Pakistan; (2) concensus on the Soviet-Pakistan cultural agreement (which was later signed in Rawalpindi on 5 June 1965); (3) non-proliferation of nuclear weapons; (4) China's rightful place in the United Nations; (5) condemnation of colonialism and imperialism in all forms and manifestations; (6) promotion of personal contacts between the Soviet and Pakistani leaders.[19]

Ayub Khan's assessment of his visit to the Soviet Union, in a larger historical sense, highlighted the geography of Soviet

Central Asia: 'Even though our civilization and culture had close connections with Central Asia, 200 years of British occupation had wiped out these connections. My visit was essentially intended to recover lost links.'[20] Lastly, Ayub concluded that Sino-Soviet conflicts would continue, even though Premier Kosygin described them 'not of an organic nature.'[21]

The establishment of broad understanding and cooperative relations with the Soviet Union laid the foundations for a new Soviet policy toward Pakistan, which was underlined by evenhandedness, and even impartiality, between India and Pakistan. This new policy was amply reflected during the India-Pakistan war, which broke out on 4 September 1965—almost 3 months and 23 days after Ayub's visit to the USSR—when India launched an attack on Lahore.

The Soviet Union supported the ceasefire, and invited the leaders of India and Pakistan to Tashkent in order to terminate the consequences of hostilities and to re-establish normal relations. Unannounced, Ayub Khan visited China to thank their leaders for support, who gave their blessings to the Tashkent conference but cautioned Ayub 'to beware of the Soviet desire to exploit the situation to their advantage.'[22] Moreover, Chinese leaders were critical of the way that the Pakistani army had handled the war against India. This criticism did not please Ayub, but the Chinese evaluation was objective, and had well-grounded facts on its side.

When the Tashkent conference started on 3 January 1966, the Soviet attitude was impartial toward India and Pakistan; however, the atmosphere of the conference, the Soviet insistence that both sides must settle their problems, especially when India had refused to settle the Kashmir issue, compelled Ayub to accept the status quo *ante bellum*. To India, it implied Pakistan's relinquishment of territorial claims in Kashmir (despite the repetition of verbal pretentions); and to Pakistan, a defeat in the battlefield, and at the negotiation table. The Soviet Union emerged as an influential power in South Asia which had legitimate claims in settling the affairs of South Asian states, hoping that these countries would eventually line up against China.

During the next four years (1966-70), Soviet-Pakistan relations functioned like a roller-coaster; they ascended to the peak, and then plunged to the lowest level when the secessionist movement in East Pakistan gained momentum in 1971. The potential military and economic strength of India led the Soviet Union to support India as a counterweight to China. India had thus become the centrepiece of Soviet policy towards South Asia. Much the same factors in the power calculations led the Soviet Union in 1971 to support India in Bangladesh. (On the other hand, the United States, on whom Pakistan was dependent, had declared an arms embargo against Pakistan after the war of 1965; this embargo remained effective until after 1971, when it was only partially lifted.)

During 1966-70 the Soviet Union improved its relations with Pakistan in the areas of (1) cultural exchange; (2) trade; (3) industrial development assistance; and finally, (4) a limited military sale/aid to Pakistan.

1. Cultural Relations: Nine academic, cultural and artistic agreements signed by the Soviet Union and Pakistan, succeeded in establishing viable programmes which continued to flourish overtly, as well as covertly.

In the Soviet Union, in a relatively short period of time, literary works of Marxist and non-Marxist poets and litterateurs, including Faiz Ahmad Faiz, Josh Malih-Abadi, Saadat Hasan Manto, Ahmad Nadeem Qasmi, Hafeez Jalandhri, Sufi Tabassum, Hamza Shanwari and Qalander Mohmand, have been published in original and in translation at least three hundred times. Poet-philosopher, Muhammed Iqbal's works have been published in thirty editions.

The Soviet-Pakistan Friendship Society in the USSR, an officially recognized organization, has its counterpart in Pakistan. Each year both societies celebrated Pakistan's Independence Day and the Soviet Union's October Revolution Day. In December 1976, Lahore and Dushanbe, capital of Tajikistan, were declared twin cities. Between 1976 and 1981, students of Lahore's Punjab University and Dushanbe's Tajikistan State University were encouraged to exchange an academic year with each other.

Table 1
Industrial Assistance to Pakistan

Description of project	Allocations	Date of credit
1. Oil exploration	30 million $	4 March 1961
2. Import of Soviet agricultural machinery	11 million $	17 June 1964
3. First general credit	50 million $	7 April 1965
4. Second general credit for these projects (1) Guddu thermal power station of 210 MW capacity over the Indus River. (2) A high-voltage transmission line more than 1000 km long. (3) Fifteen broadcasting stations of different capacity (including one for Islamabad and one for Quetta). (4) Two plants for the production of electrical machinery with an annual capacity of 20 000 tons of electrical Equipment. (5) A combined railroad–highway bridge over the Rupsu river. (6) Geological surveys to prospect for solid minerals.	85 million $	6, 9 Sept. 1966
5. Karachi steel mill (financing the cost of machinery and equipment (1971 allocation was $ 200m was increased to $ 493m)	493 million $	22 Jan. 1971
6. Karachi steel mill (additional credits for twelve years at 2.5% interest)	160 million $	October 1974
7. Karachi steel mill (USSR to provide equipment and construction material)	Rs. 5230 million	26 July 1975

Sources: George Ginsburg and Robert M. Slusser (eds.), *A Calendar of Soviet Treaties* (Rockville, Maryland: 1981); R.K. Jain (ed.), *Soviet–South Asian Relations, 1947–1978* (Atlantic Highlands, New Jersey: 1979).

The most remarkable feature of this cultural enterprise between the two states was the extensive programme in the USSR of instruction in Urdu, Pakistan's national language. Urdu was taught in the elementary and secondary schools in Moscow, Leningrad, and particularly in the schools of Central Asian cities—Tashkent, Bukhara, Samarkand, Alma-Ata and Dushanbe. Last, but not least, the Soviet Institute of Oriental Studies in Moscow, and its counterparts in Central Asian Republics, have produced

Table 2
Soviet Arms Supplies to Pakistan

Year	Number	Description	Financial Arrangement
Aircraft 1968-71	12	MI-8	u.c. $504 000 approximately, repayable over 10 years
Armoured fighting vehicles 1969 (1969–70)	150 (20)	T-54/55 PT-76	

Source: SIPRI, *Arms Trade Registers: The Arms Trade with the Third World* (Stockholm: 1975), pp. 38, 40.

respectable scholars (including Yuri V. Gankovsky, Vyacheslav Belokrenitsky, Vladimir Moskalenko, and Railya Muqeemjanova) on Pakistan's history, culture and contemporary political developments.

2. Trade Relations: Twenty-five trade agreements were generally in the nature of barter trade, and their total cash value in rubles/rupees was really insignificant. Most of them were negotiated between 1952 and November 1959. Trade began to improve by 1965, and then declined in the 1970-72 period; it picked up again in 1973 and almost disappeared after 1979, when the USSR intervened in Afghanistan.

3. Economic and Industrial Assistance: The Soviet industrial and economic aid to Pakistan became substantial from 1961 to 1979. This aid was related to some minor and some major industrial projects, as shown in Table 1. As can be determined from the Soviet commitment of financial industrial resources, the most impressive and visibly prestigious industrial project is the Karachi steel mill which contributed significantly to the industrial progress of Pakistan. The plant was completed in 1985.

4. Military Assistance: To Pakistan the litmus-test of Soviet relations was the parity or rough equivalence of the delivery of military equipment, which would enable Pakistan to maintain a fairly credible level of military preparedness in comparison to India.

A one-shot agreement in July 1968 on the sale of Soviet arms to Pakistan was signed in Moscow during the visit of the Chief of Staff of the Pakistan Army, General Yahya Khan. But it was never repeated. The details of this agreement included those shown in Table 2.

Bangladesh Crisis

Soviet-Pakistan relations continued to develop fairly smoothly when the USSR had begun to treat India and Pakistan on the basis of an approximate equality. Pakistan adopted a foreign policy which came to be known as 'bilateral equations' or 'equidistance' from three major powers. This policy attempted to maintain the formal alliance structure with the United States and the states in the Middle East. Simultaneously, Pakistan tried to retain and nurture informal understandings with China. This period (1966-71) was, from Pakistan's viewpoint, underlined by this 'ideal' foreign policy. But ideal situations in international diplomacy develop rarely, and do not last indefinitely. Internal political developments in East Pakistan shook the entire equilibrium and brought into play political forces which operated to the total disadvantage of Pakistan. A review of these realignments is not only significant for deeper understanding of Soviet-Pakistan relations, but also has direct bearing on Pakistan's security.

The East Pakistan crisis started in December 1970, when general elections were held in Pakistan, and ended in January 1971—a period of twelve months—when Bangladesh came into existence. The emergence of Bangladesh is attributed to several factors, including:

1. the separation of East and West Pakistan by 1000 miles of Indian territory;
2. linguistic and ethnic differences between the peoples of East and West Pakistan;
3. lack of economic, social and political development, generating a sense of deprivation, or oppression in East

Pakistan, which has now come to be recognized as Bengali nationalism;
4. Yahya Khan's inept handling of Sheikh Mujib and his Awami League followers, which ended in the imposition of Martial Law on 26 March 1971, arrest of Sheikh Mujib, the disbanding of the Awami League, the influx of '10 million' Bengali refugees into India, which led to the establishment of a Provisional Government in India, and the proclamation of independence on 10 April 1971;
5. the determination of India to intervene militarily in East and West Pakistan to defeat Pakistan's armed forces in order to establish the 'sovereign' state of Bangladesh;
6. and finally, the USSR's diplomatic and military support to India, which deterred both the United States and China from coming to Pakistan's aid, when India launched its attack.

India's motives for the dismemberment of Pakistan are easy to understand. To India, Pakistan was a thorn in her ideological flesh, and had been a threat to her security since 1955, when Pakistan started to receive military aid from the United States. India wanted in South Asia what Kenneth Galbraith (former US Ambassador to India) has called the 'North American formula', where there is one big power, like the United States, and a number of smaller ones arranged around it, which 'can maintain an equilibrium on the Indian sub-continent'. India resented attempts first by the US and then by the Soviet Union to try to equate India with Pakistan. Far more explicitly and abrasively, Mrs Gandhi publicly reformulated the North American formula in a press conference in London on 1 November 1971: 'Nothing will work if people [i.e.major powers] continue to equate India and Pakistan. We are tired of this equation which the western world is making...we are not equal and we are not going to stand for this kind of treatment.'

In 1971, the Soviet Union opted for the North American formula, while the United States and China opposed it. Why? Essentially, the Soviet Union reacted to (a) the US initiative to normalize its relations with China and (b) Pakistan's role in the process of this normalization.

For twenty years, relations between the United States and China had been deadlocked; while Sino-Soviet relations had steadily declined very intensely since the Sino-Indian conflict of 1962. At this time, the Soviet Union, disregarding its ideological and political ally's security needs, sided, like the United States, with India. By 1970, the political isolation of China was complete, while internally it had suffered self-inflicted wounds of the Cultural Revolution. China also felt threatened by the Soviet build-up on the 4000-mile common border. By 1970, China's orientation fundamentally changed; instead of looking at the United States in ideological terms, it began to regard her in geopolitical perspectives. Obviously, China decided to lessen the number of its potential and real enemies and wanted to lessen Soviet pressure with the help of a partner. Such a counterweight to the Soviet power could only be provided by the United States.

Bogged down by the war in Vietnam, the US had resolved to free herself from the burdens of Asia, yet she was determined to shape a new type of state relations where China could make a very substantial contribution. The Chinese were interested, as Henry Kissinger has pointed out, in discussing the global balance of power with the United States.[23]

In January 1970, Yahya Khan sent to Nixon a copy of the Pakistani Ambassador's conversations with Premier Zhou En-lai. This memorandum of conversations revealed that Zhou was primarily concerned about the Soviet threat, and considered the US a lesser danger. Finally, the Chinese government conveyed an official invitation to Nixon through Yahya Khan, which Pakistan's Ambassador had delivered to Kissinger on 27 April 1971. China agreed 'to receive publicly in Peking a special envoy of the President (for instance, Mr Kissinger) or the US Secretary of State, or even the President of the US.' Zhou further advised that Yahya Khan's good offices should continue to be used, and all technical arrangements should be made through Pakistan.

Nixon decided to send Kissinger as his emissary; and informed the Chinese government that Kissinger would 'arrive in China on 9 July and leave on 11 July 1971, flying in a Pakistani Boeing Aircraft from Islamabad to Peking.'[24] Simpleminded Yahya Khan 'personally reviewed each detail of my [i.e. Kissinger's] departure; he put the full facilities of his government at our disposal'. On 9 July 1971, Foreign Secretary Sultan Muhammad Khan escorted Kissinger to Chaklala Airport, where he boarded the Boeing 707 of the Pakistan International Airlines (PIA). Commenting on Yahya's role, Kissinger made a comment which cannot be improved upon: 'Yahya was a bluff, direct soldier of limited imagination caught up after the convulsion in East Pakistan in events for which neither experience nor training prepared him. He made grievous mistakes. Yet, he performed a great service for our country...'[25]

However, an appropriate question may be asked: Did he serve Pakistan's interests? That was supposed to be his primary responsibility.

The Soviet reaction was not slow in coming. On 9 August 1971—exactly thirty days after Kissinger took off from Chaklala for Peking—the Soviet-Indian Friendship Treaty was signed to last for twenty years. Pakistan concluded that the treaty would restrain India in East Pakistan. A remarkable assessment indeed for its 'farsightedness'!

Any novice in diplomacy would have recognized that the Soviet Union had exploited a strategic opportunity in creating an Indo-Soviet counterweight to the emergence of a US-China entente, in which Pakistan was to play a subordinate role. The operational Article IX of the Treaty was crucial. It called upon the signatories to refrain from giving assistance to any third country taking part in an armed conflict with the other, and committed each side to consult immediately with a view to taking 'appropriate effective measures' in case either party was attacked or threatened with attack.

An Indian analyst has pointed out that 'in the discussions which preceded the signing of the Treaty, the Soviet Union concurred with the Indian view that the Treaty would apply if

Pakistan, with or without Chinese support, attacked India in retaliation against Indian assistance to the Mukti Bahini; the Soviet Union regarded the Bahini as a liberation movement and support to it as just and defensible.'[26] Publicly, on 28 October 1971, the Indian Foreign Minister stated that the USSR would give 'total support' to India in case of a conflict with Pakistan.

In the Indo-Pakistan conflict of 1971, the USSR effectively demonstrated Chinese impotence, and completely humiliated Pakistan, a friend of China and the United States. Five months later Bangladesh became a reality, when the Awami League leaders rode to Dhaka on Indian tanks, and Mujib flew in from Delhi after thanking Mrs. Gandhi for having made him a 'triumphant hero'. Nearly five years later, in August 1975, Mujib, his family and the Awami League's leadership were hacked to death by the dissident elements in the Bangladesh Army.

Pakistan recognized Bangladesh as an independent country and then began to restructure its relations with the Soviet Union under the leadership of Z. A. Bhutto.

Bhutto's Dynamic Bilateralism

After the Indo-Chinese War of 1962, and Indo-Pakistan conflict of 1965, Zulfikar Ali Bhutto had come to adopt a bilateral orientation for Pakistan's foreign policy. This policy was to replace Pakistan's exclusive commitment to the United States. Three basic objectives of this foreign policy included: (1) a policy of friendship and good faith with China; (2) good relations with the United States and the Soviet Union; (3) the strengthening of relations with the Third World, especially Muslim states and the neighbouring countries.[27] Bhutto's order of priorities assigned both the US and the USSR the second position. In order to underline this shift in foreign policy, Bhutto had emphasized that Pakistan should terminate (1) the Mutual Defence Agreements and other pacts with the US; (2) withdraw from SEATO and CENTO. However, this rearrangement of orientations was enunciated between 1966 and 1969, when he was out of power and was engaged in formulating the policies of the Pakistan People's Party (PPP), which he had founded in 1967.

Bhutto came to power in December 1971 when certain realities had to be factored into his calculations: (1) Indo-Soviet Treaty of Friendship of August 1971; (2) Indian military intervention in East Pakistan with Soviet diplomatic support, and the delivery of much needed weapons; (3) defeat of Pakistan's army in Bangladesh; (4) Chinese and US support to Pakistan during this crisis, even though it was not strong enough to intimidate India, as, for example, Chinese support had been in the Indo-Pakistan conflict of 1965.

The US had refused to honour the Executive Agreement of 1959 to help Pakistan in Bengal. Despite these negative developments, Sino-US entente had come into existence, for which Pakistan had played a substantial supportive role. Pakistan was punished by the USSR for this role. However, Bhutto acknowledged in the National Assembly debate (14 July 1972) that Nixon had moved the Seventh Fleet to the Bay of Bengal to warn India that the US 'would not allow the dismemberment of West Pakistan' or the destruction of the Pakistan Army. This credible threat had forced India to accept ceasefire in West Pakistan.[28] US contribution in protecting the territorial integrity of New Pakistan was thus greatly appreciated.

In light of these factors, Bhutto decided to activate Pakistan's participation in CENTO, and Regional Cooperation for Development (RCD), and did not repudiate the Executive Agreement of 1959, which became the foundation of support to Pakistan, when the Soviet Union intervened in Afghanistan in December 1979. However, Bhutto withdrew from SEATO and the British Commonwealth of Nations and joined the movement of non-aligned nations. In other words, the United States became the first co-priority along with China. Bhutto stated that 'by maintaining friendly relations with all the great powers on the basis of principles and not expediency, Pakistan hopes to avoid involvement in disputes and struggles between them. It is part of our new policy that we should refrain from participating in multilateral pacts directed by one bloc of power against another.'[29] Bilateralism, in theory, implied a great deal of flexibility, but how Pakistan's continued participation in CENTO would be compatible with this bilateral approach couldn't be determined. In any case, this dilemma was resolved by Iran in 1979 when CENTO was put to rest.

Bhutto visited the Soviet Union twice in a period of five years (1972-7). The first visit from 16-18 March 1972 nearly broke the ice. Both states agreed to (1) restore Pakistan-Soviet trade and (2) to continue cooperation in geological prospecting, in building a metallurgical works in Karachi, and in power engineering; and (3) both states expressed similar views on the Arab-Israeli conflict, withdrawal of foreign troops from Indo-China, termination of the arms race, and keeping nuclear disarmament under effective control. The third category of issues was not directly of significant interest to Pakistan, but concerned the USSR in the United Nations, where identity of views ensured Pakistan's vote on the Soviet side. However, Bhutto's land reforms, nationalization of banks, insurance companies and other privately owned industries were greatly admired in the Soviet Union.

On his second visit, 24-26 October 1974, Bhutto was cordially received, and Premier Alexei Kosygin stated forthrightly: 'We are satisfied with the way our bilateral relations have been developing in recent years.' The USSR assured Bhutto of further industrial assistance to Pakistan, and supported Bhutto for normalization of the situation in South Asia by virtue of the Simla Agreement (July 1972), the Delhi Agreement (August 1973), and the Tripartite Agreement (April 1974) between India, Bangladesh and Pakistan. Instead of supporting Afghanistan over the Pashtunistan issue in the manner and style of Nikita Khrushchev, the Soviet Union joined Pakistan in expressing the hope that 'the differences between Pakistan and Afghanistan will be settled by peaceful means through negotiations.'[30]

Finally, Kosygin stated approvingly that 'Objective conditions exist for the development of Soviet-Pakistan relations.' The expression of these views clearly vindicated Bhutto's conception of bilateralism. How Bhutto would have applied this framework of bilateralism of relationship to the new developments in Afghanistan, when the 'revolution' took place in April 1978, and then the Soviet Union intervened in December 1979 to protect this 'revolution', one would never know.

Soviet Debacle Over Afghanistan: Pakistan Moves Back to the United States

Exactly nine months after Zia's *coup d'état* against the Bhutto government, the People's Democratic Party of Afghanistan's (PDPA) Khalq-faction toppled the Daud regime in Afghanistan. The initial Soviet reaction to the coup in Pakistan was objective—neither particularly 'sad' at Bhutto's overthrow, nor jubilant over Zia's emergence to power. Only a modest disapproval of the military regime was expressed by the Soviet commentators saying that 'the periods of civilian rule were most favourable for Pakistan.' The Soviets took Zia's initial commitments at face value: (1) 'Democracy is the only way to save our country'; (2) neither Zia, nor the Army, had any political ambitions; (3) the constitution was suspended and not abolished, while the elected President Chaudhry Fazl Elahi remained head of state; (4) elections were promised to be held in October 1977; (5) Zia had declared that there would be no change in Pakistan's foreign policy.

If the Daud regime had continued in Afghanistan, probably Zia, under the Foreign Office's guidance, would have continued Bhutto's foreign policy of bilateralism, especially in regard to the Soviet Union. From 1977 to 1979, relations between the United States and Pakistan were strained, because of (1) Bhutto's charge that the US had attempted to destabilize his government; (2) US insistence that Pakistan should not develop nuclear weapons; (3) the fact that, under US pressure, the French government cancelled the contract for the reprocessing plant in August 1979; and (4) the US Embassy in Islamabad was burned down by an infuriated mob when rumors circulated that the US and Israel had captured the Holy Mosque in Mecca. Lastly, (5) from April 1978 to December 1979, though Pakistan and the US shared a common perception that the Afghan revolution was essentially a 'Communist takeover', the US had refused to develop a contingency plan of cooperation with Pakistan in order to deal with the Afghan developments.

With the Soviet intervention in Afghanistan (December 1979), the US position in regard to Afghanistan radically changed, and Pakistan welcomed this change. Why? Several factors entered into this calculation. (1) The consolidation of the Soviet hold on Afghanistan along with the Indo-Soviet Treaty of Friendship (August 1971) would enable the two powers to crush Pakistan in their future pincer movement; (2) Afghanistan, with the accretion of Soviet protection and support for its armed forces, would become unmanageable for Pakistan; (3) Ideologically, Pakistan would become vulnerable to a 'socialist' revolution. Finally, (4) A domestic determinant of Zia's foreign policy—his need to have a powerful patron in order to prolong his rule—entered into the calculus of decision-making.

In return for US economic and military aid, Zia doggedly pursued four major objectives in regard to the Soviet Union and Afghanistan and relegated bilateral relations with the Soviet Union to the background: (1) complete withdrawal of Soviet forces from Afghanistan; (2) repatriation of approximately 3 million Afghan refugees; (3) maintenance of the Islamic character of Afghanistan; and (4) the restoration of the non-aligned status of Afghanistan's foreign policy. Starting in 1980, the UN General Assembly overwhelmingly voted to endorse these principles. The UN, through the appointment of the General Secretary's Special Representative, initiated the negotiating process between the four powers—USSR, USA, Afghanistan and Pakistan—which finally hammered out accords for the Afghan settlement, in Geneva in April 1988. The Soviet forces were withdrawn by February 1989, but the Soviet supported government of Najib survived, assuring the continuation of war by the Mujahideen (Peshawar-7, the so-called Mujahideen's political parties located in Pakistan).

However, two years later in December 1991, the Soviet Union collapsed.

The Soviet Collapse

The Soviet collapse was inexorably moving toward its climax during 1989-91. When it came, the world finally realized that the menacing giant had feet of clay, and had collapsed under the weight of its societal and economic contradictions. The system was based upon fear and a system of rewards for those who supported it. The fear was systemic, and was generated by instruments of control, including the CPSU's political monopoly, censorship and surveillance through the KGB. By exercising total control over the nationalized economy, the Communist Party of the Soviet Union (CPSU) established the priority in allocations which invariably favoured the military-industrial complex, and rewarded certain other segments of society which helped to work this system. Gorbachev, when he came to power in 1985, called it 'the Stalinist totalitarian bureaucratic system.' He believed that during the 1970s and early 1980s, the Soviet 'economy was failing and beginning to slip back.'[31]

In order to reform the Soviet system fundamentally, Gorbachev initiated the policy of perestroika (restructuring) and glasnost (openness), which he thought would usher in an era of democratic socialism—the real objective of the Leninist revolution. Consequently, the removal of the Stalinist model of the Soviet Union was Gorbachev's avowed objective. With no alternative system to replace the old model, Gorbachev's policies unravelled the Soviet Union. Whatever his aspirations, Gorbachev could not have foreseen that he was destined to preside over the loss of the USSR's 'empire' in Eastern Europe and the collapse of the Soviet Union.

The disintegration of the Soviet Union accompanied the fall of Gorbachev in December 1991. The factors which led to this denouement were (1) the opposition of the CPSU and corruption within its ranks; (2) decline in the economy; (3) the policies of perestroika, which dismantled the Stalinist mould of the USSR's political system; and (4) the unrelenting march of the republics for secession and independence. Collectively, these factors hastened the demise of the Soviet Union. However, the *coup de grâce* to the USSR was given by the Gorbachev-Yeltsin rivalry. A junta of Gorbachev's former top aides[32] started a coup against him on 18 August but it failed by 21 August when he returned from the Crimea to Moscow, where the balance of power had radically shifted in Yeltsin's favour. Probably, the precipitating factor for the short-lived coup was the new union treaty, which was to be signed by six of the fifteen republics on 20 August in the Kremlin. The draft of the Union Treaty transferred substantial autonomy to the Republics, while it retained powers of sovereignty for Moscow.

Yeltsin pushed Gorbachev to the sidelines. On 24 December 1991 Yeltsin and the Presidents of ten other republics met at Alma-Ata to reaffirm the dissolution of the USSR and to proclaim the birth of the Commonwealth of Independent States.

The decline and fall of Soviet power had a direct impact on developments within Afghanistan. One week after the Soviet Union recognized the independence of the Baltic Republics of Lithuania, Latvia and Estonia, Gorbachev's new Foreign Minister, Boris D. Pankin, joined US Secretary of State, James A. Baker, in September 1991 to end weapons delivery to the Afghan combatants by 1 January 1992. This commitment did not bind Pakistan or Saudi Arabia, China or Iran, to follow the US-USSR announcement. The Soviet decision demoralized the Najib regime, while the developments within the Soviet Union convinced all Afghans that the Najib regime's days were numbered. In recognition of this unavoidable eventuality, the UN Secretary-General's special emissary in Afghanistan, Benon Sevan, pressured Najib to announce that he would resign and hand over power to an interim government, outlined in February 1992 a peace programme, envisaging a conference in Geneva between tribal leaders, monarchists, Mujahideen and the Najib regime's representatives, without Najib's participation. This conference was to nominate an interim president and government to take power in Kabul by the early summer of 1992. In early April, Sevan accelerated the timetable. Now his plan was for a pre-transition council of around fifteen prominent, but politically neutral, Afghans to take over power in Kabul before the end of April. Najib's decision was made not exclusively under Sevan's diplomatic pressure. The collapse of the Soviet Union was the main catalyst in convincing his generals that he was no longer useful. They prepared to switch sides. Unwisely, Najib also started to tinker with the new ethnic equilibrium which had developed in northern Afghanistan. Lastly, Najib's Watan Party, mostly the Parcham faction of the PDPA, deserted him.

In the north, the Uzbeks, Tajiks, Turkomen, Hazaras and Ismailis had established, since 1979, local autonomy. In January 1992 Uzbek and Tajik generals in the northwest rebelled rather than accept their replacement by Pashtun officers as Najib had attempted. In March, the powerful Jozjani Uzbek militia, based in Mazar-i Sharif, rebelled against the government and seized control of the city and neighbouring provinces. The militia, led by the well known General Abdul Rashid Dostam, an Uzbek, then joined with local Mujahideen to form a military council to administer their new fief. The best known Mujahideen Commander, Ahmad Shah Massoud, a Tajik, who had run much of the Tajik northeast for years, joined in an 'alliance' with General Dostam. Already, the Hazaras had created a mini-state in Hazarajat in Central Afghanistan.

The regime's garrisons elsewhere sought to protect themselves by making alliances with local Mujahideen. By 23 April only Jalalabad and Kabul remained in the regime's control. Here also Najib's demoralized associates and military officers started to negotiate with the Mujahideen the terms of surrender. Powerless to stop the defections, and lacking any solid support in Kabul, Najib not only resigned but attempted to flee during the night of 15 April. He was turned back at the airport by General Dostam's militia, who had already established their control at the airport and in the environs of Kabul. Sevan gave him asylum in the UN office in Kabul, and then tried to arrange for Najib to join his family in India, but did not succeed.[33]

After the fall of Najib, the Mujahideen started to march victoriously into Kabul on 24 April. A day later, the Mujahideen leadership in Peshawar announced the formation of a 50-member interim council with Professor Sibghatullah Mojaddedi (the AIG's President) as the new President of Afghanistan for two months. He was to be followed for a period of four months by Professor Burhanuddin Rabbani, who would arrange a *loya jirga* (grand assembly) in order to lay the groundwork for general elections in Afghanistan. A major step toward transfer of power was taken when on 28 June 1992 Rabbani took over presidency from Mojaddedi, and was re-elected by the *loya jirga* in December 1992.[34]

With the Mujahideen's total victory over the Soviet-installed government in Afghanistan, the Soviet Union/Russia endured a humiliating defeat. Internationally, the Soviet-Indian partnership suffered a major setback, while the US-Pakistan coalition triumphed. A few hours after Mojadidi's assumption of power in Kabul on 28 April, Pakistan's Prime Minister, Nawaz Sharif, along with the Chief of the Army, and the Inter-Services Intelligence, made a lightning two-hour visit to Kabul and congratulated President Mojaddedi on the Mujahideen's victory. Both addressed a joint press conference, and emphasized the need for cooperation and peace in Afghanistan.

However, Pakistan's strategic thinkers were already speculating on the possibilities of trade and economic partnership beyond Afghanistan's frontiers, with the Central Asian states. The concept of strategic depth, including Afghanistan and the Central Asian states, which was so popular with Pakistan's military planners, now seemed to appear on the horizon. Fraternal Afghanistan thus became a linchpin in the architectural design of South West Asia's relations with Central Asia, and Pakistan's secure niche in it. However, this 'secure niche' remains only a hope while the conflict in Afghanistan continues to rage. In 1998, it looks possible that the Taliban's government in Kabul would be able to establish peace over all of Afghanistan, and follow a fraternal policy toward Pakistan.

Pakistan's Relations with Post-Soviet Russia (1991-1998)

During this brief span of time, Pakistan's relations with Russia were marked by a strange attitude of indifference toward Russia. Actually, it was the best time to cement relations with this Eurasian power. Also, soon after 1991, it was the best opportunity for Pakistan to unlock India's claim on an exclusive friendship with Moscow by virtue of its Treaty of Friendship of 1970. Russia could have become an alternative source of military hardware for Pakistan, as it has been for India. Thoughtlessly, those opportunities were squandered by Pakistan.

At least three factors were responsible for Pakistani diplomacy's irresponsible indifference: (1) internal political instability atrophying diplomatic initiative in the Foreign Office; five prime ministers, including Benazir Bhutto and Nawaz Sharif, twice alternated each other, and then were dismissed unceremoniously by the President, with an interim prime minister in-between serving a brief term of three months each; (2) Pakistan's syndrome of dependency on the United States, which was strengthened by the ongoing conflict in Afghanistan. Mistakenly, Pakistan believed, at least until 1995, that probably a semblance of tattered strategic relationship of the past could still be maintained; (3) lack of Pakistan's expertise on Soviet/ Russian developments, which made it well nigh impossible for Pakistan to have a realistic assessment of Russian capabilities, and its assets and liabilities.

India, once again, signed a Treaty of Friendship with Russia, rightly asserting that India always perceived the Soviet Union and Russia as pre-eminently the same power. Thus, India padlocked its friendship with Russia, leaving Pakistan out on the sidelines. With the rise of the Taliban movement in Afghanistan in 1995, and their almost total conquest of the Turkic north, Russia and the Central Asian states, especially Uzbekistan and Tajikistan, clamoured in 1998 the penetration of Islamic fundamentalism into the CIS (Commonwealth of Independent States.) Russia claims to head the CIS, and rightly or wrongly perceives the borders of Tajikistan as its ideological and strategic frontiers.

Despite the dissolution of the Soviet Union, Russia still remains a significant Eurasian power, which contains 22 autonomous states. Almost half of them are Turkic in ethnic origin and Islamic in faith. Located in the Volga-Ural basin and highly industrialized, the most significant and politically sophisticated of these autonomous states are Tatarstan and Bashkortostan. In Asia, Russia enjoys disproportionate power— it inherited from the USSR 90 per cent of the oil, nearly 80 per cent of the natural gas, 62 per cent of electricity, 70 per cent of the gold, 70 per cent of the trained workers,[35] and 65-70 per cent of the territory. Its industries, while most of them obsolete by American standards, are appropriate to Pakistan's level of industrial development.

During December 1991-1994, a fierce debate raged in Russia between Atlanticists and Eurasianists. Under Foreign Minister Andrei Kozyrev, the Atlanticists perceived Russia's future with the West, naively attempting to adopt Western liberal democracy and 'sharing' strategic partnership at the global level with the United States. Against them were arrayed the Eurasionists, who defined Eurasia as lands occupied by Russia and Central Asian states. Culturally, they perceived Russia neither in Europe nor in Asia, but as 'a distinctive Eurasian cosmos' in symbiosis of one combination or another: (1) Slavic-Turkic; (2) Irano-Turanian, and (3) Ugro-Mongol. They derided the Atlanticists for their west-oriented foreign policy, which consigned Russians 'to another bout of suffering from an inferiority complex,' not only in relations with the West, but also with respect to Japan and China. Also, they saw danger to Russia from the independent Central Asian states because, through the latter, politicized Islam penetrated 'the lower and middle Volga regions' including Bashkortostan and Tatarstan.

Clearly, the Atlanticists lost out, when the United States admitted in 1998 the former Warsaw Pact 'allies' of Russia,— Poland, Hungary and the Czech Republic—into NATO. The Eurasian view has prevailed in Russia, whose orientation also collides with American oil interests in the Caspian Sea region, and Central Asia. Consequently, the developments in Afghanistan have pitted Russia (as well as Iran) against Pakistan's interests, while India is supportive of Russia. Ironically, in Eurasia the old cold war 'alliances' are resurfacing in a slightly different version.

To forestall these developments, proposals were made (in which this author was intimately involved) to significantly improve Pakistan's relations with Russia. But to no avail, Pakistan's diplomacy remained atrophied, reflecting lack of initiative and creative thinking in the conduct of its foreign policy. In June 1994, three proposals were submitted to Prime Minister Benazir Bhutto, and then with some appropriate modifications, they were resubmitted in April 1997 to Prime Minister Nawaz Sharif through the courtesy of Pakistan's President Muhammad Rafiq Tarar.

Prime Minister's Visit to Russia and Tatarstan

Benazir Bhutto was scheduled to visit Russia in October/November 1994. It was suggested that she should also visit the autonomous Republic of Tatarstan with the concurrence of Russia. In addition to normalizing relations with Russia and restarting economic relations, Pakistan should cultivate special relations with Tatarstan. Why? Being a highly industrialized republic, Tatarstan produces helicopters, MIG fighters, automobiles, electronics, and many other industrial products which Pakistan could use. Tatarstan also produces large quantities of oil, which it has started to export.

In February 1994, Tatarstan signed a treaty of co-existence and autonomy within a federal arrangement with Russia. According to this treaty, it acquired substantial authority in dealing with foreign states, especially in matters of economic and trade relations.[36] Pakistan's Prime Minister(s)' visit to Tatarstan would have laid the foundation of enduring relations with this republic, where India had no influence.

As of 1998, neither Benazir Bhutto nor Nawaz Sharif, visited Russia, let alone Tatarstan. Under friendly persuasion, the Tatar government took the initiative in August 1995 of sending an exploratory delegation to Pakistan, which was to be headed by Tatarstan President, Mintimer Shaimiyev's senior Political Adviser, Rafael Khakimov, a man of superb diplomatic skills. This delegation was to explore between 15 December 1995-15 January 1996 the possibility of establishing trade relations, and cultural exchanges. (At the personal level, this author obtained invitations for the Tatar delegation from Pakistan's Chamber of Commerce in Lahore, and Islamabad's Pakistan Forum, to be their hosts). Pakistan's Ambassador to Russia, Tanvir Ahmad Khan, made a special visit to Islamabad to persuade Benazir Bhutto to give clearance to the Tatar delegation. Unfortunately, his entreaties were ignored, and Tatarstan's initiative was aborted.

Establishing the Russian Centre for Pakistan Studies in Moscow

In Moscow, especially between 15-20 June 1994, extensive exploratory conversations were held at the prestigious Russian Institute of Oriental Studies in order to establish a Russian Centre for Pakistan Studies. To Russian scholars, the model of the American Institute of Pakistan Studies was presented, which this author had established in the United States in 1973 with the assistance of Prime Minister Zulfikar Ali Bhutto. The Russian Centre was to promote scholars' exchanges between Russia and Pakistan in order to promote Russian and Pakistan studies in the two countries. The funding was to be provided by Pakistan (50 per cent) and Russia (50 per cent).

Russian scholars led by internationally known scholars, especially Yuri V. Gankovsky and Vyacheslav Belokrinitsky, submitted this proposal to the Russian Government for its approval. Despite all the financial problems and economic difficulties, the Yeltsin government agreed to establishing the

Russian Centre for Pakistan Studies and to provide 50 per cent of its funding. Pakistan's government remained undecided!

Treaty of Friendship with Russia

Indeed, Russia signed for the second time the Treaty of Friendship with India, but the infamous security article, which was directed in the 1970s against Pakistan and China, was eliminated. Clearly, Russia was not prepared to continue the old strategic partnership with India. Until 1994, Russia was equally interested in signing a similar treaty with Pakistan. If this treaty were to be signed in that year (as it was privately proposed), then Russian friendship with Pakistan would have become the co-equal of that with India, and the Indian monopoly of friendship with Russia would have been set aside. After 1994 this golden opportunity disappeared.[37]

Clearly, this brief survey indicates that Pakistan's diplomacy took no advantage of the opportunities which had become available immediately after 1991.

Belatedly, Pakistan signed in July 1997 four agreements with Russia in the fields of (1) culture; (2) science and education; (3) consular relations, and (4) illicit trafficking of drugs. These non-political agreements did not raise the level of bilateral political cooperation significantly, but were in the style of interaction between the two states, which existed during the cold war. One agreement, however, was politically significant, and it pertained to Afghanistan. Pakistan offered Russia to participate in confabulations in Islamabad, which would also include China, Iran, Tajikistan, Turkmenistan, Uzbekistan, and the United States. This conference is proposed to be held under the United Nations' auspices in order to encourage an inter-Afghan dialogue for power sharing between the Taliban and the opposition.[38] These agreements were signed in Moscow by Pakistan's Foreign Minister, Gohar Ayub Khan, and Yevgeny Primakov, who subsequently became Russian Prime Minister.

Despite these positive steps, Russia-Pakistan relations have not achieved the cordiality which might break India's exclusive friendship with Moscow.

NOTES

1. National Assembly of Pakistan, *Parliamentary Debates*, Vol. I (26 March 1956), p. 76.
2. Firoz Khan Noon in 1946, quoted in A.B. Rajput, *The Muslim League: Yesterday and Today* (Lahore: 1948), p. 109.
3. For Mir Laik Ali's mission to the United States, see Secretary of State's communication to Pakistani Ambassador (Ispahani), Washington, D. C., dated 17 December 1947, in *Foreign Relations of the United States, 1947*, Vol. III, (India & Pakistan Section) (Washington, D. C. : 1972) pp. 172-3 (hereafter called FRUS).
4. For these assessments, starting with 'the Pentagon Talks of 1947', see *FRUS*, 1947 (Near East and Africa Section) (Washington, D. C. : 1971), Vol. V, pp. 484-1305; Vol. XI (1952-4) (Washington, D. C. : 1983), pp. 1057-161.
5. George McTurnan Kahin, *The Afro-Asian Conference, Bandung, Indonesia*, April 1955 (Ithaca: Cornell University Press, 1956), p. 54.
6. Henry Kissinger, *White House Years* (Boston: Little, Brown & Co., 1979), pp. 895-1488.
7. Aide Memoire presented by the Soviet Ambassador to the Prime Minister of Pakistan, 14 April 1958; R. K. Jain (ed), *Soviet South Asian Relations, 1947-1978* (Atlantic Highlands, N. J.: Humanities Press, 1979), Vol. II, p. 10.
8. V.V. Balabushevich, 'India posle razdela', *Mirovoe Khoziaistvo i mirovaia politika*, No. 12 (December 1947), p. 55, as cited by Jerry F. Hough, *The Struggle for the Third World* (Washington, D. C.).
9. T.N. Kaul, *Diplomacy in Peace and War: Recollection and Reflections* (New Delhi: Vikas, 1979), pp. 12, 15.
10. Igor V. Khalevinski, *USSR and Pakistan* (Moscow: Glavnaja Redaktsija Vostchnoy Litratury, 1984), p. 20.
11. Ibid., p. 21.
12. For details, see Hafeez Malik, 'Marxist Literary Movement in India and Pakistan', *Journal of Asian Studies* (Ann Arbor, Michigan), June 1967, pp. 649-63.
13. W.W. Rostow, *Open Skies: Eisenhower's Proposal of 21 July 1955* (Austin: University of Texas, 1982), pp. 62-3.
14. Michael R. Beschloss, *May Day; Eisenhower: Khrushchev and the U-2 Affair* (New York: Harper & Row, 1986), p. 256.

15. Ibid., p. 60.
16. Agha Shahi, 'Pakistan's Relations with the United States', in Hafeez Malik (ed.) *Soviet-American Relations with Pakistan, Iran and Afghanistan* (New York: St. Martin's Press, 1987), p. 164.
17. *Dawn,* 9 May 1960.
18. 'Moscow Radio Broadcast to India and Pakistan, 31 January 1962', in Jain, *Soviet South Asian Relations,* pp. 25-6.
19. 'Foreign Minister Bhutto's Interview with a Correspondent', *New Times* (Moscow) 25 January 1965.
20. Jain, *Soviet South Asian Relations,* pp. 33-8.
21. Muhammad Ayub Khan, *Friends, Not Masters* (London: Oxford University Press, 1967), p. 174.
22. Khan, ibid., p. 113.
23. Kissinger, *White House Years,* p. 690.
24. Ibid., pp. 714-15.
25. Ibid., p. 739.
26. Pran Chopra, *India's Second Liberation* (Cambridge, Mass. : MIT Press, 1974), p. 100.
27. Zulfikar Ali Bhutto, *The Myth of Independence* (London: Oxford University Press, 1969), p. 145.
28. Zulfikar Ali Bhutto, *Speeches and Statements,* 1-30 July; September 1972 (Karachi: Govt. of Pakistan, 1972), p. 31.
29. Zulfikar Ali Bhutto, 'Pakistan Builds Anew', *Pakistan Affairs* (New York), April 1973, p. 552.
30. Ibid.
31. Mikhail Gorbachev, *The August [1991] Coup,* (New York: Harper Collins, 1991), pp. 102-3.
32. These aides were: (1) D. D. Baklanov, First Vice-Chairman of the Defence Council; (2) V. A. Kryuchkov, Chairman of the KGB; (3) V. S. Pavlov, Prime Minister; (4) B. K. Pugo, Minister of Internal Affairs; (5) V. A. Starodubtsev, Chairman of the Peasants' union; (6) A. I. Tizyakov, President of the Association of State Enterprises; (7) D. T. Yazov, Minister of Defence; (8) G. I. Yanayev, Vice President of the USSR. 'Statement by the Soviet Leadership', *Pravda* and *Izvestia,* 20 August 1991.
33. 'The Afghans' Nervous End-Game', *The Economist,* 25 April 1992; for details on these developments, see Afghan Information Centre: *Monthly Bulletin,* Peshawar: No. 132-5, March—June, 1992; Edward A. Garga, 'Afghan President Ousted as Rebels Approach Capital', *The New York Times,* 17 April 1992.
34. Donatella Lorch, 'Rebels Agree on Interim Rule for Kabul', *The New York Times,* 25 April 1992; Mushahid Hussain, 'Afghanistan: Smooth Transition', *The Economist,* 10 July 1992.

35. Vladislav Zubok, 'Tyranny of the Weak: Russia's New Foreign Policy', *World Policy Journal* (Vol. IX, No. 2, Spring 1992), p. 195.
36. For details of this treaty see Hafeez Malik, 'Tatarstan's Treaty with Russia: Autonomy or Independence', *Journal of South Asian and Middle Eastern Studies*, (Vol. XVIII, No. 2, Winter 1994), pp. 1-36.
37. Based on Malik's personal correspondence with the Governments of Pakistan, Russia and Tatarstan.
38. *Dawn*, 10 July 1997.

13

Foreign Policy: Relations with the West, China and the Middle East

Abdul Sattar

Pakistan entered upon the world stage with aspirations founded in the history and culture of its predominantly Muslim people. Heir to a universalist civilisation with an over-arching sense of human community, the nation looked forward to friendly cooperation with other countries. The Pakistan movement sought freedom from British colonial rule and the right of self-determination for the Muslim people in areas where they constituted a majority, upholding the right of all nations to freedom and independence. Quaid-i-Azam Mohammad Ali Jinnah, the leader of the Pakistan movement and the first head of state, was a man of reason, well-versed in law and logic, and a votary of the democratic system of government with equal rights for all, free from discrimination on grounds of race, religion or sect. Other mentors of the nation, too, envisioned a progressive polity. In the latter part of the nineteenth century, Syed Ahmad Khan successfully exhorted the Muslim community to end its sullen attitude toward the British conquerors, learn English and acquire contemporary knowledge without which they were relegated politically and deprived of opportunities for economic advancement. Allama Mohammad Iqbal, a humanist scholar deeply read in history and philosophy, used the vehicle of inspiring poetry to inculcate pride in humanity's capacity to mould its own destiny. While holding fast to Islamic moorings, he urged the Muslim community to open the door to adaptation and reconstruction of religious thought so as to re-embark on the road to social dynamism and economic progress.

Proud of having achieved Pakistan 'peacefully by moral and intellectual force,' Jinnah believed in the human capacity to achieve peace with justice. 'We believe in the principle of honesty and fair play in national and international dealings,' he said, pledging that 'Pakistan will never be found lacking in extending its material and moral support to the oppressed and suppressed people of the world and in upholding the principles of the United Nations Charter.'[2]

Solicitous of friendly relations, specially with fellow Muslim nations, Pakistan harboured no 'prejudices in the international sphere.'[3] Wishing to promote close relations with countries of Asia and the Middle East, Pakistan also looked to the West for cooperation for its economic development. It was opposed to policies of expansion and domination. During World War II, the Muslim League supported participation in the British defence forces to fight against the Axis powers. Jinnah expressed sentiments of friendship toward the United States which, he said, 'acted as a beacon of light and had in no small measure served to give inspiration to nations who like us were striving for independence and freedom from the shackles of foreign rule.'[4]

Pakistan bore no ill-will toward Britain but its unfair and partisan role at the time of the partition left a lasting scar. Evidently proud of having conferred unity on a vast land of disparate races, religions and languages and having built an empire bigger than that of Chandargupta, Ashoka or Akbar, Britain was loath to see its achievement undone. Then, guided by the mind set of an imperial power, it favoured the larger successor state, mentally investing it with the mantle of carrying on the Great Game. Abandoning the vaunted English sense of fair play, Prime Minister Clement Attlee's government sought to propitiate India at the expense of great harm to Pakistan. The last British Viceroy, Lord Louis Mountbatten, pursued London's preference with single-minded enthusiasm, believing that if independent India joined the British Commonwealth, its 'value to the United Kingdom both in terms of world prestige and strategy would be enormous.'[5] His ego flattered by the Congress leaders' decision to retain him as Governor-General, Mountbatten became an accomplice in their design to subject the fledgling state of Pakistan to maximum handicaps.

Relations with India are outside the scope of this chapter but a brief reference is unavoidable because the core of Pakistan's foreign policy was determined largely in the crucible of tension and conflict with this neighbour. Ascribable partly to a difficult and divisive legacy, adversarial perceptions of history, differences of religions and cultures, and the clash of political aims and ideologies, antagonism between the two countries was exacerbated by the post-partition problems. India 'dishonestly retained much of Pakistan's share'[6] of the assets of British India. Indian leaders 'persistently tried to obstruct the work of partition of the armed forces.'[7] 'What mattered to them, above all else, was to cripple and thwart the establishment of Pakistan as a viable independent state.'[8] In April 1948, India cut off the water supply in the irrigation canals that flowed from head-works on the Ravi and Sutlej rivers, menacing agriculture in Pakistan. No other problem has perpetuated antagonism and hostility between Pakistan and India more than the Kashmir question, involving India's forcible grab of the state 'in utter violation of the principles on which partition was agreed upon and effected'[9], backtracking on its solemn pledges, later sanctified in the resolutions of the UN Security Council envisaging the exercise of right of self-determination by the Kashmiri people in a plebiscite under UN auspices, and use of force and repression to perpetuate usurpation. Confronted with India's refusal to implement its pledges or accept arbitration or adjudication for settlement of differences and, instead, its penchant to resort to threat or use of force, Pakistan responded in classical style. Just as states have done throughout history, it sought to ameliorate the tyranny of imbalance of power by cultivating the sympathy and support of other states, near and far.

Relations with the United States

Needing political support as well as material assistance to ward off threats to security and to develop economic and military strength, Pakistan intuitively looked to the United States. Not only that the US alone had the resources to provide assistance while the other Great Powers were debilitated in World War II, Washington made friendly gestures upon Pakistan's independence. President Harry S. Truman sent a warm message assuring 'firm friendship and goodwill.'[10] He was 'sympathetic' in response when Ambassador Ispahani spoke about Pakistan's need 'to balance our economy, to industrialize our country, to improve health and education and raise the standard of living.'[11]

Constrained by its desperate need, Pakistan hurriedly approached the United States in October 1947 for a loan of approximately two billion dollars over five years for economic development and defence purchases in order to 'attain a reasonably independent position and...to make a fair contribution to the stability of the world order.'[12] The request drew a blank. A surprised Washington politely turned down the request but Pakistan did not give up hope. Intensifying efforts to cultivate US support in conversations with American officials, Pakistani leaders spoke about the country's strategic location, compatibility of Pakistan-US interests, 'the proximity and vulnerability of western Pakistan to Russia'[13], and importance of establishing a bloc 'as a check to any ambitions of USSR.'[14] During his visit to the United States in May 1950, Prime Minister Liaquat Ali Khan described the two countries as 'comrades' in quest of peace and democracy.

American analysts recognized the value of Pakistan's location. In March 1949 the Joint Chiefs of Staff noted the strategic importance of Karachi-Lahore area 'as a base for air operations' against the Soviet Union and 'as a staging area for forces engaged in the defence or recapture of Middle East oil areas.'[15] Assistant Secretary of State McGhee was impressed by the willingness of Pakistani leaders to support US-backed efforts to prevent communist encroachments in South Asia.[16] Pakistan's prompt support for UN action in Korea in 1950, and for the conclusion of the peace treaty with Japan in 1951 further embellished its image as America's 'one sure friend in South Asia.'[17]

Still, Washington remained unenthusiastic about economic much less military assistance to Pakistan for fear of antagonizing bigger India. Nor was this factor ever ignored even after upheavals in the Middle East and a perception of threat to the West's control over its strategic oil resources, necessitated a new policy requiring cooperation of Pakistan in arrangements for the defence of the region.

Alliances, 1954-55[18]

Revolution in Iran and nationalisation of the Anglo-Iranian Oil Company testifying to the decline of British power and prestige triggered the new United States policy of direct involvement in the defence of the region. By 1952, Pakistan came to be looked upon as a potential partner in arrangements aimed at completing the ring of containment around the Soviet Union.[19] The task of launching the major initiative was taken up by President Dwight D. Eisenhower's administration. Soon after taking office, it manifested its goodwill toward Pakistan by an immediate and positive response to the appeal for help to avert a food crisis in 1953. The president asked Congress to approve supply of one million tons of wheat. Testifying before a congressional committee, Secretary of State John Foster Dulles described Pakistan as 'a real bulwark.'[20] Congress gave bipartisan approval. Within two weeks the bill was passed and signed.

Following a tour of the region, Dulles found that Pakistan alone had a 'genuine feeling of friendship' for the United States. He suggested an alliance of the 'northern-tier' countries—Turkey, Pakistan, Iraq and Iran. But still the United States did not 'dare'[21] to give military assistance to Pakistan. State Department officials abhorred displeasing New Delhi. They said: 'India is the power in South Asia. We should seek to make it our ally rather than cause it to be hostile to us. Pakistan is distressingly weak.'[22] The American ambassador in India, Chester Bowles, warned of a 'catastrophe.' Neither Eisenhower nor Dulles was dismissive of these views but the strategic objectives in the vital Middle East claimed precedence.

Indicative of Washington's half-hearted decision to involve Pakistan in a defence arrangement, was the offer in March 1954 of a paltry $29 million in assistance. It caused deep disappointment in Pakistan. General Mohammad Ayub was 'heart-broken' and Prime Minister Mohammad Ali was most unhappy. The amount was not commensurate, they argued, with the additional risks Pakistan assumed by openly allying itself with the United States. The vehemence of Pakistani leaders' protest surprised Washington. Analogies were cited of a man leading a girl up the primrose path and then abandoning her, or of a girl chasing the man down the aisle and then complaining of gun-point marriage. Muhammad Ali gave the apt example of a man asking for a gun to shoot a mad dog and being given a needle and thread to repair a hole in the trouser. Nevertheless, Pakistan signed a Mutual Defence Assistance Agreement with the United States on 19 May 1954, under which the US undertook to provide defence equipment to Pakistan 'exclusively to maintain its internal security, its legitimate self-defence, or to permit it to participate in defence of the area.' Pakistan also proceeded to join the South East Asia Treaty Organisation (SEATO) in 1954 and the Baghdad Pact in 1955.[23]

Second Thoughts on Alliances in Pakistan and USA

A mismatch between the motivations of Pakistan and the United States was apparent from the outset of their alliance. The alliance lacked the bond of a common adversary. The American object was to contain the communist threat; that of Pakistan was to bolster itself against the threat from India. The seeds of disaffection were inherent in the ambiguous bargain. Pakistan felt it was doing the United States a favour. America was unhappy at having to displease India.

The contradiction of aims was reflected also in the defence treaties. US defence assistance was governed by laws which related to defence of the 'free world.' Pakistan expected a broader cover. SEATO was too vague to reassure. Unlike NATO, it did not provide for immediate assistance to an allied victim of aggression; the parties undertook merely to hold consultations in such a contingency. Moreover, the United States entered a reservation to restrict its commitment to consultation only to a case of communist aggression. As for the Baghdad Pact, it was orphaned at birth: the United States decided against joining the alliance; it became a member only of its military committee which got stalled on the definition of the purpose of the alliance.

The value and wisdom of the policy of alliances came under question immediately. People in Pakistan were disturbed at the price Pakistan had to pay for the alliance, politically and in pride. The country became isolated in the kindred community of African-Asian nations which were suspicious of the West and looked upon the Soviet Union as an ally in the struggle for emancipation from colonial domination and an exemplar of rapid economic development. India used Pakistani alignment as a pretext to renounce its obligation to allow a plebiscite in Kashmir. While Pakistan's allies were reluctant to use their influence in support even of the relevant Security Council resolutions, a furious Soviet Union threw its powerful weight behind India, discarding its neutral stance in Pakistan-India disputes. During their visit to India in December 1955, the Soviet Leaders, Nikolai Bulganin and Nikita Khrushchev, spited Pakistan by declaring they were 'grieved that imperialist forces succeeded in dividing India into two parts' and referred to Kashmir as 'one of the states of India.'

More painful emotionally was the denunciation of Pakistan's policy by some of the fraternal countries of the Middle East. Egypt was quick to take umbrage. Radio Cairo denounced the alliance as 'a catastrophe for Islam.'[24] Saudi radio echoed the influential Arab Voice from Cairo, calling the Baghdad Pact 'a stab in the heart of the Arab and Muslim states.'[25] The Pakistani people, who historically yearned for solidarity with the Muslim world, felt rebuked and spurned. The contradiction in Pakistan's policy came to a head during the Suez crisis. President Nasser's decision to nationalize the Suez Canal in July 1956 precipitated an international crisis. Pakistan's Western allies apprehended that Egypt's exclusive control over the maritime highway would jeopardize their vital trade interests. Losing balance, Pakistan's diplomacy placed emphasis on interests of nations 'vitally concerned with the maintenance of the freedom of navigation.'[26] This view ignored the politics of the situation which was given due weight by Ceylon, India and Indonesia though they, too, depended on the Suez Canal.

At the first London conference in mid-August, Pakistan succumbed to British and American pressure to support the suggestion for an international board to supervise the operation of the canal. The decision provoked a charge of betrayal from Egypt and ignited a political explosion in Pakistan. Pained by the obloquy Pakistan incurred, political parties, including the ruling Muslim League, censured the government's policy. Fortunately, Husain Shaheed Suhrawardy, who became prime minister at this stage, steered the government out of the storm. At the second London conference in September, Pakistan made amends by opposing the Western proposal to set up a Users' Association. Egypt was delighted by 'the return of the prodigal' but the incident left a deep scar.

Disillusionment in Pakistan accelerated as opinion in the United States began to swing away from preference for ally Pakistan to cultivation of pro-Soviet India. The policy change was illustrated in the vivid contrast between Dulles's denunciation of neutralism in 1956 as 'an immoral and shortsighted conception'[27] and Eisenhower's criticism in 1957 of the alliance with Pakistan as 'a terrible error.'[28] Opinion in Pakistan was deeply agitated. Pakistan was 'taken for granted'[29] by its allies and penalized by the Soviet Union. In contrast, neutral India was courted by both the US and USSR. While alliances cost Pakistan more than self-esteem; neutralism enhanced India's prestige. There was little comfort in Dulles's explanation that the American relationship with India was on an intellectual level whereas that with Pakistan was 'more from the heart.'[30] In Pakistan's own cultural idiom, which expects a friend to be sacrificing and supportive, the statement was unconvincing. Instead of giving unreserved support as Pakistan extended, throwing caution to the winds by joining the West in opposing 'the totalitarian concept,'[31] Washington down-graded an ally to the same level as a neutral state with a pro-Soviet tilt. The American failure to throw its weight behind a just settlement of the Kashmir dispute was a 'great disappointment.'[32]

Despite declining popular support for the alliances in both countries, it not only survived but was reinforced because of Pakistan's increasing dependence on American economic and military assistance and, more importantly, because the United States needed facilities for a communication base at Badaber near Peshawar for electronic monitoring of Soviet missile tests in Central Asia, and permission for its high-flying U-2 aircraft to use the Peshawar air base for illegal reconnaissance flights over the Soviet Union. Ayub Khan decided to accede to the American request in a secret agreement. Once again, the US administration expressed appreciation for Pakistan as a 'wholehearted ally' which undertook 'real responsibilities and risks' by providing facilities 'highly important to (US) national security.'[33] In exchange, Washington offered assurances of security protection and enhanced aid. In March 1959, the two countries signed the Agreement of Cooperation by which the US pledged, in case of aggression against Pakistan, to 'take such appropriate action, including the use of armed forces, as may be mutually agreed upon and as is envisaged in the Joint Resolution to Promote Peace and Stability in the Middle East.' Washington also agreed to provide substantial economic and military assistance to Pakistan, including F-104 fighter aircraft. Although not dissatisfied with the quantum of US assistance, Pakistan was worried about the tide of influential opinion in America in favour of India.

Americans looked upon India as a counter-model to China. Indian spokesmen encouraged the view according to which the world was supposed to be watching 'who would win—India under democracy or China under communism.'[34] Senator Kennedy forecast an apocalypse: 'If India collapses, so may all of Asia.' Aid to India was increased from $ 93 million in 1956 to $365 million in 1957[35] and a record $822 million in 1960. Deterioration in India's relations with China over Tibet in 1959, provided an additional incentive to burgeoning US support. In 1960, the US decided to provide an additional $1,276 million for the export of 12 million tons of wheat to India over the next four years. The wooing of India became even more pronounced after John F. Kennedy became president. Although he had no illusions about 'Nehru's talent for international self-righteousness'[36] he regarded India as 'the key area' in Asia. In his inaugural address he paid tribute to 'the soaring idealism of Nehru.' Viewing India as 'a potential brake on Chinese aggression'[37] Kennedy's first budget provided $500 million for economic aid to India as against $150 million for Pakistan. Soon, the United States also decided to provide a 400 megawatt nuclear power plant to India.

Pakistan continued to hope for a more balanced American approach. During his visit to the USA in July 1961, Ayub Khan emphasized the mutuality of benefits of Pakistan-US cooperation. He received a sympathetic response in the Congress and 'charmed everybody' in Washington.[38] At his suggestion, Kennedy promised to speak to Nehru in favour of a Kashmir settlement and, if unsuccessful, to support Pakistan at the United Nations. When Ayub Khan expressed concern about US military assistance to India, Kennedy replied that 'if a Sino-Indian conflict ever erupted, and India asked the United States for military aid, he would first consult with Ayub before making a commitment.'[39]

When Nehru came to Washington in November 1961, Kennedy raised the Kashmir question with him. The response was disappointing. Talking to Nehru, Kennedy said, was 'like trying to grab something in your hand, only to have it turn out to be just fog.'[40] Nehru's visit was 'the worst' by a foreign leader.[41] A month later Kennedy professed 'shock'[42] when Nehru decided to invade and occupy defenceless Goa, Diu and Daman in December 1961. 'The contrast between Nehru's incessant sanctimony on the subject of non-aggression and his brisk exercise in *Machtpolitik* was too comic not to cause comment. It was a little like catching the preacher in the hen-house.'[43] Adlai Stevenson, the US representative to the UN, soared to heights of eloquence in declaiming that 'if the United Nations was not to die as ignoble a death as the League of Nations, we cannot condone the use of force in this instance and thus pave the way for forceful solutions of other disputes.'[44] But the rhetoric proved to be hot air. Neither disappointment with Nehru nor admiration for Ayub Khan had much influence on American policy of support for India during the Sino-Indian border clash, or hostility toward Pakistan for its policy of improving relations with China.

Relations with China

Pakistan had few contacts with countries of East Asia in the early years after independence. Its decisions on issues of policy concerning the important countries of the region were based on objective merits. Pakistan was among the first countries to extend recognition to the People's Republic of China. A year later, Pakistan established an embassy in Beijing evidencing its appreciation of China's importance.

Providentially, prospects of Pakistan's relations with China escaped serious damage during the Korean crisis. The government not only denounced the North Korean attack on South Korea in June 1950 as 'a clear case of aggression'[45] it even considered sending an army brigade. The idea was abandoned because the United States balked at the suggestion for a commitment to support Pakistan in the event of Indian aggression. This decision proved a blessing. Otherwise, Pakistani troops could have been involved in fighting against the Chinese forces which came to North Korea's help after the United States decided to extend the war beyond the 38th parallel.

Pakistan's anti-communist rhetoric was largely ignored by China. Evidently it understood Pakistan's motives. Premier Zhou Enlai followed a sagacious policy, avoiding criticism of Pakistan during his visit to India in June 1954. China criticized SEATO but not Pakistan. Premier Zhou felt hurt, he told the Pakistani ambassador, because he regarded Pakistan as a friend. Still, he 'fully understood' Pakistan's circumstances.[46] Prime Minister Mohammad Ali, too, respected China's sensitivities. At the Bandung conference in April 1955, he criticized Soviet imperialism but clarified that China 'is by no means an imperialist nation.' Zhou declared that he and Mohammad Ali 'achieved a mutual understanding'[47] after the latter explained that Pakistan had no fear that China would commit aggression and, further, that if the United States took aggressive action under SEATO Pakistan would not be involved. In the joint communique issued after Zhou's visit to Pakistan in December 1956, the two prime ministers were 'happy to place on record that there is no real conflict of interests between the two countries.'[48]

Yet to appease allies, Pakistan occasionally relapsed into an improvident mode. On the issue of China's representation in the UN it supported the US-sponsored procedural manoeuvre enabling the Chiang Kaishek regime in Taiwan to continue occupying the Chinese seat. Not until 1961 did Pakistan rectify this aberration. In October 1959, Pakistan voted for the UN General Assembly resolution on Tibet which was critical of China.[49] In April 1959, Ayub Khan made the extraordinary proposal of joint defence with India. Even after Nehru ridiculed the offer by rhetorically asking 'Joint defence against whom?' Ayub Khan persisted, forecasting that South Asia would become militarily vulnerable in five years to major invasions from the north,[50] gratuitously offending both China and the Soviet Union.[51] It is a tribute to the wisdom and foresight of Chinese leaders that they continued to show extraordinary forbearance, overlooking Pakistan's aberrations. No other country has been as comprehending of Pakistan's constraints as China.

As early as 1959, Ayub Khan suggested the idea of settling the undemarcated border between China's Xinjiang province and the Northern Areas of Kashmir which were under Pakistan's control. Encouraged by China's reasonable stance in the boundary agreements with Nepal and Burma, Pakistan formally proposed demarcation of the common boundary in March 1961. The Chinese response was prompt and favourable. In May 1962, the two countries announced their decision to enter into negotiations. The talks started on 12 October 1962.[52] Conducted in a friendly spirit of mutual accommodation, the talks succeeded within two months.[53] A Pakistani official[54] recalls that after the two sides had agreed on the watershed principle, the Pakistan government, learning that grazing lands historically used by people of Hunza fell to the north of the boundary, appealed to Premier Zhou for an exception and he agreed to the allocation of an area of 750 square miles to Pakistan.

In the early 1960s, Pakistan and China drew closer[55] as the latter, too, experienced India's unreasonable attitude. Already under pressure from the United States, whose naval and air power menaced its seaboard, and the Soviet Union after an ideological rift opened between the two countries, China was faced with Indian encouragement to separatist elements in Tibet and an aggressive forward policy on the boundary issue. Beijing now understood even better than before the difficulties Pakistan confronted at the hands of imperious India backed by the Soviet Union. Though by no means so presumptuous as to enter the contest of giants, Pakistan demonstrated courage in resisting the pressures of its American ally in grasping China's hand of friendship across the Karakorum range.

Withering of Alliance with USA

Oblivious of the Sino-Soviet split, Washington viewed China as part of a monolithic communist bloc. Pulling India into the American orbit was a dominant passion of the time, and the Sino-Indian border clash in October 1962 was considered a defining moment in the history of democracy's crusade against communism. Through that prism, Washington looked askance at 'Pakistan's drift toward Communist China'[56] and applied levers of economic pressure to bring Pakistan into line. Immediately following the Sino-Indian border clash, the United States decided to rush arms to India, forgetting the promise of prior consultation with Pakistan. Military assistance continued even after China announced, to India's—and America's—utter surprise, a unilateral ceasefire and a decision to withdraw its forces back to prewar positions, returning to India 'practically all the territory their army gained.'[57]

Keen to keep Pakistan in tow while pulling India into an embrace, Kennedy wrote to Ayub to assure that the arms provided to India would be 'for use against China only.'[58] Ayub's mild reaction did not reflect the sense of outrage in the country. People felt betrayed, realizing that the arms would enhance India's offensive capability to the detriment ultimately of Pakistan. More representative of opinion in Pakistan was Foreign Minister Bogra's statement in the National Assembly describing the US decision as 'an act of gross unfriendliness.' India, he said, was keeping the bulk of its forces poised on Pakistan's border which was 'a strange method of resisting the Chinese.'[59]

America's failure to understand the Pakistani reaction was manifest also in Kennedy's suggestion to Ayub to 'signal to the Indians' that Pakistan would not embarrass them. Such a gesture, Kennedy said, would do more to bring about a sensible resolution of Pakistan-India differences than anything else.[60] Ayub decided to play a statesman, and implicitly agreed not to take advantage of the situation to press for a settlement of the Kashmir question, merely suggesting that America and Britain promote a settlement.[61] Ambassador Averell Harriman and British Commonwealth Secretary Duncan Sandys persuaded Nehru to agree to 'a renewed effort to resolve the outstanding differences...on Kashmir and other related matters.'[62] Pakistan and India held six rounds of talks in 1962-63 but no sooner had the danger of a further flare up on the border with China receded than India reverted to its policy of holding Kashmir by force. Obsessed with the aim of coopting India to contain China,

Washington and London were not prepared to expend their influence in promoting a Kashmir settlement. India had now no incentive for a settlement with Pakistan.

Instead of using what he had himself described as a 'one-time opportunity'[63] for Pakistan-India reconciliation, Kennedy decided in May 1963 to delink aid to India from a Kashmir settlement and approved a programme of enhanced military assistance. When Pakistan signed an air agreement with China in August 1963, the US called it 'an unfortunate breach of free world solidarity.'[64] The slide in Pakistan-US relations accelerated after Lyndon Johnson succeeded Kennedy. Taking a tough line, he sternly warned the Pakistani minister who came to attend Kennedy's funeral that 'Pakistan's flirtation with China was rapidly approaching the limits of American tolerance'[65], and that Premier Zhou Enlai's upcoming visit to Pakistan would jeopardize US economic and military aid to Pakistan.[66] He was no less curt with President Ayub Khan, threatening that the US would be obliged to re-examine its relations with Pakistan if it continued to develop its relations with China. In April 1964, Johnson disinvited Ayub Khan and suspended further economic assistance to demonstrate US anger at Pakistan for starting air services to China.

The final breakdown of the alliance policy came about after the alliances proved unavailing, when India attacked Pakistan across the international boundary on 6 September 1965. The SEATO council did not meet even for consultations. CENTO could not be activated. Washington took the position that neither the 1959 agreement was applicable nor the pledge it gave in the context of US arms assistance to India in 1962 reaffirming 'previous assurances that it will come to Pakistan's assistance in the event of aggression from India against Pakistan.'[67] Instead, finding its policy in South Asia in a shambles with the two countries using US arms to fight each other rather than US enemies, Washington decided to stop supply of arms to both, which hurt Pakistan more because more of its arms were of American origin. Pakistani opinion regarded the American decision as yet another betrayal. In 1968, Pakistan terminated the Badaber lease, ending the special relationship with USA.

Relations with Muslim States

Historical solidarity of the Muslim community in British India for other Muslim nations was manifest in their support for legitimate causes of North African peoples against colonialism, for the Ottoman Caliphate during and after World War I and for the Palestinian cause. After independence, Pakistan not only maintained that policy but sought to give concrete shape to its desire for close relations with the countries of the Middle East. Its contribution in support of the Arab struggle against Israeli expansionism was appreciated. But the emphasis on Arab nationalism tended to relegate non-Arab Muslim countries to the background. Moreover, Pakistan's alliance policy was considered injurious by some Arab countries. Its stance during the Suez crisis incurred wide censure.

Particularly close relations developed between Iran, Pakistan and Turkey. They became partners in CENTO which was, however, one-dimensional in its orientation. Bound by ties of history and culture, they decided to enlarge contacts and cooperation amongst them in economic and cultural fields. To that end, it was decided at a meeting of the heads of the three states at Istanbul on 22 July 1964, to establish the Regional Cooperation for Development (RCD). Over the following years, agreements were reached to jointly finance a number of industrial projects, with two or all three states agreeing to share in investment and production. Although the joint projects were relatively small, RCD symbolized the aspiration of the people of the three countries for closer cooperation.

A similar sentiment grew between Pakistan and Indonesia. Both looked upon the African-Asian solidarity movement as a better alternative to the formation of the non-aligned group which excluded not only Iran, Pakistan, Philippines, Thailand, etc. but also China, the largest and most important developing country. They cooperated closely in preparations for the second Afro-Asian summit which was aborted because of the overthrow of Ben Bella, President of the host country, in April 1965. Such commonalities of interest led the two countries to decide on the formation of the Indonesia-Pakistan Economic and Cultural Cooperation (IPECC) in August 1965. Although IPECC, like RCD, made slow progress in building cooperation, it provided a useful forum for consultation.

Israeli aggression against Egypt, Jordan and Syria in 1967 evoked strong condemnation in the world. The Muslim peoples were stirred as never before because of the Israeli occupation of Jerusalem, the first *qibla* of Islam. Mammoth demonstrations were held in Pakistan. Ardent solidarity with the victims of aggression was manifested not only in words but also in concrete ways. Pakistani military trainers in these countries volunteered their services. Pakistan's ambassador to the United Nations made a significant contribution in support of the Arab cause. In reasoned speeches, he supported resolutions in the General Assembly calling for respect for international law and for the rights of the people of occupied territories, pending Israeli withdrawal. He piloted the resolution by which Israeli measures to change the status of Jerusalem were declared invalid.

Arson, inflicting extensive damage to Al Aqsa mosque on 21 August 1969, triggered a tidal wave of anguish and outrage among Muslims throughout the world, who revere the mosque which is associated with the Prophet's Ascension. Arab and non-Arab Muslim states joined at the first Islamic summit conference held in Rabat, on 22-24 September 1969. It adopted a moving declaration reflecting the profound distress of Muslim peoples, agreed to coordinate action to secure Israeli withdrawal from all Arab territories occupied in 1967, and affirmed full support to the Palestinian people in their struggle for national liberation. Also, recognizing that common creed constituted a powerful bond between Muslim peoples, the leaders decided to institutionalize the conference and established the Organization of the Islamic Conference (OIC) with a permanent secretariat to be located in Jeddah pending the liberation of Jerusalem.

Criteria for membership of the OIC were defined against the background of India's 'pathetic importuning'[68] for invitation to attend the Islamic summit, justifying its inclusion on the ground of its large Muslim population. Recognizing the abiding concern of the Muslim community in South Asia for the welfare of their co-religionists throughout the world, Pakistan—itself being an heir to that legacy—agreed to accord representation to the Muslims of India at the conference. But when India tried to participate as a state and sent a non-Muslim envoy to the conference, it was excluded at Pakistani initiative. If the size of a Muslim population were the criterion for membership, many other states like USSR and China should have been invited to participate, their Muslim minorities being larger than the population of some of the Muslim states.

Friendship with China

After Pakistan established air links with China, it reaped a windfall in rapid development of contacts with Chinese leaders. In transit to and from countries of the Middle East, Africa and Europe, they frequently broke journey in Pakistan. Friendly conversations with their Pakistani counterparts facilitated sympathetic understanding of each other's concerns. Pakistan was thus in a position to explain the Chinese viewpoint in forums from which China was then excluded[69] which further cemented bilateral confidence. During his visit to China in March 1965, Ayub Khan was accorded an effusive welcome. Chairman Mao Tse-Tung expressed warm appreciation for Pakistan's support. The joint communique denounced the 'two Chinas' policy and reaffirmed that the Kashmir dispute 'should be resolved in accordance with the wishes of the people of Kashmir as pledged to them by India and Pakistan.'

China extended valuable support to Pakistan in the 1965 conflict with India, using vivid language to manifest friendship for Pakistan. In transit through Karachi on 4 September, Foreign Minister Chen Yi expressed support for 'the just action taken by Pakistan to repel Indian armed provocations' in Kashmir. On 7 September the Chinese foreign ministry condemned India's 'criminal aggression' against Pakistan and charged India of trying to 'bully its neighbours, defy public opinion and do whatever it likes.'⁷⁰ China further declared on 12 September that its non-involvement in the Kashmir dispute 'absolutely does not mean that China can approve of depriving the Kashmiri people of their right of self-determination or that she can approve of Indian aggression against Pakistan.' Having earlier protested against Indian 'acts of aggression and provocation' along China's border, China gave an ultimatum to India on 16 September to dismantle its military structures on the Chinese side of the border, stop incursions and return livestock and kidnapped civilians 'within three days' or it would bear 'full responsibility for all consequences.'⁷¹

The threat of expansion of the war served to inject a sense of urgency in the deliberations of the Security Council. Its resolution of 20 September demanded cessation of hostilities as 'a first step towards a peaceful settlement of the outstanding differences between the two countries on Kashmir and other matters,' and 'decided' to consider as soon as ceasefire took effect 'what steps should be taken to assist towards a settlement of the political problem underlying the present conflict.'

China's support to Pakistan at a moment of crisis made a deep impression on the Pakistani people. President Liu Shao-chi's visit to Pakistan in March 1966 was an occasion to remember. In Lahore, Karachi and Dhaka he was accorded a heart-felt welcome by enthusiastic multitudes on a scale rarely seen since independence. His description of Sino-Pakistan relations as *mujahidana dosti* (friendship in righteous struggle) aptly translated the sentiments of the Pakistani people and boosted their morale. The friendship forged in the heat of the crisis gained further strength in succeeding years.

To help Pakistan strengthen its defence capability at a time when the United States had cut off aid and even embargoed military sales, China provided, in 1966, equipment for two divisions of the Pakistan army as well as MIG aircraft for the air force. It also gave $60 million for development assistance in 1965, a further $40 million in 1969 and $200 million for the next five-year plan. Generous, because China itself was a low-income, developing country, the assistance also placed emphasis on transfer of technology to help Pakistan achieve self-reliance. The Heavy Mechanical Complex, the Heavy Rebuild Factory, the Kamra Aeronautical Complex and several other industrial plants were built with Chinese assistance. To provide a land link, the two countries decided in 1969, to build a road across the Karakorum.[73] China played a major part in the construction of the spectacular Karakorum Highway linking Gilgit in the the Northern Areas with Kashgar in Xinjiang over the second highest mountain range in the world, through the 15,800-foot high Khunjerab Pass.

Many other countries, too, criticized India for aggression, and several provided memorable assistance to Pakistan.[74] Indonesia dispatched six naval vessels. Saudi Arabia gave financial support. President Nasser echoed sympathy for Pakistan and endorsed the Arab summit's communique which called for a settlement of the Kashmir dispute 'in accordance with the principles and resolutions of the United Nations.' Prime Minister Harold Wilson was 'deeply concerned' when the Indian forces 'attacked Pakistan territory across the international frontier' though UK backtracked after India raised a storm over Wilson's remarks.

A unique characteristic of China's policy over the years has been to observe implicit respect for Pakistan's sovereignty. The Chinese leaders seldom proffered unsolicited advice. During an exchange of views with their Pakistani counterparts, they would describe their own experiences and let the Pakistanis draw the conclusions if they so wished. Even when Pakistan embarked on improvement of relations with the Soviet Union in 1960, the Chinese leaders did not try to hold Pakistan back, expressing instead understanding of Pakistan's policy.

Relations with the United States (1965-71)

Intolerant of Pakistan's developing friendship with China, President Johnson was also shortsighted in regard to prospects of US relations with China. Reacting in anger to Pakistan's air links with China, in April 1965 he disinvited Ayub Khan and suspended further economic assistance. Only a year later his Secretary of State Dean Rusk requested Pakistan's help to arrange a meeting with the Chinese foreign minister for discussions on Vietnam.[75] Two years later, in 1969, President Richard M. Nixon used Pakistan as a secret channel of communication with China.

Appreciative of Pakistan's upstanding posture in the 1950s, President Nixon also did not agree with the previous administration's policy of penalizing Pakistan for its close friendship with China. Instead, he looked upon Pakistan as an asset for exploring 'a new beginning'[76] in US-China relations. He was among the first leaders in America to detect a 'community of interests' with China, calculating that China, confronted with the 'nightmare of hostile encirclement,' might welcome 'strategic reassurance'[77] from improved relations with the United States.

The upbeat tone of Pakistan-US relations was soon manifest in US support for economic aid to Pakistan in May 1969. In August, Nixon paid a visit to Pakistan. In 1970, the US allowed sale of a limited number of B-57 and F-104 aircraft to Pakistan.

Nixon asked President Yahya Khan to convey, during his visit to Beijing in October 1970, a message to the Chinese leaders that he considered rapprochement with China 'essential.' For four months thereafter messages were passed on this channel in utter confidentiality, preparing the ground for National Security Council Assistant Henry Kissinger's secret visit to China on 9-11 July 1971.

Washington appreciated Pakistan's helpful role but it provoked a furious reaction in Moscow. In the midst of the spiralling crisis in East Pakistan, the Soviet Union concluded a Treaty of Peace, Friendship and Cooperation with India. Although not so specific as to appear an alliance, its purpose was unmistakably strategic. It committed the two sides to 'appropriate effective measures' in the event of an attack or threat of attack. The Soviet Union, in effect, provided an umbrella against intervention by China, allowing India to execute its designs against Pakistan with impunity. Moscow's object was 'to humiliate China and to punish Pakistan for having served as an intermediary.'[78]

The 1971 Disaster

Bengal played a key role in the rise of Muslim nationalism in British India. The sense of solidarity among the people of East and West Pakistan was strengthened by shared pride in the success of their common political struggle. Timely attention to the problems inherent in the distance, economic disparity and difference of languages between the two wings could have precluded alienation but Pakistani leaders failed to conceive and implement salutary policies.

The decision to make Bengali a national language along with Urdu assuaged feelings in East Pakistan but the need to ensure a sense of participation by East Pakistan in the government did not receive an imaginative political response. Not only that, very few of the administrative officials inherited by Pakistan were Bengali[79], and decision-making was centralized in distant Karachi. Delay in constitution-making and holding national elections contributed to feelings of exclusion. Following the election in East Pakistan in 1954, the United Front which won 223 out of 237 seats, asked for 'complete autonomy.'[80] The demand was ignored. Power-grabbing, first by bureaucrats and in 1958 by the army, both largely from West Pakistan, and East Pakistan's isolation during the 1965 war intensified polarization and gave a fillip to separatist trends. In March 1966, Awami League leader, Sheikh Mujibur Rahman, put forward a Six Points programme[81] which called for a new constitution under which the federal government would be responsible 'only for defence and foreign affairs.' Ayub Khan's highly centralized government equated the demand with secessionism. 'They are not going to remain with us,'[82] he said. Embitterment of the political debate fuelled extremism with Bengali elites ascribing motives of domination and exploitation to West Pakistanis and

West Pakistani opinion looking at East Pakistanis as dupes of Indian propaganda.

Alert to the storm brewing in East Pakistan, India encouraged Bengali separatism. Operatives of its secret service agency—Research and Analysis Wing (RAW)—intensified subversion and sabotage.[83] To control the deteriorating situation, the military government pursued a repressive policy which only aggravated matters. Nature, too, seemed to collude in the tragedy. A cyclone of ferocious intensity in November 1970 left death and devastation in its trail. The federal government was charged with not only incompetence but indifference to the plight of the people of East Pakistan.

In the election in December 1970, the Awami League swept the polls winning 160 out of 162 seats from East Pakistan, giving it an absolute majority in the National Assembly to claim the right to form the government. Its position on Six Points became even more rigid. Even if he wanted to compromise, Mujibur Rahman was now a prisoner of his party and his own extremist rhetoric. To force transfer of power, the Awami League ordered a sustained strike, paralyzing the government machinery in East Pakistan. Miscalculating once again, Yahya Khan ordered a crackdown in March and the Awami League raised the flag of revolt.

'Almost all nations will fight for their unity, even if sentiment in the disaffected area is overwhelmingly for secession,' observed Henry Kissinger, adding, 'So it was during our Civil War, with Nigeria toward Biafra and with Congo toward Katanga.'[84] But Yahya Khan's decision was a gamble with the dice loaded against Pakistan. It was foolish to hope that 42,320[85] West Pakistani troops could suppress 75 million people in East Pakistan, with India determined to exploit the 'opportunity of the century' to cut Pakistan into two.[86]

Indira Gandhi decided on military action but its implementation was deferred on the advice of the Indian Chief of Staff.[87] The army needed six to seven months to prepare for war. The monsoon season was too wet for operations. Besides, delay till the winter when snows would block the high

Himalayan passes would reduce the risk of China coming to Pakistan's rescue. As a further precaution, India sought to obtain a Soviet umbrella against China and assurance of its veto to stymie the UN Security Council. Meanwhile assistance to insurgency was stepped up. Tajuddin Ahmad, an Awami League leader, was installed as head of the provisional Bangladesh government in a house in Calcutta rented by RAW.[88] India began building up a rebel force called Mukti Bahini. Training camps were set up, first secretly and later openly.[89] An estimated 100,000 men were taught guerrilla skills.

President Nixon was opposed to Indira Gandhi's designs against Pakistan but he was not unsympathetic to India. During the two years of his administration, the United States gave $1.5 billion[90] in aid to India. He detested the condescension Indira Gandhi exuded, like her sermonizing father.[91] When she came to Washington on 4-5 November largely to stroke popular opposition to Nixon's policy, the conversation between the two leaders was 'a classic dialogue of the deaf.' She 'professed her devotion to peace, [but] she would not make any concrete offers for de-escalating the tensions.'[92] She protested that she was not opposed to Pakistan's existence but 'her analysis did little to sustain her disclaimer.'[93] In fact, she argued that Pakistan should not have come into being. As Nixon later recorded in his diary, Indira Gandhi 'purposely deceived me in our meeting,'[94] having 'made up her mind to attack Pakistan at the time she saw me in Washington and assured me she would not.'[95] Rarely in history has a leader told a more brazen lie than Indira Gandhi did. In retrospect, Nixon further lamented: 'how hypocritical the present Indian leaders are' and how 'duplicitous' Indira Gandhi was.

Nixon read the Indian design clearly but with American opinion outraged by the Pakistani military excesses, the establishment followed a policy of its own. Nixon acquiesced in the State Department's decision to embargo delivery of arms to Pakistan. He also approved a grant of $350 million to ease India's burden on account of refugees from East Pakistan. Nothing could dissuade Indira Gandhi from her preconceived purpose, however. Bent upon cutting Pakistan into two, she rejected Washington's efforts to promote a political settlement and 'insisted on terms that escalated by the week.'[96]

The Indian army commenced cross-border operations in November. 'From 21 to 25 November several Indian army divisions, divided into smaller tactical units, launched simultaneous military actions.'[97] Troops, tanks and aircraft were used to assist the Mukti Bahini occupy 'liberated' territory. Nixon sent another letter to Indira Gandhi informing her of Yahya Khan's offer of unilateral withdrawal, and he also wrote to Kosygin to intercede with her. She was implacable. On 29 November she told the US ambassador, 'We can't afford to listen to advice which weakens us.'

On 2 December Yahya Khan invoked the 1959 agreement asking for US assistance. The State Department argued that the agreement did not oblige the US government to give a positive response. According to Kissinger, it 'ignored all other communications between our government and Pakistan.' Their 'plain import was that the United States would come to Pakistan's assistance if she was attacked by India.'[98] He thought: 'The image of a great nation conducting itself like a shyster looking for legalistic loopholes was not likely to inspire other allies who had signed treaties with us or relied on our expressions in the belief the words meant approximately what they said.' In the event, the White House was stalled by the Department of State. Not even a statement was issued. Meanwhile, the military situation in East Pakistan grew desperate by the day. 'Yahya chose what he considered the path of honour'[99] and on 3 December ordered attack across the border from West Pakistan. This decision like others that Yahya Khan made proved disastrous.

Premier Zhou recognized that India was guilty of 'gross interference' in Pakistan's internal affairs. China continued to supply military equipment under existing agreements and extended political support to the Pakistani position in the United Nations. At the same time, it was circumspect and did not make any promises to Pakistan that it could not fulfil.

On 7 December Washington learned that Indira Gandhi was determined to continue fighting 'until the Pakistani army and air force were wiped out.'[100] Moscow encouraged New Delhi in its design, promising that it would initiate military moves against Xinjiang if China threatened India. The crisis, now involved high stakes. The threat of great power confrontation loomed over the horizon. Washington decided it could not allow Moscow to intimidate Beijing if it wanted its China policy to retain credibility. On 9 December Nixon authorized the dispatch of a task force of eight ships, including the aircraft carrier *Enterprise* from the Pacific to the Bay of Bengal. The 'objective was to scare off an attack on West Pakistan...(and) to have forces in place in case the Soviet Union pressured China.'[101] He stressed upon the Soviet government which had 'proceeded to equip India with great amounts of sophisticated armaments' to restrain India. On 12 December he sent a Hot Line message to Brezhnev saying, 'I cannot emphasise too much that time is of the essence to avoid consequences neither of us wants.'[102] To make the point more concrete, the Soviet authorities were also informed of fleet movements.

Evasive at first, Moscow finally responded on 13 December to say that they were conducting 'a clarification of all the circumstance in India.' Kuznetsov was sent to New Delhi to work for a ceasefire. On 14 December at 3 a.m. the Soviet ambassador in Washington delivered a message reporting 'firm assurances by New Delhi that India has no intention of seizing West Pakistani territory.'

Ceasefire came into effect on 16 December; Pakistan capitulated. Over 90,000 soldiers and civilians surrendered. When Indira Gandhi addressed the parliament, its members, 'delirious with joy', gave her a 'thunderous ovation'.[103] She had avenged several centuries of Hindu humiliation at the hands of Muslim sultans and emperors.

Nixon's account lends credibility to his claim that 'By using diplomatic signals and behind-the-scenes pressures we had been able to save West Pakistan from imminent threat of Indian aggression and domination.' It also raises the question if the

United States might have taken an equally tough line in regard to Indian aggression on East Pakistan. It would not have been easy. Nixon 'wanted to let the Soviets know that we would strongly oppose the dismemberment of Pakistan by a Soviet ally using Soviet arms.' But, given the nature of the American system and absence of support in the Congress, he could hardly follow a policy of intervention in aid of a brutal and hated regime in Pakistan. Even the executive branch was out of the president's control. As Nixon has testified, 'the State Department felt that independence for East Pakistan was inevitable and desirable.' However, even he 'recognized that political autonomy for East Pakistan would be the probable outcome of a political solution, and we were willing to work in that direction. The main point was that the fighting should stop and the danger of a great power confrontation should be removed.'

The New Pakistan

The 1971 war ended in disaster. East Pakistan was severed to become Bangladesh. Over 90,000 Pakistani soldiers and civilians were taken prisoner and some 5,000 square miles of territory was under Indian occupation with a million inhabitants dislocated from these areas obliged to take shelter in refugee camps. Residual Pakistan came out of the nightmare, divided and diminished, the dream of the founding fathers betrayed. Their pride in military strength shattered and their leadership exposed as selfish and incompetent, the people were bewildered and distraught. In this tortured and turbulent situation, Z.A. Bhutto was installed as president. His government had to 'pick up the pieces,' bring the nation to grips with the new reality, and rebuild morale and confidence. Above all, it needed to rehabilitate Pakistan in world esteem and rethink the failed policies at home and abroad.

For sympathy and support Pakistan turned to friends. The first country the new president visited in January 1972 was China. It offered diplomatic support and economic and military assistance. Bhutto then undertook a whirlwind tour of Islamic countries in the Middle East and Africa. They called for the unconditional release of Pakistani prisoners and withdrawal of Indian forces from occupied territories. President Nixon continued to extend a helpful hand. In a policy statement he said, 'The cohesion and stability of Pakistan is of critical importance to the structure of peace in South Asia.'[104] Britain was unsympathetic. It not only recognized Bangladesh precipitately but persuaded several countries of western Europe, Australia and New Zealand to do so simultaneously. To express Pakistan's disgust, Bhutto decided to pull Pakistan out of the Commonwealth. In March 1972, Bhutto visited Moscow in the hope of moderating its hostility. Evincing little sympathy, Soviet leaders asked that Pakistan recognize Bangladesh and negotiate with India for a 'realistic' solution of the post-war problems.

Pakistan had to sue for peace with India from a position of utter weakness. India was intent on dictating its terms. The task of Pakistani diplomacy was to minimize the price it had to pay. The limited extent of its success is manifest in the agreement signed at Simla on 2 July 1972.[105] To secure Indian withdrawal from occupied territory, Pakistan had to acquiesce in the extraordinary formulation that differences between the two countries would be settled 'by peaceful means through bilateral negotiations or by any other peaceful means agreed upon between them.' However, the Indian interpretation that this provision precluded Pakistan from seeking international redress was not consonant with the preceding paragraph of the agreement which explicitly stated that 'the principles and purposes of the Charter of the United Nations shall govern the relations between the two countries.' Under the Charter, UN members are committed to 'seek a solution by negotiation, enquiry, mediation, conciliation, arbitration judicial settlement, resort to regional agencies or arrangements, or other peaceful means.' With regard specifically to the Jammu and Kashmir dispute, the agreement provided that 'the line of control resulting from the cease-fire of 17 December 1971 shall be respected by both sides without prejudice to the recognized position of either side.'

Non-alignment, Nuclear Programme,[106] and Relations with USA

The 1971 disaster demonstrated the futility of the policy of alliances in the context of India's threat to Pakistan's security. Pakistan began to move towards a non-aligned posture. In 1972 it withdrew from SEATO. CENTO was consigned to cold storage and the 1959 security agreement with USA to a limbo. Pakistan wanted to join the Non-aligned Movement earlier but could not get admission until India dropped its opposition in 1979.

The non-aligned posture did not, of course, provide an answer to Pakistan's vulnerability to the enduring Indian threat. The division and reduction in size further aggravated the disparity in resources. The alternative Pakistan began to ponder was the acquisition of nuclear weapon capability. Development of the nuclear option became even more urgent after the Indian atomic explosion test in May 1974 demonstrated its capability to produce nuclear weapons. Nuclear weapons can be deterred only by nuclear weapons.

The decision was easier made than implemented. Pakistan possessed neither fissile material nor explosion technology. After the Indian test in 1974 industrialized countries imposed stringent restraints on export of nuclear equipment and technology. France, which had first agreed to supply to Pakistan a reprocessing plant for the separation of plutonium, succumbed to American pressure and reneged. Driven by its desperate sense of insecurity, however, Pakistan embarked upon the alternative route for the indigenous production of fissile material and began to build a plant for the enrichment of uranium.

Meanwhile, the US embarked on vigorous efforts aimed at preventing further nuclear proliferation. What vitiated Pakistan-US relations was not the principle of Washington's policy but its discriminatory implementation. Paradoxically, it accepted the *fait accompli* by India but made Pakistan the target of its new non-proliferation zeal. The Symington and Glenn Amendments provided built-in loopholes to exempt India and Israel from sanctions which were applied to Pakistan alone in 1979 to cut-off economic cooperation. Islamabad protested against this 'act of discrimination...(applying) different standards to different states'[107] but evoked no sympathy. While continuing efforts to acquire nuclear technology, Pakistan remained open to establishing a non-discriminatory non-proliferation regime in South Asia. In 1974, it proposed the establishment of a nuclear weapon-free zone in South Asia. The UN General Assembly endorsed the proposal and has continued since to adopt the resolution annually with an overwhelming majority. Only India, Bhutan and Mauritius have usually voted against the proposal. Several other proposals to foreclose or restrain nuclearization of South Asia have met with Indian rejection or stonewalling. This pattern was repeated in 1997 when India refused to sign the Comprehensive Test Ban Treaty. Pakistan, having already refrained from testing was ready to renounce testing for the future as well but decided to keep the option open in case India conducted another test, undermining the existing precarious stability in the region.

Afghanistan Crisis[108]

Few other countries are closer to Pakistan in culture and history than Afghanistan. The hope for friendly cooperation was, however, vitiated at the start. On the eve of the establishment of Pakistan, the Afghan government denounced the 1893 treaty establishing the Durand Line as an international boundary, and launched an irredenta in the guise of support for the creation of Pushtoonistan in Pushto-speaking parts of Pakistan. Afghanistan was the only country to vote against Pakistan's admission to the United Nations. In the decades that followed, relations between the two neighbours remained strained though, fortunately, tensions usually were kept under control with King Zahir Shah restraining the extremists led by his cousin, Sardar Mohammad Daoud.

Apprehensions of deterioration of bilateral relations rose in Islamabad when Daoud overthrew Zahir Shah on 17 July 1973 and designated himself as president. Aiming to use foreign support to consolidate his power at home and pursue confrontation with Pakistan, he cultivated close relations with the Soviet Union. However, the embrace soon turned into a bear-hug. The Soviets penetrated internal politics, providing support and assistance to the revolutionary People's Democratic Party of Afghanistan (PDPA). By 1976, Daoud appeared to have realized that the Soviets had an agenda of their own. To counterbalance Soviet influence, he embarked on efforts to improve relations with Pakistan, Iran, and other Muslim countries. He and Prime Minister Z. A. Bhutto exchanged visits in 1976. Bilateral relations continued to improve after General Ziaul Haq assumed power in Pakistan in July 1977. Daoud told Zia that he intended 'to mould public opinion in my country...to normalize relations with Pakistan.'[109] This policy did not, however, please Moscow or the People's Democratic Party of Afghanistan (PDPA). The contest culminated in the 'Saur Revolution' on 27 April 1978. Daoud and members of his family were murdered and Nur Muhammad Taraki was installed as president. Meanwhile, Pakistan itself was in disarray, bled white by the three-month long agitation against Bhutto for rigging the election in March 1977, and General Ziaul Haq's increasing unpopularity after he reneged on his promise to hold an election within 90 days of take-over. Making the best of a bad situation, Pakistan decided to extend prompt recognition to the PDPA regime.[110] Zia went to Kabul to meet President Taraki in the hope of mutual accommodation.

A party of intellectuals without a popular base, the PDPA was riven with rivalry between its predominantly rural and Pushto-speaking Khalq and urban-based Persian-speaking Parcham factions. Infighting led to Taraki's overthrow and murder in September 1979. His successor, Hafizullah Amin, was both headstrong and defiant of Soviet guidance. His rivals in the party and the Soviets considered him a danger to the stability of the revolution. On 26 December 1979, Soviet forces rolled across Amu Darya, Amin was executed and Babrak Karmal, leader of the Parcham faction, was installed as president. It was a clear case of blatant military intervention. When asked by a Pakistani foreign ministry official at whose invitation Moscow sent forces to Afghanistan, the Soviet ambassador in Islamabad unabashedly replied 'Babrak Karmal.'[111] Not only did Karmal hold no authority to speak for the Afghan government, he was not even in the country at the time.

The Soviet intervention provoked a deep sense of alarm in Pakistan. Suddenly the buffer disappeared. If the Soviets consolidated control, they could use Afghanistan as a springboard for a leap down the Bolan and Khyber passes to fulfil the historical tsarist ambition for access to the warm waters of the Arabian Sea. Pakistan could not acquiesce in the Soviet intervention but it could afford confrontation with a superpower even less. The horns of the dilemma on which Pakistan found itself impaled was made even more painful by internal weakness and international isolation. Bhutto's execution in April 1979 upon conviction on a charge of murder had polarized opinion at home as never before. Zia's decision to ignore appeals for clemency by foreign leaders and media antagonized almost the whole world. Pakistan's isolation was aggravated in November 1979, when a mob of youth infuriated by a false report broadcast by an unidentified radio alleging US occupation of the holy Kaaba, sacked the American embassy in Islamabad in which four staff members perished.[112]

Islamabad decided on a middle course,[113] avoiding confrontation but raising a muted voice of protest. Its statement, issued two days late, criticized the intervention as a 'serious violation' of the principles of the UN Charter but did not refer to the Soviet Union by name. Rather defensively, it explained Pakistan's 'gravest concern' in the context of its links of Islam, geography and non-aligned policy with Afghanistan, and expressed the hope that the foreign troops would be removed from Afghan soil 'forthwith.'

The United States which had earlier treated Afghanistan with neglect and ignored the rise of the PDPA to power, suddenly woke up to the dangers implicit in the advance of Soviet power to 'within striking distance of the Indian Ocean and even the Persian Gulf...an area of vital strategic and economic significance to the survival of Western Europe, the Far East, and ultimately the United States.'[114] Washington issued a strong condemnation of the 'blatant'[115] Soviet intervention. President Jimmy Carter, who was furious at the sacking of the US emabssy in November, changed his tune to extend an assurance of support to Pakistan. He proclaimed a boycott of the Moscow Olympics, and suspended arms limitation talks with Moscow. West European countries, which depended on the Gulf region for two-thirds of their oil requirements, joined their voice to denounce the Soviet intervention. Most Muslim countries condemned the Soviet intervention and many of the non-aligned countries joined in calling for withdrawal of Soviet troops.

Still apprehensive of the dangerous implications of involvement in the cold war, Pakistan hitched its diplomacy to the hope of a political settlement of the crisis through the United Nations. At its request, non-aligned members took the lead in drafting a balanced resolution strongly deploring 'the recent armed intervention in Afghanistan' and calling for 'immediate, unconditional and total withdrawal of the foreign troops.' Vetoed by the USSR in the Security Council, the resolution was adopted by a special session of the General Assembly on 14 January 1980 with 104 votes in favour, 18—mostly satellite states—against, and 18 abstentions. Significantly, despite Cuban and Indian opposition, 56 out of 92 non-aligned members voted for the resolution.

Muslim countries took a much tougher position. The OIC Foreign Ministers' meeting in Islamabad later in January issued a strong indictment of the Soviet intervention, suspended Afghanistan's membership of the OIC, and affirmed solidarity with the struggle of the Afghan people to safeguard 'their faith, national independence and territorial integrity.'

Critical to the outcome of the crisis was the opposition to the Soviet intervention inside Afghanistan. Intervention by foreign troops to protect a regime with an alien ideology transformed the resistance into a popular jihad. Despite Soviet warnings and threats, Pakistan decided to provide clandestine assistance to the mujahideen. The decision, made autonomously without foreign prompting, had complex motivations. Self-interest and solidarity with the fraternal Afghan people were certainly weighty considerations. In fighting for their own cause, the mujahideen kept the Soviets at bay from Pakistan as well. Also, President Zia liked the limelight in which he now basked internationally.

Still, Pakistan sought to save the issue from being sucked into the orbit of the cold war. The main thrust of its policy was diplomatic in orientation. To that end, the resolution proposed at the regular session of the UN General Assembly in 1980 was further toned down. It emphasized uncontroversial principles as the basis for a political solution: (i) immediate withdrawal of the foreign forces, (ii) preservation of the sovereignty, territorial integrity, independence, and non-aligned status of Afghanistan, (iii) respect for the right of its people to determine their own form of government and economic system free from outside intervention, subversion, coercion, or constraint, and (iv) creation of conditions for the voluntary return of Afghan refugees to their homes in safety and honour. It further suggested international guarantees of non-use of force against the security of 'all neighbouring countries' and efforts by the UN Secretary General to promote a political solution. This resolution, which was retained in substance for the next seven years, attracted ever greater support which increased from 111 votes in favour in 1980 to 123 in 1987. During the same period, negative votes and abstentions combined declined from 36 in 1980 to 30 in 1987.[116] Every year the Soviet Union suffered a stinging blow to its prestige.

Revival of Pakistan-US Alliance

Within days of the Soviet intervention, and without even consulting Pakistan, President Carter announced an offer of $400 million in economic and military assistance for Pakistan. Ziaul Haq's scornful if undiplomatic rejection of Carter's offer as 'peanuts' gave the wrong impression that all Islamabad wanted was a higher amount in aid. Actually, Pakistan was prepared to accept $200 million in economic aid, but the US refused to delink economic assistance from the defence component. The amount of $200 million for defence was not only incommensurate with the enhanced risks of re-involvement in the cold war, Pakistan resented the fact that the proffered aid level was determined by fear of Indian reaction, thus 'denuding it of relevance to our defensive capacity.' Even more than the amount, Pakistan sought a guarantee of American assistance in the event of Soviet or Soviet-backed Indian attack on Pakistan. It asked for the upgradation of the 1959 executive agreement on defence cooperation into a binding treaty because the 'credibility and durability'[118] of American assurances was low, due to the widely held belief that at critical junctures, especially in 1965, the United States betrayed a friend and ally. Besides, the aid package was 'wrapped up in onerous conditions' which, Pakistan was concerned, 'could affect the pursuit of our nuclear research and development.'[118]

Non-acceptance of US aid in 1980 reduced the risk of plunging Pakistan back into the orbit of the cold war. It also helped in projecting the Afghan cause in its genuine perspective of a liberation struggle. It served, moreover, to save Pakistan's relations with Iran from further strain. Iranian media perception of Pakistan as a proxy for US interests in the region was painful to Pakistanis who value Iran as a friend and a fraternal neighbour. The sincerity of Pakistan's solidarity with Iran was illustrated again in April 1980 when it expressed 'shock and dismay' at the US assault on Iran in an attempt to forcibly take out American embassy staff, and 'deplored this impermissible act which constitutes a serious violation of Iran's sovereignty.'[119]

After President Ronald Reagan succeeded Carter in 1981, the United States revived its offer of cooperation with Pakistan. The new package provided for loans and grants amounting to 3 billion dollars over five years.[120] The amount of $600 million a year for development and defence was a significant improvement over the Carter offer of $400 million for eighteen months. The new offer still did not provide a satisfactory answer to Pakistan's security concerns as Reagan, too, found Congressional opinion reluctant to support a formal security guarantee to Pakistan, but the 5-year programme generated an aura of durability around the US commitment. Besides, evincing a reassuring understanding of Pakistan's vulnerabilities as a front-line state, the Reagan administration agreed to the sale of 40 F-16 aircraft.

On the nuclear issue, the two countries maintained their formal positions, Pakistan reiterating its intention to continue research, and the US proclaiming its non-proliferation concern. But Washington turned the pressure off. Acknowledging past discrimination and expressing understanding of Pakistan's rationale,[121] it accepted Zia's assurance that Pakistan would not develop nuclear weapons or transfer sensitive technology.[122] The US administration had little difficulty in securing Congressional approval for waiver of the Symington prohibition. Senators and Congressmen who earlier targeted Pakistan for discriminatory strictures no longer commanded decisive influence.

Pakistan chose not to accept concessional loans for military sales, and instead opted to pay the market rate of interest, so as to safeguard its non-aligned credentials. Pakistan wanted also to retain its credibility as an independent actor in the hope of persuading the Soviet Union to agree to a political solution of the Afghanistan question outside the cold war context. In the event, the sacrifice won no appreciation from either Moscow or New Delhi. They denounced Pakistan even though a year earlier India had signed a deal with the USSR for the latest MIG aircraft, T-72 tanks and warships, etc. for a give-away price of $1.6 billion on soft terms though its market value was estimated by Western embassies in New Delhi at $6 billion. In retrospect,

Pakistan's more-pious-than-the-Pope posture seemed a futile and costly gesture.[123]

The Geneva Accords, 1988

UN efforts to promote a political solution began in earnest with the appointment of Diego Cordovez, a senior UN official from Ecuador, as the personal representative of the Secretary General in 1981. The situation was rather bizarre. The USSR declined to participate in the talks. Pakistan was unwilling to engage in direct talks with the regime in Kabul which it did not recognize. Cordovez persuaded Kabul to agree to indirect talks and the Soviet Union to send high level officials to Geneva to be available for consultation.

Negotiations commenced in June 1982 with exploration of the structure of a settlement that would integrate the components of the UN General Assembly resolution. An energetic, dedicated and persuasive diplomat of high calibre, Cordovez sidetracked controversy over the past by proposing agreements between Afghanistan and Pakistan on mutual non-interference and non-intervention and on voluntary return of refugees. Also, as a means of satisfying the Soviet demand for American pledge of non-interference and obtaining a Soviet commitment to withdrawal of forces, he conceived the idea of guarantees to be provided by both superpowers.

For years, negotiations made little progress. The Soviet Union was confident that its mighty forces equipped with the latest weapons would rout the ragtag mujahideen armed with antiquated rifles. Hopes for a political settlement arose in November 1992 when Yuri Andropov succeeded Brezhnev. In a meeting with Zia, he gave a 'hint of flexibility.' UN Secretary General Perez de Cuellar and Diego Cordovez who met Andropov in March received 'new encouragement' for pursuing UN mediation. Andropov counted to them the reasons why the Soviet Union wanted a solution, raising his fingers one by one as he mentioned costs in lives and money, regional tensions, setback to detente and loss of Soviet prestige in the Third World.[124] Buoyed by the positive signals, Cordovez successfully pressed the two sides at meetings in April and June 1983 to agree on the components of a comprehensive settlement. Discussions made good progress. Cordovez was optimistic about 'gradual withdrawal' of Soviet forces within a reasonable timeframe. However, when Andropov died, the Soviet-Kabul side reverted to the policy of a military solution. Mikhail Gorbachev stuck to that policy till the end of the summer in 1987.

The struggle in Afghanistan was unequal but the mujahideen demonstrated courage and resourcefulness in resistance, and did not wilt despite the increasing ferocity of Soviet pressure. Their sacrifices and stamina drew deserved praise and tribute. Assistance to them increased so as to neutralize the Soviet induction of more lethal artillery, helicopter gun ships and bombers for savage and indiscriminate destruction of villages to interdict mujahideen activities. The United States raised covert allocations for supply of arms to the mujahideen, from $250 million in 1985, to $470 million in 1986 and $630 million in 1987.[125] The American contribution was reportedly matched by Saudi Arabia. Also China, Iran and several other countries provided substantial assistance. Pakistan calibrated the flow of assistance to the mujahideen cautiously so as to minimize the risk of spill-over of the conflict, but it became bolder with time and experience. It realized that a superpower's forces could not be defeated militarily but also that attrition inside Afghanistan combined with blows to its prestige internationally offered the only hope of wearing Moscow down. Negotiations in Geneva and resolutions in OIC, NAM and the United Nations were a part of that strategy for increasing political pressure.

Diego Cordovez patiently kept the Geneva talks on track, however slow their pace. Altogether twelve sessions were held over six years. He and the Pakistani side occasionally discussed the question of a compromise between the Kabul regime and the mujahideen, but this subject was not on the agenda. UN resolutions referred to the principle of respect for the right of the Afghan people to determine their own form of government and economic system, but this was not interpreted to require replacement of the regime installed by the Soviet forces. Kabul and Moscow at first refused even to recognize the reality of internal resistance. They said 'everything comes from outside.'[126] Foreign Minister Gromyko dismissed the idea of a broad-based government in Kabul as 'unrealistic fantasies.' Cordovez himself realized the need for a compromise among the Afghans but as he said, correctly for the time, 'The UN is not in the business of establishing governments.'[127]

By late 1986, all issues were settled except the timeframe for the withdrawal of Soviet forces and, the wording of the reference to the boundary between Pakistan and Afghanistan. On the crucial issue of timeframe, the Soviet Union seemed non-serious as it waited four years for the withdrawal of its forces. The gulf was narrowed down but not bridged until after the failure of the Soviet military offensive in the summer of 1987. Mikhail Gorbachev then finally decided to abandon the misadventure.

Gorbachev and Foreign Minister Shevardnadze succeeded in winning endorsement of the party Politburo for the policy of terminating military involvement in Afghanistan.[128] The imperatives of democratic and economic reforms at home necessitated an end to confrontation with the West. The costs of the policy in human and material resources and the obloquy it entailed even in the Soviet Union's non-aligned backyard were glaringly disproportionate to any benefits that continued hold over Afghanistan might yield. In fact, the Soviet system was faltering, the cost of military confrontation and the arms race with the West, occupation of Eastern Europe, tension with China and, finally, intervention in Afghanistan had 'ruined'[129] the Soviet Union. The economy was in decline, and the new generation of communists no longer shared the pristine ideological fervour of the founders or faith in the inevitability of communism's victory.

With Gorbachev's endorsement, Najibullah proposed, in July 1987, a coalition offering the office of vice president and twelve ministries to the mujahideen. The proposal was rejected by the mujahideen alliance, however. They would have no truck with the PDPA communists and traitors. Since resistance against the Soviets still commanded priority, Islamabad, too, considered it inadvisable to press the mujahideen toward a compromise lest that should divide and weaken the Alliance.

Gorbachev announced at a press conference in Washington on 10 December 1987, that the Soviet forces would withdraw from Afghanistan within twelve months of the conclusion of the Geneva accords and, further, that during that period the forces would not engage in combat. He also delinked the question of withdrawal from an internal settlement in Afghanistan. Though he reaffirmed support for 'a coalition on the basis of national reconciliation and the realities of the situation',[130] Moscow was no longer prepared to allow the Alliance's rejectionist attitude to obstruct its decision to extricate the Soviet Union from the Afghan quagmire. Nor was it willing to undertake the removal of the Kabul regime and hand over the government to the Alliance.

The 12-month timeframe was close to the single digit proposed by Pakistan and other supporters of the struggle in Afghanistan. But just as prospects for the conclusion of the Geneva Accords brightened, dark clouds suddenly appeared on the horizon in Pakistan. President Zia took the position that the conclusion of the accords should be postponed until after agreement was reached on the formation of a government in Kabul with the participation of the mujahideen. This took not only Pakistan's foreign friends but even Prime Minister Mohammad Khan Junejo completely by surprise: heretofore Pakistan's refrain was that the only outstanding obstacle to the conclusion of the Geneva accords was a reasonable timeframe for the withdrawal of Soviet forces. Besides, making the formation of a coalition government a precondition for the conclusion of the accords was an insuperable obstacle because the mujahideen Alliance was averse to the idea of a coalition with PDPA. Now the Soviets were no longer prepared to wait. When, on 9 February, Zia pressed the visiting Soviet First Deputy Foreign Minister Yuli Vorontsov for postponement of

the final Geneva round, his comment was withering to the point of insolence. He said: 'For eight years you have been asking us to leave Afghanistan. Now you want us to stay. I smell a rat!'[131]
The logic of Zia's eleventh hour volte face was never explained. Pakistan's foreign friends were as mystified as the Junejo government. It was evident that Moscow had decided to pull out of Afghanistan. Pakistan could block the Geneva accords, but it could not prevent the Soviets from withdrawing from Afghanistan either unilaterally or pursuant to an agreement with the Kabul regime. In comparison with these alternatives, withdrawal under the accords was manifestly more advantageous. The Soviet Union would be internationally bound to withdraw its forces completely, within a prescribed timeframe and under UN monitoring. It would be legally bound also to refrain from intervention in Afghanistan, and Pakistan, too, would receive Soviet and US guarantees of respect for principles of non-interference and non-intervention.

For Moscow, the residual consideration now was the manner of disengagement so as to avoid disgrace to the Soviet Union and danger to their retreating forces. It prized the Geneva Accords as a cover to save itself from humiliation. Pakistan and the United States would be under an obligation to discontinue assistance to the mujahideen. That might save their Soviet friends from massacre. No less important was their symbolic value. A UN-sponsored agreement would provide a fig leaf to cover the Soviet defeat. Pakistan's own interests would be served by sparing humiliation to the Soviet Union, keeping open the possibility to improve relations with this superpower.

The Soviet preference for the Geneva Accords was not unknown. Islamabad used the leverage to obtain significant modifications of the texts. Realizing that Pakistan's signature on an agreement with Afghanistan would constitute recognition of the Kabul regime, and require unilateral discontinuation of arms supply to 'rebels'. Vorontsov was informed during his visit to Islamabad on 9 February, that the signing of the agreement would not constitute recognition of the Kabul regime. A diplomat of world class, confident in his understanding of his country's policy and decisive in negotiations, he instantly agreed not to make this matter an issue. Nor did he contest the logic of the view that peace in Afghanistan required all sides to discontinue arms supply. But, he convincingly explained, Moscow could not go back on its existing commitments to Kabul. 'Negative symmetry' was not feasible but when told that in that event 'positive symmetry' would ensue, and the mujahideen, too, could continue to receive supplies, he did not make an issue of this matter either. The discussion served to preclude subsequent misunderstanding between Islamabad and Moscow.

The final Geneva round began on 2 March 1988. The talks proceeded in slow motion because the Pakistan delegation did not have authorization to finalize the accords. On their part, the Soviets conveyed their agreement to reduce the timeframe for withdrawal to nine months. The Kabul representatives tried to create an obstacle by haggling over the wording of the reference to the boundary between the two countries in order to safeguard the Afghan position of non-recognition of the Durand Line. It was an artificial issue: the Geneva talks were not convened to settle the boundary problem. Pakistan had no difficulty in accepting the neutral phrase requiring the two states to refrain from the threat or use of force so as 'not to violate the boundaries of each other.'

The replacement of the Kabul regime was never a part of the Geneva negotiations but, as Diego Cordovez said in a statement issued on 8 April, 'it has been consistently recognized that the objective of a comprehensive settlement...can best be ensured by a broad-based Afghan Government' and to that end he agreed to provide his good offices. By that time Zia realized that the formation of such a government could not be made a precondition for the conclusion of the accords.

The Geneva Accords were signed on 14 April 1988 by the foreign ministers of Afghanistan, Pakistan, and the Soviet Union and the secretary of state of the United States. Pakistan and the United States declared on the occasion that their signatures did not imply recognition of the Kabul regime. The US further declared that 'the obligations undertaken by the guarantors are symmetrical' and that it retained the right to provide military assistance to the Afghan parties, and would exercise restraint should the Soviet Union do so, too. Pakistan also made the same point, and underlined the right of the Afghan people to self-determination.

The Geneva Accords marked the first time for the Soviet Union to agree to withdraw from a 'fraternal' state. Gorbachev acknowledged that the intervention was a 'mistake.' A Soviet journal blamed 'an inner group of a few Politburo members headed by Leonid Brezhnev (who), discounting the likely opposition of the Muslim world, China, the United States and the West, decided to take the fateful decision.'[132] Over 13,000 Soviet soldiers were killed and 35,000 wounded.[133] The financial drain was estimated at 100 billion rubles. A classic example of 'imperial over-stretch,'[134] the Afghanistan misadventure could well be considered the proverbial last straw that broke the camel's back. To say that, like the United States in Vietnam, the Soviet Union lost the war in Afghanistan due to pressures of domestic and international opinion is by no means to undervalue the courage and heroism of the mujahideen, and the fortitude and sacrifices of the Afghan people.

The Afghan Civil War

The Afghan people suffered grievously in the struggle to recover freedom. A million people perished and some six million people had to take refuge outside their country. The economic and human infrastructure of Afghanistan was devastated on a scale with few parallels. Already one of the least developed countries, it suffered fearful damage to agriculture, irrigation system, roads, transport, educational institutions—indeed its entire infrastructure. Nor did its travail end with the withdrawal of the Soviet force. The regime the Soviets installed under Najibullah fought on for nearly three more years. When it finally collapsed in April 1992, a struggle for succession began among the mujahideen parties. For their epic sacrifices, the Afghan people deserved a better fate than the long nightmare of internecine fighting, political disintegration and economic collapse in the wake of victory.

The mujahideen started on a hopeful note of unity after Najibullah's fall. At a meeting in Peshawar on 24 April, the Alliance leaders reached an agreement. An Islamic Council headed by Sibghatullah Mojaddedi was installed for two months after which Professor Burhanuddin Rabbani became president for four months. A transitional government was then to be formed for two years. When Rabbani refused to yield power, fighting broke out. Pakistan, Iran and Saudi Arabia joined to promote another accord among the Afghan leaders. The agreement they signed at a meeting in Islamabad on 7 March 1993, provided for the formation of a government for a period of eighteen months, with Professor Rabbani continuing as president and Engineer Gulbadin Hekmatyar to become prime minister. Although the Islamabad Accord was signed by the Afghan leaders again at solemn ceremonies during visits to Saudi Arabia and Iran, it was not implemented. The cabinet to be 'formed by the Prime Minister in consultation with the President' was not agreed upon. Prime Minister Hekmatyar felt too insecure to enter Kabul. The country was again plunged into civil war.

In 1994, a group of students of religious schools (Taliban), outraged by the 'crimes' of mujahideen rulers in Kandahar, rose to bring quick retribution to the 'criminals'. Their action evoked enthusiastic popular response. The people evidently yearned for release from the warlords who 'brought sufferings on the Afghans and violated Islamic teachings.'[135] To their surprise, the Taliban found themselves in power, and rapidly gained control over the southern provinces, restoring law and order, and gaining the support of the war-weary people. In 1995, they were invited to take over Herat, and continued to march northward as local mujahideen commanders either joined them or fled northwards. The Taliban attacked Kabul but were stalled by government forces for almost a year.

The Rabbani regime lashed out at Pakistan for supporting the Taliban, failing to understand that internecine squabbling amongst the warlords had bred country-wide disgust. On two occasions, in 1992 and 1994, Pakistan had provided good offices in collaboration with other friends of Afghanistan, to promote consensus among the Afghan leaders. The breakdown of both accords was a product of rivalries amongst them. No foreign-inspired movement could arouse the popular response that greeted the Taliban.

Pakistan's expectations for friendly relations with the government of Islamic Afghanistan received a shocking setback on 6 September 1995, when its embassy in Kabul was sacked by a government-sponsored mob. One employee was killed, the ambassador and forty officials were injured so badly as to require hospitalization, the building was burned down and embassy records burnt. Never before was a diplomatic mission subjected to such savage attack. Nevertheless, Pakistan exercised patience and refrained from retaliation. In May 1996, a visiting delegation of the Kabul government acknowledged liability for the reconstruction of the embassy but pleaded lack of resources to discharge the responsibility.

The military situation seemed stalemated, the Kabul government having successfully stalled the Taliban advance. Once again, however, the deceptive calm was shattered in mid-1996 as the Taliban burst forth, taking over the eastern Pushtoon provinces and the regional capital of Jalalabad and then pushed toward the capital. The Rabbani-Hekmatyar-Masood forces abandoned Kabul so that the Taliban entered the capital with remarkably little bloodshed on the morning of 27 September.

During the following year the opposing Afghan forces fought recurrent battles. For most of the period, the country remained divided along geographic and ethnic fault-lines, but with changing alliances and fortunes on the battlefield the situation remained in constant flux. The Taliban seemed to have consolidated control over twenty provinces inhabited mostly by Pushtoons but most of the other twelve provinces remained outside their grasp. The Uzbek militia was entrenched north of the Hindukush mountains and the legendary commander, Ahmad Shah Masood, had dug-in in the fastness of the Panjshir Valley. A simple and idealistic group with limited religious education, and lacking sophistication in their understanding of the contemporary world, the Taliban evoked global outrage by imposing stringent restrictions upon women. Their puritanical fiats antagonized also the inhabitants of the capital which was groomed by the Afghan rulers as an island of modernity in a sea of conservative and tribal countryside. The law and order situation in the areas under their control improved, however, as they disarmed the people and imposed a relatively efficient administration.

Few Islamic countries have endorsed the Taliban version of the Sharia law, but most have considered this matter an internal affair of Afghanistan. Iran openly denounced the Taliban regime, its opposition apparently founded mainly in the misperception that they were a creation of the United States and Saudi Arabia with the object of containment of Iran. Moscow's opposition to the Taliban appeared based on the apprehension that, with their religious zeal, they would pose a threat to the internal stability of the Central Asian republics. Some of these republics seemed to fear that the Taliban entertained 'aggressive designs.'[136]

All neighbours of Afghanistan favour the formation of a broad-based government in Kabul that would ensure the safety of different ethnic and sectarian segments of the population, and create conditions conducive to the return of the refugees. Peace and unity, moreover, would facilitate transit and trade as well as the construction of oil and gas pipelines, to the benefit of all countries of the region, especially land-locked Afghanistan which would earn substantial amounts in fees. This, however, is easier said than done, given the faction-ridden political reality in the country. When they had greater influence, Pakistan, Iran and Saudi Arabia promoted the 1993 Accord. Now these countries command less leverage. The UN and OIC too, have been frustrated in their efforts to promote a compromise.

The turmoil in Afghanistan has adversely affected relations among Afghanistan's neighbours. Iran and some of the Central

Asian republics have criticized Pakistan for its support to the Taliban; Uzbekistan President, Islam Karimov, openly called it 'external meddling,'[137] Iran is suspected of providing financial and material assistance and Uzbekistan of facilitating the supply of Russian arms to Uzbek and Tajik factions. Perhaps, their policy, like that of Pakistan, is explicable in the context of their desire to save themselves from the further spill-over of the Afghan civil war. Pakistan and Iran, already burdened with large populations of Afghan refugees, do not want another exodus.

A no less sinister legacy of the Afghan crisis for Pakistan is the 'Klashnikov culture' and increased production of narcotics. Modern weapons from Afghanistan have proliferated across Pakistan. Dacoits now have more lethal weapons than the police have. Hundreds of foreign citizens who came to join the jihad stayed behind in Pakistan, and some of them have indulged in acts of terrorism. The bombing of the Egyptian embassy in Islamabad in December 1995 was attributed to them. Also, agents of the Rabbani regime in Kabul have been accused of perpetrating acts of sabotage in Pakistan. A car-bomb explosion in a Peshawar bazaar killed over forty and wounded a hundred innocent persons in December 1995.

The Russian people are rightly critical of the Soviet invasion of Afghanistan as 'a great mistake.'[138] Afghans can similarly blame their communist leaders for the disaster that befell their country. Pakistanis alone have few scapegoats. They generally supported President Zia's policy with respect to Afghanistan. Few foresaw the consequences of involvement, and the grave problems that emerged in the wake of the conflict. Western supporters of the Afghan struggle, rightly critical of the Afghan warring parties, have walked away. Pakistan, once praised for 'shouldering great responsibilities for mankind...(and its) courageous and compassionate role,'[139] finds itself left in the lurch, saddled with the burden of refugees and the consequences of the strife next door.

Was Pakistan's policy misconceived? In retrospect, the answer is easy to give but, alas, humans are not gifted with prescience and policies have to be devised—and can be fairly judged—in the context of the time and contemporary knowledge. Given the history of Soviet expansionism, Islamabad's sense of alarm in 1979 was not a figment of its imagination. Pakistan was neither in a position to challenge the Soviet superpower nor could it ignore the intervention without peril to its security. An alternative to the middle course it pursued seems difficult to conceive even in retrospect. Success and failure can be a measure of policies, but human struggle cannot be appraised in isolation from the nobility of the cause. The Soviet intervention was morally wrong, the Afghan resistance was right. Pakistan's decision in favour of solidarity with the fraternal people of Afghanistan was not only morally right but also based on its enlightened self-interest.

Could the consequences of the protracted conflict in terms of the Klashnikov culture and narcotics proliferation be anticipated and obviated? Surely, these could have been minimized if not precluded. These problems as well as malfeasance and venality in transactions between the mujahideen and their friends surfaced during the struggle in Afghanistan. Priorities and vested interests did not permit timely remedies.

Were not the Geneva Accords flawed in that they did not provide for transition to peace and the formation of a government of unity for Afghanistan? The account that has been given above brings out the fact that, from the beginning, the Geneva negotiations had only the limited aim of getting the Soviets to withdraw from Afghanistan. All the parties agreed that the formation of government was entirely an internal affair of Afghanistan, and the Afghans alone had the right to decide this matter to the exclusion of the Soviet Union, Pakistan, or any other country. The United Nations was understandably reluctant to undertake this task. Until the end of the cold war it avoided assumption of a role for the promotion of reconciliation or consensus in any embattled country. Moscow and Kabul were first dismissive of any suggestion for a role for the mujahideen in the government of Afghanistan, except on Kabul's terms. When they later offered accommodation, the mujahideen rejected any truck with the Soviet puppets. Pakistan, as well as other friends and supporters, backed the mujahideen position. President Zia alone changed his view for reasons that remain obscure, though his unjustified and unlawful dismissal of Prime Minister Junejo in May 1988 provides circumstantial evidence of a personal power motivation. This was in the event even he was unable to persuade the mujahideen to meet with Diego Cordovez in pursuit of his mission of promoting a government of unity in Afghanistan.

It was probably too much to expect the mujahideen leaders to reach accommodation with the surrogate regime after the Soviets withdrew, though that might have saved the country from fragmentation. More tragic was the rivalry for personal power among the mujahideen leaders that prolonged the nightmare for the Afghan people. Also, as a result, the mujahideen themselves have been sidelined by new forces in the country. Whether the Taliban will succeed in bringing unity and reconciliation to the war ravaged country remains to be seen. Also to be watched is the effect of the Taliban success on Pakistan's relations with Iran, which believes that Pakistan wields sufficient influence with the Taliban to ensure accommodation for all the Afghan ethnic groups in the future government of Afghanistan. What is obvious by now is the futility of a king-maker role on the part of any outsider. Even a superpower failed in its attempt to impose a government on the Afghans. It would be arrogant for any neighbour to presume it might fare better.

Cooperation with Iran, Turkey, and Central Asian Republics

The Regional Cooperation for Development, formed in 1964, did not realize its potential in trade and industry due to resource constraints. After the revolution in Iran in 1979, the organization became quiescent even though it was nominally revived in 1983 under a new name—Economic Cooperation Organization (ECO). In 1992, ECO was expanded to include Afghanistan and the six Central Asian republics of Azerbaijan, Kazakhstan, Kyrghyzstan,

Tadjikistan, Turkmenistan and Uzbekistan. It has since held four summit meetings and taken ambitious decisions to enlarge the ambit of regional cooperation but achieved little progress. The first summit, held in Teheran in February 1992, endorsed the goal of 'ultimate elimination of all tariffs and non-tariff barriers' among the members and underlined the importance of development of cooperation in transport and communications, energy, industry, and agriculture. In February 1993, the ECO Council of Ministers prepared the Quetta Plan of Action elaborating proposals for enlarged cooperation in already agreed fields. The Istanbul summit held in July 1993, approved, in principle, the creation of regional shipping and airline companies, a reinsurance corporation and a trade and development bank. Agreements to implement these proposals, and on transit trade and visa simplification were signed at the Islamabad summit in March 1995. The fourth summit in Ashkabad in May 1996, agreed to streamline decision-making and strengthen the Secretariat of the organization. Turkmenistan, Afghanistan and Pakistan signed an agreement at Ashkabad for the construction of gas and oil pipelines. Civil war in Afghanistan continues, however, to preclude implementation. Earlier, Iran and Pakistan agreed to build a gas pipeline.

Meanwhile, Iran has completed the Meshad-Sarakhs-Tagen rail link with Turkmenistan, which will facilitate passenger and freight traffic between Iranian ports and the Central Asian republics. Iran has also announced a plan to build Zahidan-Kerman rail link which would connect Pakistan by railway not only to Central Asia but also via Russia to Europe. Also, Pakistan has decided to upgrade the Karakorum Highway to provide access for the landlocked Central Asian states via China to Pakistani ports. Passing through high mountains, the economy of this road link seems problematic, however. Meanwhile, the shortest, 1,600-km route from Central Asia to the Arabian Sea, via Kabul or Herat, remains blocked because of the civil war in Afghanistan.

Economic cooperation among developing countries has been a difficult goal to realize mainly because their economies are more often competitive than complementary, and the machinery and technology they need for industrialization is obtainable mostly from developed countries. Even when member states share cultural affinities, and relations amongst them are friendly, as in the case of ECO, cooperation has been problematic. Realization of economies of scale by enlargement of the market requires not only reduction of customs duties on which governments depend for revenues, but also elaborate safeguards to ensure equitable sharing of sacrifices and benefits. Moreover, as developing countries, they lack the resources required for development of rail and road networks.

Policy in the Post-Cold War World

The withdrawal of Soviet forces from Afghanistan in 1989 relieved Pakistan of the dangers and apprehensions that the advance of the Soviet superpower to Pakistan's border had triggered in 1979. But it also once again brought to the fore some of the issues that were relegated to the background because of the priority attached to the Afghanistan crisis, and confronted the country with new problems in international relations. In a world in constant flux, a decade is too long an interval even in the normal course, to permit a mere return to the status quo ante. The turn of the 1980s witnessed a sharp break in history with the end of the cold war bringing a fundamental transformation in international relations. Pakistan not only lost the dubious distinction of a front-line state, the premises of its past policy were shaken to their foundation.

The difference between Pakistan and the United States on the nuclear issue, which was by no means forgotten by Washington even during the Afghanistan crisis, once again came back to dominate centre-stage. Within a year after the Soviet withdrawal from Afghanistan, the United States reverted to the old policy with new enthusiasm. It not only reimposed an embargo on economic assistance to Pakistan as was done in 1979, it even withheld transfer of the equipment under earlier sales contracts for which Pakistan had paid in cash. Five years later, in 1995, President Clinton recognized the inequity of keeping both the equipment and the cash, amounting to over a billion dollars, but amendment of complex legislation was pursued halfheartedly by his administration, and resisted stoutly by influential senators renowned more for their attachment to nuclear non-proliferation than for their concern for consistency and non-discrimination in application of the policy. Even after the passage of two more years, the issue was only partially settled. The United States released equipment worth $368 million comprising mostly outdated arms, and refunded $200 million Pakistan had paid for equipment not yet manufactured but the amount of $658 million remained stuck, pending the sale of 28 F-16 aircraft to a third country. Meanwhile, the ban on economic assistance and military sales to Pakistan alone remains in force.

Afghanistan, caught in a protracted internal strife, continues to pose unanticipated problems for Pakistan, vitiating internal security as well as relations with other neighbours, with no prospects in sight for the realization of the dream of Afghanistan providing a bridge to the Central Asian republics.

Pakistan's relations with India seem locked in a time warp, with no surcease to Indian repression of the Kashmir struggle for their right of self-determination, and to consequent tension in Pakistan-India relations.

Recent manifestations of hatred and hostility in the West towards Muslim peoples are disturbing for Pakistan. Itself a victim of acts of terrorism, it has also cooperated in apprehension and extradition of persons charged with such crimes. Pakistan, as also other Muslim countries, does not nourish any sense of antagonism or reciprocate the atavistic spirit of crusades fanned by lobbies with vested interests. Like others in the developing world, Muslim countries have been keen to collaborate with the industrially advanced countries. They condemn all acts of terrorism, which are committed by individuals, each with a catalogue of grievances. Islam is no more responsible for such heinous acts than are Christian, Hindu, Jewish and other faiths. Regrettably, those by Muslim individuals are often used to tar the whole community.

Achievements and Failures (1947-97)

A pall of gloom hangs heavy over the record of the first fifty years of Pakistan's existence. The country's dismemberment in 1971, illustrating the abysmal failure of both domestic and foreign policies, has left a deep wound on the nation's consciousness. If dejection and demoralization is not totally unrelieved, it is because people realize the heavy odds Pakistan had to fight from the beginning. Celebration of the 50th anniversary of the nation's independence was subdued, but the self-criticism manifest in commentaries on the occasion reflected also confidence in the nation's capacity to learn from past mistakes, rectify failed policies and strengthen trends toward consolidation and progress.

Pakistan did not escape unscathed from relentless Indian hostility, but it frustrated the expectations of those Congress leaders who projected an economic breakdown of Pakistan and a collapse into India's bear hug, undoing the partition. The people of Bangladesh no less than the people of Pakistan cherish independence and retain confidence in the validity and wisdom of the 1947 partition which rescued them from alien domination. Although Pakistan is still a low income country with daunting development problems, the living standards of its people compare favourably with others in the region.

The policy of alliance Pakistani leaders instinctively followed after independence was not flawed conceptually though it suffered at times from errors of judgement. Pakistan received $4 billion[140] in economic assistance and $1.37 billion in defence support during 1954-65[141] and a further $5 billion in grants and loans during 1981-90. The assistance enabled Pakistan to fortify its defence and develop its economy. Pakistan acquired modern armour and artillery for the army, and aircraft for the air force, raising Pakistan's self-defence capability, and it was able to accelerate economic development. Not only were the benefits considerable, the costs could have been further reduced. A more circumspect leadership would have avoided abrasive statements against the Soviet Union and refrained from supine acquiescence in British pressure on Suez. Thus, the policy did not preempt friendly and cooperative relations with China.

Pakistan's disappointment with the allies was largely the product of a culture of unreserved support and sacrifice for friends. Its people and government entertained high expectations of reciprocity. If these were not realistically pitched, the lesson has been learnt and assimilated. A new strategy for peace in the region has to take cognizance of the new realities.

Achievement of nuclear capability in the face of difficult odds and obstacles has contributed significantly to Pakistan's self-confidence. Credited as a key factor in the prevention of adventurism in 1990,[142] Pakistan should make a positive contribution to preservation of peace in the future as well, especially because in the transformed global environment, it must rely on its own self-defence capacity.

Establishment of the Organization of the Islamic Conference with over fifty members and expansion of the Economic Cooperation Organization, now with ten members, is an evolution Pakistan has long desired. The meetings of these forums provide opportunities for better understanding of problems and coordination of policies on matters of common interest. If progress in economic cooperation has not been as fast as Pakistan and many other members wish, it is realized that cooperation among developing countries is inherently difficult. That is also the experience of most other such groups.

Pakistan has entered the second half century of its existence truly 'without any narrow and special commitments and without any prejudices.'[143] For better or for worse, it is once again on its own. Yet, unlike the difficult years following independence when the fledgling state was virtually defenceless and without financial resources, Pakistan can now display reliable self-defence capacity and can mobilize domestic resources for economic development. On the threshold of a new millennium, the country is, finally, coming to grips also with internal challenges of political modernization and good governance. Even critical Pakistani appraisals end on an optimistic note.

NOTES

1. M. A. Jinnah, *Speeches as Governor-General*, p. 32.
2. M. A. Jinnah, op.cit., pp. 11, 62 and 65.
3. Prime Minister Liaquat Ali Khan quoted in Sarwar Hasan, *Pakistan Horizon*, Karachi, 4 December 1951.
4. Ibid., p. 67.
5. Allan Campbell-Johnson, *Mission with Mountbatten*, p. 58, quoted in Chaudhri Muhammad Ali, *The Emergence of Pakistan*, p. 129.
6. Ian Stephens, *Horned Moon*, p. 215.
7. John Connell, *Auchinleck*, pp. 915-918.
8. Ibid., pp. 220-2.
9. These words were used by India when objecting to the accession to Pakistan of Hindu-majority state of Junagarh by its Muslim ruler but ignored while accepting accession of Muslim-majority Kashmir by its Hindu ruler.
10. *America-Pakistan Relations—Documents*, ed. K. Arif, p. 3.
11. Z. H. Zaidi, *M. A. Jinnah-Ispahani Correspondence*, p. 538.
12. Memorandum given by Mir Laik Ali Khan, *Documents*, p. 5.
13. Finance Minister Ghulam Mohammad, speaking to Assistant Secretary of State George McGhee in October 1949.
14. Ibid., p. 25.
15. *Documents*, p. 15.
16. McMahon, pp. 60-75.
17. *New York Times*, editorial, 14 September 1951.
18. The sections on alliances and the Suez Crisis have borrowed very largely from Farooq Naseem Bajwa's commendable research work, *Pakistan and the West*.
19. In May 1952 Paul Nitze, Director of State Department's Policy Planning Staff, wrote a paper deploring Western fragility in the Middle East and recommending direct US involvement in the defence of the region because British capabilities were 'wholly inadequate.' Quoted in McMahon, p. 145.
20. John Foster Dulles said:'With their religious convictions and courageous spirit, the people of Pakistan and their leaders make their country a real bulwark.' *Documents*, p. 81.
21. Briefing Senate Foreign Relations Committee on 3 July 1953 on military aid to Pakistan, Dulles said, 'We don't dare to do it because of repercussions in India.' *Documents*, p. 78.
22. Farooq Bajwa, *Pakistan and the West*, p. 87.
23. After the royal regime was overthrown in a bloody coup in 1958 and Iraq pulled out, the pact was renamed Central Treaty Organisation (CENTO).

24. *Dawn* of 22 February 1954 quoted in Burke, p. 202.
25. *Dawn* of 26 September 1955 quoted in Burke, p. 204.
26. Statement issued on 14 August 1956, quoted in S. M. Burke, op.cit., p. 185.
27. *New York Times* of 10 June 1956, quoted in Dennis Kux, p. 128.
28. Report of National Security Council meeting of 3 January 1957 quoted in Dennis Kux, p. 154.
29. Article by President Ayub Khan in *Foreign Affairs* of January 1964, extracts in *Documents*, p. 226.
30. Altaf Gauhar, *Ayub Khan—Pakistan's First Military Dictator*, p. 119.
31. Prime Minister Mohammad Ali's broadcast to the nation, 1 October 1954. Extract in *Documents*, p. 102.
32. Firoz Khan Noon, *Memoirs*, extracts in *Documents*, p. 163.
33. US Assistant Secretary of State G. Lewis Jones, quoted in Dennis Kux, p. 169.
34. India's ambassador Chagla, quoted in McMahon, p. 260.
35. In contrast US aid to Pakistan increased marginally from $162.5 million in 1956 to $170 million in 1957.
36. Arthur M. Schlesinger, *A Thousand Days*, p. 483.
37 Summary of declassified US Policy Documents on South Asia, Vol. 19, in *Dawn*, 3 September 1996.
38. Ayub 'charmed everybody,' 'ingratiated' himself with Mrs Kennedy with the gift of a spirited stallion, and 'shone' at a gala dinner. Vice President Johnson described Ayub as a 'seasoned' leader and a 'dependable' ally. Quoted in McMahon, pp. 278-80.
39. Quoted from US documents in McMahon, p. 280. Also, summary of *US Policy Documents*, Vol. 19.
40. Schlesinger, p. 485.
41. Quoted from Robert Kennedy in *His Own Words* and Arthur Schlesinger, *A Thousand Days*, in McMahon, p. 281.
42. Kennedy's letter of 18 January 1962 to Nehru, Dennis Kux, p. 197.
43. Schlesinger, p. 487.
44. Quoted in Schlesinger, p. 487.
45. *Documents*, pp. 33, 35.
46. *Hindu*, Madras, 27 November 1954.
47. Burke, p. 57.
48. Burke, p. 215.
49. Quoted from UN records in Burke, op.cit., p. 198.
50. *Time of India*, 24 October 1959.
51. On 9 November 1959, Reuter reported Ayub to have said Chinese activities in Tibet and road building in Afghanistan posed a serious threat from the north.
52. This was nine days before the first serious incident on the Sino-Indian boundary.

53. For all these dates, see Gauhar, p. 234.
54. Agha Shahi who was director general in the foreign ministry at the time narrated this to the author.
55. Mohammad Yunus, *Reflections on China*, pp. 131-32.
56. US Embassy, Karachi, press release of September 1963, quoted in Gauhar, p. 245.
57. Kux, op.cit., p. 208.
58. Kennedy's letter of 28 October 1962 to Ayub, quoted in Kux, op.cit., p. 205.
59. Mohammad Ali Bogra's statement of 22 November 1962, *Documents*, Ed. Arif, pp. 213-215.
60. Ayub Khan, *Friends not Masters*.
61. 'The assurance from Pakistan sought by the Western powers was given, though not in so many words.' Quoted from *White Paper On the Pakistan Dispute* of the Government of Pakistan in Yusuf Buch, 'Kashmir and the Big Powers' presented at the International Seminar on Fifty Years of Kashmir Dispute, 24 August 1997. (To be published in Seminar proceedings later in 1997.)
62. A statement to that effect by Ayub and Nehru was announced on 29 November 1962, ref. Gauhar, op.cit., p. 217.
63. Summary of *US Policy Documents*, Vol. 19, *Dawn*, 3 September 1996.
64. Dawn, Karachi, 24-26 August 1963, quoted in Gauhar, op.cit., p. 241.
65. McMahon, p. 314.
66. Bhutto was 'deeply upset and disturbed' at the discourtesy shown to him, gleefully noted Talbot. A White House aid thought 'Bhutto was asking for it.' McMahon, p. 307.
67. *US National Security Archives*, NEA/PAB: RKMcKEE: gn of 23 May 1977, quoted in Gauhar, p. 196.
68. *Statesman Weekly*, 27 September 1969, quoted in Burke, p. 374.
69. At the Commonwealth summit in 1964, Pakistan opposed a move to pledge joint opposition to the 'Chinese threat.' Maqbool A. Bhatty, *Great Powers and South Asia*, p. 165.
70. Gauhar, p. 347-8.
71. China demanded the return of 4 Chinese inhabitants, 800 sheep and 59 yaks India had kidnapped.
72. UN Document S/Res/211 reproduced in *Documents*, Vol. 2, pp. 115-116.
73. A jeepable road was completed in 1971, an asphalt road in 1978. The Karakorum Highway, crossing the Khunjerab Pass at 15,800 ft. (4,800 m.) was opened to adventure-travellers in 1986.
74. For details and references see Burke, pp. 338-357, and Gauhar, pp. 340-41 and 347-53.
75. Z.A. Bhutto's note for Ayub Khan, extract in *Documents*, p. 250.
76. Henry Kissinger, *The White House Years*, p. 684.
77. Ibid., p. 685.

78. Ibid., p. 767.
79. Of 101 top civil and police service officers who opted for Pakistan in 1947 only 18 were Bengalis. Though the number of those who belonged to areas of West Pakistan was also relatively small (35), the issue was politicized so that any non-Bengali was dubbed as a 'Punjabi.'
80. The Lahore Resolution adopted by the Muslim League on 23 March 1940 demanded that contiguous Muslim-majority 'units' in the northwestern and eastern zones of British India should be 'grouped to constitute 'Independent States' in which the constituent units shall be autonomous and sovereign.' This rather vague concept clarified as the Pakistan idea caught the imagination of the masses. The 1946 convention of the elected legislators with a clear popular mandate left no doubt that Pakistan was to be 'a sovereign independent state.' For texts of resolutions see Syed Sharifuddin Pirzada, *The Pakistan Resolution* (Pakistan Publications, Karachi, 1968).
81. Text of original and revised formula reproduced in Siddiq Salik, *Witness to Surrender*, pp. 215-217.
82. Gauhar, p. 411.
83. Asoka Raina, *Inside RAW*, p. 49.
84. Kissinger, p. 852.
85. Salik, p. 101. (This figure did not include local raisings for paramilitary formations.)
86. K. Subramaniam, Director of the official Indian Institute of Defence Studies and Analyses said on 31 March: 'What India must realize is the fact that the break-up of Pakistan is in our interest, an opportunity the like of which will never come again.' *The Hindustan Times*, New Delhi, 1971 reported him to have also spoken of a 'chance of the century.' Quoted in Salik, p. 97.
87. Sisson and Rose, p. 209.
88. Raina, p. 54.
89. Salik, p. 100.
90. Kissinger, p. 848.
91. Nixon was not alone in finding Nehru insufferable. Secretary of State Dean Acheson said he was 'One of the most difficult men with whom I have ever had to deal.' Quoted from Acheson, *Present as the Creation*, pp. 439-40 in McMahon, p. 56. Truman considered Nehru 'disagreeable' and Kennedy who publicly praised Nehru's 'soaring idealism' found his sense of superiority 'rather offensive.'
92. Richard M. Nixon, *The Memoirs* of, Vol. 1, p. 651.
93. Kissinger, p. 880.
94. Nixon, p. 652.
95. Ibid., p. 658.
96. Ibid., p. 857.
97. Sisson and Rose, p. 213.

98. Kissinger, p. 895. In footnote 7 on p. 1488, he further says: 'Assurances were given by by the Kennedy and Johnson administrations, including a letter from President John F. Kennedy to President Mohammed Ayub Khan on Jan. 26, 1962; an aide memoir presented by the US ambassador on 5 November 1962 a public statement by the State Department on 17 November 1962; and an oral promise by President Lyndon Johnson to Ayub Khan on 15 December, 1965.'
99. Kissinger, p. 896.
100. Kissinger, p. 901.
101. Ibid., p. 905.
102. Ibid., p. 910.
103. V. Longer, *The Defence and Foreign Policy of India*, p. 215.
104. Statement on Policy for the 1970s, issued on 3 May 1973, *Documents*, p. 207.
105. For a first-hand account and analysis of the Simla agreement, see the author's 'Simla Agreement: Negotiation Under Duress' in *Regional Studies*, Islamabad, Autumn 1995, pp. 28-45.
106. For a more comprehensive study on the subject, see this author's article 'Reducing Nuclear Dangers in South Asia: A Pakistani Perspective' in *The Nonproliferation Review*, Winter 1995, Center for Nonproliferation Studies, Monterey, California, pp. 40-55, and Regional Studies, Islamabad, Autumn, 1994.
107. Statement by Pakistan Foreign Office, 7 April 1979, *Documents*, p. 347.
108. For a more detailed account, reader may refer to the author's article 'Jihad to Civil War' in *Afghanistan—Past, Present and Future*, pp. 460-491.
109. K. M. Arif, *Working With Zia*, p. 203. (Daoud made the remark to Zia.)
110. Agha Shahi, *Pakistan's Security and Foreign Policy*, p. 4.
111. Ibid., p. 6.
112. Statement by Pakistan Information Ministry, 21 November 1979, *Documents*, p. 366. For cost of rebuilding the embassy Pakistan paid $13.94 million. In addition US claimed $7.245 million for other property lost. Statement by US State Department, 12 November 1981, *Documents*, p. 366.
113. Shahi, p. 8.
114. President Carter's statement, 21 January 1980, *Documents*, p. 372.
115. Statement by US Department of State, 26 December 1979, *American Foreign Policy—Basic Documents*, 1977-80.
116. For detailed table see Riaz M. Khan, p. 40.
117. President Zia on NBC-TV, 18 May 1980, *Documents*, p. 394.
118. Statement by Foreign Affairs Adviser Agha Shahi, 5 March 1980. *Documents*, pp. 388-90.
119. Pakistan Foreign Office Statement, 25 April 1980, *Documents*, p. 392.

120. The package included $ 150 million in economic aid for F'82 and about $3 billion for economic assistance and military sales credits for the period F'83-F'87.
121. In testimony before a Congressional committee on 27 April 1981 Deputy Assistant Secretary of State Jane Coon acknowledged the injustice of past US policy, saying that sanctions were 'applied in the case of one country—Pakistan.' A few weeks later, Assistant Secretary of State James Buckley exuded understanding of Pakistan's perception that the threat to its security 'could not be met by conventional and political means.' For texts of statements, see *Documents*.
122. US Department of State, 16 September 1981, *Documents*, p. 457.
123. The interest differential was initially 8 per cent on $300 millions a year. Fortunately, interest rates declined in subsequent years, and the package which was carefully negotiated so as to increase the grant component for economic support funds did not prove 'back-breaking.' The follow-up agreement which remained in force only for 3 years until 1990 at a level of $700 million a year provided for military sales credits at a concessional rate.
124. Riaz M. Khan, p. 107.
125. Selig Harrison, *Inside the Afghan Talks*, p. 31. Also, Bernett R. Rubin, *The Search for Peace in Afghanistan—From Buffer State to Failed State*, pp. 63-65; slightly different figures in Riaz M. Khan, p. 88.
126. Quoted by Diego Cordovez, Bernett R. Rubin, p. 40.
127. Rubin, p. 43.
128. Shevardnadze told Secretary of State George Shultz on 16 September 1987: 'We will leave Afghanistan...I say with all responsibility that a political decision has been made.' Quoted from Shultz, *Turmoil and Triumph*, p. 1090 in Rubin, p. 83.
129. Statement by Foreign Minister Eduard Sheverdnadze in a meeting of the Central Committee of CPSU, after cataloguing the thousands of billions of rubles USSR spent on occupation of Eastern Europe, creating defence infrastructure on the border with China, and in Afghanistan. Author's memory.
130. Riaz M. Khan, p. 234.
131. This exchange took place on 9 February 1988 in author's presence.
132. *Literaturnaya Gazeta*, Moscow, 17 February 1988, quoted in Agha Shahi, p. 93.
133. K. M. Arif, p. 327, based on statements by General Alexei Lizichev and Prime Minister Nikolai Ryzhkov.
134. Paul Kennedy, *The Rise and Fall of Great Powers*.
135. Mulla Mohammad Umar, Taliban leader, quoted by Rahimullah Yusufzai in *The News*, 4 October 1996.

136. Uzbekistan President Islam Karimov, speaking at the OIC Summit in Ashkabat on 14 May 1997, reported in *The News*, Islamabad, 15 May 1997.
137. Ibid.
138. K.M. Arif, p. 327, quoting Eduard Sheverdnadze's statement in *Izvestia* of 19 February 1989.
139. President Ronald Reagan's, speech welcoming President Zia to Washington, 7 December 1982, *Documents*, p. 481.
140. US economic aid, quoted from Foreign Operations Appropriations, 1964, in Burke, p. 255.
141. *Documents*, pp. 285-86, Statement by James Noyes, Deputy Assistant Secretary for Defence, on 20 March 1973. Part of the aid was used to build Multan and Kharian cantonments and Sargodha air base.
142. A crisis was threatened in the spring of 1990 because of reported Indian plan for air raids on Pakistan as a means of deterring Pakistan's alleged assistance to Kashmiri freedom fighters. As it could have triggered a war between the two countries now possessing nuclear capabilities, President Bush sent Robert Gates on a successful mission of preventive diplomacy.
143. See note 3.

14

India-Pakistan Relations and the Problem of Kashmir

Robert G. Wirsing

Introduction

Pakistan and India are presently marking the fiftieth anniversary of the accession crisis, a series of remarkably controversial events, occurring near the end of October 1947, that set in motion a protracted dispute between them over the former princely state of Jammu and Kashmir. In contrast with the annual marking of this anniversary in the preceding years of this decade, its observance this year occurs against a background of shifting—and, at least in some respects, promising—atmospherics in the India-Pakistan relationship. True, the observance is likely to pass without any sign—either in the Valley (or Vale) of Kashmir in the Indian-controlled sector of the state or on the Line of Control (LOC) dividing that sector from the Pakistan-controlled portion of the state—of serious let-up in the violence that has been emblematic of this relationship from the beginning. Renewed dialogue between the senior leaders of the two countries over normalization of this relationship has been underway for several months, however, and there has been considerable speculation about a possible breakthrough in regard even to the explosive subject of Kashmir itself.

It had been the two sides' refusal to budge from irreconcilable positions on Kashmir that had brought the last round of bilateral talks between them on 2-3 January 1994, to an abrupt and acrimonious end. In that round, the seventh in a series of foreign secretary talks begun in 1990, the Pakistanis insisted that the behaviour of Indian security forces in counter-insurgency operations (the 'human rights issue,' in other words) be at the top of the agenda, while the Indians were equally emphatic that the talks focus on Pakistan's cross-border aid to the separatist Muslim guerrillas (the 'terrorism issue'). The talks were broken off after scarcely seven hours were spent at the negotiating table over the two days. The standoff persisted for over three years until both sides had undergone a change in government.

The first change to occur was on the Indian side, where the United Front (UF) leader H.D. Deve Gowda replaced P.V. Narasimha Rao as prime minister in the wake of the Congress party's trouncing in the national elections of April 1996. Deve Gowda promptly noted his willingness to reopen the foreign secretary talks with Pakistan. It was not until the Pakistan Muslim League (PML) leader Nawaz Sharif took over from Benazir Bhutto in Islamabad in February 1997, however, that a thaw in the relationship began to take shape. Deve Gowda communicated to the new Pakistani prime minister that his offer of talks still stood; and Nawaz Sharif responded in the same spirit. At the end of March, Pakistani Foreign Secretary Shamshad Ahmad met in New Delhi with his since-retired Indian counterpart, Salman Haider, setting a dialogue once again in motion. But before this initial round was concluded, the UF government's restless parliamentary ally, the Congress-I party, had yanked the rug out from under Deve Gowda's patchwork coalition and the talks ended on 31 March, not surprisingly in some confusion.

Elevation to the prime ministership in early April of Inder Kumar Gujral, Minister of External Affairs in the Deve Gowda government and author of the so-called Gujral Doctrine that encouraged India to 'go more than halfway' in dealing with its smaller neighbours, assured the survival of the initiative towards Pakistan in the reconstituted UF government. Talks between the two governments were quickly resumed: Pakistani Foreign Minister Gohar Ayub Khan met with Gujral, who retained the external affairs portfolio for himself, at a meeting of the Non-

Aligned Movement (NAM) foreign ministers in New Delhi in the second week of April; and in early May, the two prime ministers themselves met in a glare of publicity at the South Asian Association for Regional Cooperation (SAARC) summit at Male, capital of the Maldives Republic. This last meeting ended with the promise to resume foreign secretary-level talks at the end of June and, of particular importance, with an agreement in principle to constitute a number of joint 'working groups' to consider all outstanding issues between the two countries. In the subsequent meeting of the foreign secretaries in Islamabad near the end of June, agreement was reached to form eight such groups. Kashmir, to the amazement of most observers, was identified as one of the eight issues to be considered. This was the first time since the Simla Agreement in 1972 that India and Pakistan had formally agreed upon Kashmir's explicit inclusion on the agenda for talks between them.[1] [See Figure 1.]

Figure 1
Direct Bilateral Talks between India & Pakistan, on or Including Kashmir, 1947-1997

Date	Auspices/Location	Level	Outcome
1 Nov.-8 Dec. 1947	Joint Defence Council/ Lahore, New Delhi, Lahore	Governors-general & prime ministers	No agreement reached. Abandoned in favour of UN intercession.
25-27 July 1953	Karachi	Prime ministers	Preliminary discussions only.
17-20 Aug. 1953	New Delhi	Prime ministers	Expert committees approved, plebiscite endorsed. No agreement reached in follow-on correspondence.
14-18 May 1955	New Delhi	Prime ministers	No agreement reached. Further talks called for.
19-23 Sept. 1960	World Bank/ Karachi	Prime ministers	Indus Waters Treaty signed. No progress on Kashmir.

27-29 Dec. 1962 16-19 Jan. 1963 8-10 Feb. 1963 12-14 Mar. 1963 21-25 Apr. 1963 14-16 May 1963	Rawalpindi, New Delhi, Karachi, Calcutta, Karachi, New Delhi	Ministers (railways & foreign)	Joint Communique issued at end of sixth round reported no agreement.
1-2 Mar. 1966	Rawalpindi	Foreign ministers	Terminated upon failure to agree on Kashmir's inclusion in formal agenda.
28 June-2 July 1972	Simla	Prime ministers	Kashmir excluded from formal agenda. New cease-fire line (LOC) agreed. Commitment to final settlement of Kashmir included in peace treaty.
2-3 Jan. 1994	Islamabad	Foreign secretaries	Seventh round in series commenced in 1990. Kashmir implicitly included on agenda. No progress reported. No further meetings scheduled.
28-31 Mar. 1997	New Delhi	Foreign secretaries	First round in fresh series. 'All issues' on agenda. Further meetings planned.
9 Apr. 1997	NAM conference/ New Delhi	Foreign ministers	Commitment to bilateral talks reaffirmed.
12-14 May 1997	SAARC summit meeting/ Male (Maldives)	Prime ministers	Commitment made to resume foreign secretary-level talks. Plan announced to constitute joint 'working groups' to consider all outstanding issues.
19-23 June 1997	Islamabad	Foreign secretaries	Second round in series. Agreement announced to form eight 'working groups' to consider major issues between them, including Kashmir.
15-18 Sept. 1997	New Delhi	Foreign secretaries	Third round in series. No agreement on any issue except to hold another round of talks.
23 Sept. 1997	UN General Assembly/ New York	Prime ministers	Commitment made to take action to end border skirmishes in Kashmir.

A third round of foreign secretary talks was held in New Delhi in the middle of September. No agreement was reached at this meeting in regard to commissioning of the proposed working groups. In fact, by then the search for a suitable 'mechanism' or framework for the talks was already showing signs of wear in the face of accumulating contradictions in the political and military signals being sent out in the region. In a speech in Srinagar on 26 July, for instance, Prime Minister Gujral reportedly said that his government was 'ready for unconditional talks with misguided elements in the Kashmir valley so that peace returns to the paradise on Earth'.[2] The first public offer of unconditional talks to be made by an Indian leader since the outbreak of militant violence in 1989, Gujral's comment drew immediate and welcoming reactions, including some from leaders of the militant movement's political umbrella organization, the All Parties Hurriyat (Freedom) Conference (APHC).[3] On the very next day, however, Gujral appeared to execute an about face when he corrected himself by adding the proviso that the militants should first lay down their arms before talks to end the rebellion could begin.[4] The contradictions were starker—and more threatening to the laboriously wrought but still hesitant normalization initiatives just getting underway in the region—on the military side of things. On 22 August, in between the second and third rounds of foreign secretary talks, artillery exchanges broke out between Indian and Pakistani forces at a number of points along the entire length of the LOC.[5] The skirmishing, which produced fairly heavy casualties on both sides and which continued off and on into October, provided an ominous background to the meeting in New York in late September of the Indian and Pakistani prime ministers.[6]

While there were thus few, if any, observers prepared to predict on the fiftieth anniversary of the Kashmir conflict that the hoped-for breakthrough in India-Pakistan relations was at hand, the atmosphere was still sufficiently promising to keep alive at least the possibility of some improvement. This chapter is based in part on research on the subject of Kashmir conducted during five visits to South Asia over a period of nine months from September 1996 to May 1997. During these five visits, the author held discussions on Kashmir with a total of 169 individuals in 3 urban centers in India (New Delhi, Jammu and Srinager) and 5 in Pakistan (Islamabad, Rawalpindi, Lahore, Karachi and Sialkot). Visits were made to both the Kashmir and Jammu divisions of the Indian state of Jammu and Kashmir, in the course of which the author observed directly Phase II of the 1996 state assembly elections in that state. With the cooperation of the Pakistan army, the author made site visits to the Pakistan side of the Line of Control (Jammu and Neelam Valley sectors) and received briefings on the Kashmir issue at corps, division, brigade, and wing levels. Consider the question whether this relatively promising atmosphere is likely to be converted, at any time in the near future, into substantive progress towards the normalization of relations between these two arch rivals and, in particular, towards a settlement of the Kashmir dispute. Research focuses, first, on the perceptions of political elites in both countries of the need and desirability of change in the relationship, second, on the priority each side appears to assign to Kashmir in the overall scheme of normalization initiatives; and, third, on the domestic political constraints on the two governments' capacities for moving in the direction of reconciliation. It concludes by urging a number of immediate practical steps that need to be taken in the region before movement of that kind can realistically be expected.

Elite Perceptions

This and succeeding sections of this chapter draw upon a co authored report, *1947-1997: The Kashmir Dispute at Fifty: Charting Paths to Peace*, in the drafting of which the present writer participated. Prepared for the Kashmir Study Group, a non-governmental organization formed in late 1996, the report summarizes findings and presents recommendations in regard to Kashmir based on two visits to South Asia in the spring of 1997 by a five-member study team. The team's members, in addition to the author of this paper, were former Ambassador Howard B. Schaffer, Dr Joseph E. Schwartzberg, Dr Ainslee E. Embree, and Dr Charles Report, the named co-authors bear no responsibility whatsoever either for the contents of the present argument or for the particular interpretations this writer has placed on these contents. India and Pakistan are under considerable pressure nowadays to normalize their relationship and, in particular, to end the state of armed confrontation that presents both a constant threat of renewed war between them as well as a major financial burden. The pressures on them have not been identical, however, a feature of their relationship which is itself problematic.

Pakistan

Pressure for a change in policy appears to be far greater on the Pakistan side, where an array of 'compulsions'—the economy foremost among them—has formed in recent years to create an unprecedented crisis for Pakistan's leadership. Pakistan's alarming economic dilemmas—including a rapidly mounting external debt, an unfavourable balance of trade, a depressingly low economic growth rate, and an unprecedented decline in large-scale manufacturing output—have obviously placed the country under great strain; but these unfavourable economic indices clearly were not the end of Pakistan's difficulties. It had also to contend with the fact that Prime Minister Nawaz Sharif's massive electoral mandate in February 1997 could no more than paper over the frailty and latent instability of Pakistan's democratic institutions; that the country's never-resolved issue of its religious identity was now surfacing with disturbing frequency in widespread sectarian violence; that India seemed to have outplayed Pakistan diplomatically, leaving Pakistan isolated on the question of Kashmir and unable to secure firm and reliable backing of its Kashmir policy from any powerful members of the international community, including its traditional allies China, Iran, and the United States; and that Pakistan was in no position militarily to challenge India's possession of Jammu and Kashmir.

In these circumstances, the Government of Pakistan's regional policies have themselves inevitably been brought under the increasing scrutiny of Pakistanis. These policies, in particular those directed towards the state of Jammu and Kashmir, have acquired a patina of orthodoxy over the years that resist serious criticism; but the resistance is clearly weakening.

The government's declared position on Kashmir directly challenges the Indian claim that the state of Jammu and Kashmir is now and has been since its accession to India on 26 October 1947, an integral part of the Indian Union, and that nothing agreed to by India in UN Security Council resolutions at that time or in any subsequent instrument alters this status or in any way qualifies Indian sovereignty over the state. Pakistan has modified its position occasionally as its conflict with India evolved; but there has been little public deviation from four core postulates, namely:

(1) That the state of Jammu and Kashmir, as formally acknowledged in the UN Security Council resolutions of 13 August 1948 and 5 January 1949, is now and has been since the end of British rule over the Subcontinent, disputed territory;
(2) that the content of talks between India and Pakistan over the future status of the state should be focused upon securing the right of self-determination for the Kashmiri people via conduct of a free, fair, and internationally supervised plebiscite, as agreed in the aforementioned UN Security Council resolutions;
(3) that the plebiscite should offer the people of Kashmir the choice of permanent accession of the state to either Pakistan or India; and
(4) that involvement of members of the international community in the process of negotiating the future status of the state should not be ruled out.

Defence of this formal position by members of the Pakistani ruling classes has never been uniformly vigorous; but, at least until recently obvious deviation from or outright rejection of it was extremely rare, at least in public. It was still being described as nearly sacrosanct by some of the author's informants, especially those of the older, Partition-era generation, during the past year. Striking, however, was the nearly universal tendency of most informants, including some at the highest levels of government, to allow for serious revision—in some instances the wholesale discard—of the official position on Kashmir. To ensure promised anonymity, the identities of the author's informants have been concealed.

One of the milder but most widely-shared revisionist views, one that had the support of informants representative of virtually every point on the ideological compass, pertained to the plebiscite. A unitary plebiscite embracing all regions of the state of Jammu and Kashmir, as had been envisioned in the original UN Security Council resolutions, now struck practically everyone as impractical. Higher government officials, in particular, seemed to consider it essentially a dead issue. In its place many of the author's respondents, including some influential persons notorious for extremely conservative opinions on the Kashmir question, expressed approval for regional or even district-wise plebiscites that would allow Kashmiri Muslim sentiment in the Valley to be separately registered and, potentially, justify breakup of the state along ethno-religious lines. This would amount to resurrecting something akin to the 'regional plebiscites' proposal, never formally accepted by Pakistan, made by UN mediator Sir Owen Dixon in 1950.[7] This proposition is probably less revisionist than appears on the surface, however, since the Government of Pakistan, according to comments made to the author by an official of the Foreign Office, had itself already moved quietly in that direction. On 18 January 1994, he said, Islamabad had presented the Government of India with an unofficial 'nonpaper'—one of two such documents conveyed to Indian leaders at the time, detailing proposed Pakistani terms for resuming talks with India—dealing with modalities for holding a plebiscite. One of its paragraphs, he said, expressed Pakistan's willingness to consider new and innovative methods to ascertain the will of the people. This meant, he observed, that the method of measuring the popular will was negotiable.[8]

Unquestionably radical, however, was the suggestion, made with startling frequency by very senior—both retired and active—members of Pakistan's bureaucratic and political establishments (albeit by a minority of the author's interlocutors), that the whole idea of plebiscite might well be jettisoned and, instead, that the LOC be endorsed as the permanent international boundary between Pakistan and India. This proposal has the status of conventional wisdom on the Indian side, of course; but in the contemporary Pakistani political milieu, it bordered on heresy.

Admittedly, the author's informants displayed varying degrees of firmness and enthusiasm for the LOC option. A prominent leader of an opposition political party put the most bluntly favourable reading on it: If Punjab and Bengal could be divided at Partition, he asked, why couldn't Kashmir be divided at the LOC? Why should a small fraction of the region's population, he added, hold a billion hostage? A key member of the ruling Pakistan Muslim League party offered the tantalizing speculation that perhaps 'down the road'—and provided India met other conditions-he could even see the LOC as a permanent border between India and Pakistan. A retired and highly respected army general, on the other hand, took a rather more equivocal position: Pakistan could not get the whole of Kashmir, he conceded, but the Valley had to be granted self-determination. 'Maybe,' he said, 'Pakistan can have the Valley. But one must be realistic.' Getting the Valley would be *very* difficult .' At the same time, the Valley's retention by India on *India's present terms*, he observed, was out of the question. Some kind of autonomy for Kashmir was possible, however. The Valley could aspire to *maximum* autonomy in some sort of loose federation. Kashmir as a whole should have a 'special status.' Taking this last point a step further, a senior serving diplomat among the author's

Pakistani informants indicated that even Pakistan's traditional interpretation of the plebiscite—that it should offer the people of Kashmir the strictly bifold choice of permanent accession of the state to either Pakistan or India—was up for reconsideration. The third option of independence, he averred, was being given serious attention in Pakistan *at the highest level*.

It would be a serious mistake to interpret these somewhat startling observations as evidence that Pakistan was preparing to abdicate entirely from its long-standing claim to Kashmir. Heard in Pakistan with considerable frequency, in fact, was the sentiment that normalization of relations with India, no matter what compulsions Pakistan faced, would not translate into any such behaviour. Pakistan is 'not prepared to yield an inch...,' declared a retired member of Pakistan's foreign affairs bureaucracy, echoing many of the author's respondents. 'Pakistan, for the sake of peace, doesn't have to yield an inch on its Kashmir position.' Pakistan, he insisted, will not acquiesce to India's occupation of Kashmir; but it will not go to war. 'We are not so down and out that we have to surrender...We are not under that kind of compulsion.'

All things considered, however, the Pakistanis interviewed by the author, as a group, evinced surprising willingness to rethink Pakistan's long-standing official position on Jammu and Kashmir and, where necessary, to shed or at least recraft those aspects of it that had proven unproductive. The words of a very senior politician of Azad Jammu and Kashmir, albeit less guarded than most, perhaps captured the essence of this spirit best. While pointing out his very strong reservations about the desirability of Kashmiris remaining within the Indian Union, he stated emphatically that he was 'prepared to reconsider the whole situation [in Kashmir]...There can be a via media,...a new way of looking at a problem [that could] accommodate both India and Pakistan.' Kashmir needed to be rethought. 'We are prepared,' he said, 'to do anything to facilitate movement towards settlement....Let us forget 1947, 1948. Let us be reasonable.'

Nothwithstanding such accommodating sentiments, none of the author's respondents in Pakistan expected clear sailing in the direction of normalizing relations with India, even less that the Kashmir conflict would soon be removed from the regional agenda. Few went quite as far as an academic, one with experience as a professional diplomat, who said that he did 'not foresee a Kashmir solution at all. We should plan for a future in which everything remains frozen...India will not yield an inch.'[9] But most expressed varying degrees of pessimism. Indian Prime Minister Gujral was described by several as a 'wolf in sheep's clothing'—a good public relations man, perhaps, and a man who gave the appearance of being conciliatory; but one, nevertheless, whose response to Nawaz Sharif in the end would be—as a very senior, now retired, diplomat put it—mainly diversionary, affecting atmospherics only, while in fact taking an unyielding stance on the core issue of Kashmir. When all was said and done, he said, India would not negotiate the future of Jammu and Kashmir on the basis of terms required by Pakistan.[10] Said another, a professional analyst: The Government of India wants only to buy time, time to crush the militants and to assure preservation of the status quo. For Gujral too, he said, no matter what he may say, 'Kashmir is a non-issue.'[11]

Even when a more kindly view of Gujral was taken, it did not produce greater optimism. As a senior member of the Pakistan government put it, Prime Minister Gujral was one thing, the Indian establishment another. It was more rigid, more entrenched. Gujral, he estimated, had probably no more than a year to rule, probably less. The Congress, representing the Nehruvian tradition, would take about that long to repolish its electoral image. Whereas the present non-Congress government welcomed change in India-Pakistan relations, a Congress government, still burdened with a Nehruvian concept of India's potential world role, likely would not. Unfortunately, he said, the potential for compromise, symbolized by Gujral, was receding in India under the weight of Hindu nationalism.[12]

India

The government of India's official and abbreviated position on the state of Jammu and Kashmir, as publicly and frequently expressed in the present decade by its highest leadership, contains three basic postulates, namely:

(1) That the state of Jammu and Kashmir is now and has been since its accession to India on 26 October 1947 an integral part of the Indian Union, and that nothing agreed to by India in the UN Security Council resolutions of 13 August 1948 and 5 January 1949, or in any subsequent instrument, alters this status or in any way modifies Indian sovereignty over the state;
(2) that the future status of the state, aside from the question of Pakistan's 'vacation of aggression' against it, is an exclusively domestic matter to be resolved, as Indians typically put it, 'within the four corners of the Indian Constitution'; and
(3) that talks between India and Pakistan in regard to the future status of the state should be held within a strictly bilateral framework and in conformity with the Simla Agreement of July 1972.

Notwithstanding the bellicose rhetoric that crops up occasionally in India on commemorative occasions when speakers (not excluding recent prime ministers) unashamedly lay claim to the whole of pre-Independence Jammu and Kashmir, the Indian government has made it clear on numerous occasions and over a lengthy period of time that it is, as a practical matter, willing to settle with Pakistan for the territorial status quo in Jammu and Kashmir—that is, for retention by both sides of territories currently held and for acceptance of the LOC dividing these territories as the permanent international border. This position was implicit in the Simla Agreement and the Indian government has scarcely wavered from it since then.

Indians interviewed by the author during the past year displayed a confidence, at times bordering on smugness, with regard to India's position on Kashmir that stood in marked contrast to the somewhat disillusioned and generally pessimistic outlook on Kashmir witnessed on the Pakistan side. While there was ample recognition in India that the political alienation of Kashmiri Muslims was both acute and widespread, and that steps taken thus far by the government to address this alienation fell far short of requirements, Indians appeared largely convinced, nevertheless, that militant separatism in the Valley had been effectively contained by the armed forces and that in due course it would be eliminated. Modest support for the extension of greater autonomy to the peoples of Kashmir was expressed by some of the author's Indian respondents; but this support was most often described in terms of a general devolution of central powers to the states, not as a concession to Kashmir alone. Aside from minor modifications of the LOC in order to rationalize the boundary, there was practically no support expressed for the transfer to Pakistan of any territory from the Indian-held portion of Jammu and Kashmir. Neither, moreover, was there any significant support expressed for the grant of independence to any part or all of this territory.

In sum, the author uncovered little dissent in India from the government's announced position on Kashmir. On the contrary, there were fairly numerous signs of growing confidence in India that, provided the government exercised prudence and patience, the Kashmir dispute would sooner or later be settled essentially on India's terms and that there were no urgent grounds for compromise.

Underlying this relatively uncompromising—even triumphalist—sentiment among Indians was the frequently voiced perception that India was in a powerful position to ward off any challenge to its control of Kashmir from Pakistan or elsewhere. Common to most of those interviewed, in fact, was the perception that the principal foreign backer of the Kashmiri cause, Pakistan, was a nation in social, economic, and political tatters. Neither Pakistan's imminent collapse nor its sudden acquiescence to Indian terms on Kashmir was predicted by any of the Indians interviewed by the author. Prevalent among them, however, were the beliefs that Pakistan had lost the strategic advantages granted it by the cold war; that its reputation in some quarters as a breeding ground for Islamic fundamentalist and anti-Western inclined terrorists lent force to Indian allegations of Pakistan's sinister role in Kashmir; that it was now under heavy US (and other foreign) pressure to accommodate India on Kashmir; that it was confronted nowadays with popular alienation among Kashmiri Muslims—those in Pakistan-controlled Azad (Free) Jammu and Kashmir as well as those in the Indian-controlled sector—that rivaled the alienation felt against India; and that its overall position on Kashmir, both internal and external, was steadily weakening and should not, therefore, command serious Indian attention. Put more succinctly by a highly-regarded New Delhi intellectual, what all this meant was that 'Pakistan's ability to do damage to India is very limited.'[13]

Normalization Priorities

These two widely shared Indian views, first that India should not and need not budge from its traditional position on Kashmir, and second that India's rival over Kashmir is a nation presently under severe duress, have helped to generate fairly strong interest in India recently in the cautious extension to Pakistan of the Gujral Doctrine—the view that India, in dealing with its smaller neighbours, should be willing to make non-reciprocal concessions. Support for the government's initiatives in this direction, begun during the short-lived UF government of H.D. Deve Gowda (April 1996 to April 1997) by then External Affairs Minister (Since April 1997 Prime Minister) Gujral, was voiced very frequently by the author's Indian interlocutors. With some notable exceptions, however, they understood it to have as its objective not the resolution of the Kashmir issue, which they almost uniformly considered quite beyond reach in the near term, but the sequestering of that issue from the cluster of issues falling under the rubric of normalization and its quick dispatch to the 'back burner' of India-Pakistan relations—a position it had occupied, or so Indians tend to claim, from 1972 until the outbreak of the uprising in 1989.

A vocal but small minority argued that of the two neighbours India, being the bigger, more powerful, and more stable party to the dispute, was in the better position to accelerate the process of normalization. Pakistan's policy-making machinery was paralyzed, and for it the risks of failure were greater. This group gave a maximalist interpretation to the Gujral Doctrine, seeing it as the opening wedge to a new and more stable South Asian political order. A number of these respondents urged the thinning of Indian security forces in Kashmir. One of the best-known and respected respondents argued that India's policy initiatives thus far towards Pakistan had, in fact, been entirely too limited. What was needed was not the lifting of visa restrictions against Pakistan, but a robust and broadly conceived set of initiatives pertaining not only to Kashmir but to nuclear weapons, missile production, and expanded regional co-operation.[14]

The majority of the author's respondents, however, dissented from the principle that because India is bigger and more powerful it should be the first to offer concessions. While they welcomed normalization of relations with Pakistan, it was not given topmost priority or held worthy of significant sacrifice, certainly not when it came to Kashmir. These Indians typically gave a minimalist interpretation to the Gujral Doctrine, one that envisioned progress on the Pakistan front in small and relatively risk-free increments, focused on issues where substantial agreement already existed or was easy to gain. 'Expand areas of agreement,' said one professional Pakistan-watcher, 'so that areas of disagreement seem smaller.' Then, he said, things will gradually fall into place. If Siachen proves too difficult, he observed, then set it aside. If academic exchanges can be arranged, or media exchanges, or scientific exchanges, then do that.[15]

The Trade Issue

New Delhi's 'normalization *sans* Kashmir' initiative officially includes a number of relatively minor and presumed 'confidence building measures,' such as the easing of visa requirements, release of fishermen captured in contested coastal waters, and the promotion of cultural exchanges. Its centrepiece, however, is economic—the promise of movement towards GATT-mandated, tariff-free trade between the two countries. The author's Indian respondents observed very often that the steady expansion of co-operative trading mechanisms between India and Pakistan would very likely result in expanded recognition on both sides of the border of their Kashmir-transcending common interests and common problems. That would eventually lead, according to this logic, to a softening of time-hardened positions on Kashmir and heightened possibility for arms reductions—developments that promised a significant 'peace-dividend' down the road for the hard-pressed economies of both. In the meantime, as one respondent put it, 'Pakistan is under duress...it will have to enter into trade and commerce with India in order to lift the siege'.[16]

Representatives of Indian commercial organizations who spoke to the author tended toward bullishness on the potential scope for India-Pakistan trade. Legal trade between India and Pakistan, they pointed out, was extremely small—in 1994 amounting to $64 million, or only one-eighth of that between Bangladesh and India. Illegal (or 'unauthorized') trade, on the other hand, was, relatively speaking, substantial—at present, by their estimate, falling in the vicinity of $500 million. The loss to Pakistan implicit in this, they observed, was substantial: Pakistani businessmen were having to pay more for the Indian goods they imported via third-party go-betweens, and of course the Pakistan government collected less revenue. There was, they said, 'tremendous' potential for two-way India-Pakistan trade: Pakistani manufacturing firms need have no fear that Indian goods would flood the Pakistani marketplace. Among potential Pakistani exports with marketing potential in India they listed:

handicrafts, light engineering goods, leather-wear, cotton goods, raw materials for chemicals, sporting goods, dried fruits, and natural gas. They conceded that there was a significant element of non-complementarity of the two economies; but this, they said, was easily exaggerated and, in any event, the similarities in their economies only went to demonstrate the need for joint ventures between them.[17]

When the subject of expanding trade with India came up in the author's discussions in Pakistan about normalization, the idea in general was almost universally applauded. However, when it came to the terms that would govern expansion, the seeming consensus rapidly evaporated. Liberal intellectuals among the respondents were among the most enthusiastic backers of trade with India. Echoing sentiments often heard on the other side of the border, one of them urged, for instance, that Kashmir should be put on the back burner for some years. In that period, trade with India should be encouraged, along with travel and cross-border cultural exchanges. As contacts developed between the two rivals, mutual fears would decline. And then Kashmir could be dealt with.[18] Ideological conservatives, for their part, were just as insistent that Kashmir's priority among Pakistan's objectives not be sacrificed on the anvil of trade. Said one influential respondent: There can be no trade or normalization with India until Kashmir is solved; it is 'impossible.'[19]

The most common view encountered in Pakistan, however, was that trade should indeed be promoted with India, but slowly, and that it should be looked upon neither as a cure for India-Pakistan hostility nor as a substitute for a Kashmir policy. It was essential, according to most who commented on this issue, that steps be taken at the same time as trade was opened to protect vulnerable sectors of Pakistani commerce and industry. The Pakistani business community was split down the middle on this issue between traders and industrialists, with smaller industrialists in particular understandably concerned that Pakistan's unrestricted opening up to more heavily subsidized, more lightly taxed, and more cheaply produced Indian products would spell grief for themselves. But opposition to trade expansion with India was actually more complicated than that. As a businessman explained it, Pakistan's garment manufacturers, for instance, while enthusiastic about lifting restrictions on the import from India of cotton fabric and yarn, were far from eager to encourage lifting the ban on the import of Indian finished cotton garments. By the same token, whereas Pakistan's textile manufacturers were eager to gain access to India's cheaper raw cotton, their lobbying on this point naturally got a cold reception from Pakistan's own cotton producers, who happened to be powerful in Parliament.[20]

The fact was that the Pakistani business community, having suffered for fifty years through twenty-two different governments, each with its own economic policies, was weak and not generally competitive economically. As a result, some Pakistani businessmen were inevitably tempted to exploit the Kashmir issue in order to guard their industry's flanks. Having 'grown up in a hothouse of government patronage and corruption,' commented a senior journalist,' businessmen are inevitably apprehensive about major change in government policy, but nevertheless 'realize the benefits of normalizing relations with India'.[21]

In sum, while sentiment was strong that Pakistan's economic relationship with India ought to improve, so too was the feeling that the improvement should be worked out step by step and with the long-term health of the Pakistani business community uppermost in mind. Trade, it was felt, was no panacea for Kashmir and would scarcely touch the deeper antagonism between India and Pakistan rooted in Partition. While expanded trade with India was seen as a good idea, it was not expected to drive the engine of normalization.

Siachen Glacier Issue

Perhaps equally high on India's normalization wish-list is settlement of its conflict with Pakistan over possession of the

Siachen Glacier, which, until fighting broke out between Indian and Pakistani forces in April 1984, was a little known and rarely visited tract of about 1,000 square miles in a remote and largely uninhabited stretch of the Karakoram Mountain Range. Since 1985, there have been six rounds of talks over Siachen at the defence secretary level between India and Pakistan. The last two of these—in 1989 and 1992—focussed on very detailed proposals covering disengagement and redeployment of forces, as well as boundary delimitation and marking.[22] In spite of huge costs and spectacular damage to what had been a pristine high-altitude wilderness, no lasting agreement has yet been reached. The potential for renewed diplomatic activity over Siachen resurfaced last June when the two sides agreed to its inclusion among the eight major issues to be dealt with by the proposed working groups. [See Figure 2.]

Figure 2
Direct Bilateral Talks over Siachen between India and Pakistan, 1985-1997

Date	Auspices/Location	Level	Outcome
17 Dec. 1985	New Delhi	Prime minister[I] & President [P]	Agreement to hold defence secretary level talks on Siachen.
10-12 Jan. 1986	Rawalpindi	Defence secretaries	First round in series. Resolved to seek negotiated settlement in accordance with Simla agreement of 1972.
10-12 June 1986	New Delhi	Defence secretaries	Second round.
4 Nov. 1987	SAARC conference/ Katmandu (Nepal)	Prime ministers	Agreement to revive suspended meetings of defence secretaries on Siachen.
19-20 May 1988	Islamabad	Defence secretaries	Third round.
23-24 Sept. 1988	New Delhi	Defence secretaries	Fourth round.
15-17 June 1989	Rawalpindi	Defence secretaries	Fifth round. Agreement to work towards comprehensive settlement of Siachen issue based on redeployment of forces. Next round scheduled at New Delhi.
16-18 June 1989	Islamabad	Foreign secretaries	Scheduled fifth round held

			parallel to defence secretary talks. Pakistan foreign secretary publicly declared agreement on withdrawal of forces from Siachen. Denied by India.
9-10 July 1989	New Delhi	Military commanders	Technical talks on forces redeployment.
16-17 July 1989	Islamabad	Prime ministers	Results of fifth round of defence secretary talks approved. Defence secretaries directed to work toward comprehensive settlement in accordance with Simla agreement and based on redeployment of forces. Military authorities directed to continue talks on forces redeployment.
18-20 Aug. 1989	Rawalpindi	Military commanders	No progress reported. Siachen talks suspended.
16-19 Aug. 1992	New Delhi	Foreign secretaries	Sixth round of foreign secretary talks. Resumption of Siachen talks proposed.
4-6 Aug. 1992	New Delhi	Defence secretaries	Sixth round. Detailed examination of redeployment. No agreement reached. No further round scheduled.
19-23 June 1997	Islamabad	Foreign secretaries	Second round in current series. Siachen included among eight major issues on agenda of proposed 'working groups.'

To the prompt solution of the thirteen year old dispute over Siachen, most of the author's respondents in India gave strong support. Indeed, very few seemed to dissent from the observation of a retired senior civil servant, with intimate knowledge of Kashmir's security environment, that continued fighting over Siachen was 'sheer insanity.'[23] Conspicuous among the Indian respondents, however, was the insistence that the Siachen's obvious geographic proximity to the troubled Kashmir valley not be construed to imply its political inseparability from the larger dispute. Like every other category of normalization, the Siachen dispute, regardless of its location, had to be *delinked* from the quagmire in its own neighbourhood to achieve the lofty objective of regional co-operation.

Siachen is viewed rather differently on the Pakistan side of the border. While a government spokesman in Islamabad assured the author that Pakistan was keen to settle the Siachen dispute with India and emphasized that it would be wrong for Pakistan to use it as an opportunity to 'bleed' Indian armed forces, Pakistani respondents commenting on the Siachen issue generally perceived it to be one of the few Kashmir-related issues in which Pakistan held the upper hand. Typical were the remarks of a retired general turned political analyst. 'Indians,' he said, 'are under terrific logistical pressure [at Siachen] to maintain their forces.' India's costs are 'much, much higher' than Pakistan's. The Indian press, he said, had reported that Siachen was costing India Rs 6 crores (roughly US$ 1.7 million) per day.[24]

Consistent with that judgement was the commonly expressed view that a reasonable agreement over Siachen, one that would satisfy the interests of both sides, would not be especially difficult to achieve. Fighting over Siachen, as a retired army general observed, was 'pointless.'[25] Moreover, as he and other Pakistani respondents saw it, Pakistani negotiators had already displayed their willingness to strike a fair bargain over Siachen in 1989 and again in 1992, only to see the agreements fall victim to a loss of political will in New Delhi. The Government of India, it seemed to them, sought agreement over Siachen only when under duress. At the moment, said one, Siachen 'is a weakness in India's position, so the Indians want to talk about it.'[26]

Pointedly mentioned by several Pakistani respondents, however, was the fact that Pakistan's consent to a renewed effort to negotiate Siachen would not be cheaply bought. Settlement of Siachen now, said the general-turned-analyst quoted above, would be a major concession by Pakistan requiring a major quid pro quo. India's lifting of visa restrictions on Pakistani travellers, he commented, or its encouragement of cultural exchanges with Pakistan were, in comparison with Siachen, but minor issues.

In sum, what united most Pakistani respondents commenting on Siachen was the conviction that the Government of Pakistan would be well advised to move towards negotiations with India provided such a move was a carefully conceived element in a larger strategic package—a package that, in one way or another, linked Siachen to Indian concessions on the larger root or core problem of Kashmir. Pakistan was 'willing to include Siachen among four or five Kashmir related problems,' observed a retired army general, 'but not to delink it.'[27] The piecemeal and sequestered approach favoured by India, in other words, which envisioned treating Siachen essentially on its own as a confidence building measure, received, for the most part, little support in Pakistan, where the favoured approach was more holistic. As a senior journalist expressed it, Pakistanis were averse to delinking Kashmir from the normalization process, for that would consign Kashmir to a political limbo, which was just what the Indians wanted.[28]

Confidence-Building Measures (CBMs) in Kashmir

In fact, although even some Pakistani respondents listed renewed negotiations over Siachen as a potentially fruitful CBM, by far the most commonly identified—and insisted upon—measures involved concessions by India relating directly to the situation in the Indian-controlled parts of Jammu and Kashmir. They included the following:

(1) India's acknowledgment that Kashmir is disputed territory.
(2) Reduction in size of Indian security forces in Kashmir.
(3) Release of detained Kashmiri militants.
(4) Termination of Indian security forces' 'cordon and search' operations in Kashmir.
(5) Enforcement of stricter curbs on human rights abuses.
(6) Greater transparency in regard to Kashmir via expanded media coverage or increased monitoring by international human rights groups of India's compliance with human rights standards.
(7) Opening of talks with leaders of the All Parties Hurriyat Conference (APHC).
(8) Initiation of joint Indo-Pakistani patrolling of the LOC.

The first of these—acknowledgment by India that Kashmir is disputed territory—is the most generic and also one of the most emphatically endorsed CBMs. Not much could be achieved without it, said many of the author's Pakistani interlocutors, and nothing else would more clearly communicate India's readiness for serious negotiations. What stands out about the other recommended measures, however, was the modesty (or realism) of the expectations that appeared to underlie most of them. In the first place, many of the respondents described them as face-saving gestures—in other words, as measures that would allow Pakistan to ease itself down from the often hardline public positions taken on Kashmir in past years. Secondly, in urging India to implement the above CBMs, most respondents, including those occupying sensitive government posts, chose remarkably moderate language. The Indians, said a senior government official, should 'at least symbolically reduce forces' in Kashmir.[29] Even a 10 per cent improvement in the situation in Kashmir might do, said a prominent member of the ruling Pakistan Muslim League party. India, he said, must give some assurance about troop withdrawals, even partial withdrawals. Alternatively, he suggested, international human rights groups, like Amnesty International, could be authorized access to the Valley. What was essential, he emphasized, was 'some degree of restraint by India' in Kashmir.[30] After all, observed a senior member of the foreign affairs bureaucracy, Prime Minister Nawaz Sharif, in accepting the principle of *simultaneity* in negotiations with India (in other words, that other issues entailed in normalization might be dealt with alongside those relating to Kashmir) has himself already made a major concession that deserved a reciprocal gesture from the Indian side.[31] The gesture, cautioned a leading journalist, had to be convincing. Indian withdrawal of forces from Kashmir, for instance, couldn't just be a token. That wouldn't work. To strengthen Nawaz Sharif's hands in Pakistan, he said, India has to *give*.[32]

When asked whether bolder experiments in India-Pakistan reciprocity, such as opening the LOC to more liberal—if not free—transit by Kashmiris, should be added to the list of CBMs, the characteristic reply of the Pakistani respondents, like that of a leading Azad Kashmiri political figure, was extremely sceptical. The free transit option, he commented, was 'a very, very remote possibility.'[33] In sum, while few respondents deviated from the expectation that India would have to make concessions on Kashmir, most made it clear that they did not expect India, in making them, to 'give away the store.'

Domestic Political Constraints

Thus far, we have observed that there are substantial differences in the fundamental perceptions of the need for change in India-Pakistan relations that Pakistani and Indian elites bring to discussions of normalization. We have also seen that there are considerable differences, too, in the ordering of each side's priorities when specific normalization initiatives are considered. The discussion turns now to consider the domestic political constraints under which the two governments labour and in the face of which normalization initiatives have to be pursued. Here, too, we discover important differences but also some common ground.

Public Opinion and the Media

A common theme among Indians critical of the government's Kashmir policies was that the Indian media, with some notable exceptions, have for all practical purposes observed a blackout on honest reporting about Kashmir: There simply wasn't any free discussion of Kashmir going on in India. Many journalists are corrupt and easily bought off, said one respondent, and there was a pervasive anti-Muslim communal bias to steer others away from Kashmir.[34] The media, said a human rights activist, avoid the torture issue. In fact, he claimed, 'since the 1950s no individual on the street in India has been told the truth about Kashmir.' No one in parliament, he said, was willing to speak out on Kashmir.

A few, he said, were willing to act privately but not publicly. This 'conspiracy of silence,' he maintained, had paralyzed the government's Kashmir policy. Its staggering problem now was: How to change course in a democratic society, where government was caught in a trap of its own making.[35]

A professional analyst and defender of the government's Kashmir policy among the author's Indian respondents gave a more positive slant to the issue. He argued that, while it was true that the Indian press exhibited little passion about Kashmir, this was evidence of 'a certain degree of maturity [on the issue]... [The press] does not push [the issue] under the carpet...There is a consensus [on Kashmir] that these are *domestic* problems.' The Indian press, he said, had an aversion to third-party interference in Kashmir. It was convinced, he said, that the Government of India would ultimately be able to resolve the problem, and that this resolution was likely to come about not as a result of any special concessions to the Kashmiris but via reform of centre-state relations nationwide.[36]

Many of the author's Pakistani respondents expressed views on the role of the media in shaping popular and elite opinion in Pakistan in terms highly reminiscent of the more disparaging comments heard in India about the Indian media. The Pakistani press, said a retired and very senior diplomat, has played a 'terrible' role in regard to Kashmir, one consisting in large part of inflaming public opinion.[37] An intellectual active in the peace movement stated that the government was not getting much support for its initiative from the press, which was still generally hawkish. The Urdu-language press was the worst, he suggested, but there was in fact little support for normalization even in the English-language press.[38] 'Most of the press,' commented a senior journalist, 'suspects Nawaz Sharif of kowtowing to India.'[39] Allowing that the print media do provide some leadership, if only in English and to a tiny elite, another prominent journalist with many years in editorial posts observed that in Urdu-language journalism no one promoted liberal, democratic views. Orthodoxy, he said, was already so successful (profitable, in other words) that there was no interest in redesigning it. The Kashmir issue, he stated flatly, was never openly discussed in Pakistan.[40]

With respect to the Pakistan Parliament's contribution to raising public consciousness about normalization and Kashmir, an ex-diplomat among the author's respondents stated that while there were a handful of parliamentarians sympathetic to the Prime Minister's normalization initiative, overall the normalization lobby was weak.[41] Echoing him, a retired general commented that, with the exception of a few individuals, there was little awareness among Pakistan's political leadership of the gravity of Pakistan's current situation. What had to be more generally realized, this respondent suggested with unusual candour, was that, in many respects, Pakistan simply could not match India. Pakistanis did not understand, he observed, what their country had to do as a small nation. And those who did understand, he noted, were reluctant to speak out.[42]

On the Pakistani public's own view of Kashmir and normalization, there was some divergence of opinion. Some respondents felt that public opinion in regard to India and the Kashmir conflict was so deformed by years of propaganda and the suppression of facts that it now formed a huge obstacle to normalization. Capturing this sentiment was the comment of a peace activist that Pakistanis today were simply unable to analyse Kashmir objectively: propaganda against India—that it wanted to reabsorb Pakistan—had fostered deep insecurity. Pertinent facts—as in regard to Pakistan's less-than-innocent role at the time of Kashmir's accession or the build-up to the 1965 war—had been systematically hidden, he said, from public view.[43] Reinforcing this observation, a serving diplomat reflected that the younger generations in both India and Pakistan, far from having been emancipated from the deeply-entrenched hostility and distrust of their elders, had instead been weaned on vicious media and schoolbook propaganda that had produced mutually opposed and mainly negative stereotypes. Even educated young Pakistani professionals, he said, tended towards dogmatism on the subject of India.[44]

At odds with that point of view was the opinion, expressed by numerous Pakistani respondents, that the principal trend in Pakistani public opinion in connection with Kashmir, far from being blind hostility for India, was sharply declining interest in Kashmir. Many Pakistanis, commented a respected member of the legal profession, were starting to feel that their own future was in jeopardy. The conventional emphasis on Kashmir's liberation, he said, was 'not as resolute as it used to be.'[45] Pakistani interest in Kashmir has diminished, claimed a prominent journalist. At Kashmir-related events, one saw only small audiences. Television coverage was modest. 'There is almost no public support for the Kashmir cause,' he asserted, 'anywhere in Pakistan.' What support for it existed was to be found only in small pockets in a few urban centres such as Lahore. Pakistani youth as a class, he said, were not interested. Kashmir, he claimed, had not been a key issue in either the 1990 or 1993 elections; nor had it figured much in the 1997 elections. Pakistanis, he declared, were amenable to change over Kashmir.[46] Agreeing with that sentiment, a prominent opposition political leader observed: There is not as large a body of Pakistanis thinking emotively about Kashmir today as there was twenty years ago. There was awareness now of its cost to the economy, he said, and that there was need for bold India-Pakistan initiatives.[47]

The existence of significant regional variations in public outlook on Kashmir was claimed by several respondents. Among Sindhis, stated a senior journalist, echoing others, Kashmir was probably not an issue. At the popular level, he suggested, it probably wasn't much of an issue either in Baluchistan or the North West Frontier Province. Even in the southern Punjab, he added, there was little interest in Kashmir. It was only in northeastern Punjab, especially urban Punjab (and most especially Lahore) where substantial consciousness about Kashmir existed. Lahore was the media centre of Pakistan. Residing there were many ethnic Kashmiris. It was a religiously conservative city—and the powerful media organs in Lahore were in the hands of religious and political conservatives. That, he said, was what had kept the Kashmir issue alive.[48]

An Azad Kashmir political figure offered the ironic observation that even in Azad Kashmir support for the Indian Kashmir cause was far from unqualified. Many Azad Kashmiris, he claimed, favoured keeping a fairly low profile in the current difficulties across the Line of Control. The right wing Jama'at-i-Islami forces and some youths, he said, did put stress on Azad Kashmir's unity with the Valley. But generally, he insisted, the people of Azad Kashmir were not very enthusiastic about assisting Kashmiris in the Valley if that meant risking themselves.[49]

Did public opinion really matter when it came to Kashmir? 'Not at all,' said a journalist, expressing the viewpoint of several respondents. 'There is no civil society in Pakistan,' he stated, 'no organized action.' The government was free of virtually all constraints from the non-governmental sector. It consulted only the businessmen, because they could shut down the shops. But it didn't listen to journalists, students, or academics. The educated community he observed, is 'completely out of opinion-making processes.'[50] Commenting in the same vein, a serving diplomat said that so long as the Prime Minister had the army's backing, he could do virtually anything in regard to Kashmir. The army, he said, would have struck a bargain with the government protecting its stake in return for allowing some concessions on Kashmir. Public opinion, along with the rightist political parties, was containable by the army.[51]

Casting some doubt on the foregoing views were the comments of a prominent PML leader, who pointed out that the Pakistan government in fact had limited space in which to maneuver. True, he conceded, the government had been given a strong mandate from the people in the February election; but Punjab province, he pointed out, was the most crucial province to the Prime Minister and he could face serious problems if he were seen by most Punjabis as surrendering to India. Pakistani public opinion, he insisted, was strongly supportive of the government's existing Kashmir policy; and there were strong pro-Kashmiri lobbies in Pakistan—in the business community, the legal profession, the civil service, and military. Nawaz Sharif had the political advantage at the moment, he said, but it was limited.

The author's soundings in Pakistan suggested that the opportunity for a major shift in Pakistan's Kashmir policy, while present in principle, was both heavily conditioned by expectations of a similar shift in India's policy and likely to be fairly short-lived. Any significant deviation from the policy status quo would be quickly detected and subject to resistance. The strongest opposition would most likely come from the Lahore-based press, which is, ironically, among the staunchest supporters of the Nawaz Sharif government—a source of support that the government cannot ignore. The government's mandate to rule was far more fragile than either the size of the vote for it or its command of seats in the National Assembly would imply. Perceptive individuals among the author's respondents were confident that the Prime Minister's mandate would gradually weaken, and when it did, they said, it would grow increasingly imprudent for the government to expend scarce political capital on a project as risky as Kashmir. The unyielding opponents of any alteration of policy, though they are today a dwindling minority, and Nawaz Sharif's numerous political opponents would find common ground to exploit this perceived weakness.

Pakistan: Political Role of the Army

Conceded by virtually all of the author's Pakistani respondents commenting on the issue, irrespective of their background, was that the Pakistan army had and could be expected to retain a commanding role in forming and implementing Pakistan's Kashmir policy. The following comments, quoted or closely paraphrased, were representative:

> [Senior member of legal profession] The army has 'areas of special concern' to it—Afghanistan, for instance, which is handled by the armed forces and Inter Services Intelligence Directorate (ISI). Since Kashmir is also heavily a security matter, so in regard to it too 'no

decision can be taken without the army's going along with it...No political leader can take the risk of annoying them.'

[Senior journalist] 'Any civilian government in Pakistan would have to seek approval [for its Kashmir policy] of the army.'

[Peace-movement activist] Pakistan's political leadership is hostage to the military; the ISI commands greater information than anyone else and thus dominates decision-making. One must understand the military's role to understand Kashmir and its solution.

[Senior diplomat] In addition to nuclear weapons, Afghanistan, and relations with the United States, the army GHQ takes a leading role in framing policy on Kashmir. Initial drafts of policy positions are, of course, formulated and then discussed in the Foreign Office. But, on relations with India, the army continues to exercise considerable influence on policy. It is well equipped to do so. In terms of resources, budget, and capabilities, between the India cell of the army's ISI and the South Asia Division of the Foreign Office, there is no comparison. Especially in regard to the current initiative on Kashmir, the Prime Minister must have the blessings of the army. The army and the ISI clearly dominate policy on Kashmir.

Was the army likely to obstruct the Prime Minister's initiative towards normalization? The answers to this question varied considerably, even though, more often than not, the army was portrayed in an unfavourable light. Perhaps the most insightful and nuanced comments were those of a senior journalist, with extensive military contacts, whose views are cited here at some length:

The current army chief [General Jehangir Karamat] differs from his predecessors. He thinks 'we've gone too far in Kashmir; we need to pull back a bit...' However, he insists that Pakistan's Kashmir policy must be a product of discussions that include the army and the ISI. There should be no movement to settle Siachen, for instance, until and unless the agreement is the product of a careful, systematic review of state policy.

The rank and file of the army favour retaining the status quo in Kashmir. Up to the rank of major, they are mainly unqualified hardliners. Colonels and above, on the other hand, betray a seeming divergence of views: Some are unabashed hawks, while others favour dialogue with India. But even seeming moderates will usually qualify their remarks heavily. Thus, in large part the army is 'a bastion of conservatism.' The COAS himself is not inflexible on the issue of Kashmir. As far as Siachen is concerned, for instance, General Karamat would have no problem concurring with a settlement so long as it were part of a larger strategy. The army does recognize that Pakistan is on a 'weak wicket'—that the economy is in shambles. This does influence its judgment.

The army doesn't want to be attacked by the press as being too secular or too soft on Kashmir. General Karamat wants, above all, that the army remain strong. He wants to avoid an attack on the defence budget.

The best measure for India to take to win the army's concurrence with normalization would be to pull some troops out of Kashmir.[52]

Should one expect the Pakistan army/ISI, for its part, to suspend covert operations in Kashmir in order to encourage settlement? No, said the journalist quoted above, the ISI won't stop. Its leaders want the leverage this supplies. Only in case of a full settlement of Kashmir, he suggested, would the ISI relent. Essentially concurring with this observation, an intellectual with close ties to the foreign affairs bureaucracy said that the Pakistan army had already lowered the threshold of the military's involvement. Nevertheless, it would keep the insurgency in Kashmir going. It had to, he insisted; it couldn't just turn it off. The insurgency provided too good a resource for that. The army, he said, would maintain it, but at a lower level.

India: Electoral Trends

There are two interrelated electoral trends in India that have a direct bearing on the potential for progress towards normalization in India-Pakistan relations. The first of these is the fragmenting of the political party system and electorate. A by-product of the gradual decline of the so-called 'Congress system' of one-party dominance that characterized Indian politics during the first two or three decades following independence, this trend has been underway since the late 1960s. Its spread in the 1990s features an accelerated rate in the decline of the Congress party's political standing at both the state and national levels; the rapid proliferation of regional political parties, many of them rooted in ethno-linguistic, caste and sectarian identities; and the consequent emergence of coalition politics. The capture of most of India's twenty-five state governments by regional parties is a matter of record. But there are now twenty-eight political parties in parliament (Lok Sabha), the largest number ever, and, as may be observed in Table 1, the ranks of the regional parties among them are rapidly growing. They currently occupy 45% of the ruling fourteen-party United Front's parliamentary seats, a position symbolizing the heightened bargaining leverage they now enjoy in the coalition arrangements and hung parliaments prevailing in New Delhi.

Table 1
Seats in Lok Sabha Won by Regional (State, Caste, Ethnic) Parties in General Elections of 1989, 1991, and 1996

[Total seats = 543]

Party	Seats in 1989	Seats in 1991	Seats in 1996	Primary regional base
Telegu Desham Party/TDP	2	13	16	Andhra Pradesh
Asom Gana Parishad/AGP	-	1	5	Assam
Dravida Munnetra Kazhagam/DMK	-	-	17	Tamil Nadu and Pondicherry
All India Anna DMK	11	11	-	Tamil Nadu
Shiv Sena	1	4	15	Maharashtra
Haryana Vikas Party/HVP	-	1	3	Haryana
Samata Party/SP	-	5	8	Bihar, Uttar Pradesh
Bahujan Samaj Party/BSP	3	2	11	Punjab, Uttar Pradesh Madhya Pradesh
Akali Dal	6	-	8	Punjab
MGP	1	-	1	Goa
SDF	-	-	1	Sikkim
Jharkhand Mukti Morcha/JMM	3	6	1	Bihar
Total	27	43	86	

Source: *India Today*, 31 May 1996, p. 46.

The second trend, visible in Figures 3 and 4, is the rise to political prominence in the last several years of the Bharatiya Janata Party (BJP)—a Hindu nationalist organization born in 1980. Its rise no doubt signals the spread of conservative religious nationalism in India; but the spread is far from being either geographically or socio-culturally universal. In fact, the BJP's forward march is fundamentally a north Indian, forward caste, and Hindu nationalist phenomenon much more than what the BJP styles itself to be—an Indian nationalist movement. It represents, understood in this light, the communalization—not nationalization of politics and is thus part and parcel of the larger process of political fractionalization that is taking place in India.

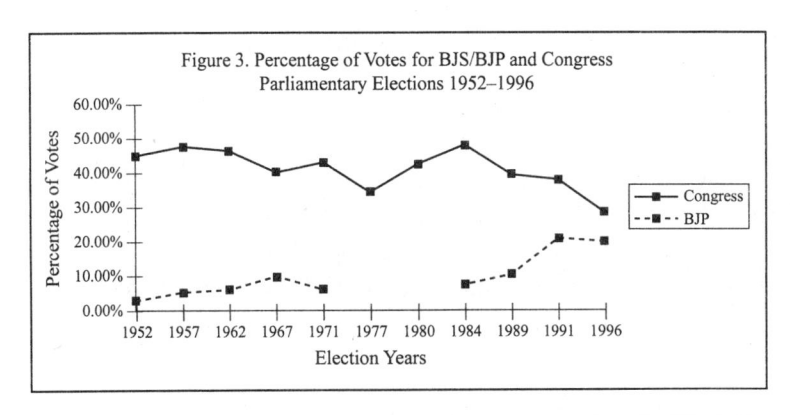

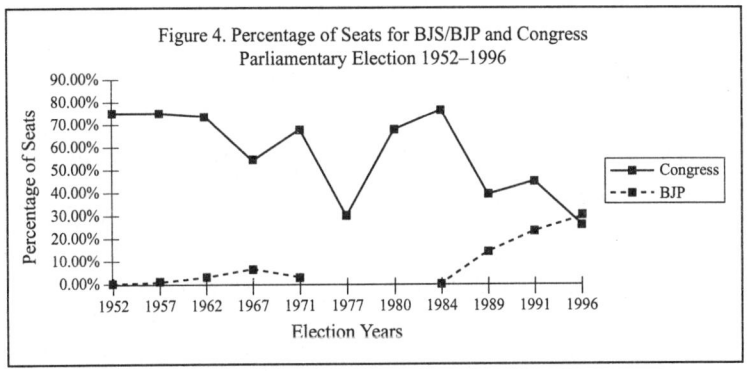

Figure 3. Percentage of Votes for BJS/BJP and Congress Parliamentary Elections 1952–1996

Figure 4. Percentage of Seats for BJS/BJP and Congress Parliamentary Election 1952–1996

Sources: Adapted from Robert L. Hardgrave, Jr. & Stanley A. Kochanek, *India: Government & Politics in a Developing Nation*, Fifth Edition (Fort Worth: Harcourt Brace Jovanovich, 1993), pp. 314, 319-21 and *India Today* (31 May 1996), pp. 22-27.

The BJS contested the 1977 and 1980 elections as part of the Janata Party coalition. The BJP was formed in April of 1980.

While its ability to capture power at the Centre, particular in its own right, is thus highly problematic, as the largest party in parliament the BJP unquestionably occupies a pivotal position when it comes to overseeing the government's initiatives in regard either towards Kashmir or normalization of relations with Pakistan. Its ability last summer to embarrass the UF government over Gujral's appointment to a senior advisory position of the outspokenly pro-normalization intellectual Bhabani Sen Gupta testified to its political clout.[53]

Together these two interconnected trends spell a potentially prolonged period of relative political instability and policy paralysis in India—a period in which bold initiatives, as would clearly be required to manoeuvre India-Pakistan relations onto a more positive path, would surely strike India's political leadership as risky if not entirely out of place. India's domestic political circumstances, to put it very simply, are more likely than not to put a damper on the serious application to India's western border of the Gujral Doctrine.

Conclusions

The governments of India and Pakistan have taken significant steps during the past year in the direction of normalizing their relationship. For the first time in decades, they have agreed explicitly to Kashmir's inclusion in discussions between them. There are signs in both countries that recognition is growing of the steep price both pay for their continuing standoff. There is evidence on both sides, moreover, of some willingness to compromise—on the Pakistan side, at least, even in regard to Kashmir. Both governments are seriously constrained, however, not only by serious differences in the way each conceives the problem of normalization and in the order of priority each assigns to particular elements of it, but also by the tensions that exist between each of them and powerful forces, whether political or military, in their own populations. In a way, they are captives of conflict perhaps as much as they are progenitors of it.

Particularly disturbing in this context is the high potential that exists for the derailment of the revived process of normalization talks. Given their pre-existent and inherent frailty, their survival in the face of acute provocation, such as is currently occurring along the LOC, seems slender indeed. Each government accuses the other side of having precipitated the recent military action. Each also accuses the other side's government of having lost control of the situation—Pakistanis insisting 'that the latest clashes have been instigated by hardliners in the Indian Establishment,' Indians insisting just as vehemently that Nawaz Sharif has been overridden by 'the top brass of Pakistan's politically ambitious armed forces.'[54]

Mutual recrimination begins to crowd out the earlier gestures of peace. 'Bureaucratic culture in both countries,' commented Michael Krepon recently,

> ...continues to place a premium on parrying new initiatives, not championing them. The impulse remains strong to address matters on a rhetorical plane, rather than to deal constructively on matters of substance. Opposition figures look for openings, not to improve bilateral relations, but to exploit such initiatives for political advantage. Nor does it help that, when high-level meetings take place, firing across the Line of Control seems to increase.[55]

While the sympathies of *India Today*, India's premier news magazine, are never in doubt, in its most recent account of the firing on the LOC, its observation that 'hope for an improvement of relations between Islamabad and Delhi is fast waning' can hardly be doubted.[56]

In the face of all this, there is an obvious urgency to the quest for practical and immediate measures for keeping the newly restarted process of negotiations on track. A number of such measures are outlined in a recent report, *1947-1997: The Kashmir Dispute at Fifty: Charting Paths to Peace*, in the writing of which this author participated.[57] I conclude this paper by taking particular note of two of them:

> One obvious and immediate requirement is the institutional 'hardening' of the process of dialogue now underway—its safeguarding, that is, from the kinds of attack upon its utility and credibility that are routinely witnessed during periods of heightened tension, as is occurring now, between India and Pakistan. The 'peace policies' endorsed by both sides are in desperate need of reinforcement. In particular, bilateral talks in regard to them need to be removed from the glare of publicity, given a fixed venue, and

held frequently. It may be that they should be held abroad, perhaps in one of the smaller South Asian capitals; but in any case they need to be held in a protected environment.

A second equally obvious and immediate requirement is the strengthening of peacekeeping machinery on the lengthy border between India and Pakistan. One way to accomplish this, of course, is via an upgrading of the existing peacekeeping force—the United Nations Military Observer Group in India and Pakistan (UNMOGIP)—both in terms of numbers of personnel and the redesign and expansion of its present mission. Prime Minister Nawaz Sharif called for exactly such upgrading, of course, in his speech to the UN General Assembly on 22 September. Specifically, he called upon India to permit UNMOGIP officers to monitor the LOC from the Indian side, a responsibility which they have been barred by India from performing ever since 1972, while at the same time calling upon the United Nations to enlarge the number of observers.[58] Indians may be excused for thinking his proposal disingenuous, not only because India has for decades strenuously opposed 'internationalizing' the Kashmir dispute, but, more importantly, because UNMOGIP officers, even when they did have access to the LOC from the Indian side, largely—and by no means solely because of India's failure to co-operate with them—failed in their mission of peacekeeping. A potentially more reliable way to accomplish the peacekeeping task, I believe, would be for India and Pakistan to regionalize peacekeeping responsibilities—that is, to constitute their own peacekeeping force (call it Joint Border Security Group, for instance), for the time being to augment but eventually perhaps to replace the UNMOGIP. After nearly fifty years of frustrated efforts at international peacekeeping, it is surely time to shift the burden to the South Asian region, specifically to the region's principal peacebreakers.

NOTES

1. John F. Burns, 'India and Pakistan to Hold Talks About Kashmir,' *The New York Times* wire-service, 24 June 1997.
2. 'Indian Leader Proposes Talks on Kashmir,' *The Washington Post*, 27 July 1997, p. A28.

3. Ranjan Roy, 'India-Kashmir Hopes,' Associated Press news-wire report, New Delhi, 27 July 1997.
4. Tahir Ikram, 'Pakistanis Flay Gujral "Somersault" on Kashmir,' Reuters wire-service report, Islamabad, 28 July 1997.
5. Manoj Joshi, 'Stoking the Embers,' *India Today International* (8 September 1997), pp. 36-9.
6. 'Leaders of India, Pakistan Meet During UN General Assembly,' Associated Press wire-service, 23 September 1997.
7. For background on Sir Owen Dixon's 'regional plebiscites' proposal, see Josef Korbel, *Danger in Kashmir*, revised edition (Princeton: Princeton University Press, 1966), pp. 170-76; and Alastair Lamb, *Kashmir: A Disputed Legacy*, 1846-1990 (Hertingfordbury: Roxford Books, 1991), pp. 171-75.
8. Interview, Islamabad May 1997.
9. Interview, Islamabad May 1997.
10. Interview, Islamabad May 1997.
11. Interview, Islamabad May 1997.
12. Interview, Islamabad May 1997.
13. Interview, New Delhi, March 1997.
14. Interview, New Delhi, March 1997.
15. Interview, New Delhi, March 1997.
16. Interview, New Delhi, March 1997.
17. Interviews, New Delhi, April 1997.
18. Interview, New Delhi, May 1997.
19. Interview, Lahore, May 1997.
20. Interview, Lahore, May 1997.
21. Interview, Lahore, May 1997.
22. For background on the Siachen negotiations, see Robert G. Wirsing, *India, Pakistan, and the Kashmir Dispute: On Regional Conflict and Its Resolution* (New York: St. Martin's Press, 1994), pp. 75-83, 195-216.
23. Interview, New Delhi, April 1997.
24. Interview, Islamabad, May 1997.
25. Interview, Rawalpindi, May 1997.
26. Ibid.
27. Interview, Rawalpindi, May 1997.
28. Interview, Islamabad, May 1997.
29. Interview, Islamabad, May 1997.
30. Interview, Islamabad, May 1997.
31. Interview, Lahore, May 1997.
32. Interview, Lahore, May 1997.
33. Interview, Islamabad, May 1997.
34. Interview, New Delhi, April 1997.
35. Interview, New Delhi, April 1997.
36. Interview, New Delhi, April 1997.

37. Interview, Islamabad, May 1997.
38. Interview, Islamabad, May 1997.
39. Interview, Lahore, May 1997.
40. Interview, Karachi, May 1997.
41. Interview, Islamabad, May 1997.
42. Interview, Islamabad May 1997.
43. Interview, Islamabad, May 1997.
44. Interview, Lahore, May 1997.
45. Interview, Lahore, May 1997.
46. Interview, Karachi, May 1997.
47. Interview, Lahore, May 1997.
48. Interview, Islamabad, May 1997.
49. Interview, Islamabad, May 1997.
50. Interview, Lahore, May 1997.
51. Interview, Lahore, May 1997.
52. Interview, May 1997.
53. *India Today International*, 15 September 1997.
54. Manoj Joshi and Ramesh Vinayak, 'Border Firing: War on Peace,' *India Today International*, 13 October 1997, pp. 18-24.
55. Micheal Krepon, 'Opportunities for Indo-Pak Ties,' Southern Asia Internet Forum, Article IV, 14 October 1997.
56. Zahid Hussain, 'Pakistani Policy: No Meeting Point,' *India Today International*, 13 October 1997, p. 22.
57. The report makes twelve recommendations, all of them focused on relatively near-term steps aimed at the restoration of 'normal civil life' in Kashmir. 'Final stage' measures aimed at the long-term resolution of the dispute are deliberately excluded. *1947-1997: The Kashmir Dispute at Fifty: Charting Paths to Peace* (New York: Kashmir Study Group, October 1997).
58. Barbara Crossette, 'Pakistan Asks India to Open Talks on "No-War" Pact,' *The New York Times* wire-service, 23 September 1997.

Contributors

Khalid Mahmud Arif is a former Commander of the Pakistan Army, from 1984-1987. Born in 1930, he joined the Pakistan Army in 1949 as a Second Lieutenant in the armour branch. He is a graduate of the Command and Staff College, Quetta; the National Defence College, Rawalpindi, and the Armor School, Fort Knox, Kentucky, USA. He participated in the Indo-Pakistan wars of 1965 and 1971, earning a decoration in the former. He has been awarded the Nishan-i-Imtiaz (Military) and the Sitara-i-Basalat.

Craig Baxter is Professor Emeritus of Political Science in the Department of Politics at Juniata College, Huntingdon, Pennsylvania. A career diplomat in the US Department of State, Baxter retired as Consul General. He is an author of several books and numerous articles.

Afak Haydar is Professor Emeritus of Political Science and Public Administration and Associate Dean Emeritus of the University College at Arkansas State University. For several years, he served as the Treasurer of the American Institute of Pakistan Studies.

Javid Iqbal was Justice of the Supreme Court of Pakistan from 1986-1989. Before this position, he served for several years as the Chief Justice of the High Court of the Punjab at Lahore. In 1994, he was elected as a Member, to the Senate of Pakistan. An author of several books and articles, Senator Iqbal has travelled extensively in different parts of the world lecturing on Islamic political philosophy, human rights, democracy and justice, ideology of Pakistan, and the philosophy of Iqbal.

Walid Iqbal earned his law degrees from the University Law College in Lahore and Harvard Law School. Currently, he is an Attorney-at-Law at the prestigious law firm of Sullivan and

Cromwell in New York. He specializes on the security and foreign policy issues of Pakistan.

Munir Ahmad Khan, the former Chairman of the Pakistan Atomic Energy Commission, died in 1999. In the 1970s, under the leadership of Zulfikar Ali Bhutto, he led the Pakistan Atomic Energy Commission to extensively develop Pakistan's nuclear capability.

Dennis Kux is a former Ambassador. He is currently Executive Director of the Association for Diplomatic Studies, Arlington, Virginia. A member of the American Foreign Service since 1955, Mr Kux has served in both India and Pakistan and worked as Country Director for India in the US State Department. His other assignments include Director of the Center for the Study of Foreign Affairs, Deputy Assistant Secretary for Intelligence Coordination, and Deputy Director for Management Operations (the last three at the US State Department). Dennis Kux has been a Visiting Fellow at the National Defence University (1990-91) where he researched and wrote *Estranged Democracies*.

Robert E. Looney is a professor at the Naval Postgraduate School of the Department of the Navy in Monterey, California.

Hafeez Malik is Professor of Political Science at Villanova University in Pennsylvania. From 1961 to 1963, and from 1966 to 1984, he was Visiting Lecturer at the Foreign Service Institute of the US Department of State. An author/editor of several books and numerous articles, he is, since 1971, President of the Pakistan-American Foundation; founding Director (1973-88) of the American Institute of Pakistan Studies, and since 1977 Editor of the *Journal of South Asian and Middle Eastern Studies*, and Executive Director of the American Council for the Study of Islamic Societies since 1983.

Abdul Sattar is presently Foreign Minister in the Caretaker government since 12 October 1999. He is a retired diplomat, having served in the Foreign Service of Pakistan from 1953 to 1992. He was appointed Ambassador to Austria (1975-78), India (1978-82 and 1990-92) and the Soviet Union (1988-90) and as

Foreign Secretary, Ministry of Foreign Affairs, Islamabad, Pakistan (1986-88).

Anwar H. Syed is Professor Emeritus of Political Science at the University of Massachusetts, Amherst. He served as editor of *Polity*, the journal of the Northeastern Political Science Association, between 1981 and 1986, and has taught at the Universities of Pennsylvania and the Punjab. His articles have appeared in numerous professional journals and he has authored several books.

Robert G. Wirsing is Professor of Political Science and International Relations at the University of South Carolina. He had also been Visiting Professor of International Studies at the US Army John F. Kennedy Special Warfare Centre, Ft. Bragg, North Carolina. He had published several books and numerous articles.

S.M. Zafar is a senior advocate of the Supreme Court of Pakistan and has held a position in the Punjab Bar Council [1964-1969]; was President of the High Court Bar Association [1976-77]; and elected President of the Supreme Court Bar Association [1977-78]. He was formerly Minister of Law and Parliamentary Affairs, Government of Pakistan, from 1965-69. Currently, he is also Chairman of the Human Rights Society of Pakistan.

Index

A

Abadi, Josh Malih-, 328
Abdullah,Talha bin, 250
Acheson, Secretary of State Dean, 289, 409
Advani, L.K., 181
Affan, Osman bin, 249, 251
Afghanistan, 26, 27, 101, 106, 117, 139, 156, 160, 186, 208, 221, 252, 255, 258, 301, 302, 303, 304, 306, 308, 313, 317, 318, 323, 324, 325, 330, 336, 337, 338, 339, 341, 342, 343, 344, 346, 349, 350, 351, 381, 382, 383, 384, 385, 387, 388, 389, 390, 391, 392, 393, 394, 396, 397, 398, 399, 400, 401, 402, 403, 408, 410, 411, 442, 443
Agni, 164
Agresto, John, 80
Ahmad, Waqar, 108
Ahmad, Qazi Husain, 260
Ahmad, Shamshad, 414
Ahmadis, 257, 264, 278, 282
Ahmed, Aziz, 108
Al Aqsa Mosque, 368
al-Husaini, Allama Arif Husain, 253, 267
al-Khairi, Habib Wahab, 74
al-Khattab, Umar Ibn, 24, 249
Albright, Madeleine, 22, 306
Ali, Prime Minister Chaudhry Muhammad, 33, 36, 108, 125
Ali, Chief Justice of Pakistan Yaqoob, 64, 69
Ali, Mir Laik (of Hyderabad), 317, 406
Ali, Ambassador Salman, 324
Ali, Syed Abid, xi
All Parties Hurriyat (Freedom) Conference (APHC), 417
All-India National Congress, 7, 316
All-Pakistan Progressive Writers' Association, (PPWA), 316, 322
Amendment (13th), 103
American Institute of Pakistan Studies, x, 347
Amin, Hafizullah, 382
Andropov, Yuri, 388
Anglo-Iranian Oil Company, 356
Anjuman Sipah-e-Sahaba, 268
Annan, Kofi, 180
Ansar, 24
anti-Bhutto electoral alliance, 107
anti-Communist security pacts, 289
Arbab, Niaz, 114
Arif, Khalid Mahmud, 6, 19, 82
Army Welfare Trust, 120
Asma Jilani vs. Government of Punjab, 67, 68, 70, 80
Ata Turk's abolition of the Ottoman Caliphate in 1922, 2
Attlee, Prime Minister Clement, 353
Attock Conspiracy case, 124
Auqaf Acts, 39
Awami League, 42, 66, 129, 130, 132, 142, 299, 334, 337, 373, 374, 375
Awami National Party, 136
Awan, Zubair bin, 250
Ayesha, 251, 279
Azad, Abul Kalam, 7
Aziz, Sartaj, 108

INDEX

B

Badaber, listening post at, 292
Baghdad Pact, 27, 291, 293, 318, 319, 357, 358
Bahini, Mukti, 335, 375, 376
Bahriya Foundation, 120
Baker, James A., 341
Bakr, Hazrat Abu, 275
Ball, Under Secretary of State George, 295
Ballistic Missiles, 163
Balochistan, 126; security duties in (1973-77), 119
Bandung Conference, 319
Bangladesh, 15, 18, 26, 42, 43, 66, 98, 132, 137, 138, 147, 148, 153, 282, 311, 313, 317, 328, 331, 332, 335, 336, 337, 375, 378, 379, 404, 429
Barelvi, 245
basic democrats, 38
Basra, Riaz, 254, 255, 257
Baxter, Craig, 16, 20, 126, 147, 148, 282
Bay of Bengal, 300, 336, 377
Beg, Mirza Aslam, 107, 304
Ben Bella, 367
Belokrenitsky, Vyacheslav, xi, 330, 347
Bengal, vii, viii, 4, 5, 8, 10, 12, 13, 14, 15, 41, 146, 300, 317, 336, 373, 377, 422
Bhabha, Dr, 150, 151
Bharatiya Janata Party (BJP), 446
Bhutto, Benazir, 60, 71, 72, 73, 78, 104, 134, 140, 143, 212, 218, 240, 303, 304, 344, 346, 347, 414; Benazir government, 107, 112
Bhutto, Begum Nusrat, 59, 70, 80
Bhutto, Zulfikar Ali, xii, 17, 42, 44, 47, 66, 68, 70, 73, 76, 88, 98, 106, 129, 153, 183, 296, 300, 335, 347, 350; land reforms, 337

Biria, Maulana, 278, 280, 286
Blair, Prime Minister Tony, 184
Block, W., 215, 242
Bogra, Muhammad Ali, 55
Bohras, 264, 275
Boundary Commission, 13
Bowles, Chester, 357
Braibanti, Ralph, xi
Brelvi school of Islam, 136
Brezhnev, Leonid, 394
British Commonwealth of Nations, 336
British Indian Army, 127
Brown, Senator Hank, 305
Brzezinski, Zbigniew, 302
Bulgarian, Nikolai, 358
Burmese Sanction Regulations, 176
Bush, Vice President George, 25, 303

C

Cabinet Mission Plan, 9
Carter, President Jimmy, 301, 384
Caspian Sea region, 346
Central Treaty Organization (CENTO), 293, 318
Central Asia, ix, x, 105, 139, 160, 164, 239, 252, 318, 321, 324, 325, 327, 343, 346, 360, 401; Central Asian republics, 400, 401, 403
Central Intelligence Agency (CIA), 292
Chaghai, 186, 187, 188
Chaghai-Pokhran sanctions, 188
Chaudhry, Zaheer, xi
Chaudhry, President Fazal Elahi, 89, 338
Chief Martial Law Administrator, 37, 42, 49, 63, 64, 69, 86, 97, 99, 116, 293
China, ix, 25, 26, 27, 107, 151, 154, 157, 158, 159, 164, 166, 167, 169, 175, 179, 181, 187, 189, 234, 294, 295, 296, 297, 298, 299, 318, 319,

326, 327, 328, 331, 332, 333, 334, 335, 336, 337, 341, 345, 348, 352, 360, 361, 362, 363, 364, 365, 366, 367, 369, 370, 371, 372, 373, 375, 376, 377, 378, 389, 397, 400, 408, 411, 412, 419
Clinton, President Bill, 184, 305
Communist Party of Pakistan (CPP), 316, 322
Communist Party of the Soviet Union (CPSU), 340
Comprehensive Nuclear Test Ban Treaty (CTBT), 22, 168, 191, 192, 194
Conference on the Peaceful Uses of Atomic Energy, 152
Congress ministry, 94
Congress Party, 316, 320
Constituent Assembly, 5, 6, 10, 16, 17, 18, 30, 31, 32, 34, 35, 36, 41, 42, 43, 44, 47, 54, 55, 56, 59, 61, 62, 63, 66, 87, 95, 96, 105, 127, 128, 129, 130, 132, 146, 147, 317
Constitution 1973, 71; constitutional crises, 18, 20, 61, 75, 76, 118; constitutional framework, 54
Cordovez, Diego, 388, 389, 393, 400, 411
Cornelius, 62, 64, 65
Criminal Law Amendment Act 1908, 38
Cripps, Lord Privy Seal Sir Stafford, 8

D

Daoud, Prince Mohammad, 381
de Cuellar, UN Secretary General Perez, 388
Defence of Pakistan Rules, 66
Delhi Agreement (August 1973), 337
Deoband Dar al-Ulum, 8
Deobandi attack, 257
Dixon, Sir Owen, 421, 451

Dobbin, Fr. Edmund J., x
Dosso's case, 59, 64, 65, 70, 75
Dostam, General Abdul Rashid, 342
Dulles, Secretary of State John Foster, 289, 310, 356, 406
Durand Line, 381, 393
Durrani, Lt-Col, 67

E

East Bengal, vii, viii, 7, 8, 13, 141, 146, 317
East Pakistan Legislative Assembly, 94, 95
Economic Cooperation Organization (ECO), 400
Egypt, 91
Eighth Amendment, 46, 53, 71, 89, 90, 100
Eisenhower, Dwight D., 289, 310, 356
Ellis, Fr. Kail C., x
Engineering and Research Laboratories (now A.Q. Khan Research Laboratories), 184
Enlai, Chinese Premier Zhou, 26, 319, 363, 366
Estonia, 341
Eurasia, 26, 313; Eurasian power, ix, 344, 345; Eurasianists, 345
Executive Agreement of 1959, 320, 336
Eximbank, 177, 187

F

Faiz, Faiz Ahmad, 322, 328
Family Laws Ordinance, 39
Farooqi, Maulana Zia-ur-Rehman, 281, 283
Farooqi, Salman, 108
Fatchett, Derek, 180
Fatima, Hazrat, 275, 283, 284
Fauji Foundation, 120

Federal Court, 18, 35, 48, 60, 62, 63, 117
Federal Shariat Court, 70, 74
Federation of Pakistan vs. Malik Ghulam Mustafa Khar, 71
Fifth Amendment (notified on 15 September 1976), 68
fiqh, 245, 253, 259, 263, 266, 267, 268, 269, 272, 274, 275, 279, 281, 282, 285; fiqh of Abu Hanifa, 254; fiqh-e-Jafariya, 254
Fissile Cut Off Treaty (FCOT), 168
Fissile Materials Control Treaty (FMCT), 192
Ford, Gerald, 300
Fourth Amendment (notified on 25 November 1975), 68
Fundamental Rights, 65, 71

G

Gandhi, Tushar, 183
Gandhi, Mahatma, 7, 8
Gandhi, Indira, 117, 374, 375, 376, 377
Gankovsky, Yuri V., xi, 330, 347
Gauhar, Altaf, 108, 125, 407
Geneva accords, 391, 392
Ghazali, 246
Gilgit, 10, 371
Gorbachev, Mikhail, 350, 389, 390
Government of India Act, 18, 34, 35, 61, 127
Gowda, H.D. Deve, 414, 427
Green Revolution, 201, 202, 205
Gross Domestic Product (GDP), 197, 204, 211, 222, 229, 237
Gujral, Inder Kumar, 414
Gupta, 173, 448
Gurdaspur district, 13
Gwartney, 215, 216, 217, 218, 242, 243

H

Haider, Salman, 414
Hakim, Dr Khalifa Abdul, 3, 28
Hanifa, Abu, 245, 246, 254
Haq, Mahboobul, 108
Haq, Chief Justice Anwar-ul, 70
Haq, General Ziaul, 17, 18, 24, 45, 50, 69, 111, 115, 184, 263, 382; General Zia, 53, 57, 87, 89, 100, 101, 103, 107, 117, 265, 266, 281, 283; Zia era, 100, 106, 208, 22; General Zia's death, 212; President Zia, 87, 301, 385, 393, 400, 402, 412; Zia administration, 117, 223; Zia regime, 136, 140, 214, 223, 226;
Hasan, Chief Justice Dr Nasim, 64, 74
Hashmat Ali vs. Lt-Col Muhammad Shafi Durrani, 67
Hausman, Susan K., xi
Haydar, Afaq, xi, 23
Hekmatyar, Engineer Gulbadin, 395
Helms, US Senator Jesse, 22, 172
Huddle, Ambassador Kalhr, 288
Hudood ordinances, 266, 267, 281
Hunbal, Imam, 245, 246, 275
Hunza, 10, 325, 364
Husain, Imam, 275
Husain, Saddam, 256
Husain, Mufti Jafar, 267
Hussain, Begum Syeda Abida, 272

I

India, vii, viii, ix, 2, 3, 4, 7, 8, 9, 10, 11, 12, 13, 14, 15, 17, 18, 19, 20, 21, 22, 23, 26, 27, 28, 29, 33, 34, 35, 40, 51, 54, 59, 61, 82, 83, 85, 88, 93, 94, 96, 98, 101, 104, 105, 113, 125, 127, 128, 129, 136, 138,

INDEX

139, 140, 147, 149, 150, 151, 152, 153, 154, 155, 156, 157, 158, 159, 160, 161, 162, 163, 164, 165, 166, 167, 168, 169, 170, 171, 172, 173, 174, 175, 176, 177, 178, 179, 180, 181, 182, 183, 184, 185, 186, 187, 188, 189, 190, 191, 192, 195, 199, 212, 223, 252, 258, 261, 264, 282, 287, 288, 289, 290, 291, 292, 293, 294, 295, 296, 297, 299, 300, 301, 304, 306, 307, 308, 309, 310, 311, 312, 315, 316, 317, 318, 319, 320, 321, 323, 325, 326, 327, 328, 330, 331, 332, 333, 334, 335, 336, 337, 342, 344, 346, 347, 348, 349, 350, 353, 354, 356, 357, 358, 359, 360, 361, 362, 363, 364, 365, 366, 367, 368, 369, 370, 371, 372, 373, 374, 375, 376, 377, 379, 380, 381, 387, 408, 409, 410, 411, 412, 413, 414, 415, 417, 418, 419, 420, 421, 422, 423, 424, 425, 426, 427, 428, 429, 430, 431, 432, 433, 434, 435, 436, 437, 438, 439, 440, 441, 442, 443, 444, 445, 446, 447, 448, 449, 450, 451, 452

Indian Army, 33, 42, 112, 127
Indian Central Legislative Assembly, 93
Indian Constitution, 174, 425
Indian Independence Act (of 18 July, 1947), 9, 13, 30, 31, 41, 59, 85
Indian Military Academy, 112
Indian National Congress, 85
Indo-Chinese War of 1962, 335
Indo-Pakistan conflict of 1971, 335
Indo-Pakistan war over Kashmir, 326
Indo-Soviet counterweight, 334
Indo-Soviet Treaty of Friendship (August 197), 336, 339
Indonesia-Pakistan Economic and Cultural Cooperation (IPECC), 368

Intelligence Bureau (IB), 105
Inter Services Intelligence Directorate (ISI), 106, 442
interim constitution made in 1972, 88
International Atomic Energy Agency (IAEA), 152, 153, 156
International Development Agency (IDA), 178
International Monetary Fund (IMF), 178, 190, 191, 193, 212, 213, 214, 218, 219, 220, 231, 235, 242, 243
Iqbal, Walid, 22, 172
Iqbal, Muhammad, vii, 1, 69
Iqbal, Javid, x, 16, 17, 61
Iqbal, Chief Justice Sardar Muhammad, 69
Iran, 16, 25, 27, 101, 186, 244, 246, 247, 251, 252, 255, 256, 258, 263, 266, 267, 271, 274, 276, 278, 280, 281, 282, 291, 293, 305, 318, 337, 341, 346, 349, 350, 356, 367, 382, 386, 390, 393, 398, 399, 400, 401, 404, 405, 419
Ishaq, Khalid M., 111
Islamabad Accord, 395
Islami Jamhuri Ittehad (IJI—Islamic Democratic Alliance), 143
Islamic Advisory Council, 57
Islamic fundamentalist Taliban movement, 306
Ismailis, 24, 264, 275, 342
Ispahani, Ambassador, 355
Israel, 291, 339, 380

J

Jafri, V.A., 108
Jalandhri, Hafeez, 328
Jamaat-e-Islami, 8, 260
Jamiat Ulama-i Hind, 8
Jamiat-ul-Ulema-i-Islam, 136
Jamiat-ul-Ulema-i-Pakistan, 136
Jan Sangh Party, 181

Jatoi, Ghulam Mustafa, 143
Jhang, 25, 254, 255, 263, 267, 268, 269, 270, 271, 272, 281, 283, 286; Haq Nawaz of, 254
Jhangvi, Maulana Haq Nawaz, 263, 268, 269, 270, 271, 272, 281, 284
Jilani, Malik Ghulam, 66
Jinnah, Mohtarma Fatima, 98, 141
Jinnah, vii, xi, 1, 2, 4, 6, 7, 8, 9, 10, 11, 12, 13, 14, 15, 16, 19, 21, 24, 28, 29, 30, 31, 34, 51, 56, 82, 91, 93, 95, 96, 128, 129, 130, 134, 141, 146, 288, 307, 316, 317, 320, 321, 352, 353, 406, 412; Governor-General Mohammed Ali, 287
Johnson, Lyndon, 25, 295, 296, 297, 298, 311, 320, 366, 371, 406, 407, 410
judicial review, 65, 68, 116
Junagarh, 406
Junejo, 46, 47, 71, 87, 100, 111, 133, 135, 143, 144, 391, 392, 400
Jurisdiction of Courts (Removal of Doubts) Order, 66, 68

K

Kabul, Rabbani regime in, 398; Kabul regime, 389, 391, 392, 393
Kaishek, Chiang, 363
Kalat, 94, 120, 138
Kapitsa, Soviet Ambassador Michael, 325
Karachi Nuclear Power Plant (KANUPP), 154
Karachi steel mill, 329, 330
Karakoram Mountain Range, 432; Karakorum Highway, 371, 401, 408
Karamat, General Jehangir, 443, 444
Karbala, 249, 250, 251, 275, 276
Karimov, President Islam, 398, 411

Karmal, Babrak, 383
Kashmir, 413, 415, 416, 417, 418, 419; Kashmir valley, 10, 11, 417, 433; Jammu and Kashmir, 10, 28, 113, 288, 379, 413, 418, 420, 421, 423, 424, 425, 426, 427, 435; Kashmir question, 354, 361, 365, 421; Kashmir dispute, 83, 96, 104, 309, 360, 369, 370, 371, 379, 418, 426, 450; Kashmir conflict, 166, 417, 424, 439; Kashmir settlement, 361, 366; Kashmir problem, 166, 288; Indian occupation of, 27; Confidence-Building Measures (CBMs) in, 435
Kasuri, Ahmad Raza, 70, 100
Kennedy, 25, 147, 148, 262, 283, 293, 294, 295, 296, 298, 311, 320, 361, 365, 366, 407, 408, 409, 410, 411
Khalevinski, Igor V., xi, 351
Khalid Malik vs. Federation of Pakistan, 72
Khan, Ayub, 16, 17, 18, 20, 37, 38, 39, 40, 41, 50, 52, 53, 54, 55, 59, 63, 64, 65, 66, 68, 69, 73, 84, 86, 87, 88, 96, 97, 98, 102, 103, 112, 114, 115, 117, 122, 123, 125, 131, 136, 140, 141, 148, 152, 199, 202, 204, 223, 224, 225, 265, 272, 290, 291, 293, 294, 295, 296, 297, 298, 310, 311, 325, 326, 327, 328, 329, 330, 350, 357, 360, 361, 362, 363, 365, 366, 369, 372, 373, 407, 408, 410, 414
Khan, General Tikka, 115
Khan, Liaquat Ali, 7, 14, 17, 32, 33, 91, 105, 129, 288, 321, 355, 406; assassination of, 96, 249
Khan, Abdul Qayyum, 135
Khan, Sultan Muhammad, 334
Khan of Kalat, 138

INDEX

Khan, General Agha Muhammad Yahya, 17, 18, 41, 42, 48, 53, 54, 55, 66, 67, 68, 73, 84, 88, 91, 98, 103, 111, 115, 123, 124, 131, 152, 298, 299, 331, 332, 333, 334, 372, 374, 376
Khan, Pakistan's Foreign Minister Zafrullah, 288
Khan, Brigadier Siddique, 114
Khan, Roedad, 76, 108
Khan, General Gul Hassan, 115
Khan, Major-General Akbar, 114, 322
Khan, Haji Saifullah, 71, 80
Khan, Gohar Ayub, 348, 414
Khan, Nawab Mohammad Ahmad, 99
Khan, President Ghulam Ishaq, 72
Khan, Tanvir Ahmad, 347
Khan, Munir Ahmad, 21, 149
Khan, Maulvi Tamizuddin, 59, 62, 64, 75
Khokar, Ambassador Riaz, 306
Khomeini, Ayatollah, 247, 256, 260, 267, 271, 284
Khrushchev, Nikita, 323, 337, 358
Khulafa-e-Rashideen, 273, 275, 277
Kissinger, 298, 299, 300, 312, 320, 333, 334, 349, 350, 372, 374, 376, 408, 409, 410
Kohl, Chancellor, 180
Kosygin, Premier Alexei, 327, 337, 391
Kozyrev, Foreign Minister Andrei, 345
Krepon, Michael, 449, 452
Krishak Sramik Party (KSP), 129
Kux, Dennis, 25, 287, 310, 412

L

Lahore High Court, 45, 67, 69, 70, 71, 72, 74, 76, 99
Lahore Resolution, 4, 14, 409
Land Reform Regulations, 39
Lashkar-e-Jhangvi, 254

Law of Libel, 110
Laws (Continuance in Force) Order, 37, 64
Lawson, 215, 242, 243
Legal Framework Order (LFO), 41
Leghari, President Farooq Ahmed Khan, 75, 79, 111, 144
Line of Control (LOC), 413
London Suppliers Group (LSG), 155
Looney, 23, 195, 242
loya jirga, 343

M

Madison, James, 261, 262
Majlis-e-Shura, 253
Majlis-i-Ahrar, 8
Mahmood Khan Achakzai's case, 75
Mahmud, Masood, 108
Malik, Hafeez, xi, 1, 25, 26, 28, 313, 349, 350, 351
Malik, 246; Malikis, 275
manazra, 269
Manto, Saadat Hasan, 328
Marshall, George C., 287, 317
Martial Law, 17, 18, 37, 38, 41, 42, 44, 45, 46, 49, 50, 51, 52, 53, 54, 55, 56, 58, 59, 63, 64, 65, 66, 67, 69, 70, 71, 84, 86, 88, 94, 97, 98, 99, 100, 111, 115, 117, 119, 123, 127, 271, 293, 332
Masood, Ahmad Shah, 397
Maulana Maudoodi's case, 8, 65
Muawiya, Yazid Ibn, 275
Mazari, Balakh Sher, 144
McConaughy, Walter, 296
McGhee, George, 309, 355, 406
Mecca, 301
Mehdi, 64, 246, 248
Ministry of Science and Technology, 21, 153
Mirza, Colonel Iskandar, 108
Mitha, Commanding Officer General, 67

Mohammed, Governor-General Ghulam, 95, 97, 111, 265, 289, 307, 310
Mojaddedi, Professor Sibghatullah, 343, 395
Moscow Olympics, 384
Moskalenko, Vladimir, 330
Mountbatten, Lord, 11, 26, 30, 320
Movement for the Restoration of Democracy (MRD), 53, 119
Muhajir Qaumi Movement (MQM), 119, 135, 136, 138
Mujahideen, 106, 339, 341, 342, 343
Mujib, Sheikh, 66, 98, 132, 137, 299, 332, 335, 375
Munir, Chief Justice Muhammad, 18, 28, 36, 47, 62, 64, 65, 75, 76
Muqeemjanova, Railya, 330
Murray, Senator Patty, 190
Musa, General Muhammad, 115
Muslim League, xi, 7, 8, 9, 13, 14, 40, 46, 52, 53, 58, 72, 75, 91, 93, 94, 95, 96, 128, 129, 130, 134, 135, 141, 143, 307, 349, 353, 359, 409, 414, 422, 436; All-India Muslim League, vii, 4, 51
Mutual Defence Assistance Agreement, 357

N

Nahj-al-Balagha, 251
Najafi, Mr Ghulam Abbas, 272
Najibullah, 390, 394, 395
Naqvi, Maulana Sajid, 272
Naqvi, Ghulam Raza, 254, 255, 257
Nasser, President, 359, 371
National Assembly, vii, 40, 43, 46, 47, 55, 59, 65, 66, 68, 71, 72, 73, 74, 75, 79, 86, 87, 89, 133, 134, 135, 141, 142, 143, 144, 260, 261, 272, 311, 316, 336, 365, 374, 442
National Awami Party, 133
NATO, 345, 358

Nazimuddin, Khawaja, 33, 34, 55, 97, 129, 146, 264, 288, 289
Nehru, 7, 9, 85, 93, 150, 151, 174, 288, 289, 290, 291, 295, 320, 321, 361, 362, 363, 365, 407, 408, 409, 424
Nethercutt, George R., 190
Niazi, Maulana Kausar, 266
Nichols, General, 151
Nishter, Sardar Abdur Rab, 7
Nixon, Richard, 298
Nizam-e-Mustafa, 263, 265, 266, 272, 281
Non-Aligned Movement, 302, 414
Non-Proliferation Treaty (NPT), 21, 151, 155, 157, 158, 159, 161, 163, 165, 167, 168
Noon, Firoz Khan, 316, 349, 407
North West Frontier Province, 253, 440
Nuclear capability, 21, 149, 162
Nuclear Free Zone, 154, 157
Nuclear Proliferation Prevention Act of 1994, 175

O

Oakley, Robert, 190, 312
Objectives Resolution, 16, 31, 32, 34, 41, 44, 47, 56, 57
October (Coup) Revolution, 37; October Revolution Day, 328
Official Secrets Act, 110
Organization of Islamic Conference (OIC), 300, 368, 384, 386, 391, 399, 412
Ottoman Caliphate, 2, 367
Overseas Private Investment Corporation (OPIC), 177

P

Pakistan Resolution, vii, 4, 409
Pakistan National Alliance, 44, 52, 135, 142

INDEX

Pakistan Army, 19, 66, 97, 98, 106, 112, 113, 124, 125, 142, 290, 322, 331, 336
Pakistan movement, 52, 352
Pakistan People's Party, 42, 58, 89, 112, 299, 336
Pakistan, Military Assistance Program for, 322; Armed Forces of, 69; demand for (1940), 93; military aid for, 297; Sunni-Shia conflict in, 247; Constitution of the Islamic Republic of (1956), 63; Pakistan national movement, vii; Federation of, 59, 60, 62, 71, 72, 80, 81; dismemberment of, 332, 378; Islamization of the laws in, 266; Indian military intervention in East, 336; secessionist movement in East, 328; Supreme Court of, x, 37, 50, 63, 78, 90; Pakistan and Turkey, 290, 367
Pakistan Democratic Movement (PDM), 52
Pakistan Muslim League, 40, 46, 53, 58, 75, 141, 414, 422, 436
Pakistan Atomic Energy Commission, 21, 153
Pandit, Madam Vijyalakshmi, 321
Panjshir Valley, 397
Pankin, Foreign Minister Boris D., 341
Pashtunistan, 139, 323, 337
Patel, Sardar Vallabhbhai, 7
People's Democratic Party of Afghanistan (PDPA), 338, 396; Khalq-faction, 338
Perestroika (restructuring), 340
Peshawar High Court, 72
Platt, Nicholas, 190, 312
Pokhran, 173, 174, 175, 176, 177, 178, 179, 181, 182, 183, 184, 185, 187, 188
Political Parties Act of 1962, 38, 141
Pressler, Senator Larry, 303; Pressler amendment sanctions, 304, 308
Primakov, Yevgeny, 348
Prithvi missile, 164
Prophet, house of the, 250
provincial autonomy, vii, 1, 43, 49, 61, 132, 137, 299, 341, 342, 346, 373, 378, 422, 426
Province of East Pakistan vs. Muhammad Mehdi Ali Khan Panni, 64
Provisional Constitutional Order of 1981 (PCO), 45
Punjab, vii, 5, 10, 12, 14, 25, 28, 43, 67, 73, 77, 94, 105, 125, 134, 139, 141, 144, 147, 179, 199, 200, 253, 256, 257, 258, 260, 262, 263, 267, 268, 272, 282, 283, 289, 316, 328, 422, 440, 441, 446, 448

Q

Qadianis, 264, 282
Qasim, Muhammad Bin, 139
Qasmi, Ahmad Nadeem, 328
Qazi, A.G.N., 108
Quantico Panel, 323
Quetta Plan of Action, 401
Quit India campaign, 8
Quran, 57, 248, 261, 268, 273, 278, 280; Quranic exegesis, 268
Qureshi, Moeen, 144

R

Rabbani, Professor Burhanuddin, 343, 395; Rabbani regime, 396, 398; Rabbani-Hekmatyar-Masood forces, 396; Rabbani regime in Kabul, 398
Rahman, Mujibur, 137
Rann of Kutch skirmishing, 307
Rao, P.V. Narasimha, 414
Raphel, Robin, 303

Rashid, Rao Abdul, 108
Rawalpindi Conspiracy case, 20, 114, 124
Reagan, President Ronald, 387, 412
Regional Cooperation for Development (RCD), 367
Rehman, Maulana Fazalur, 49
Rehman, Zia-ur-, 67, 68, 281, 283
Rehman, Hamood-ur-, 67
Representation of the People Act, 1976, 71
Research and Analysis Wing (RAW), 374
Rockefeller, Governor, 323
Round Table Conference, 41
Roy, Arundhati, 183, 193
Rusk, Secretary of State Dean, 372
Russia, viii, ix, x, 25, 26, 158, 164, 167, 170, 181, 187, 190, 287, 313, 314, 316, 324, 343, 344, 345, 346, 347, 348, 349, 351, 355, 401
Russian Centre for Pakistan Studies, 347, 349
Russian Institute of Oriental Studies, 349

S

Sadiq, Ahmad, 108
Sahaba (the companions of the Holy Prophet), 269
Sajjad, Wasim, 144
Salim, Shah Ismail Sultan, 252
Sandys, British Commonwealth Secretary Duncan, 365
Saqifa, banu Sa'ida, 24
Sattar, Ambassador Abdul, 25, 26, 27, 352
Saudi Arabia, 252, 255, 256, 258, 263, 307, 341, 371, 389, 401, 403, 404
Saur Revolution on 27 April 1979, 389
Seaboarg, Dr Glenn, 151

SEATO, 290, 291, 300, 310, 318, 319, 325, 335, 336, 357, 358, 363, 366, 380
Second and Third Five-Year plans, 203
Security Agreement of 1959, 293, 302, 380
Sevan, Benon, 341, 342
Seventh Amendment (notified on 16 May 1977), 69
Shafaiees, 275
Shah, Chief Justice Sajjad Ali, 74, 78, 79
Shah, King Zahir, 381
Shah, Mohammad Raza, 266
Shah, Pir Ali Mardan of Pagara, 46
Shahabuddin, Justice, 38
Shaheen Foundation, 120
Shahi, Foreign Minister Agha, 114, 302, 312, 350, 408, 410, 411
Shanwari, Hamza, 328
Shariat Court, 57, 70, 74, 253
Sharif, Nawaz, 60, 72, 73, 74, 75, 77, 78, 79, 81, 103, 104, 111, 134, 143, 144, 184, 186, 212, 214, 219, 220, 240, 304, 305, 343, 344, 346, 347, 414, 419, 424, 436, 438, 441, 442, 449, 452; Shahbaz, 256
Sherpao, Aftab Ahmad Khan, 72, 80
Shevardnadze, Minister, 390, 411
Shia imams, 246; Shia doctrines, 244, 245, 261, 268; Shia belief, 245, 246, 247, 248, 251, 270, 282, 284; Shia-Sunni relations, 248; clergy, 258; Shia ulema, 246, 258, 278; Shia-Sunni conflict, 23, 24, 271, 284; Shia-Sunni split, 24, 244; Shia-Sunni rift, 266; Shia-Sunni divide, 265, 266; Shiaism, 29, 252, 271, 281; Shias, 2, 5, 138, 262; anti-Shiaism, 272, 281; Shia revolution, 267, 268; Shia fiqh, 267, 279; Shia Zakireen (preachers), 276, 264, 266, 267,

268, 269, 270, 271, 272, 275, 276, 277, 278, 279, 280, 281, 282, 283, 284, 286
Siachen, 428, 432, 433, 434, 435, 443, 444, 451; Siachen Glacier Issue, 431; Siachen dispute, 433, 434
Simla, agreement signed on 2 July 1972 at, 379
Sindh Chief Court, 62
Sino-India war, 307; Sino-Indian conflict, 294, 326, 333, 361; Sino-Soviet relations, 333; Sino-US entente, 336
Sipah-e-Muhammad, 254, 257
Sipah-e-Sahaba Pakistan (SSP), 263, 268, 271, 281
Six Points Programme, 91
Sixth Amendment (notified on 4 January 1977), 69
Socialist movement, 3
South Asian Association for Regional Cooperation (SAARC), 415
South East Asia Treaty Organisation (SEATO), 357
Soviet Institute of Oriental Studies, 329
Soviet vetoes, 299
Soviet Union, viii, ix, x, 15, 25, 26, 27, 98, 105, 117, 156, 176, 287, 292, 295, 296, 299, 313, 314, 315, 316, 317, 318, 319, 320, 321, 322, 323, 324, 325, 326, 327, 328, 332, 333, 334, 335, 336, 337, 338, 339, 340, 341, 342, 343, 344, 345, 355, 356, 358, 359, 360, 363, 364, 371, 372, 377, 382, 383, 386, 388, 389, 391, 392, 393, 394, 395, 400, 405; Soviet Union's October Revolution Day, 328; Soviet collapse, viii, 340; Stalinist model of the Soviet Union, 340; Soviet leaders, 321, 379; Soviet totalitarianism, 3; Soviet/Russia-Pakistan relations, 26; invaded Afghanistan, 156;
Soviet Central Asia, 318, 321, 324, 325, 326
Soviet-Indian Friendship Treaty, 334
Soviet-Pakistan Friendship Society, 328
Soviet-Pakistan relations, 319, 325, 326, 328, 331, 337
SSP militants, 258, 259
St. Laurent, Prime Minister Louis, 174
Stalin, 316, 320, 321, 322, 340, 341; Stalinist totalitarian bureaucratic system, 340
State vs. Dosso, 67, 80
Stetsenko, A.G., 321
Stevenson, Adlai, 362
Subrahmanyam, K., 300, 312
Suez crisis of 1956, 27
Sufyan, Muawiya bin Abu, 250
Suhrawardy, Hussain Shaheed, 14, 146
Sunnah, 57
Sunnis, 5, 138, 244, 247, 248, 249, 250, 251, 252, 253, 259, 260, 262, 264, 268, 269, 270, 271, 275, 276, 279, 280, 282; Sunni fiqh, 274; Sunni doctrine, 246
Supreme Court, x, 17, 18, 19, 37, 38, 40, 41, 42, 43, 45, 46, 47, 48, 50, 53, 54, 55, 57, 63, 64, 65, 66, 67, 68, 69, 70, 71, 72, 73, 74, 75, 76, 77, 78, 79, 81, 89, 90, 98, 100, 111, 112, 116, 133, 134, 143, 144
Syed, Anwar H., 23, 244
Symington and Glenn Amendments, 380

T

Tajikistan, 328, 344, 345, 348
Talib, Ali ibne Abu, 245, 247, 248, 249, 250, 251, 259
Taliban, 258, 306, 347, 348, 351, 395,

396, 397, 398, 400, 411; Taliban government, 347
Tamizuddin, Maulvi, 35, 59, 62, 64, 75
Taqiyya, 247; taqiyya (dissimulation), 246
Taraki, Nur Muhammad, 382
Tarar, President Muhammad Rafiq, 346
Tashkent, 40, 297, 327, 329; Tashkent Declaration, 40, 98
Tatarstan, 345, 346, 347, 351
Taylor, General Maxwell, 296, 311
Tehrik-e-Khatm-e-Nubbuwwat, 272
Tehrik-e-Nifaz-e-Fiqh-e-Jafaria, 267, 272
Tehrik-i Nizam-i Mustafa, 52
Tehrik-i-Pakistan, 52
Thackeray, Bal, 182
Thant, UN Secretary General, 297
Total Factor Productivity (TFP), 227
Tripartite Agreement (April 1974), 337
Trudeau, Prime Minister Pierre, 174
Truman, President Harry S., 287, 321, 355; Truman's policy, 307
Tse-Tung, Mao, 369
Turkey, 27, 290, 318, 356, 367, 400
Turkish national assembly, 2
Turkish-Pakistan security accord, 291
Turkmenistan, 348, 401

U

U-2 plane, 325; U-2 incident, 293, 325, 326
United Nations (UN), 120, 148, 155, 288, 299, 302, 326, 337, 348, 353, 361, 362, 368, 371, 376, 379, 381, 384, 391, 401, 416, 450, 451, 452; UN General Assembly, 168, 287, 339, 381, 388, 416, 450, 451; General Assembly, 299, 302, 363, 368, 384, 385; UN Security Council, 104, 174, 288, 354, 375, 420, 421, 425; resolution on Tibet; 363;
United States, viii, ix, x, xi, 21, 22, 23, 25, 27, 39, 147, 148, 151, 156, 157, 158, 176, 177, 178, 180, 190, 208, 211, 238, 287, 288, 289, 290, 291, 292, 293, 296, 299, 300, 301, 302, 303, 304, 305, 306, 307, 308, 309, 310, 313, 314, 316, 317, 318, 320, 322, 325, 326, 328, 331, 332, 333, 335, 336, 338, 344, 345, 347, 348, 349, 350, 353, 355, 356, 357, 358, 359, 360, 361, 362, 363, 364, 365, 370, 371, 372, 375, 376, 378, 384, 386, 387, 389, 392, 393, 394, 397, 402, 403, 419, 443
United Nations Military Observer Group in India and Pakistan (UNMOGIP), 450
Urdu, 15, 94, 105, 135, 138, 186, 260, 261, 282, 283, 284, 285, 286, 329, 373, 438
US Arms Control and Disarmament Agency, viii
ushr, 2, 253, 254, 266, 281
USSR, 26, 154, 170, 320, 321, 323, 324, 325, 326, 327, 328, 329, 330, 331, 332, 335, 336, 337, 339, 340, 341, 345, 349, 351, 355, 359, 369, 384, 389, 412;aerial inspection of, 324
Uzbekistan, 344, 348, 399, 402, 412

V

Vajpayee, 179
Volga-Ural basin, 345
Vorontsov, Yuli, 391, 392
Voznesensky, Nicholas A., 316, 317

W

Wahabis, neo-, 245, 246
Wakhan Corridor, 325
Waldheim, Kurt, 180
Warsaw Pact, 345
Watan Party, 342
Wheeler, Mortime, 139, 147
Wirsing, Robert, 27, 28, 413, 451
World Bank, 140, 144, 145, 148, 178, 179, 190, 193, 209, 212, 214, 238, 241, 243, 296, 415
World Bank Pakistan consortium, 296
World Gross National Product (GNP), 317

X

Xinjiang, 319, 325, 363, 371, 377

Y

Yazdani, Murdi Abbas, 254, 260
Yazid, 248, 249, 250, 251, 275, 276
Yeltsin, Boris, 341, 347
Yi, Foreign Minister Chen, 369

Z

Zafar, S.M., 16, 17, 30, 59, 60
Zaheer, Sajjad, 322
Zaheer-ul-Islam Abbasi case, 124
Zaidi, Ijlal Haider, 108
Zhou, Premier, 26, 319, 333, 363, 364, 366, 376; Zhou's visit to Pakistan in December 1956, 363
Zonal Martial Law Administrator, 67